A
Social
History
of
England
1851–1975

A
Social
History
of
England
1851–1975

François Bédarida

TRANSLATED BY

A. S. Forster

METHUEN
LONDON AND NEW YORK

First published as *La Société Anglaise 1851–1975*
by Librairie Arthaud, Paris
© 1976 B. Arthaud
English translation first published in 1979 by
Methuen & Co. Ltd
11 New Fetter Lane, London EC4P 4EE
Published in the USA by
Methuen & Co.
in association with Methuen, Inc.
733 Third Avenue, New York, NY 10017

© 1979 Methuen & Co. Ltd

Photoset in V.I.P. Palatino by
Western Printing Services Ltd, Bristol
Printed in Great Britain
by William Clowes & Sons Limited
Beccles and London

British Library Cataloguing in Publication Data

Bédarida, François
A social history of England, 1851–1975. –
(University paperbacks; 672).
1. England – Social conditions – 19th century
2. England – Social conditions – 20th century
I. Title   II. Series
309.1′42′081   HN385

ISBN 0–416–85910–0
ISBN 0–416–85920–8 Pbk

. . . this scepter'd isle, . . .
This fortress built by Nature for herself
Against infection and the hand of war,
This happy breed of men, this little world,
This precious stone set in the silver sea,
Which serves it in the office of a wall, . . .
Against the envy of less happier lands;
This blessed plot, this earth, this realm, this England, . . .

WILLIAM SHAKESPEARE, *Richard II*

This is a letter of hate. It is for you, my
countrymen. I mean those men of my
country who have defiled it. . . . You are
its murderers . . . I carry a knife in my
heart for every one of you. Macmillan,
and you, Gaitskell, you particularly . . . .
Till then, damn you, England. You're
rotting now, and quite soon you'll
disappear. My hate will outrun you yet
. . . I wish it could be eternal. . . .

JOHN OSBORNE, Letter to *Tribune*, 1961

Contents

List of plates x
Acknowledgements xi
Preface xiii

Part I The Power and the Glory: 1851–80 1

1 INDUSTRIALISM TRIUMPHANT 3
　The festival of work and industry 3
　Unlimited growth 8
　Malthus forgotten 12
　On the urban front 16
　London 20
　Green England: the unchanging countryside 25
　Material civilization: the dividends of progress 31

2 THE MERITS OF HIERARCHY 36
　Classes and structure: Marx or Palmerston? 36
　An aristocratic country 41
　The irresistible ascent of bourgeois England 48
　The popular classes 56
　Unionism and social integration 66

3 POWER AND CONSENSUS 73
　The social dynamic 73
　Was England revolution-proof? 75
　The individual and the State: liberalism triumphant 81
　A Christian land 85
　England *über alles* 92

Part II The Old World Resists: 1880–1914 97

4 THE CRISIS OF VICTORIAN VALUES 99
　The great climacteric: appearance and reality 99
　Laissez-faire challenged 103
　Traditional beliefs and new modes of behaviour 109
　Women make themselves heard 116

5 FROM OLIGARCHY TO DEMOCRACY? 125
   The aristocracy on the defensive 125
   The awakening of Caliban 132
   The slow march of democracy 139

6 THE SPLENDOUR AND SQUALOR OF A GOLDEN AGE 144
   Angliae est imperare . . . 144
   Inequality: opulence and deprivation 148
   Education and class 153
   Sex and death 158
   The end of *Pax Britannica* 162

Part III Through Storms and Crises to Recovery: 1914–55 165

7 THE SEARCH FOR SECURITY AND STABILITY 167
   Twentieth-century blues 167
   For King and Country: from Flanders' mud to the disillusion
      of peace 170
   Economic vicissitudes 174
   The battles of Labour 182
   'Their finest hour': from Armageddon to the New
      Jerusalem 186
   The Welfare State 191

8 THE IMMUTABLE CLASS SYSTEM 200
   The Establishment 200
   Bourgeois and petit-bourgeois 205
   The working class 209
   Rich and poor: an island of lords or a country of Mr Smiths? 213

9 THE SLOWLY CHANGING SOCIAL LANDSCAPE 226
   Neo-Malthusian fluctuations 226
   Urbanization, suburbanization and town-planning 231
   The schools: democratization or élitism 235
   Secular encroachment on religion 241

Part IV A Disrupted Society: 1955–75 247

   The end of old England? 249

10 THE FRUITS OF AFFLUENCE 253
   The cornucopia of neo-capitalism 253
   Winds of revolt and spiritual quests 257
   Youth, family life, religion 262
   The emancipation of women: progress or stagnation? 269

11 DECADENCE OR WISDOM? 274
  Sic transit gloria Britanniae . . . 274
  The threat of stagnation and disruption 276
  Class, State and power 281
  An art of living? 287

  Conclusion 290
  Postscript 1975–9 296
  Notes to the text 299
  Notes to the plates 313
  Chronological table 317
  Bibliography 333
  Index 344

List of plates

1. Panorama of Leeds, seen from Richmond Hill (1885)
2. London Bridge in 1895
3. Hydraulic presses for a ship's launching
4. Liverpool: Lime Street Station
5. Gustave Doré: 'A poor quarter of London'
6. F. M. Sutcliffe: 'Old houses in Whitby'
7. London prostitutes (1857)
8. Votes for women: an endless labour
9. Arrest of a suffragette
10. *Fin de siècle* trip by bicycle
11. Haymaking in Berkshire (1910)
12. The luxury of the aristocratic life: Harewood House
13. The War in Flanders (1917)
14. and 15. Tomorrows that bring disillusionment
16. A 'hunger march'. The Jarrow workers on their way to London (1936)
17. The 'Two Nations'
18, 19 and 20. Leisure scenes: from the Edwardian to the inter-war period
21. Shelter in the Underground (1940)
22. Churchill as war leader
23. In the City of London
24. Pub scene
25. Two elders
26. Open-air oratory
27. Urban development in the 1970s: Thamesmead
28. A traditional street
29. Rural landscape in Yorkshire (1974)
30. In a Midlands mining town
31. Pop festival
32. The Beatles
33. Francis Bacon: 'Portrait of Isabel Rawsthorne standing in a Soho street' (1967)
34. In the heart of London

Acknowledgements

We would like to thank the following institutions, companies and private individuals for granting reproduction permission.

Plates
Bill Eglon Shaw, The Sutcliffe Gallery, Whitby for pl. 6; Black Star Publishing Co. Ltd for pl. 34; The Central Press Photos Ltd for pl. 17; Fotogram for pls 4 and 10; Gernsheim Collection, Humanities Research Centre, The University of Texas at Austin for pl. 12; Greater London Council Photograph Library for pls 2 and 27; Imperial War Museum, London for pl. 13; The John Hillelson Agency Ltd for pls 28 and 30 © Richard Kalvan/Magnum, pl. 23 © Michael Hardy, pls 24 and 25 © Henri Cartier-Bresson, pls 26 and 31 © Josef Koudelka; The Labour Party Library, London for pls 14 and 15; The National Maritime Museum, Greenwich for pl. 3; Photographie Giraudon, Paris for pl. 33; Popperfoto, London for pls 19, 22 and 32; Radio Times Hulton Picture Library, London for pls 1, 5, 9, 16, 18, 20 and 21; University of Reading, Museum of English Rural Life for pl. 11; Viva, Paris for pl. 29 © Yves Jeanmougin.

Figures
Her Majesty's Stationery Office for Figures 14 and 15.

Preface

Je cherche à déchiffrer le plus indéchiffrable
des peuples, le plus moral, le moins familial,
le plus mobile, le plus adapté, le plus franc et
le plus hypocrite. Où est le principe?

Elie Halévy[1]

To many people an enterprise such as the writing of this book would appear to present an impossible challenge. No one is more aware of this than the author. By its content and by its intent the book purports not only to describe the evolution of modern English society in its broad patterns, but to provide a critical assessment of this evolution, in order to interpret and explain the history of the nation. An arduous task in any circumstances, but especially so for a foreigner, for it must seem utterly presumptuous.

The social make-up, the attitudes and behaviour, the psychology of the English people during these one hundred and twenty-five years provide such a tangle of data, fleeting and contradictory at the same time, that the task may seem hopeless. As soon as one tries to analyse the true nature of the islanders, it vanishes; and in contact with it one constantly has the feeling that it cannot be grasped. This impression has indeed been shared by all those who have sought to penetrate the nation's secret. Even Baron von Bülow, when he was Prussian envoy in London, used to say to his compatriots who asked him his views on the country: 'After spending three weeks in England, I was quite ready to write a book about

it; after three months I thought the task would be difficult; and now that
I've lived here three years, I find it impossible.'[2] About forty years later,
the radical novelist Jules Vallès echoed this sentiment when he confessed
on his first visit to the English capital: 'After a three weeks' stay in London
I became aware that, to be able to talk about England, a stay of ten years
would be necessary.'[3]

The British too have felt puzzled when trying to characterize and
understand their own civilization. Asking himself in 1940 what constituted the particular nature of the English nation, and how it differed from
other nations, George Orwell concluded: 'Yes, there is something distinctive and recognisable in English civilisation. It is a culture as individual as
that of Spain. It is somehow bound up with solid breakfasts and gloomy
Sundays, smoky towns and winding roads, green fields and red pillar-
boxes. It has a flavour of its own.' But such peculiar features, Orwell
rightly went on, cannot be properly understood outside the historical
setting:

> It is continuous, it stretches into the future and the past, there is
> something in it that persists as in a living creature. What can the
> England of 1940 have in common with the England of 1840? But then,
> what have you in common with the child of five whose photograph
> your mother keeps on the mantelpiece? Nothing, except that you
> happen to be the same person. And above all it is *your* civilisation, it is
> *you*.[4]

So it is easy to understand why foreign observers have often hesitated
before launching into mastering the labyrinth without Ariadne's
thread – even, and indeed above all, when they have wished to be
solicitous and sympathetic to the object of their study. For the more
scrupulous they are, the more they feel condemned to look in from
outside. Thus Elie Halévy, in the introduction to his great *History of the
English People in the Nineteenth Century*, admitted his foolhardiness at once
and confessed his fears in these terms:

> Frenchmen, I am undertaking a history of England. I am attempting the
> study of a people to whom I am foreign alike by birth and by education.
> Despite copious readings, visits to London and to the provinces, and
> frequent intercourse with different circles of English society, I have
> nevertheless been obliged to learn with great difficulty, and in a man-
> ner that would seem necessarily artificial, a multitude of things which
> even an uneducated Englishman knows, so to speak, by instinct. I fully
> realize all this. Nevertheless I am firmly convinced that the risks I have
> taken were risks well worth the taking.[5]

Indeed a historian must surmount these obstacles and difficulties. In his own defence Halévy mentioned the 'useful faculty of astonishment' which a foreigner, looking from the outside, preserves towards the subject of his study. It is undeniable that such an approach encourages a critical mind and the will to ask questions and explain. Moreover, following the lead of another clever student of English politics and society, Jacques Bardoux, one can add another argument: 'Distance allows one to observe calmly and to judge dispassionately. Space is as important as time in giving perspective. A channel, when one wants to scrutinise and understand, is as valuable as a century. It ensures, or it ought to ensure, clarity of vision and calmness of judgment.'[6]

For my part, it is in this spirit that I have undertaken this work. It is for the reader to decide how good a job has been done.

Let me now try, at whatever risk, to make a list of the key problems which we have made a point of emphasizing in the pages to come. It will at least be a first step towards clarifying the field of investigation, and a way of tracing out in broad strokes the framework of our study.

(1) The history of England shows a national continuity. A territorial continuity, first of all, thanks to the rampart of the sea, but above all a political continuity. Comparison with all the other great nations of continental Europe is instructive on this point. Why did England escape not only revolutions, bloody violence and attempts at totalitarianism, but also internal upsets, civil discord and drastic changes of regimes and institutions?

(2) In a society of such clear-cut class distinctions, where social mobility has not been as real as some have made out, how has the ruling oligarchy – aristocratic at first, and later bourgeois – succeeded in keeping its influence as well as its prestige, and all this with the full acquiescence of the masses?

(3) How can one explain the fact that the working class – as powerful in numbers as in organization – fought so vigorously and doggedly, and yet so often accepted compromise when its loyalty to the representative system gave it such a key numerical advantage?

(4) How far was power democratized? Who ruled the country a century ago? Who rules today? Exactly how much power did the State have throughout this period? Was it as feeble (at least up to 1914) as has been maintained? How was the link between State, capitalism and the Establishment preserved?

(5) An unusual balance was kept between the individual and the collective, between liberty and constraint, between individualism and the pressure of the consensus. What were the elements which made up this equilibrium? How were the aspirations to individual independence ('the freeborn Englishman') reconciled with a community spirit (itself

reinforced by the pressure of conformity)? In this area, what role was played by religious beliefs?

(6) How did an imperial vocation and the dynamism of an expansionist society settle into the national consciousness ? And, when the time came for England to give up her world role, how did she make the change from pride to humility? Under what conditions did the shift take place towards a new model of society limited to a medium-sized island and above all jealous of 'the quality of life'?

(7) What really changed between 1851 and 1975, either in social structure or in the public mind? How did England adapt, by its internal and external development, to the new conditions of the contemporary world – economic, political, intellectual and spiritual? What part was played in this process by religion and the decline of religion, by ideologies and scales of value? And what happened to the consensus of the old days?

Of course this book can only bring partial answers and very modest offerings of interpretation to questions of such wide scope. We would feel well satisfied if the pages that follow helped to open up certain paths of investigation and shed some beams of light on an area that is wrapped in obscurity.

Let us, however, confess to one ambition. I would wish through this work to help get rid of some traditional clichés, to which people refer as if they were gospel. Let us put an end to pseudo-explanations deriving from the 'national character' of the British! How often their 'taste for compromise', their 'sporting spirit in politics', their 'golden mean', their 'pragmatism', their inveterate 'traditionalism' and other stereotypes are invoked! As if these concepts explained everything by dint of repetition, when of course their first characteristic is to explain nothing at all. They also absolve one from asking the real questions, such as why tradition prevailed at one juncture and not at another, why such and such compromise or reform or pressure group won the day and not others. So much repetitive parrot-talk. . . . It behoves us therefore to cast aside all easy and misleading catch-phrases and to press on to *real* analyses by uncovering the *real* forces at work – structures, classes, hierarchies, ethical codes, ideologies, sacred and profane beliefs. There we shall find solid ground for explanations, far from conventional views and superficial clichés. After all, was it not the method followed by our illustrious predecessors, all those French pioneers in the discovery of England who gave us analytical models that were rigorous, profound and penetrating, and whose names were Alexis de Tocqueville, Léon Faucher, Hippolyte Taine, Emile Boutmy, Moïsei Ostrogorski, Paul Mantoux, André Siegfried, André Philip, and of course, greatest of all, Elie Halévy?

Two clarifications to end up with, so as to explain and justify my limits, both in space and time. First of all, I have deliberately chosen to speak of

'English' society. Not that I underestimate the role played by Scotsmen, Welshmen and Irishmen in the development of the kingdom, but until recently, among the British as well as among foreigners the word 'England' certainly had a generic meaning.[7] The best proof is that, up to the nineteenth century, neither the Scots nor the Irish hesitated to use the word to describe the United Kingdom. Even in the twentieth century Bonar Law, though he was half Scottish and half Canadian by birth, had no qualms about calling himself 'Prime Minister of England'. Also, on great historic occasions it is the word 'England' that has always prevailed, from Nelson at Trafalgar ('England expects every man to do his duty') up to Leo Amery shouting the famous plea to Arthur Greenwood, the Opposition spokesman, in the dramatic Commons debate of 2 September 1939 – 'Speak for England!'. The truth is that no term is satisfactory, for even 'Great Britain' is defective, as it excludes Northern Ireland.

In all events I have centred the book on England, but where the destinies of the Scots and the Welsh and even the Irish follow on the destiny of the English, their history has been taken into account. Elsewhere I have left them out, preferring to concentrate on the major partner rather than to let my attention be distracted by particular details. In the same way the Empire has been left out of our field of study, except where its existence affected the national consciousness.

As for the period covered, the choice of 1851 was an obvious one, for the mid-century represented a turning-point for England, when economic conditions were reversed and social stability re-established. From that moment the triumphs of Victorianism could impose itself freely. After the endless storms of the period 1815–50 during which they nearly lost the helm of the storm-tossed ship, the governing classes felt sudden relief that no tidal wave had wrecked the vessel, and they entered calmer waters. Now the 'SS England' could with pride and assurance sail forward with the wind behind her. On the other hand, 1975 seems to mark no visible break in the historical evolution of English society. This being so I would like to look on my description of the years 1955–75 as being tentative, waiting to be completed and indeed revised in the light of future events. For my part I will take refuge behind the authority of Daniel Defoe who, two hundred and fifty years ago, in the preface to his *Tour* made this excellent comment:

After all that has been said by others, or can be said here, no description of Great Britain can be what we call a finished account, as no clothes can be made to fit a growing child; no picture carry the likeness of a living face; the size of one, and the countenance of the other always altering with time: so no account of a kingdom thus daily altering its countenance can be perfect. . . .'[8]

I The Power and the Glory: 1851–80

1 *Industrialism triumphant*

The festival of work and industry

1 May 1851. Extraordinary excitement in London. Around Hyde Park the atmosphere is festive. A motley crowd gathers in the spring sunshine – respectable citizens in top hats, working men in cloth caps, tradesmen in their Sunday best, foreigners from all over Europe. Smart turn-outs pass by, and soon high society and all the celebrities are there. Suddenly a party makes its way through the vast assemblage amid loud cheers – it's the Queen! In great state Victoria, accompanied by Prince Albert, arrives at this splendid show which England has put on – the Great Exhibition of London. Silver trumpets sound out under the vault of the Crystal Palace. A solemn prayer invokes 'the ties of peace and friendship among nations', and the sovereign slowly tours the stands of the Exhibition amid the palm-trees and the flowers and the unfurled flags of all nations to the continuous applause of the crowds.

In a letter to her uncle King Leopold of Belgium written the day after this memorable ceremony, Queen Victoria was proudly able to describe 1 May 1851 as 'the greatest day in our history', adding that it was 'the most beautiful and imposing and touching spectacle ever seen'.[1] And Palmerston echoed her feelings: 'a glorious day for England' – words that well conveyed the general feeling of national success. Thanks to the technical progress and creative energy displayed at the Exhibition, the whole country felt itself raised to the forefront of humanity and imbued by Providence with a mission to lead mankind on its way. Was this the pinnacle of the Victorian era? Yes certainly, but even more it was one of the great moments of English history. For to grasp the full significance of the Great Exhibition, the very first of the universal exhibitions (it lasted from May to October 1851 and welcomed 6 million visitors), it is not enough to regard it, for all its brilliance, simply as a display of material progress in England. Certainly it showed off the superiority of England's enterprise, in terms of manufactured goods, trade and capital, as well as the professional ability of her engineers, designers and workpeople. But its importance went much further. For the country which gave birth to the Industrial Revolution, 1851 marked a celebration as well as a turning point.

On the one hand the Great Exhibition celebrated Great Britain's entry into the era of the industrial society. Machinery and town life from now on assumed more importance than the old agrarian civilization. John Bull, the latter-day Prometheus, had won from nature the secret of power, steam taking the place of fire. This time, however, instead of defying the Creator, the might of man remained subservient to Him. The justification of technology, repeated loud and often, was its work for the progress of the species. Thus, hardly had the industrial system made its appearance in the life of the country than it assumed a hallowed role and became closely bound up with morality.

On the other hand the 'Great Exhibition of the Works of Industry of All Nations', to give its correct title, coincided with the start of a phase of great economic prosperity and social peace. What a contrast there was between the 1840s and the 1850s! Ten years of chaos and conflict, dominated by fear and famine (the 'Hungry Forties') were to be followed by ten years of prosperity and confidence, studded with a thousand marvels (the 'Fabulous Fifties'). The prime reason for the Exhibition's success was that it took place in a tranquil atmosphere – peaceful competition between nations abroad and renewed social harmony at home.

From now on the prosperous classes could breathe freely. For the popular outbreaks of yesterday had never ceased to haunt them – Peterloo, 'Captain Swing', the Bristol riots, and just recently the Chartist marches. With these in mind on the eve of the Great Exhibition the pessimists foresaw the worst excesses – pilfering, brawls, even riots. Wouldn't the display of such treasures excite the worst instincts of the mob? Wouldn't criminals from the underworld emerge to take advantage of the occasion? True, the Government took precautions on the opening day. Whole regiments of Hussars and Dragoons, and battalions of Fusiliers were brought in from the provinces to bivouac in the suburbs. Batteries of artillery were kept in reserve in the Tower of London. Several Guards' battalions were massed inside Hyde Park as well as some cavalry. Finally 6,000 policemen were mobilized. However no incident disturbed law and order either that day or at any time during the Exhibition. When the lamps were finally extinguished, the nation was proud to learn that in six months not a flower had been picked!

The attitude of the masses caused surprise at first, but people soon felt reassured and comforted. The social scene had indeed changed. Instead of a Theatre of Cruelty, it was a Theatre of Harmony that held the stage. Had England finally achieved lasting social peace? For twenty years an endless chorus of complaint about pauperism had made itself heard against a backcloth of proletarian squalor, but from 1851 onwards the tune was to change. With one voice everyone sang the praises of hard work and industrial success, and compliments for the workers were the order of the day. Hardly a word was breathed about the 'dangerous classes'; they had now disappeared from the scene. In their place the 'labouring classes' took the limelight. Wasn't it touching to contemplate 'the fustian jackets and unshorn chins of England' enjoying a peaceful picnic on the grass in Hyde Park instead of dreaming of how to overthrow society, when the outward signs of triumphant Capitalism were laid out a few feet away from them?

One must recognize that the Exhibition profited from a combination of favourable circumstances. While general confidence resulted from the strong economic recovery which began in 1851, most of the great battles which used to divide the nation into rival camps had now ceased to rage. With free trade in force since 1846, Chartism in retreat, Irish agitation broken by the failure of the Young Ireland movement, and the tragedy of the Great Famine, classes and parties no longer had the same motives to oppose each other. Somewhat to their surprise but with considerable self-satisfaction Englishmen woke up to the fact that they were almost the only people in Europe to have escaped the disturbing revolutions of 1848. Inevitably the *Zeitgeist* also underwent a profound change. Now was the time for science, the arts, and peace. People were ready to listen attentively to official spokesmen, such as the organizers of the Exhibition, when they affirmed that the future did not lie in Utopian demands or in fratricidal quarrels, but that progress and welfare depended above all on individual effort and on peace, both national and international.

The Exhibition itself was a stupendous festival of technology. The organizers wanted to present a whole panorama of human activity, and to that end divided the exhibits into four sections: raw materials, machinery, manufactured goods and fine arts. But of course the achievements of *homo britannicus*, creator of the first industrial society, were entitled to pride of place. Of the 14,000 exhibitors, 7,400 represented Great Britain and her colonies, and 6,600 the rest of the world. It was a triumph for the Age of the Machine. On every side the primacy of metal and coal asserted itself. People like Ruskin might mourn in vain the transformation of old

England into 'a land of the Iron Mask'.[2] The island had indeed been transformed, as Michelet said, into 'a mass of coal and iron'. The machine reigned supreme. The crowds gaped in admiration at the locomotives, at the models of metal bridges, hydraulic presses, giant lenses for light-houses, the latest refinements in machine-tools devised by the pioneers in precision engineering (Whitworth, Fairbairn, Armstrong) and the great Nasmyth steam hammer that was able at one moment to come down with the full weight of its 500 tons and at another to crack delicately the shell of an egg. There were machines of every sort – for threshing corn, for crushing sugar cane, for making soda water, for folding envelopes, for rolling cigarettes, and so on.

To technical objectives were added aesthetic and moral ambitions. What the organizers wanted was to unite the useful, the beautiful and the good. On entering the show the visitor was greeted by two symbolic figures: on one side a giant statue of Richard Coeur de Lion, national hero and perfect knight, the personification of courage, and on the other, an enormous block of coal weighting 24 tons, representing power! Some exhibits aimed to unite industry and art, others sought above all to speak to the imagination, from the dazzling 'Crystal Fountain', a transparent structure 10 metres high in the centre of the Exhibition, to the fabulous Crown diamond, the Koh-i-Noor.

Yet, amid all these achievements of the technological age, the most spectacular success was the very building which housed the whole show, the famous Crystal Palace. It was an edifice of staggering dimensions – 520 metres long (three times the length of St Paul's Cathedral), 125 metres wide with a display capacity of 9,000 square metres in which there was plenty of room to arrange the 109,000 exhibits.[3] Withal the building was light and airy, thanks to its construction of metal and glass. A building of genius devised by an amateur self-made man, the former gardener Pax-ton, the Crystal Palace was a remarkable combination of the classical canons of taste – symmetry and simplicity of design – and the functional-ism of modern construction methods. Conceived as a cathedral of indus-try and designed in the form of a Latin cross with a wide transept, this gigantic temple of glass was at once admired for its imposing beauty. It was greeted with a chorus of praise, accompanied by an abundance of religious parallels. Some saw 'the greatest temple ever built for the arts of peace'. For a German visitor it was the sanctuary of *Weltkultur*. A French-man wrote that the old dream of Babel had come to pass, but instead of a mixture of tongues, 'the fusion of interests and minds has been achieved'.[4] An American admirer saw in the Great Exhibition the apoca-lyptic vision of the New Jerusalem that had appeared to St John on Patmos.[5] Others in more pagan vein talked of a magician's palace.

At the dawn of the new half-century the country was bathed in optimism. There was a firm belief that the year 1851 prefigured an age of peace, progress and universal happiness. The nation was inspired by a grandiose vision of man's power, a power capable of mastering matter without falling into materialism, since his activity was constantly referred to the Almighty. Just as the entrepreneurs and manufacturers at the Exhibition were proud of having achieved a synthesis of beauty and function, so it was asserted that there was no difficulty in reconciling dominion over Nature with surrender to God. Progress and the Bible were not incompatible. The future seemed to belong to those who, like the British, knew how to combine the hand of God with the right arm of Man. In fact all these half-scientific homilies should be interpreted as so much quasi-religious worship of the genius of industry. This was well expressed by the popular poet and song-writer Mackay in the verses set to music by Henry Russell:

> Gather, ye Nations, gather! From forge, and mine, and mill!
> Come, Science and Invention; Come, Industry and Skill!
> Come with your woven wonders, the blossoms of the loom,
> That rival Nature's fairest flowers in all but their perfume.
> Come with your brass and iron, your silver and your gold
> And arts that change the face of earth, unknown to men of old.
> Gather, ye Nations, gather! From ev'ry clime and soil,
> The New Confederation, the Jubilee of toil.[6]

There is another lesson to be drawn from the Great Exhibition if you take it as the symbol of an emergent industrial system. The triumph of the machine launched the era of the masses. Some acute minds understood it at the time, and the Great Exhibition gave a foretaste of that era on the material as well as the human level. Everything was multiplied both in manufacture and in selling. Development progressed rapidly, from the making of one object, or possibly a hundred, to a thousand and then a million. Who had ever imagined standardization on such a scale as to produce 300,000 plates of glass to build the Crystal Palace, all of identical shape and size, or the sale on the refreshment stand of a million bottles of soda-water, lemonade and ginger beer, all manufactured by the house of Schweppes? In the *Revue des Deux Mondes*, a French visitor to the Exhibition commented subtly on England's success in adapting herself to the necessities of mass consumption, while France continued to specialize in producing for the luxury market: 'It is very odd. An aristocratic country like England is successful at supplying the people, whereas France, a democratic country, is only good at producing goods for the aristocracy!'[7]

On the human level too, quantity was the dominant theme. The railways and technical improvements meant that crowds of people could come together in a way that had never before been seen. In this respect the Great Exhibition was a huge popular festival – a real party for the people. It was the opposite of the splendid displays at Versailles or Windsor which were reserved for a small privileged circle. This was a democratic show laid on for the inquisitive masses gathered together in festive mood. It was not simply a deliberate (and successful) attempt on the part of Prince Albert, the chief organizer of the enterprise, to build a bridge between the monarchy and the machine, between the court and the labouring masses. For at the same time it managed to unite all classes, especially the workers, in their admiration for the industrial system, and this integrated the whole nation into the structure of a 'liberal' society. That was the political significance of the Exhibition. It conferred a smiling appearance on a dominating Capitalism and adorned it with every creative virtue. The trading economy, now launched on its triumphant career, could ignore the odd signs of revolt that cropped up here and there, and could concentrate on drawing the maximum profit from the successes of industrialism.

So it was from sound knowledge that one of the most influential celebrators of progress and the liberal destiny of England, the great Whig historian Macaulay, asserted that 1851 'will long be remembered as a singularly happy year of peace, plenty, good feeling, innocent pleasure, national glory of the best and purest sort'.[8] Who then showed concern for the other side of the coin? Who paid attention to the victims – the multitude of the crushed and the oppressed? Who noticed that in that same year, in the heart of Africa, the soldiers of Her Majesty were engaged in bloody battles to annex the country of the Kaffirs to the Empire and turn poor black peasants off their lands? Who felt indignant that on Christmas Day 1851 it was necessary to organize a charity gathering in the heart of London, at Leicester Square, so that 10,000 poor families of the district could have a bit of roast beef and plum pudding washed down with a cup of tea?

Unlimited growth

'With Steam and the Bible the English traverse the globe' was the proud boast of one of the Great Exhibition guides.[9] Indeed the growth of the economy seemed miraculous. The national income was multiplied by eight in the course of the century, while the population only went up by four. A doubling of the income per head occurred in the second half of the century. The great 'Victorian prosperity' began in 1851 under the influence of the world rise in prices, and it went on until 1873. Even the difficult times after that date did not halt this dynamic progress. In the thirty years between 1851 and 1881 the national product rose from £523 million (£25 per inhabitant) to £1,051 million (£35 per inhabitant).[10]

Each key sector showed an advance. Exports? They were £55 million in 1840–9; they went up to £100 million in 1850–9, to £160 million in 1860–9 and to £218 million in 1870–9. Railways? 6,000 miles had already been built by 1850; in 1870 the total had reached 14,000 miles. Cotton? Imports of raw cotton (the best gauge of textile activity) increased in weight from 300 million lbs in 1830–9 to 800 million in 1850–9, to 1,250 million in 1870–9. The merchant fleet? The tonnage of British shipping plying the world was 3.6 million in 1850; it was 6.6 million in 1880, of which 40 per cent was steam against less than 5 per cent in 1850. Metals? The production of cast iron rose from 2 million tons in 1850 to 6 million in 1875.[11] In all directions it was a breathless, almost intoxicating race for growth and profit. Coalmines, foundries, blast furnaces, shipyards, cotton mills, woollen mills, linen and jute factories, arsenals, cement works, cutlery workshops, makers of shoes, precision instruments and furniture, all competed with each other to produce goods more and more cheaply and exported them to the four corners of the earth. Hence the proud feeling of success, smugly expressed by the inventor of the term 'Victorian'. 'The Englishman lives . . . to move and to struggle, to conquer and to build; to visit all seas, to diffuse the genius of his character over all nations. Industry, Protestantism, Liberty, seem born of the Teutonic race – that race to whom God has committed the conservation as well as the spread of Truth and on whom mainly depend the civilization and progress of the world.'[12]

These were the external signs of growth. We must now analyse its effects so that we can try to extract an answer to the question – why was England supreme? For the key result of that growth from a macro-economic point of view, was England's dominant position in the world, a position which was only reinforced by the advances of the period 1850–75. In the middle of the century the country entered what Walter Rostow has described as the 'mature' stage, that is to say that it was now able to produce beyond the key 'take-off' sectors by applying techniques of management and accumulated investments to a wide variety of economic activities. As a nation on the move Great Britain was continuously able to extend her resources and strengthen her leading position. That is why she was variously called 'the Workshop of the World', 'the Industry State' and even 'the Fuel State'.

Thanks to the alliance of industry and commerce, to entrepreneurial skill and tenacity, to individual enterprise and the collective guarantees of *Pax Britannica*, England drew advantage from a whole range of economic stimuli. Sure of herself and of the blessing of heaven, she not only outstripped all other nations including the most highly industrialized, but it was often she who stimulated their development. In 1860 England produced nearly 60 per cent of the coal and steel in the world, more than

50 per cent of the cast iron and nearly 50 per cent of the cotton goods. In 1870 the United Kingdom produced one third of the world output of manufactured goods, and the national income per inhabitant was higher than in any other country. The French, although relatively rich, achieved only 60 per cent of the average individual income of the English. To illustrate this supremacy one can simply quote individual cases; for instance the railway construction magnate Thomas Brassey who, in twenty-five years, built 7,000 kilometres of line over four continents. The great bankers of the City competed in power with crowned heads, whom Disraeli described admiringly as 'mighty moneylenders whose *fiat* sometimes held in balance the destinies of kings and empires'.[13] Among the key-points of European development it was the London-Birmingham-Manchester axis that held the lead without serious rival. In his book *L'Europe sans rivages*, F. Perroux powerfully evoked the extraordinary thrust of British trade which, with the support of the City of London, permeated the arteries and circulation of world commerce, continuously extended it bounds of influence, centralized information and banking facilities, and fixed prices that were expressed in a dominant currency, i.e. sterling, which was everyone's favourite. Such was the supreme power and leadership of a nation which 'living rather grandly, having worked hard and possessing immense strength, . . . could address the world'.[14]

We must now try to understand the overall reasons for this growth and progress: what are the factors that explain English supremacy at this time? One must hark back to the past to answer this question. For it is beyond doubt that the English in the middle of the nineteenth century continued to draw full benefit from the series of advantages which had made their country the cradle of the Industrial Revolution. Only they were not simply content to hang on to those trumps they held in their hands at the outset. The combination of a multiplying and accelerating upward growth gave the British economy an even faster impetus and rhythm than any other, and placed her in a leading position ahead of all competitors.

The list of advantages enjoyed by prosperous Albion is a long one: a remarkable abundance of natural resources thanks to a sub-soil rich in coal and iron-ore, many waterways, a climate favourable to textile fibres, surrounding seas at the cross-roads of the world's trade-routes; a strong current of innovation that encouraged advanced techniques with high productivity, supported by well-qualified engineers, technicians and workmen; a trade network of proven value with vast foreign markets spread over five continents, and a colonial empire both rich and extensive, all served by a merchant fleet without rival in number and variety of vessels; a vast accumulation of capital and profitable investments; ample

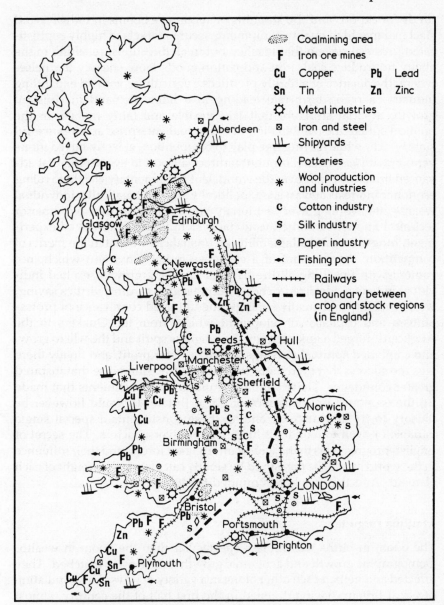

Map 1.   Economic geography of Great Britain in 1851

The demarcation line (taken from Caird) separates the pastures from the arable lands in England – the stock-raising areas (with high rents) in the west, and the lands under cultivation in the east.

funds for export, and the stimulus of successive booms in railways and steel making; high quality equipment, secure markets, a highly sophisticated financial system that reached out in all directions, resulting in the ability to produce coal, iron and cotton goods more cheaply than elsewhere; the alliance of a highly productive agriculture with an expanding industry; a rising birth-rate leading to a home demand in constant growth; a social structure that was flexible and fairly mobile; in the political sphere the combination of individual enterprise and a powerful state which, while leaving free play to competition, cleverly mixed intervention with *laissez-faire*, brought indirect support to everything that advanced British interests over the world, lent parliamentary weight to ruling economic interests and assisted, politically and diplomatically, individual wealth and world power; a human capital characterized by superior technical know-how; an educational system which encouraged experiment, innovation and adaptability; an unshakeable belief in the merits of competition; the pressure of a collective moral conviction which, not content with upsetting all the barriers opposing growth, exalted individual initiative, idealized riches, and praised as cardinal virtues saving, work, mobility and creative energy; the unforced connivance of protestantism and capitalist development which, from the Quakers to the Anglicans, forged a link between the religious spirit and the will to grow, and combined spiritual strivings with a taste for profit; and finally there was the success that bred more success and the confidence that inspired greater confidence. These were the multifarious constituents that made up the economic pre-eminence of Great Britain. It would however be illusory to try and discover among these constituents a special single variable or even to look for a hierarchy of diverse factors. The secret of English progress was in the web of interrelated forces, and their influence in the world cannot be measured by simply calculating the weight of each element. And that is what astounded the world.

Malthus forgotten

The boom in births was no less spectacular than the boom in wealth. Demographic growth and economic growth were closely matched. They affected and helped each other along in a variety of ways. The population of Great Britain, having doubled in the first half of the century, almost doubled again in the second half. The census in fact registered 20.8 million inhabitants in 1851 (as opposed to 10.5 million in 1801) and 37 million in 1901. If one looks at the three 'nations' of the island, one sees that England has the lion's share with 16.9 million souls in 1851 (against 8.3 million in 1801) and 30.8 million in 1901. The Welsh, who numbered half a million at the end of the eighteenth century, reached 1 million in

1851 and 1.7 million in 1901. Here the population explosion was accompanied by a remarkable geographical concentration, for by 1901 half the population were living in the county of Glamorgan. The latter had more inhabitants than the other eleven Welsh counties put together, whereas in 1851 it contained only 10 per cent of the total. In Scotland, where emigration had a greater effect and where the population also tended to concentrate in one region, the Lowlands, the number of inhabitants increased at a slower rate. There were 2.9 million Scotsmen in 1851 (as opposed to 1.6 million in 1801) and 4.5 million in 1901 – an increase of 55 per cent compared with increases of 69 per cent in Wales and 82 per cent in England.

The rhythm of its increase kept Great Britain at the head of the European league. She maintained the ample lead she had won at the time of the population explosion. From 1851 to 1881 her annual rate of increase, which was around 1.3 per cent, put her at the head of Europe, equal to Holland and Denmark, well above Prussia, Belgium, Italy and Russia, and leaving France a long way behind. Having underlined demographic potency as a major trait of British society, one ought perhaps to spell out its elements. It was the coexistence of three characteristics which gave the population of England in the middle of the nineteenth century its particularly original make-up: a number of old persistent patterns dating from the pre-industrial demographic regime, a stabilization of the forces at work in the great flood of growth, and finally new migration movements heading overseas.

Table 1 The age distribution of the population of England and Wales, 1821–1971

	1821	1851	1881	1911	1931	1951	1971
0–9 years	27.9	24.8	25.7	20.9	15.8	15.7	16.8
10–19 years	21.1	20.5	20.6	19.0	16.6	12.6	14.2
20–29 years	15.7	17.5	16.8	17.3	17.1	14.2	14.1
30–39 years	11.8	13.2	12.7	15.3	14.7	14.6	11.6
40–49 years	9.4	9.8	9.8	11.5	13.1	14.9	12.5
50–59 years	6.6	6.9	7.0	8.0	11.1	12.1	12.0
over 60 years	7.5	7.3	7.4	8.0	11.6	15.9	18.8
	100.0	100.0	100.0	100.0	100.0	100.0	100.0

Among the long-standing characteristics one must mention the preponderance of young age groups, the traditional structure of households and the general fertility. A young country (in 1871 four out of five Englishmen were under 45 and one out of two were under 21), England maintained an age pyramid until after 1880 which was very similar to the one that prevailed, according to Gregory King's estimates, at the end of the seventeenth century. There was the same proportion of young people and probably much the same proportion of elderly. There was little practice of birth control. As for the average size of households, far from showing a new style of family (i.e. smaller families instead of extended families), the works of Peter Laslett have shown a steady continuity from the seventeenth to the end of the nineteenth century – 4.7 persons per household in 1851, the same as the average between 1650 and 1750.[15] Contrary to what has often been thought, not only did industrialism and urbanization contribute nothing to a reduction in the size of households (in fact just the opposite, as the urban family in the nineteenth century tended to be a bit larger than the classic rural family) but indeed recent evidence shows that the composition of households simply followed the traditional model. Only a minority of households extended over three generations and included collateral relations (i.e. aunts, nephews cousins); most of the time they were 'nuclear' families, centred on two generations. Michael Anderson's detailed study of Preston, a typical industrial town in Lancashire, whose family size was noticeably larger than the national average (5.4 persons per household) still showed that three-quarters of the families consisted only of parents and children.[16]

In this great population explosion, which has been called the 'demographic revolution', everyone knows that the central mechanism was the variable effect of three factors: birth-rate, death-rate and marriage-rate. In mid-nineteenth-century England, one sees these factors becoming relatively stable. Between 1840 and 1880 the curves on the graph hardly vary at all. Hence the numerical expansion was both strong and regular.

After the slow decline in the first third of the century the death-rate seems to have reached a plateau at around 22–3 per '000. No doubt the plateau tilts downwards a little, but until 1875 there is no decisive alteration to be seen. Neither public health nor medical science brought about a spectacular change. Infant mortality did not vary. Another proof of stability was the insignificant change in life expectancy. While in 1841 it was 40 years for men and 42 years for women, it increased by only one or two points in the course of the next thirty years and only just reached 44 years and 48 years at the end of the century. On the marriage side, i.e. marriage-rate and average age of marriage, the fluctuations were insignificant. Finally the birth-rate kept up its high level with splendid regularity, for the five-year averages remained consistently between 35 and 36 per '000 up to 1875.

The result of all this was that the demographic factors, which more or less stabilized just before the mid-century, remained unaltered until 1880 and resulted in a remarkable increase in numbers. Around that date

300,000 new souls were added to the population of Great Britain every year. The main reason for this was the large gap between the number of births and the number of deaths – three births for every two deaths. For one birth followed another pell-mell. In the public mind the traditional picture of the family reigned supreme. The large family was the rule. Wasn't it the law of nature? For example in the cohort of marriages celebrated between 1861 and 1869, amounting to a million and a half couples, an average of 6.2 children was produced.[17] At this time more than one family out of six consisted of 10 children or more. On the other hand only one out of eight families had 1 or 2 children.

Fertility, vitality, activity – the social side of life echoed the biological. This outpouring of young human beings required new horizons and a field of expansion broader than an island with a rising population could offer. The national territory was not enough. Energy and ambition sought fresh territories overseas in which to work. There was, of course a long tradition of distant trade and pioneer colonization, but there was a change of scale in the middle of the nineteenth century. Emigration, occurring in successive waves (1851–4, 1863–6, 1869–74, 1880–4) became a prodigious phenomenon.

Up until 1840 the flow of departures had stayed at a modest level; and emigrants had been recruited mostly from the Celtic lands. From then onwards there was a distinct change. Emigration absorbed at least one third of the excess of births over deaths. And it was now England's turn, after Scotland and Ireland, to become an important source of leavers. It is certainly difficult to arrive at an accurate number of people who left their native land for good, because many returned and the statistics do not distinguish between the different subjects of the United Kingdom. Nevertheless we can reckon that the number of English and Scots who left between 1850 and 1880 to people the new Anglo-Saxon lands came to more than 3 million. If the currents of emigration (in which a distinct preponderance of males must be noted – three out of five) had their ups and downs of intensity, they showed a striking regularity in their destinations. Two-thirds of emigrants started life again in the United States, one-fifth in Australia and New Zealand, one-tenth in Canada. Around 1875–80 we see a new current, albeit a very small one, towards South Africa. The preference for America persisted steadily until 1895. The change only came about in the last years of the century, when quite quickly the share of the United States dropped to half of the total and then declined further, to the advantage of Canada and South Africa. So all over the world there sprang up Anglo-Saxon homes where myriad links were kept up with the motherland in the spheres of finance and exchange, of sentiment and institutions, of religion and culture, and of language and civilization.

At the same time emigration appeared as a remedy for pauperism and economic difficulties. It offered a safety-valve to the threat of social breakdown. It provided an outlet which channelled both the despair of the unemployed and the appetite of those who looked for profitable ventures; and in addition it accorded a special means of spreading English influence throughout the world and of making the human capital of the nation bear fruit – 'the best affair of business in which the capital of an old and wealthy country can engage' said John Stuart Mill.[18] In his *Notes on England*, Taine recounts with admiration a meeting with two young people, born into a family of twelve children, who are getting ready to leave for New Zealand to be sheep farmers: 'Impossible to describe their energy, their ardour, their decisiveness . . . one feels a superabundance of energy and activity, an overflowing of animal spirits.' He concludes: 'Here is a fine way of entering life. Many risks are taken, the world is wide open, and one skims off the cream.'[19]

For side by side with the hunger that drove the surplus mouths overseas there existed a well-to-do emigration, less numerous but very active. This was the emigration of managers who went out to Egypt, to India, to the Rio de la Plata or to China. In the four corners of the globe you came across these pioneers, on the Colorado as well as on the Yangtse, in Lagos or Beirut, in Winnipeg or Singapore. For some of them expatriation was only temporary. They intended to come back home after a few years, their fortunes made, or at least having accumulated a modest pile. For others it was a departure for good, sometimes cheerful, sometimes endured with resignation and that sadness which one sees in the faces of Ford Madox Brown's painting, 'The Last of England'.

Creative energy was thus abounding everywhere, abroad as well as at home. Growth gave rise to enterprise, which in its turn bred confidence for further ventures. Travel, which for some meant a voyage as far as the Antipodes, became the symbol of a society of movement, adventure and expansion.

On the urban front

As the first country to arrive at an industrial civilization, England was also the first to experience a predominantly urban way of life – the one that was to become the lot of all the advanced nations. Her peculiar experience was to arrive at this stage very early and at the same time on a massive scale. Indeed it was around 1845 that the traditional town-country pattern was reversed. The long domination of the country then came to an end, and the predominance of towns started. Once this tendency had got under way, the imbalance in favour of towns very rapidly asserted itself. The urban population, which just formed the

majority in 1851, was very far ahead 40 years later, when three Englishmen out of four were townsmen. In less than half a century England became an urban nation. But in this leap forward the change
was not simply numerical. The transformation was even more one of
the quality of life than of mere numbers. In the course of this urbanization a new visual scene emerged together with a new system of social
relations and a new lifestyle – in brief a new civilization came into
being.

Table 2 Urban and rural populations in England and Wales in the nineteenth
century[20]

	Urban and rural populations as a percentage of the total population								
	1801	1841	1851	1861	1871	1881	1891	1901	1911
THE POPULATION LIVING IN TOWNS									
of over 100,000 inhabitants	11.0	20.7	24.8	28.8	32.6	36.2	39.4	43.6	43.8
of 50,000 – 100,000 inhabitants	3.5	5.5	5.9	6.1	5.6	7.3	8.6	7.5	8.0
of 20,000 – 50,000 inhabitants	4.8	6.8	7.0	7.4	9.6	9.4	9.2	9.9	10.4
of 10,000 – 20,000 inhabitants	4.7	5.3	6.4	6.6	6.6	6.6	7.1	8.1	7.9
of 2,500 – 10,000 inhabitants	9.8	10.0	9.9	9.8	10.8	10.5	10.2	8.9	8.8
TOTAL URBAN POPULATION	33.8	48.3	54.0	58.7	65.2	70.0	74.5	78.0	78.9
TOTAL RURAL POPULATION	76.2	51.7	46.0	41.3	34.8	30.0	25.5	22.0	21.1
No. of towns with over 100,000 inhabitants	1	7	10£	13	17	20	24	33	36
No. of towns with 20,000 – 100,000 inhabitants	16	48	55	66	88	108	118	141	165

The urban front now developed three special characteristics – fast
rhythm of growth, new types of living quarters and a new ordering of
space. To take growth first, the rate was so remarkable that one can only
talk of galloping urbanization, and the figures bear this out eloquently.
Table 2 shows on the one hand the spectacular rise of the urban population (in absolute terms it tripled between 1850 and 1900), and on the other
hand the supremacy of the large towns in the expansion.
    Side by side with the large towns whose wealth dated from the begin-
ning of the Industrial Revolution (between 1851 and 1901 Manchester
grew from 340,000 inhabitants to 650,000, and its huge suburb, Salford,
from 65,000 to 220,000; the Liverpool area went up from 400,000 to
700,000, the Birmingham area from 230,000 to 760,000; in Scotland, Glasgow leapt from 360,000 to 920,000) one can see the swift rise of towns of
second rank, which assumed the role of regional capitals. In the second
half of the century Leeds increased from 170,000 to 430,000, Sheffield
from 135,000 to more than 400,000, Newcastle from 90,000 to 250,000 and
Hull from 85,000 to 240,000. Others held their old positions, e.g. Bristol
with 330,000 inhabitants in 1901 as against 140,000 half a century earlier.
Among the fastest growing towns we should mention Leicester, in the

Midlands, (60,000 souls in 1850, 210,000 in 1901) where new engineering industries joined the traditional hosiery activity; Stoke-on-Trent in the heart of the Potteries, up from 65,000 to 215,000; and the textile centres of Nottingham and Derby. Some towns rose up out of nothing. Coal created Cardiff, ironworks Middlesborough and Barrow-in-Furness, the railways Crewe and Swindon.

Throughout the country, apart from the extreme north of England and Scotland, there was one prevalent type of habitation: that of the individual house. The 1851 census remarks on this subject that 'the possession of an entire house is strongly desired by every Englishman, for it throws a sharp, well-defined circle round his family and hearth – the shrine of his sorrows, joy, and meditations.'[21] This indicates a profound longing for domestic independence, expressed even by humble folk in the well-known saying 'my home is my castle'. Of course living quarters of this kind tended to give rise to an individualist mentality, without lessening in working-class areas a lively spirit of solidarity and mutual help among families.

Houses varied considerably in size and comfort according to the social class and income of the occupants. In middle-class areas one found terrace houses next to each other all along a street, or detached houses standing in their own large gardens. The latter style was favoured by the more prosperous families, being a vision of the aristocratic country house on a small scale. A more economic solution was often adopted in the lower levels of the middle class – pairs of 'semi-detached' houses joined together and separated from their neighbours. The spacious Victorian terrace houses, usually built in the classical style with a profusion of columns, balconies and stucco facings but occasionally displaying the Hanseatic, Flemish or Tudor mode, were nearly always built with an identical interior plan. The distribution of rooms was an exact reflection of the orders of society. The lower classes, i.e. the servants, for their day-time work occupied the basement ('below stairs') where the kitchen, the pantry and the servants' hall were situated, and in the evening they went up to the third or fourth floors to sleep. The ground floor and the first two floors were the domain of the masters. The dining-room and an occasional room were usually on the ground-floor; the drawing-room, where the lady of the house presided, was on the first floor; and the bedrooms of the parents and children on the second floor.

In the poorer quarters, i.e. in most of the town, the workers' dwellings also followed a more or less fixed plan. They nearly always consisted of small two-floor brick houses, aligned in terraces and separated from the next row at the back by a small yard or a bit of garden. These houses sometimes had two rooms on each floor, but more often a single room or 'one up, one down'. From the end of the eighteenth century onwards, it also often happened that the builders took to backing houses one against the other to save ground. This 'back-to-back' technique was a calamity denounced by all experts in hygiene, which is why from 1850 onwards most local authorities ruled out the system, but the back-to-backs took a long time to disappear. In Nottingham for example, around 1850, there were 8,000 such houses, i.e. two-thirds of the dwellings in the town. The scourge of urban squalor was not confined to this type of construction. Slums resulted from overcrowding, itself the product of poverty and high rents, and from 'jerry-building', a cut-price way of building on badly drained soil with no solid foundations and using materials of poor quality. The result was that whole districts were made up of hovels without air or water, and without sanitation beyond a common sewer. Rubbish and filth gathered in these fetid cess-pits, and encouraged vermin and epidemics of every kind. Urban misery reached the depths of degradation.

Property speculation played an important role in the development of towns. First it was a fruitful sector for investment because of rapid expansion. The return on building was a regular 6 per cent. At the same time the fast growth of the towns gave a boost to ground values which continued to be high and on the increase even up to our own times. However, quite apart from the effect of rising land values, the spatial layout and the Victorian urban scene are above all explained by the system of land ownership and the methods of building development. The ground landlords often possessed vast estates. When a landlord decided to parcel out all or part of his property, he usually got in touch with a 'speculative builder' who took charge of the development.

There were two consequences to this. First of all, the uniform appearance of urban houses in England – mass-produced, all the houses in the same street or the same district resemble one another in design and size. The resulting impression is one of monotony which strikes all foreigners. Bernstein recalls in his memoirs that Marx, who was very short-sighted, regularly entered the wrong house when he came back to his district of Kentish Town from the British Museum.[22] Secondly the landlord, whether he was a private individual or an institution, usually imposed a general scheme for the construction of the houses and the street lay-out, together with a mass of specifications, so that, paradoxically, private initiative tempered the natural anarchy of urban development. It is therefore, a mistake to suppose that Victorian towns were simply the products of chance. At the estate level they were not without plan or direction. Laissez-faire and the profit motive were joined together to produce a certain degree of control. It would be more sensible to talk of a mosaic of small enterprises rubbing shoulders with one another, a curious mixture of order in detail and chaos in the general plan. Victorian town development was thus tempered by a degree of private planning which took over some of the traditions of the aristocratic urbanism of the classic period. In the end, towards the close of the century, public authority planning started to assert itself.

This form of 'mosaic' development inevitably led to each district, and even each street in a town, acquiring a special character, and so gave rise to social segregation. Even before it was built one could see the destiny fixed for an area, and in a social system as strictly defined and hierarchical as Victorian England, the differentiation became mandatory. It is well known that every town reflects in its layout and architecture the society from which it springs. In Great Britain's case the methods of town development as well as the prevalence of horizontal construction led to an urban geography that underlined social divisions more than in any other country. Far from bringing different social groups together, the British town contributed to isolation, not to say apartheid. There was indeed a contradiction here with the ambitions of society which aimed, as we shall see, at a closing of the ranks round a political and moral consensus. On the contrary, urban life led to local loyalty – to the neighbourhood, to the street, to the group of houses or the district – and to the strengthening of class distinctions. As against this the extreme diversity of the towns – large conurbations like Manchester, Birmingham or Glasgow, medium-sized industrial cities like Halifax, Huddersfield or Barrow-in-Furness, small peaceful towns like York or Oxford, resorts like Brighton or Scarborough, etc. – led to a host of regional and local nuances.

London

Standing apart, in a class by itself, was the capital – the 'Metropolis'. It was an enormous mass which by its extent and the number of its inhabitants and buildings far outstripped all other towns in the world, without a possible rival. London seemed to be the incarnation of the Industrial Age. Its population passed the million mark when the century was just two years old. It was the first town since the fall of Rome to reach this total. In 1851 there were 2.4 million Londoners; in 1881 there were 3.8 million, and for the whole conurbation of Greater London the total was even 4,750,000. It was at the turn of the century that the town itself, i.e. the County of London, reached its maximum of 4.5 million according to the census of 1901, while Greater London, whose growth was no less spectacular, counted 6.6 million inhabitants. This ocean of houses stretching as far as the eye could reach induced a feeling of immensity that almost overwhelmed the beholder – a source of fear as well as of admiration. The vision that constantly sprang to the minds of the Victorians was that of the great cities of antiquity, such as Tyre, Nineveh, Palmyra, and, above all, Babylon. Byron's phrase 'the modern Babylon' became the standard way to express, depending on the context, the grandeur, the power, the wealth, the vice or the corruption of this monster city. When Ozanam visited London for the 1851 Exhibition, he saw there, after Rome and Paris, 'the third capital of modern civilization'. Most Englishmen, being less eclectic and more jingoist, soon set up their own clichés and described their capital as 'the centre-point of the civilized world', 'the wonderful centre of the world's trade', or, alluding to the gigantic con-centration of wealth 'the Golden City'. London was represented as the microcosm of the universe, 'the World City'.

However, the concentration was so vast and so diverse, so fragmented and contrasted, that it was difficult to form a concrete idea of the whole. Mayhew, the most famous researcher of the mid-century, had the notion of trying an ascent in a balloon above the giant town. From that special vantage-point he observed in fascination the 'Leviathan metropolis with a dense canopy of smoke hanging over it'. But even from there it was impossible, he reported, 'to tell where the monster city began or ended, for the buildings stretched not only to the horizon on either side, but far away into the distance . . . where the town seemed to blend into the sky'. He went into ecstacies at the sight of 'this vast bricken mass of churches and hospitals, banks and prisons, palaces and workhouses, docks and refuges for the destitute, parks and squares, and courts and alleys, which make up London'. Indeed the observer was struck less by the quantities of houses than by the countless mass of human beings of all conditions, assembled in this small area where the threads of millions of human destinies crossed each other. At this level social analysis, as so often happened in that moralizing age, was coloured by ethical considerations of the good and bad results of such a concentration of humanity, a 'strange conglomeration of vice, avarice and low cunning, of noble aspira-tions and humble heroism'. From his balloon the journalist, comparing his airy position to that of an 'angel's view' takes to meditating on this 'huge town where perhaps there is more virtue and more iniquity, more wealth and more want, brought together in one dense focus than in any other part of the earth'.[23]

The area of the town continued to spread like an oil patch advancing by capillarity, with some fingers shooting out along the axes of the main roads and railways. In its gradual advance the town engulfed ancient villages, market gardens and pastures, driving farms and their fields ever further out. Urbanization took over whole tracts of land in its progress. Private estates, often of considerable acreage, were suddenly given over to development. In this way the fashionable new districts of Kensington and Paddington, extending the West End further west, were constructed, while to the north substantial houses sprang up in St John's Wood, Hampstead and Islington. On the east side and on the flat lands south of the Thames, the working-class quarters predominated with their long monotonous lines of small grey houses. The East End grew towards Mile End, Poplar and Hackney, while on the south bank of the river the spaces between the ancient boroughs of Southwark and Greenwich were filled

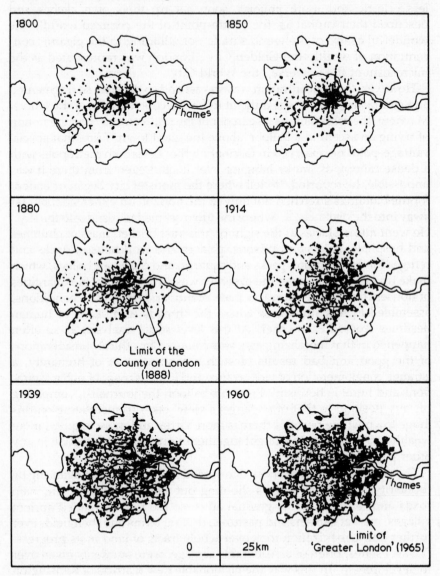

Map 2. The growth of London[24]

in with housing, and new districts such as Battersea and Camberwell developed at the same pace. Further south, near the first line of Surrey hills, the solid suburbs rose up amid greenery, with their comfortable detached villas in the middle of large shady gardens.

What was completely new from the mid-century onwards was the movement of the population away from the central districts. The zone most affected was the City and its adjacent areas. While the City's population from 1801 to 1851 was very stable with an almost constant figure of 130,000 inhabitants (which gave a considerable density – over 1,000 people per acre on average, and in certain areas up to nearly 2,000), it suffered a rapid decline in the second half of the century as a result of the building of railway stations and even more of the growth of warehouses and office blocks. In 1881 there were no more than 51,000 inhabitants, in 1901 27,000. The City started to live on a double rhythm – a diminishing night population and a day population of growing numbers and frenzied activity. A 'day census' revealed the daytime presence of 170,000 people in 1866 and 300,000 in 1891.[25] A similar pattern developed in other parts of the historic heart of London – the Strand, Holborn, Soho. In all, between 1851 and 1881, the central districts lost 135,000 people, and towards the end of the century the process was even more rapid. So began a special division of urban space which in the twentieth century was to lead to a contrast between business centres and residential areas, as well as to daily migrations that became both more numerous and longer in distance. However, in the second half of the nineteenth century, these daily journeys were on a small scale – they amounted to less than 50,000 in 1854.[26] Only the well-to-do, i.e. those who had the means to use the omnibus, the train or better still the personal vehicle, could allow themselves to live at a certain distance from their work. All the rest, and particularly the workmen who travelled on foot, were forced to find lodgings near their place of work, with all that this entailed for popular housing – overcrowding, high rents and the spread of slums.

Two phenomena dominated the organization of collective living in London: the total absence of municipal government at town level, and the violence of urban contrasts. London was a huge sprawl without unity, broken up into a multitude of small autonomous districts – civil parishes governed by vestries, unrepresentative and without effective powers. The capital suffered from its division between the City on the one hand, administered by its 'Corporation', a closed oligarchy of businessmen with age-old prestige, and on the other the chaos, not to say anarchy, of a mass of small local authorities, entangled, inefficient and often corrupt – the 'Bumbledom' denounced by Dickens. Until 1888 no remedy was applied to the scandalous under-administration and under-equipment of the world's largest town, for the only reform ever voted (The Metropolis

Management Act of 1855 creating the Metropolitan Board of Works) confined itself to correcting the worst abuses relating to drainage and traffic.

Laissez-faire likewise triumphed in the social sphere. Hence the astonishing contrasts which surprised every visitor. Firstly there were the contrasts between districts. The town was in effect made up of various towns. So it took in the City, world centre of finance and trade, Westminster, the headquarters of the government and heart of the Empire, the industrial zones of the centre and the East End (where garments, shoes, jewels, furniture, silk and timber were made up, and where boats, vehicles, precision instruments, etc. were manufactured) and the south whose specialities were machine-tools, tanning, fire-arms and so on. Beyond London Bridge started the Docks, an immense and very active port, the first in the world. To these wharves and warehouses ships would steam, carrying cargoes from the four corners of the globe: tea, ivory, spices, wine, wood, furs, grain and coal. There was a ceaseless movement of ships on the Thames, an everchanging scene which the brush of Whistler immortalized around 1860 in a series of watercolours. 'A wonderful medley of masts, sails and rigging', remarked Baudelaire, 'a chaos of fog, furnaces and gushing smoke – the profound and complicated poetry of a vast capital.'[27]

Another contrast, and a much more violent one, was the marked difference between opulence and poverty, which went far beyond the standard antithesis of West End and East End. The lines of social hierarchy were drawn with great precision. In 1851, only one Londoner in twenty-five belonged to the 'upper-class', while the 'lower classes', of which the vast majority were manual workers, formed more than four-fifths of the population. In the fine houses of the aristocracy of Belgravia and Mayfair there were parties and a social life of exceptional brilliance, especially in 'the Season', while every day, in Hyde Park, Rotten Row provided an elegant meeting-place for the gentlemen and ladies of society when mounted on horseback. Yet, not a mile from these glamorous scenes where money flowed like water, there were thousands of human beings squatting in filth and misery. Apart from the pockets of poverty which were dotted about the wealthy districts, there were whole areas delivered over to the poor, nearly all the East End and the area that bordered the Thames on the south. Yet, to counter current romantic visions of 'the mysteries of London', we must carefully distinguish between two categories of population. On the one hand there was the majority made up of workmen and small tradespeople who, in spite of conditions that were difficult and often sombre, did manage to make some sort of a living and had no contact with the world of crime. On the other, there was the underworld, whose size and influence has often been unduly exaggerated. It is certainly true that the size and anonymity of the English capital encouraged the existence of a host of castaways and down-and-outs. There were crowds of bad hats, young criminals escaped from detention, sailors who had jumped their ships, pickpockets, prostitutes from innumerable brothels, and above all the left-overs of a society that was merciless to the unfortunate. There were cripples, hard-core unemployed, beggars in rags, hangers around soup-kitchens and night shelters – in short, a world of outsiders on the margin of society, a latent menace to law and order. It was a universe of the starving and destitute which charitable organizations, always anxious to preserve respectability, tended to keep in existence rather than alleviate. It took an optimistic liberal economist like MacCulloch to calculate that one Londoner out of six died in a workhouse, a hospital or a lunatic asylum.

So one can see why the maelstrom of London provoked views that were so passionate and so contradictory. These opinions varied from the invective of critics like Ruskin who spoke of 'that great foul city – rattling, growling, smoking, stinking – a ghastly heap of fermenting brickwork, pouring out poison at every pore',[28] to the enthusiasm of the admirers of a varied and fascinating town, a true epitome of England at the peak of liberalism. It was to the latter that Henry James belonged when he saw in the movement of the capital 'the rumble of the tremendous human mill'.

Green England: the unchanging countryside

The spectacular advance of the towns should not lead us into thinking that the countryside was fading away. In hundreds of ways, directly or indirectly, the old green England continued to hold a privileged place in the life of the nation. First of all, in the physical sense, by its preponderance. The urban areas covered at most only a twentieth of the country's surface. Elsewhere the rural expanses prevailed, as the centre of traditional country life and ancestral influences. Wherever you went in England you found fields and pastures, peaceful flocks and large trees, endless hedges and earth roads, small villages and thatched farms. Such was the almost uniform pattern of the countryside. 'Nothing but green' was Taine's description. On the other hand the forests, despoiled in former times for naval construction, occupied very little space, and no effort was made to replant them.

The age-old traditions of rural civilization were also solidly entrenched in habits of thought and in social relations. Land ownership remained the prime source of authority, prestige and influence. In spite of the powerful intrusion of commercial and manufacturing capitalism from the eighteenth century onwards, it did not succeed in upsetting the old idea, dating from the origins of agrarian society, that land was the fundamental asset. So it followed that power should belong to the owners of the soil. Furthermore labour on the land was endowed with a thousand virtues and continued to symbolize labour in its purest form.

Everything was impregnated with the rural spirit – mentalities, ways of thought and language. Even the two main foundations of the national culture – classical antiquity for the educated élite and the Bible for all – helped to strengthen the primacy of the country. Biblical echoes and Virgilian tags commended the peace of the fields while they strengthened the conviction that there resided the true habitat of man. Not that it can have been very easy to compare the rubicund drovers of herds of short-horns to shepherds of Arcadia! But these bucolic impulses, brought up to date by capitalism and revitalized by agricultural science, came alive again by their association with progress and well-being. Furthermore, as people saw the enormous increase in yields arising from the agricultural revolution, how could they not marvel at the results which even the inhabitants of the Promised Land could not have imagined in their wild-est dreams? And the prestige of the countryside was raised even further by 'the taste of the wealthiest and most influential section of the nation for rural life' which was noticed by the Frenchman Léonce de Lavergne, a great admirer of English agriculture.

In certain respects ruralism even gained ground instead of retreating. As industrial civilization tightened its grip, an ardent quest for nature began to develop, as a sort of defence reaction. People felt a growing need for the country as an antidote to the urban environment. Hence the love of greenery, of gardens and lawns. 'The town-dweller does all he can to cease being a town-dweller' observed Taine as early as 1860. And after that the process never ceased to gain strength, making a profound mark on town architecture and town life. In this superiority granted to the country over the town we see a sign of green England's resistance to the spread of black England, much more than a nostalgia for the past. The country, admitting a material defeat, took a spiritual revenge on the town by winning men's hearts.

It is certainly true that the population of the countryside began to diminish in a marked way. Not that the abolition of the Corn Laws in 1846 struck a fatal blow to agriculture. That is a legend that must be con-tradicted. Supported by favourable conditions, the working of the land successfully survived free trade; and the 'Victorian prosperity' from 1851 to 1873 benefited as much from agriculture as from industrial and com-mercial enterprise. Nevertheless the pull of the towns was stronger. Towards the middle of the nineteenth century the rural exodus began to take a new turn. Here and there losses in manpower occurred, for the departures outstripped the natural population growth. In his study of rural depopulation J. Saville has shown that it was in the 1851 census that for the first time purely agricultural counties (e.g. Wiltshire in England and Montgomeryshire in Wales) showed a drop in population.[29] In the following decades, the same tendency affected East Anglia, Cornwall and most of the Welsh counties. However, one must not exaggerate this tendency because, according to Bowley's estimates, in the second half of the nineteenth century, the total rural population went down by less than 10 per cent, having grown by 50 per cent in the first half.[30] So ritual lamentations on deserted villages should be greeted with some reserve. Nevertheless, even if in absolute figures the drop was slow, in relative terms the story was very different. In 1871 the proportion of the rural population to the urban population was exactly the reverse of what had obtained at the beginning of the century: one-third countrymen and two-thirds town-dwellers, as against two-thirds and one-third. The number of workers in agriculture, which was just over 2 million in 1851 dropped to 1.6 million in 1881, and their proportion in the total labour force fell between those two dates from one-fifth to one-eighth. (At the end of the eighteenth century it was two-fifths.) Even more marked was the retreat of agriculture within the economic activity of the country. From 1851 to 1881, with an equal turnover (rather more than £100 million) agriculture saw its contribution drop from one-fifth to one-tenth of the national income.

Yet rural society held its own. It kept its cohesion in a remarkable way. One of its characteristics was its homogeneity arising from a shared life in contact with nature and the land, and from the survival of semi-feudal traditions. Another was its fundamental variety, seeing that the rural community, made up of three layers, was divided into three blocks whose limits could not be crossed. In appearance there was nothing in common between a country gentleman – rich, civilized and treated with the respect that surrounded old families – and the poor illiterate day-labourer who toiled all day on the land. Yet they were bound together by a sense of solidarity that went far beyond patronage on one side and dependence on the other.

For the originality of the British countryside lay in the fact that a highly capitalist agriculture developed, without a break, within the framework of an earlier structure, that is to say the feudal and aristocratic system. This system, entrenched in its near-monopoly of the land and its alliance with the Church, managed to survive in many institutions and even more in modes of conduct, while adapting itself to the requirements of new methods of production. This explains the three-layer structure of rural society, each man in his own station, and the three levels defined with the utmost exactitude. It was thus a society characterized by a stable and rigid hierarchy with very little mobility indeed.

At the top of the pyramid were the landed capitalists, the owners of the soil. Aristocrats belonging to the peerage or the gentry, drawing most of their income from land rents, they lived in their manor, hall or country house, leaving the task of running their properties to their agent. In the centre of the hierarchy were the farmers who paid rent on their farms in exchange for a lease. Working their land made them both employers of labour and producers, and more or less members of the middle class. Finally, at the bottom of the social scale, was the world of hired farm-workers. Labourers, ploughmen, shepherds, farm servants and the like, they formed an agricultural proletariat, plentiful and submissive, generally very poor and exploited. These 'agricultural labourers', on

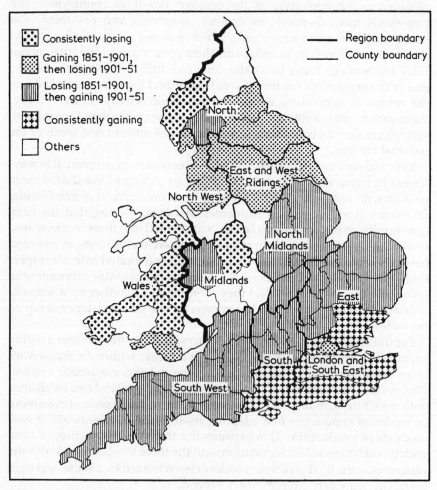

Map 3. Internal migration in England and Wales, 1851–1951[31]

whose efforts depended the working of the soil, were very often neglected, if not actually ill-treated.

Let us consider the respective sizes of the three elements that made up
the rural world. One can reckon that in 1851 the landlords did not number
more than a few thousand. The tenant farmers, who rented their land,
amounted to a quarter of a million, while the wage-earners numbered
about 1,250,000 agricultural labourers. Two conclusions can be drawn
from this analysis. Firstly, the extreme simplicity of the social pyramid,
from the wide spread of the base up to the narrow point of the summit.
Secondly, one sees that the three levels of the social hierarchy faithfully
reproduce the fundamental division of English society into three classes:
aristocracy, middle class and manual workers.

Later on, in the detailed study of social stratification, we will find each
of these categories placed at its national level (see chaps 2 and 3).
However, to understand the rural world and its cohesive strength fully,
one would have to view at the same time the horizontal divisions – the trio
landlords/tenant farmers/labourers – and the vertical unity, the result of
the integrating powers of the old society of the soil. For the existence of a
rural community did not derive solely from a certain unity of interests
among all those who lived on the same land – in other words, the landed
interest. Tradition and style of life also counted. In fact, despite enormous
differences in income and standard of living, in power and culture, the
rural world felt itself united in its association with nature and the earth, by
the immemorial rhythm of the seasons and the days, and perhaps even
more by the weight of age-old customs, both of castle and of cottage ('The
rich man in his castle, the poor man at his gate'). Hence the common
acceptance of an order considered unchangeable and ordained by the
Creator, symbolized every Sunday in church by the squire and his family
in their own pew, the farmers in their comfortable decent seats, while the
labourers, crowded and standing, were relegated to the back of the aisle.

The preciseness of the social structures reflect the relative simplicity of
agrarian structures, in spite of regional differences. A country of large
estates and medium-sized farms is how one might summarize the situation in England in the second half of the nineteenth century. The enclosures were just about at an end, for the simple reason that there was not
much left to enclose. On the contrary there was a reversal of the century-
old tendency after 1870, as shown in a new interest in the preservation of
common grounds. The 'commons', now considered as green open spaces
to be preserved, acquired a sudden importance, forerunners of the 'green
belts' and the special land reserves. In spite of this tentative effort, the
concentration of property, which had continued uninterrupted since the
eighteenth century, reached its peak around 1875–80. Certainly the small
independent farmer did not disappear entirely, but he was hard pressed

from all sides and only survived in patches, generally in the hilly regions like the Lake District, Devonshire, Wales and the marshy Fens. These 'yeomen', who inherited from freeholding forebears and worked the land themselves (they were the only people who could reasonably be called peasants) only held a very small portion of England's soil, from 12 to 15 per cent.

We are fairly well informed on the ownership of landed property at that time thanks to an inquiry carried out on the orders of Parliament in 1873. This document, nicknamed the 'New Domesday Book' after the famous land register set up by William the Conqueror, was in effect the first official survey of land distribution to be carried out since 1086. It came into existence because evidence was required to refute attacks regularly mounted by the Radicals. They took up the arguments developed at length by the free traders and the Chartists in the 1840s and denounced the aristocratic monopoly of land ownership. In the event, the evidence of the inquiry, far from refuting these attacks, revealed a much higher degree of concentration than had been thought, and brought grist to the mill of the enemies of aristocracy and privilege. Shortly afterwards Joseph Chamberlain was to launch his famous attack on idle landowners who 'toil not neither do they spin'. In fact the extraordinary power and wealth of the landlords shows up with blinding clarity, however one presents the figures. Four-fifths of the soil of the United Kingdom belonged to less than 7,000 people, and the owners of more than 1,000 acres held two-thirds of the land under cultivation in Great Britain.[32] In England and Wales half the land was in the hands of 4,200 owners, while one quarter belonged to 360 magnates whose domains extended to more than 10,000 acres each. In Scotland, the concentration was even greater since 24 owners possessed between them a quarter of the country, with one estate passing the fabulous figure of one million acres, and 350 individuals shared two-thirds of the soil.[33] It was not possible for smallholders, although they numbered a million, with patches often not larger than a pocket handkerchief, to counterbalance the power concentrated in the hands of the minority of landlords. So everywhere the great estates dominated without rival.

A very different situation obtained for the size of farms. Usually the great estates were broken up into farms of modest size, all the more because the richest landlords rarely owned continuous stretches of land. Indeed their estates often spread over several counties. In 1851, out of a total of 215,000 farms, the small units were the most numerous, 90,000 being of between 5 and 20 acres; but one should note that they only covered 8.6 per cent of the area under cultivation. It is true, on the other hand, that their number tended to grow. In the twenty-five years following they almost doubled, but without occupying more than 14 or 15 per cent of the total. The first place was occupied by medium-sized farms. There were 45,000 farms of 50–100 acres, occupying 13 per cent, and 54,000 farms of 100–300 acres occupying 45 per cent of the total surface. This category remained pretty stable, and still occupied three-fifths of the land under cultivation at the end of the century. Finally large farms, the favourite scene for 'high farming', made up a very important proportion, i.e. one third of the total surface in 1851, with 12,000 farms of 300–500 acres covering 17.5 per cent, 4,000 farms of 500–1,000 acres covering 11.5 per cent and nearly 800 farms of more than 1,000 acres covering 5 per cent of the total surface. In 1885, large farms continued to account for nearly 30 per cent of all cultivated land.[34]

During the wave of prosperity which lasted from 1851 to 1873, equipment and methods of farming were gradually modernized. There was an effort to put into practice the maxim laid down by the great agronomist and recognized authority, Caird: 'High farming – the best substitute for Protection'.[35] One sign of prosperity was the rise in estate revenue and the land values. Rents, already rising since 1835, continued to increase until 1879. The rise was between 25 and 45 per cent, according to the region. For producers, whether tenant farmers or landowners, this resulted in high profits. The lot of the labourers, on the other hand, hardly changed at all.

The growth of demand at home both stimulated and diversified production. A line of demarcation continued to separate the England of cereal crops to the east and south, consisting mostly of wheat, from the England of pasture lands to the west and south-west; but meadow lands and cattle-breeding never ceased to make headway. Around 1870, 43 per cent of all agricultural land consisted of grass and, out of the ploughland making up the rest, one third was taken up with artificial pastures and root crops for forage. On the other hand rural craftsmen suffered severely from the competition of mechanized industry. A village carpenter, victim of the slump, complained that, 'But for the coffins, he would starve!'[36] And yet the world of the village, sheltered and peaceful, with its traditional patterns, retained its way of life without being too shaken by contemporary material change.

Material civilization: the dividends of progress

The English might freely recognize the superiority of their French rivals in matters of artistic refinement, manners, fashion and gastronomy, but they were justified in claiming for themselves the role of pioneers in all that concerned practical life and the open air. Indeed they were responsible for two inventions that were to spread throughout Europe – domestic comfort and sport. As Rimbaud wrote:

Ce sont les conquérants du monde. . . .
Le sport et le confort voyagent avec eux.[37]

In this area innovation generally started in high society. The middle classes imitated it until eventually, with the lapse of time and with the requisite standard of living, it reached the less privileged. In society, remarked a Victorian, ideas rise upwards from below, while manners descend from above. Some of the innovations, however, were so important in themselves that they turned everyone's habits upside down at once. This was true of railways which, in revolutionizing travel, transformed people's existence. Who could refuse the advantages of speed, in spite of some discomfort in the third class? The number of passengers rose from 5 million in 1838 to 54 million ten years later. In 1854 it passed 100 million; in 1869 it reached 300 million and, in 1876, 517 million.[38] The change occurred without a transitional period. At one blow the old methods of transport were abandoned. In 1841 a journey by coach from London to Exeter took 18 hours; after 1845 it took $6\frac{1}{2}$ hours by express train. At the same time the fare for the journey went down from £4 to £2 10s. first class.

Towards 1860–70 the existence of railways began to produce a profound change in living habits. Until then a suburban residence had been the privilege of a very few well-to-do people, owners of a carriage and pair. Now the number and frequency of suburban trains allowed many prosperous bourgeois to live far from their work in comfortable houses away from the smoke, the noise and the turmoil of the centre. When they began the English suburbs were a preserve of the rich, and so conferred social prestige on their inhabitants.

The railway did not, however, only serve the daily commuters. It also transformed leisure. From the middle of the century onwards excursions to the seaside became more and more frequent. Excursion trains poured out hordes of day-trippers onto the beaches of Margate, Gravesend and Brighton. Other longer journeys took Englishmen onto the Continent in growing numbers. Thomas Cook started his business in 1845 and towards 1870 his name became a household word. In 1857 the Alpine Club was founded, and the number of climbers increased rapidly, combining sport with travel. Winter holidays in the South of France became fashionable, and Queen Victoria helped to launch the Côte d'Azur by her visits there. Other travellers crossed the oceans, and Jules Verne paid a deserved tribute to the British in making Phileas Fogg in *Round the World in Eighty Days* the model of the intrepid and determined globe-trotter.

In domestic life the middle classes did their best to combine utility with comfort. In that bourgeois age there was more concern for usefulness than elegance. Everything solid and practical was appreciated. It was the heyday of large comfortable armchairs, sofas and ottomans. Mass production turned out thousands of pieces of furniture, washing facilities and household utensils. As a sign of the desire for comfort and visible wealth, one found in homes a profusion of curtains, draperies, carpets, hangings, pouffes, lamps, overmantels, etc. The habit of taking baths became general. This usually meant a tub into which hot or cold water was poured. Frequent cold baths were recommended for hardening children, starting with the most delicate. About 1865 the daily bath became a habit in high society, the middle classes being satisfied with one a week. As for bathrooms, they did not appear until the end of the century, but the flushing water closet became general after 1850.

A mass of minor innovations contributed to the change in lifestyle, easing and simplifying the daily round. In 1840 the modern postal system was created with the introduction of a stamp paid for by the sender – the 'Penny Post'. The number of letters sent quadrupled in ten years. At about the same time the steel nib replaced the goose quill, and blotting paper replaced sand. People started to use 'little sacks of paper, called envelopes' instead of sealing folds with wax. Matches of sulphur or phosphorus (they were called 'lucifers' or 'prometheans') took the place of tinder-boxes, and in 1845 Browning's poem *Meeting at Night* celebrated the new invention, which was already in general use:

> . . . the quick sharp scratch
> And blue spurt of a lighted match

Other innovations which transformed material life around 1840–50 were cheap soap, sewing machines, and gasoline for lamps instead of colza oil. Cigarettes were introduced by English soldiers returning from the Crimea, where they had acquired the habit from their French comrades-in-arms. However the smoking-room, the area dedicated to the pleasure of tobacco, did not make its appearance until the last third of the century. Then it became the rule.

Food consumption increased among the middle classes and, to a certain extent, among the working classes. Treatises on domestic economy became widespread, from the culinary advice given by a French chef, Soyer, who through his good reputation was given the job of catering for the 1851 Exhibition, to the classic *Household Management* by Mrs Beeton, published in 1861 and endlessly reprinted. The habit of copious breakfasts consisting of tea, toast, eggs, fish, ham, etc. became established. Even among workmen breakfast was far from negligible. Afternoon tea was a Victorian novelty. Launched by the Duchess of Bedford, it won over the aristocracy and from there spread among the bourgeoisie in the middle of the century. Consumption of food by the masses did not grow during the first half of the nineteenth century, but prosperity after 1850 brought rapid improvement. The annual consumption of sugar per person rose from 18 lbs at Victoria's accession to 54 lbs in 1870–9, and tea from 1½ lbs to 4¼ lbs. As for beer every Englishman drank an average of 20 gallons (90 litres) a year around 1830; fifty years later he drank 36 gallons (165 litres). Consumption of tobacco also increased between those dates, going up from 14 ozs to 1½ lbs (375 to 630 grams) per person.[39]

In a country which was covered by more and more houses, streets and smoke, urban life made physical exercise almost a necessity. The need for recreation in the open air became imperative. Up till then such sports as had existed had reflected the spirit of rural civilization, whence they sprang. They were generally violent and involved the rearing and killing of animals. In aristocratic circles the traditional pastimes were shooting, fox-hunting, fishing and especially horse-racing, which had the additional lure of gambling. There were the classic races like the Derby, the St Leger, Ascot and, after 1839, the Grand National. The working classes entertained themselves with sports that were equally violent – wrestling, boxing, and above all fights between animals, e.g. cocks, dogs and rats, and bull-baiting.

Towards the middle of the nineteenth century, under the influence of the public schools, team games appeared which provided exciting recreation for the spirit as well as the body. The fashion was now for refined games controlled by rules. The idea was to take exercise that was beneficial in its appeal to endurance, team spirit and manly qualities. Sport became a school for character. Its association with making money was frowned on, and one played for pleasure and not for the betting. In matches it was the sense of competition and fair play that were important. Submission to rules was felt to have moral and disciplinary value, and there was the additional advantage that a larger number of people could take part in refreshing exercise.

Social divisions were as clearly marked out in these new sports as they were in the old. Among the gentleman's games were cricket, an ancient game that now acquired great prestige (even giving rise to the expression 'it's not cricket'), rugby football, first played at Rugby School (the Rugby Union was founded in 1871), golf, imported from Scotland in 1869 (whence its name 'Scotch golf'), rowing (the Oxford and Cambridge Boat Race became an annual event around 1856), and polo around 1870. Athletics started at Oxford in about 1850. Croquet became fashionable at the same date. As for lawn tennis, it was invented in 1874 and codified shortly afterwards by the Wimbledon All England Croquet and Lawn Tennis Club. By the end of the century tennis and bicycling had become the great recreations of the middle classes.

The favourite game of the working classes was association football or 'soccer' which quickly outstripped 'rugger' in popularity. The Football

Association was constituted in 1863. As in the case of rugby, rules were standardized all over the country, and those who wanted to keep to their local customs had to give in. Thanks to the shorter working week, public matches were soon played on Saturday afternoons, at first between local clubs and later internationally. So, instead of the spontaneous and brutal anarchy of old-time sport where individual prowess counted, games took their place among disciplined activities which submitted to a code of collective conduct. Rational and social controls checked the impulses of instinct, and the individual voluntarily integrated himself to the group. In short, civilized sport took the place of traditional undisciplined sport.

2 The merits of hierarchy

Classes and structure: Marx or Palmerston?

Writing in 1854, Marx observed that, of all countries, Great Britain was the one in which 'the despotism of capital and the slavery of labour' had reached their most advanced stage. The disappearance of intermediate classes left only 'the millionaire commanding whole industrial armies and the wage-slave living only from hand to mouth' to face each other head-on. 'In no other country the war between the two classes that constitute modern society has assumed so colossal dimensions and features so distinct and palpable.'[1]

For its part, the Victorian *Weltanschauung* did not rest on such a dualist structure born of the remorseless dialectic of property and hired labour, but on a tri-dimensional conception of society made up of a number of free-moving elements. Let us listen, for instance, to Palmerston, the quintessence of mid-Victorianism, developing his views, as he so often did, on the social system of his country. The occasion was a prize-giving at an Industrial Exhibition in 1865. The happy balance, he affirmed, which characterized England, derived from the unique combination of a recognized hierarchy and a social mobility that was sometimes effective and sometimes only potential. In a constitutional monarchy, he went on, you needed an aristocracy of rank – the nobility – and an aristocracy of wealth – the bourgeoisie. Underneath were to be found the common people. There anyone could aspire to raise himself to the very highest level, provided that he devoted to that end the talent, the industry, the perseverance and the good conduct that were necessary. 'Wealth', said Palmerston, 'is, to a certain extent, within the reach of all.' Consequently all ambitions were permitted. Every member of society, whatever his position, carried in his knapsack the baton of a minister, a general or a Lord Chancellor (these were Palmerston's words). Furthermore, those who failed to reach these summits could take comfort, for their efforts would not have been in vain. By cultivating the faculties with which Providence had endowed them, they would attain self-respect and domestic happiness, combined with the feeling of being useful to their country. A singularly optimistic vision, based on the dynamics of a social order that was triangular (aristocracy, bourgeois élite, lower orders) and open (everyone free and dependent on his own willpower). It was the principle of the 'career open to talent'. Why not conclude, as Palmerston did in effect, with this Guizot-like exhortation: 'Go on, gentlemen, and prosper!'[2]

So, in the face of laissez-faire capitalism at its zenith, Marx described a divided and rigid society, the prey of ineluctable forces, which was split into two antagonistic classes; while Palmerston, on the contrary, depicted a society that was flexible, welcoming, mobile and comprised of different levels, where exchanges upwards and downwards were constantly taking place. A great debate indeed, which for a century has never ceased to divide historians, sociologists and political theorists. . . . In fact the debate is a double one, for it embraces two different, though interrelated, problems. The first question concerns the social structure. How many classes were there in nineteenth-century England? Of whom and of what were these classes composed? In this connection the most varied positions have been taken up. Some think that there were only two classes, others that it was a three-class system, while others again go up to five, or even more. Occasionally it has been denied that one can even distinguish classes at all, because of the lack of internal consistency. So should one talk of a bipolar, a tripolar or a multipolar society? Or, if one prefers another metaphor, should one describe the social set-up as a duet, a trio or an orchestra? The second question, which takes us away from the static plane of stratification to the dynamic plane of mobility, is how far society was in fact open, with opportunities to pass from one level to another. Was it so easy? And did it happen so often?

It is perfectly true that the literature of the time is full of talk about 'bridges' and 'stepping-stones'. But, in the end, weren't the barriers more numerous than the rungs for the man who wanted to climb up the social ladder? One can reasonably query whether social mobility was quite as flourishing as the Victorian high-priests made out.

To see the matter clearly we must first take a closer look at the notion of class in its historic development. When and how did the word penetrate the language, and when did it come into current usage? To what extent did the movement of society shape the concept? And, above all, did the terms used by the people of the time accurately reflect the social reality? The mid-nineteenth century was a period of transition, when two terminologies were used concurrently. Together with the modern word 'class', eighteenth-century terms continued to be used. During that time one talked sometimes of 'orders' and sometimes of 'ranks' and 'degrees'. When one wanted to designate social groups with a common economic base, such as associations in trade or pressure groups, one used the word 'interest'. So there was the 'landed interest', consisting of landlords or those who drew their revenues from the land, the 'City or banking interest', the 'cotton interest' (Lancashire manufacturers), etc. Around 1850, all these terms were in full vigour, (for example the phrase 'lower orders' was constantly used to describe the popular masses), and it was only in the last third of the century that they went into decline.

The term 'class' however began to assert itself and gradually came to dominate.[3] It made its first appearance, usually in the plural, at the end of the eighteenth century and was first applied to the bourgeoisie, when one talked of 'the middling and industrious classes'. Then came the turn of the world of labour. After 1830 the expression 'working classes' became usual. In fact the new title's success was not simply due to its providing a convenient description of the social groups that resulted from industrialization, but probably more so because it gave expression to a new consciousness. During the 1830s and 1840s there came into being, both among the workers and the middle classes, a new and very lively feeling that they belonged to a distinct social category, quite easy to define, whose interests were opposed to those of the old governing aristocracy. The class struggle, far from being a Marxist theory grafted artificially onto the social reality, did correspond to life as it was actually lived. On the ideological level the first people to have developed the notion of the class struggle were, as E. P. Thompson has pointed out, the spokesmen of radicalism. The use of the term 'class' by a bourgeois reformer like Cobden in his fight against the aristocracy was at least as trenchant as its use in Engels' critique of the manufacturing bourgeois, or in the Chartists' fiery protests against the double oppression of noblemen and capitalists. The result was that, in the middle of the nineteenth century, it became common practice to define the British social system in terms of an edifice with three storeys (just as there were three classes on the railways): on the ground floor were the popular classes, i.e. the manual workers of the town and countryside (the lower or working classes); on the first floor the bourgeoisie (the middle classes); and on the top floor the aristocracy and the 'haute bourgeoisie' (the upper classes). Should one deduce from this that the new terminology reflected a major upheaval in the heart of society? In other words, did a society of class replace a society of orders under the impact of the Industrial Revolution? In our view this was in no way the case. English society in the eighteenth century was, like Victorian society, a society of classes even if the classes were described by other names. The difference was that modern terms began to supplant old terms, even though the latter did manage to survive for several decades.

So we come back to our first question: how were the social classes in Victorian England demarcated and distributed? If we define classes by three major criteria – (1) the position in the system of production, i.e. occupation, income and standard of living; (2) a collective consciousness of belonging to a certain class; and (3) the sharing of common values by virtue of way of life, education and status – two points, in our opinion, emerge with clarity. Firstly, the validity of a triangular structure as a model for English society in the nineteenth century. It seems to us that this stratification into three layers gives us a truer vision of the social kaleidoscope than would a dual construct. Not that one should be too rigid about it, for people have too often turned this image into a stereotype. Other dividing lines – religious (Anglicans and Dissenters), political (Tories, Whigs and Radicals), social (town and country), national (Scots, Welsh, Irish) – serve to complicate the social scene by multiplying the fronts, the antagonisms and the alliances. That is why there is wide variety within each class, and it may well be that the coherence of each class was more external, as an attitude to others, than internal.

The dualist theory, it is true, belonged to an old tradition which included, beside the precursors of socialism, such people as Charles Hall at the beginning of the century ('The people need only be divided into two classes – the rich and the poor'[4]), representatives of Young England and social Toryism (Disraeli expressed himself in exactly the same terms when he enunciated his famous thesis of 'the two nations'), and most of the Chartists, themselves the heirs of Cobbett's Jacobin language which vehemently denounced 'reducing the community to two classes: masters and slaves'.[5]

As far as Marx's analysis of English society is concerned, one should note that, while he elaborated the concept of a dialectic featuring two antagonistic classes, he did not misunderstand the role of the aristocracy. For Marx, the whole English political system was precisely the fruit of a compromise between the two sections of the governing class, the aristocracy and the bourgeoisie. One can even go further. To the very last chapter of *Capital*, which remained incomplete, Marx referred his whole theory of the production process to the trilogy property rent/profit/labour by affirming that England offered the most elaborate example in

the world of the three great classes of modern society: landlords, capitalists and wage-earners.

Indeed Marx was here only following the tradition of British economic
thought. It was among the classical Scottish economists of the eighteenth
century, Sir James Steuart, John Millar and above all Adam Smith that the
concept of three classes in society first saw the light of day.[6] They were the
first to define a social class by its economic structure – the type of
production and of income – and to launch the trio of landlords, manufacturers and labourers. This tripartite theory gained ground so rapidly
that Stuart Mill in 1834 took to chiding those who, he said, 'revolve in
their eternal circle of landlords, capitalists and labourers, until they seem
to think of the distinction of society into those three classes as if it were
one of God's ordinances not man's'.[7] Whatever the differences in vocabulary, there was the same triple division which one finds in Carlyle
when he distinguishes 'Workers, Master Workers and Master Unwork-
ers', in F. D. Maurice ('the aristocracy, the commercial classes and the
working classes') or again in Matthew Arnold with his famous trilogy of
Barbarians (the aristocracy), Philistines (the bourgeoisie) and the
Populace (the workers).

There is a second characteristic which emerges extremely clearly. The
three-layer structure of English society in the nineteenth century drew
much of its strength from the deeply embedded sense of hierarchy that
existed in men's minds and habits. It was a vertical society, fundamentally inegalitarian, where each person, from the grand feudal *seigneur* to
the humblest hand, became impregnated with the consciousness of his
own 'station'. As early as the 1830s, Tocqueville had remarked: 'The
French spirit is to want no superior. The English spirit is to want inferiors.
The Frenchman lifts his eyes about him with anxiety. The Englishman
drops his in acquiescence.'[8] It was not simply that hierarchy appeared as a
necessity – it was seen as a benediction endowed with a thousand virtues.
The stricter it was, the more readily it was accepted; in fact it seemed even
more desirable that way. Writing an essay on equality in 1878, Matthew
Arnold noted how unpopular the term was.[9] In the same period,
although he was on the way to becoming an Englishman by adoption,
Henry James could not help being struck by the rigorous social stratification, bristling with barriers and different levels: 'The essentially hierarchical plan of English society, is the great and ever-present fact. . . .
There is hardly a detail of life that does in some degree not betray it.'[10]

The moment has come to analyse the three classes of this hierarchy,
asking ourselves at the same time whether the optimistic assertions of the
liberals on the mobility of the social organism corresponded to reality, or
whether, on the contrary, they were not rather one of the forms of 'the
opium of the people'.

An aristocratic country

Burke, the political philospher of the landed interest, once wrote that noblemen were 'the incarnation of tradition' and were like 'the great oaks that shade a country and perpetuate their benefits from generation to generation', while commoners 'creep along the ground, bellying into melons that are exquisite for size and flavour, but like annual plants perish with their season'.[11] With the advent of an industrial society and the progress of democratic ideas one might imagine that such a view of the world would be overthrown for ever. Nothing of the kind. The aristocracy continued to form the 'Corinthian capital', to take another of Burke's images, at the top of the social column. In spite of furious attacks mounted against it since the end of the eighteenth century by Jacobin and radical forces, of either bourgeois or popular origin, the aristocracy succeeded in keeping its dominant position without having to consent to much loss of power. Honours, respect and, to a very large extent, wealth and political power came its way. Furthermore there had always been a close link between the aristocracy and the Church of England, both in theory and in practice. The old alliance of squire and parson retained its strength and showed the double attachment of the nobility to Church and Crown.

We must now once and for all refute the clichés of the liberal historians, and in particular the cleverly fostered legend of a bourgeois England in 1832 usurping the position of the old aristocratic England. Even though the Reform Bill of that year and the repeal of the Corn Laws in 1846 went a long way to curbing the power of the old ruling oligarchy, they kept the essentials of their privileged position. In the second half of the nineteenth century, England remained socially, economically, politically and mentally an aristocratic country. 'We are', confessed as stout an enemy of noble privilege as Cobden 'a servile, aristocracy-loving, lord-ridden people, who regard the land with as much reverence as we still do the peerage and baronetage'.[12] It is very true of course that the balance of power gradually tilted in favour of the middle classes to the detriment of the landed aristocracy. Yet for the latter the years 1850–80 were a splendid Indian summer. Hardly anyone thought of questioning the nobility's position of superiority. In some ways one might talk of consolidation, both of riches and prestige. Country gentlemen's memories of the period were those of a blessed age, hardly touched, as the nineteenth Lord Willoughby de Broke recalled, by the 'symptoms of industrialism' and 'the untoward manifestations of the thing called democracy'.[13]

It would certainly be absolutely wrong to represent the aristocracy as being composed of a single block. Within its ranks there were several levels. There were marked differences of income, living standards and status, whether one looked at the nobility at the top (a small minority consisting of very substantial landlords and holders of ancient hereditary titles), or at the lower strata of gentry and squirearchy. Yet they all shared the advantages of birth, landed property, the income arising therefrom and the rank attached to it. All led a life of leisure – a gentleman was by definition someone who did not work. All obeyed an unwritten code of conduct, inherited with their land. Together they formed the community of 'the gentlemen of England', privileged to be 'well born' and recognized by their 'inferiors' as the best and noblest of the land. However great was the distance separating a duke (there were 27 in 1873, of which 4 drew incomes from their land in excess of £100,000 and 13 between £50,000 and £100,000) from a modest village squire, whose revenue just touched £1,000 a year, they were still united by a thousand fine threads. 'They have', wrote Cracroft in 1867,

> 'a common blood, a common education, common pursuits, common ideas, a common dialect, a common religion and – what more than any other thing binds men together – a common prestige, a prestige growled at occasionally, but on the whole conceded and even, it must be owned, secretly liked by the country at large.'[14]

It is precisely this spirit of semi-feudal reverence which largely explains the persistence of power of the aristocracy in England – and indeed traces of it continue to manifest themselves even today. This collective attitude provoked Thackeray's sardonic outburst in his *Book of Snobs* (1848): 'What a Peerage worship there is all through this free country!'

What is it that denoted the aristocracy? An estate? A name? Or recognition by others, whether equals or inferiors? To put it another way, were the criteria objective or subjective? If one leaves aside the noblemen in the strictest sense, that is to say the families of peers who qualified automatically, and ignores the strict rules governing the transfer of land (primogeniture, entail and settlement), the answer is far from simple. There are however two essential conditions. First of all landed property, that is to say the possesion of an estate of adequate size. It was a necessary condition because only land could confer high status. As a hero of Trollope neatly puts it, 'land gives so much more than rent. It gives position and influence and political power, to say nothing about the game.' But that alone was not enough. A man newly rich, who had acquired vast properties, did not automatically enter the circle of nobility. He had to fulfil a second condition, that of an established position, which alone gave him recognition and status. So a family of bankers and manufacturers would only join the ranks of the gentry after the presence of two or three generations on their land. On the other hand an ancient lineage, combined with an uninterrupted patriarchal tradition at the manor house, was certain to make the village folk touch their forelocks, even when it was accompanied by only modest wealth. This psychology was not the result simply of inherited vanity or exclusivity. Over and above a haughty defence of privilege, there was the desire to assimilate, by a kind of reproductive process, those who aimed at aristocratic status. For to join the gentry it was necessary to adopt their style and behaviour, in short to assume the personality of the squire.

This is what made the nobility an assimilating force without in the least detracting from the power of tradition, in fact gaining strength from it. It was a class that was both open and inveigling. In fact, in the English social system, entry into the landed aristocracy had no bottom limit as far as the gentry were concerned. There was no limit in theory to entry into the peerage, but in practice ennoblement outside the ranks of the gentry was very rare indeed. The English were pleased to point out that their aristocracy did not form a caste, or even a closed order in the style of the French nobility of the Ancien Régime. Nevertheless, access continued to be only sparingly granted, partly because the golden rule of an élite is to perpetuate itself without dilution, and partly because entry depended on conforming to an existing model. The statistics are there to prove the point. The real aristocracy, i.e. the great landed proprietors, whose estates exceeded 10,000 acres and who for the most part belonged to the peerage, numbered from 350 to 400 families. The gentry and the squire-archy, whose estates ran from 1,000 to 10,000 acres, amounted to about 3,000 families.[15]

What is so extraordinary, one might ask, about a society with a rural tradition giving importance to the notion of heredity and consequently defining its ruling élite on the basis of land wealth and pedigree? In fact, the aristocratic principle went much further than that. It arrived at a point where the whole of society gave precedence to status that was *transmitted* rather than *acquired*. On the one hand birth erected the barrier of rank, underlining the irremediable gulf between the aristocracy and the common people. On the other hand, membership of an old family that was 'established' and therefore rooted in the past was considered to confer on its members, for reasons of heredity and environment, certain innate personal capabilities, such as leadership, a sense of honour, chivalry, in short the capacity to run the country. People willingly closed their eyes to the reverse side of the coin – the pride, corruption, dissipation, waste and insolent luxury. The habit of looking at the aristocracy as the repository of a natural superiority had become ingrained with time. The aristocracy itself was so imbued with its own eminence that it responded with equal certainty. As the ruling class it was very conscious of its role, its privileges and its duties. Why should the vocation of the élite be altered? Besides, in spite of all its faults, could it not be justly proud of its success in history?

Was it not the class which had carried English power to such heights, defeated Louis XIV and Napoleon, conquered India, provided the country with its military heroes like Marlborough and Wellington, and its statesmen like Pitt, Castlereagh, Palmerston and Salisbury?

So one can see that supremacy of the aristocracy rested essentially on two pillars: landed wealth and the prestige of birth. This is what we now have to consider in more detail. The first decisive factor is that their estates made the noblemen the richest class in the country. Patricians and plutocrats were still largely synonymous. This was the cardinal fact which persisted until the 1880s, as it had for centuries. Of course one could name several banking or industrial magnates capable of matching the very highest ranks of the aristocracy, but these would be the exceptions to the rule. As a class the aristocrats occupied almost exclusively the top rungs of the income ladder. Their great landed wealth, whose extent we have already indicated, made them, as the main owners of the soil, not only the richest in land but also the richest in total wealth. The domains of the landlords, which were generally well managed, brought in very substantial incomes to their owners. It is generally reckoned that an acre of cultivated land brought in an average of £1 a year. So the sum is easy to work out. The great landowners (those with 10,000 acres and over) received enormous revenues, over £10,000 a year. Take the upper gentry, with their estates of 3,000–10,000 acres, and the squires, with their 1,000–3,000 acres: all these proprietors found themselves in the £1,000–£10,000 income bracket, which put them in the thin layer of the richest people in the country (0.25 per cent of the population).

Furthermore, the wealth of the nobility had long ceased to be based purely on land, even though rents continued to constitute the main element. Firstly the landlords did not confine themselves simply to making their agricultural assets profitable. They also invested in overseas trade, banks and, more recently, railway companies. Their estates gained most of all in value through the development of towns, mines, railways and docks. Coal-mining, for example, brought unheard-of wealth to the Duke of Northumberland and the Earl of Durham. In 1856 Robert Stephenson worked out that, out of £286 million invested by the railway companies for line construction in twenty-five years, one quarter of the sum had been spent on purchasing land. The beneficiaries were of course the owners of the land. The aristocracy also found another source of wealth on an even larger scale. Urban development, far from reducing the relative importance of the old landed fortunes, had the effect of increasing it. In London three giant landlords owned between them a sizeable section of the West End; the Duke of Portland owned most of the area south of Regent's Park (he also owned the mines of Kilmarnock and the port of Troon in Scotland), Covent Garden and most of Bloomsbury belonged to the Duke of Bedford, and the Marquis of Westminster's properties extended all the way from Mayfair to Pimlico. In the same way urban rents went to fill the coffers of the Marquis of Bute, who owned a part of Cardiff and Glamorgan, and of Lord Derby, owner of whole sectors of Liverpool and other towns in Lancashire. The interests of Lord Salisbury were represented in Liverpool as well as London. As for the Duke of Norfolk he held several districts of Sheffield, an important area in the centre of London, and coalmines too. Nine-tenths of the £120,000 income of Lord Calthorpe came from owning Edgbaston, a residential suburb of Birmingham.

However, as a general rule, agricultural receipts provided four-fifths of the nobility's income. Throughout our period they increased steadily, thanks to the rise in rents up to 1879. Among the richest of the grandees figured the Marquis of Bute (£230,000 gross a year), Sir John Ramsden (£175,000) and Lord Derby (£163,000). It was said that the Marquis of Bredalbane could cover 33 leagues on horseback in a straight line without leaving his estates. The fourth Duke of Northumberland, who owned 166,000 acres in Middlesex, Devonshire and, above all, Northumberland (he held one-eighth of the county) drew a net sum of £90,000 a year from his farmlands and £20,000 in royalties from coalmines, and in his lifetime spent more than £300,000 on Alnwick Castle. Another patrician, the seventh Duke of Devonshire, owning 200,000 acres spread over 11 English and 3 Irish counties with a gross revenue of £180,000, was at the same time president of the Haematite Company and of the Institute of Iron and Steel. It was he who took the initiative in developing the steel complex at Barrow-in-Furness. On top of this he owned a substantial part of the seaside resort of Eastbourne. Having managed his assets in a shrewd and modern way, the Duke left a fortune of £1,800,000 at his death. He was an important figure in the Liberal Party, and in the Palladian setting of Chatsworth presided with imposing presence over one of the most sumptuous country houses in England.[16]

The squires also lived in the middle of their domains in a much more modest, but still comfortable setting. They were surrounded by their servants in their hall or manor house, and their influence spread over the whole neighbourhood. The difference was not simply in the level of income, it was even more a question of lifestyle. For the gentry lived in the country all year round and did not visit London for the Season. Their existence was more restricted because they lived far from the capital and the cosmopolitan universe of high society. They were therefore much more conservative, both in their behaviour and in their opinions. But they did benefit, as much as the aristocrats did, from the aura attached to an ancient name, which made the lord of the manor a creature apart.

So feudal prestige was indeed the second pillar of aristocratic power. Grand or not, the nobility constituted the natural élite in the eyes of the vast majority. Everything encouraged this reverence – social pressure, education, institutions and the many networks that encouraged a sense of dependence among both the humblest and the most sophisticated. This applied as much to the spontaneous respect shown by servants, lasting long after their departure from their master's service, to the vanity of bourgeois parvenus who were proud to consort with titled people. Sometimes this attitude turned to absurd and fawning admiration, as it did in Mr Meagles, whose foolishness is ridiculed in *Little Dorrit*. He was the person who, in spite of all the humiliations he endured at the hands of a snobbish group, repeated in awe-struck tones: 'Yes, but in what high-class company!' Even when these reverential instincts took on less naïve and more sophisticated forms, they still invested the aristocracy with an unassailable prestige. A patriarchal idea of social relations persisted deep down in men's consciousness which meant that all classes, even the rich and cultured bourgeois, responded to the paternalism of the noble-man.

Was it deference or servility? That is the great question that is crucial for the future of English society. Ever since the eighteenth century, supporters of the 'Establishment' and advocates of egalitarian democracy have faced each other on this issue. Bagehot, who championed deference without hesitation, stated the paradox without being able to explain it: 'I do not think', he wrote, 'there is any country in which all old families and all titled families received more ready observance from those who were their equals – perhaps their superiors – in wealth, their equals in culture, and their inferiors only in descent and rank'.[17] On the opposite political side, the Radicals continued to launch regular attacks on aristocratic privilege in order to eradicate it, or at least to reduce it, but without much success. Patrician prestige survived all the severe blows directed against it between 1815 and 1848. After 1850 there were even signs of an increase in sentiments of deference. It seemed a long time since Feargus O'Connor inveighed against the clique of aristocratic parasites and profiteers whose venison, he claimed, was stained with the blood of orphans and whose claret was redolent of the tears of widows. There certainly remained a strong tradition of hostility to those whom John Bright, the idol of the middle classes, called 'the landlords and great possessors of the soil'. This attitude was to be found either latent in the popular consciousness or explicit among intellectuals like Thackeray, T. H. Green and Matthew Arnold. However Cobden, the leader of the great anti-aristocratic campaigns, was to recognize quite clearly the ineffectiveness of such an attitude. 'The citadel of privilege in this country is so terribly strong owing to the concentrated mass of property in the hands of the comparatively few' and the upper classes 'never stood so high in relative social and political rank as . . . at present'.[18] So, while the bourgeois conception of property, in the Roman style, triumphed in commerce and industry, the land was run on the system of feudal property rights with its law of primogeniture and its leasehold system that denied security to lessees. What better example could there be of the survival of aristocratic tyranny than the Game Laws which gave the squire exclusive rights to the hunt, even though it was an ordinance that was deeply resented and regularly transgressed?

What added to the prestige of the aristocracy was the elegance of their way of life. There was the daily ceremonial of the great house, both refined and elaborate; the luxury of the carriages, the stables and the hounds; an abundance of servants (up to fifty in the most important families, but a minimum of four or five in a simple household); shooting parties, riding, ritual visits exchanged with neighbours, church on Sundays – that was the rhythm of the days and seasons. For the wives and daughters there were also good works in the parish, visits to farmers' families, the village school, the sewing circle, and the whole family could enjoy the excitement of receptions, the great county balls, the house parties, the garden parties and the thrill of riding to hounds. For the grandest, the London Season was an occasion for splendid parties and it introduced a cosmopolitan atmosphere. The tradition of the Grand Tour developed as more and more people travelled abroad. High Society (one called it 'Society' for short) developed a taste for luxurious residences, rivalled each other in artistic refinement and elaborate decor, amassed paintings, statues, porcelain, tapestries, and silver, and continued the tradition of English parks and gardens in great style. In such a setting a touch of originality, not to say eccentricity, was not amiss. It was felt that it gave an agreeable finish to an aristocratic figure – witness the case of Lord Hertford, the great collector and *bon vivant*, whose humorous invitation to one of his French friends was reported by Taine: 'I have a castle in Wales. I have never seen it, but I am told it is very beautiful. Every day twelve places are laid for dinner and the carriage is ready at the front door in case I might arrive. Do go and stay there – it won't cost me a penny.'[19] An exceptional case perhaps, but in the social body it was the duty of the well-born, besides being patrons, to be conspicuously lavish. The floodlights were turned on the great families at all levels, from the Duke of Omnium to the obscurest squire, and it was up to them to assume the role of stars in society. With some surprise a French observer, Léonce de Lavergne, came to the conclusion: 'In France, when a landowner aspires to play a role, he must leave his property and manor. In England he must stay there.'[20]

The irresistible ascent of bourgeois England

Meanwhile, at the centre of the social structure, the middle classes relentlessly pressed forward their advantages. They were possessed by a tireless dynamism. Looking back in 1851 at the distance they had come in half a century, they were bound to feel self-satisfied at the really spectacular progress they had made. However envious the middle classes might be of the aristocracy, they, as the standard-bearers of industrialism and progress, could only feel complete confidence in the future. Wasn't it the start of a golden age of the bourgeoisie whose progress was as irresistible as the spread of machinery? Their numbers, their role in the economy, their political successes filled them with pride. While the total number of the aristocracy came to a tiny figure, 40,000 – 50,000 people, the middle class added up to a respectable section of the country's population: 4 million souls, or more than one-sixth of the total. United by a lively consciousness of their common destiny, the bourgeois felt more and more that they were the main contributors to national prosperity, for those activities which depended on them – industry, commerce and the upper ranks of administration – were gaining every day on agriculture. As good disciples of Ricardo, they considered the entrepreneur above all as the intitiator of the economic cycle, the creator of wealth and the agent who gave the impulse to initiative, management and risk. Here was the capitalist proclaimed benefactor of society . . . In political and intellectual life, in the movement of ideas, in the code of behaviour that prevailed in society, the middle classes, dignified, austere, efficient, could easily weigh their growing influence and measure the advance of their two darling children, liberalism and individualism. Optimism round about 1850 was at full flood. Some time back, during the battle for the Great Reform Bill, Brougham in a lyrical outburst had proclaimed the middle classes to be 'the wealth and intelligence of the country, the glory of the British name'.[21] Now the ideas had become evident truths, an expression of 'the pride of an order' according to Disraeli in *Coningsby*. Listen for instance to Thackeray loftily proclaiming in 1857 that he belonged to 'the class of lawyers and merchants and scholars'. All his sympathies, he declared, went to those beings who made their way by work and struggle, 'the middle and educated classes of our country'.[22]

In a society as dynamic and creative as mid-Victorian Britain, what gave the bourgeoisie such confidence was the certainty of having on their side both history and the moral law. Wasn't English history during the last two centuries in effect the history of progress and liberty, whose champions were precisely those middle classes? Such was the smug message of Macaulay's *History of England*, a book that had an enormous success. The future therefore belonged to these middle classes. Furthermore, as the industrialists and merchants by virtue of their economic functions united the interests of consumers and producers, they personified the common interest in direct opposition to the aristocracy who represented selfish sectional interests. In the words of Cobden, the middle classes 'have no interest opposed to the general good, whilst, on the contrary, the feudal governing class exists only by the violation of sound principles of political economy'.[23] Anyone who was so firmly convinced of being of great public service found his social position completely justified and even hallowed. A new aristocracy was springing up – the knighthood of industry. Let each strive to fight the good fight! Make way for ability in the race for possessions and power! Here was the end of the old order, traditional and stable, in which each was chained to his condition from birth onwards. Now it was a headlong rush, full of aggression and confidence, towards the world of money and merit (surely the same thing for a true liberal). In the old days, wrote the historian J. A. Froude, each individual had to 'do his duty in that state of life to which it had pleased God to call him'. Now a new social system prevailed: 'to push on, to climb vigorously on the slippery steps of the social ladder, to raise ourselves one step or move out of the range of life in which we were born, is now converted into a duty.'[24]

What exactly does the notion 'middle class' cover? Some have made out that it amounts to a vague concept and point out above all the imprecision of the borderlines, both up towards the upper class and down towards the manual workers. This imprecision, they say, renders all rigorous demarcation impracticable. But doesn't this view indulge in the specious argument which rules out all classification? One should point out that the bourgeoisie themselves conspired to confuse the issue in that they, as opposed to the aristocracy, energetically refused to freeze the social triad and sought on the contrary to make the hierarchy as fluid as possible. Let us try to examine the matter a bit more closely. The first point, which is almost a truism, is that this class, being 'middle' by definition, is differentiated from the other two classes, the 'superior' and the 'inferior'. However, it does not follow from this purely negative description that the social category in question is necessarily amorphous. The second point to consider is a more positive one, namely that to establish the contours of the bourgeoisie there are in fact three relatively precise criteria one can use. First of all, the consciousness of a common identity which was a sentiment deeply felt by members of the middle class. In addition, they often found themselves in opposition to the other two classes, and this strengthened their cohesion or, more precisely, their class-consciousness. Secondly, membership of the middle class was linked to a certain type of occupation. Finally it implied a comfortable standard of living. A bourgeois income ranged on average from £150 a year (£100–£120 would be the absolute minimum) to £1,000 a year, though in the very rich bourgeoisie it could be much higher. This income, which was never the fruit of manual labour (that was absolutely taboo) came from a job in the economic sectors of distribution, transport and services, both public and private, which was remunerated in the form of profits or fees or salary, but never as a weekly wage. Other signs of the bourgeoisie were a degree of education and the employment of servants – two indispensable conditions to mark their separation from the common herd.

One should mention two more traits in order to complete the picture. In religion, Nonconformity claimed the majority of members of the middle class, though there were also a good many Anglicans among them. The dissenting sects, notably the Congregationalists, the Baptists and the Methodists, found a main centre of activity in the middle classes who provided the 'chapels' with their big battalions and their ministers. This was one more point of conflict with the aristocracy who were always firm supporters of the Established Church, and was the source of the strict morality which permeated all bourgeois existence. The ethical style of the middle classes was indeed severe. The accent was above all on effort, discipline and work. In that England of frock-coats and top hats, clothes were of a sombre colour and discreet cut. One got up early, the manager was at the factory by 7 am and the working day was long. The week-end was still unknown and the main activity of Sundays was to respect 'the Sabbath'. More beer was drunk than wine or madeira. And leisure time was mostly spent with the family and at home.

Yet the bourgeoisie was far from forming one solid block. On the contrary it was subdivided into several main and subsidiary layers, for in its midst it developed complex hierarchies which existed in parallel. One can adduce two sorts of divisions – economic ones, relating to occupation, and socio-cultural ones relating to income level, lifestyle and status. To take the first case, the nineteenth century saw an addition to the two great old categories that had existed for centuries – trade and the professions. The new category that had emerged from the Industrial Revolution were the leaders of industry – the manufacturers, the ironmasters, etc. This category, which was growing rapidly, cast its net fairly wide over the social scale, for it included the small manufacturer in charge of a modest factory as well as the big industrialist controlling hundreds of workers and probably several factories. The old commercial professions themselves had become diversified. One found jostling with each other the merchant aristocracy of dealers in grain, wood, wool and linen linked by rank and business to the shipowners, the bankers and their staff, and the varied world of retailers, tradesmen and small shopkeepers.

As for the professions, their range, which was originally very narrow, was also growing and their numbers were rapidly increasing. They included army officers, clergymen and senior civil servants together with the members of the liberal professions strictly defined – doctors, solicitors, etc. Originally there were only three groups, those of the old 'learned professions', Divinity, Physic and Law, but it became customary to add the officers of the army and navy. There followed other employments which succeeded in getting their qualifications and status recognized (for the protection of a profession always leads to the establishment of special preserves), such as architects, civil engineers, naval engineers, chemists, veterinary surgeons, actuaries, accountants, and so on. Furthermore, as the needs of industrial society became continuously more varied, one notes in the second half of the century a proliferation of teachers, journalists, writers, publicists and artists. While Nonconformist ministers graduated to the ranks of the bourgeoisie, the civil service made little progress. In 1853 there were 42,000 civil servants of whom two-thirds were in the lower grades such as copying clerks and postmen.

At the same time other lines of separation – social, cultural and psychological – made a jig-saw puzzle of the bourgeoisie, delineating contrasts and gradations that were sometimes hardly visible and sometimes considerable. To start with, there were marked differences in income, which could be traced on a five-point scale, and consequently living standards varied greatly. Besides, there were subtle differences in the status of employments. The remuneration might not differ, but whereas one profession was regarded as honourable, a similar one was viewed with disdain. So there was a firm prejudice against tradesmen; the world of the shop still bore a 'base' image. In general, business was considered unworthy of a gentleman until well on in the century. However one must certainly draw distinctions. High commerce and finance always had the edge over industry; a banker or a merchant automatically ranked higher than a manufacturer, however great the power of the latter. More respect was accorded to a brewer or a West Indian planter than to an ironmaster. In the professions, the old trio of barristers, clergymen and service officers retained their former prestige. They were all jobs compatible with gentlemanly status, which is why these activities formed, within the middle class, a sort of enclave for the gentry, especially for the younger sons, as well as providing a springboard for those on their way up to the upper classes.

And so was built a delicately balanced hierarchy where bridges and barriers alternated. Mobility was counterbalanced by a mass of prejudices and taboos. For simplicity's sake one can, however, distinguish three degrees. At the top, the upper middle class was drawn from the big business centres: bankers, merchants of the City of London, Liverpool and Bristol, industrialists with large factories in Lancashire and Yorkshire, directors of railway companies, magnates in mining and public works, important ironmasters, and shipowners in Liverpool and Glasgow. There were also representatives of the professions in their ranks such as successful lawyers and doctors, and best-selling authors. This upper crust of the bourgeoisie, whose income was always higher than £800 a year and sometimes reached £4,000–£5,000 or more, led a splendid life, mixed with the aristocracy, was recognized by it, married daughters into it, took part in the life of 'Society' and began to found real bourgeois dynasties.

On the next level down was to be found the 'middle middle class' – what you might call the true bourgeoisie. Strong in numbers it included most industrial employers (generally owners of their own firms), the world of the professions (solicitors, barristers, doctors, civil engineers, university professors and public-school masters, literary men), wholesale merchants, managers in commerce, accountants and senior clerks of the central or local government services. Their incomes ranged from £300 to £800 a year, the professions generally heading the group. In other words it was a class that was well off. Their confidence in the future was based on professional competence, hard work and shrewd investment through their solicitor. Their homes were comfortable, their children's education was well organized. Life went on in their large commodious houses, with as many servants as were necessary, in accordance with moral principles inculcated at an early age – a sense of economy, a rigid code of behaviour, and the fear of God.

Finally, at the bottom of the hierarchy, the lesser bourgeoisie or 'lower middle class' brought together small employers, shopkeepers, bank clerks, office workers, minor civil servants, schoolmasters, travelling salesmen, railway staff, and so on. Here there was an obsession with status. At all costs one had to show one's respectability and distinguish oneself from the common herd, to the point of aping without discrimination the life and habits of the superior classes. Taine, when going through the suburbs of Lancashire towns, describes 'the neat lawns, the little gates, the painted fronts . . . a gimcrack luxury which seems to belong to an upstart who adorns himself in trash rather than in objects of real quality'.[25] The prevailing values were high seriousness, a rather ungenerous virtue, and the spirit of self-respect. Their well-regulated lives did not leave much room for fantasy. The pity of the upper and solid middle classes descended relentlessly on this stratum of society. They regarded the lower middle class as being made up of third- or fourth-grade businessmen (contaminated moreover by direct contact with merchandise and cash), dim scribblers and mediocrities sick with ambition. Yet parvenus were to be found at every level of the middle classes, and in a sense the whole of bourgeois society could be put into that category. They were the chosen targets for *Punch* caricatures as well as for the corrosive satire of Dickens. Who can forget the Veneerings, the new-rich couple so cruelly depicted in *Our Mutual Friend*?

The reason why there were so many newly rich was that the middle class grew rapidly both in numbers and in wealth. Starting with the censuses and the income tax statistics, one can get a general idea of the development of its strength. In spite of some areas of uncertainty, the calculations carried out by J. Stamp, J. A. Banks and G. Best trace out the overall movement, which amounted to a swift improvement. So between the periods 1848–53 and 1868–73 the total amount of incomes in excess of £150 per annum rose by 70 per cent while the population of the country went up by only 25 per cent. According to G. Best, the growth was more marked for the lower and middle bourgeoisie whose incomes overall doubled between 1851 and 1871, than it was for the upper bourgeoisie, whose incomes went up by only 50 per cent. H. Perkin, on the contrary, sees an opposite tendency – a faster enrichment for the higher categories.[26] Another proof of bourgeois prosperity was the growing number of servants. In twenty years (1851–71) the number went up by 60 per cent, i.e. two and a half times faster than the population.

The conquering and deserving middle classes moved relentlessly on. The forces that had set them on the move kept up their momentum. On the economic level it was technology and enterprise; on the psychological and moral side it was hard work, competition and discipline. The triumph of industrialism gave the middle classes a series of opportunities for self-assertion that they seized greedily. With the levers of power in their hands the bourgeois set themselves up as the promoters of the economy. They gambled heavily on the system of unlimited competition and sanctified the race for money, power and advancement. Marx and Engels were no doubt thinking of this middle-class dynamism (Engels indeed had had first-hand experience of it in Manchester) when they extolled in the *Communist Manifesto* the creative force of the bourgeoisie which 'has demonstrated the capacity of human activity'. For his part, Jaurès praised its magnificent role of midwife to a new world and its power of revolutionary activity,

> breaking down the old framework, dissolving all the old forces and beliefs, turning the habits of the world upside down and continuously renewing its techniques, unleashing the tragic beauty of unlimited productive forces . . . and throwing the whole great sleeping forest of tradition into its monstrous, ever-stirring furnace.[27]

The other achievement of the bourgeoisie was to have imposed their scale of values on society. The managers of the economy were also the professors of ethics – a brand of ethics marked in depth by evangelicalism and puritanism, and founded on work, sacrifice, thrift and discipline. The hour of virtue sounded on Victoria's accession. Whether they liked it or not, the aristocracy had to conform. What a triumph to have shed disapproval on the laziness and loose morals of the upper class with all the forces of social pressure! In the middle-class creed, two articles were inscribed in letters of gold – individual effort and the spirit of enterprise and competition. This rivalry was not evoked in the abstract, as in treatises of economy, nor was it a battle between anonymous firms. It was a real struggle, a personal one between individuals of flesh and blood in the arena. As for the spirit of enterprise it easily found its theoretical justification in the reigning philosophy. Just as on the ethical side there was a firm belief in the direct responsibility of each human being for his own destiny, so there was an equally firm belief in the economic responsibility of the individual. Everyone here on earth had the fate he deserved.

Such was the gospel preached by Samuel Smiles in his bestseller *Self-Help* (1859) and repeated in his other books with symbolic titles – *Character* (1871), *Thrift* (1875), *Duty* (1880) – as well as in the three-volume *Lives of the Engineers* (1862) which spread the cult of the heroes of the Industrial Revolution. With its strong moralizing style, *Self-Help* was the expression *par excellence* of the middle-class ethic (Smiles was a general practitioner of radical background). The work develops one idea relentlessly, namely that the decisive factor in men's lives is personal effort: 'Their happiness and well-being as individuals must necessarily depend mainly upon themselves – upon their own diligent self-culture, self-discipline, and self-control – and, above all, on that honest and upright performance of individual duty, which is the glory of manly character.'[28] Thus individualism, supported by austere and righteous conduct, was set up as a guarantee of success in this world, and salvation in the next – a remarkable alliance between order and discipline on the one hand, and mobility on the other. It was this same morality that Beatrice Webb, born in the high manufacturing bourgeoisie of Lancashire, had heard preached around her in her youth with such sincerity and fervour: 'It was the bounden duty of every citizen to better his social status; to ignore those beneath him, and to aim steadily at the top rung of the social ladder. Only by this persistent pursuit by each individual of his own and his family's interest would the highest general level of civilization be attained.'[29] Based on these principles there developed a world of hard-working businessmen – tough, egotistical, merciless in the pursuit of profit, hard on themselves as well as on others, and at the same time efficient, confident and sure that they were advancing on the right road. These men concentrated their disapproval equally on privileges and monopolies, idleness and corruption, the aristocracy being castigated both morally and economically. In all branches of economic life they extolled *laissez-faire*, striving to extend the word 'free trade' to free trade in labour and land. They also tried to put the maximum limit on State intervention in relations between capital and labour, so that the principle of free contract could prevail in place of the old paternalist 'master and servant' relationship. The Master and Servant Act was first modified in 1867, then replaced in 1875 by the Employers and Workmen Act. In brief, their dream was to introduce the notion of mobility everywhere – mobility of capital, mobility of skills, mobility of jobs.

So it was the golden age of the captain of industry. It was he who was the figurehead of mid-Victorian society, the hero that public opinion liked to set up as an example, as if he were on the same level as an explorer or a missionary. If he was of humble origin, people saw in the success of a self-made man the reward of will-power and perseverance. When on the contrary he was born in easy circumstances, they said that he knew how to make his talents bear fruit. Indeed if the spirit of enterprise flourished between 1820 and 1880, it was because, as S. Checkland has emphasized, unusually favourable conditions offered unheard-of opportunities to creative temperaments. Formerly the captain of industry only had a limited range of techniques at his disposal, and it was difficult, except in very successful enterprises, to develop a business to the full. After 1880 freedom of personal action in business was to be hampered by new forms of concentration and a number of complex external factors; but in the middle of the century intitiative reigned supreme. For the ambitious all hopes were reasonable, as for the enterprising young man in *Alton Locke*, who, 'fired with the great spirit of the 19th century . . . resolved to make haste to be rich'.[30]

Indeed there were numerous examples of daring leaders of industry on whom fortune smiled and whose ship came home on the great swell of capitalism. Take for example the metallurgist Fairbairn, one of the great engineers, who managed a factory of 600 workers in Leeds; or Samuel Morley, the Nonconformist hosiery magnate who employed 8,000 workers in Nottingham and the Midlands – an outstanding figure. He owned the radical *Daily News* and had one of the greatest fortunes in England, which he used to support philanthropic and religious foundations, the Liberal Party and even the campaigns of certain trade-union leaders. In Liverpool the shipowner Samuel Cunard managed to impose not only his port but also his shipping lines on the Transatlantic route. Even more instructive was the case of Thomas Cook. He was a simple Baptist preacher by origin and, while chartering a special train for a Temperance outing in 1841, had the idea of setting up organized travel. Thirty years later his name was known all over Europe. John Player had the idea of putting a sailor's head on his packets of tobacco – a piece of publicity that was seen all round the world. It was the same success story for the Quaker chocolate manufacturers Cadbury, Fry and Rowntree in the Midlands and York, Keiller in Dundee with his marmalade, and Colman with his mustard.

Side by side with the entrepreneurs who quickly became known to the general public for their popular products, there were also the figures who struck the imagination by their technical prowess. There was Isambard K. Brunel, builder of bridges, docks, tunnels and ships (his *Great Eastern*, the largest ship in the world, was launched in London in 1858). There were the Siemens brothers, pioneers in machinery, metallurgy and above all electricity, who built dynamos, cables and so on. Sir George Hudson, 'the Railway King', crashed sensationally in 1854 and returned to nothing after starting with nothing. Another railway king succeeded him in the person of Edward Watkin, great man of enterprise as well as Liberal MP. He was carried away by his dream of a Channel Tunnel and would have linked England to the Continent if the British Government had not taken fright in 1881 and stopped the operation. For a manufacturer's career, what better model than Joseph Chamberlain's? Starting work at eighteen, he built up the Birmingham branch of his family firm making nuts and screws. Thanks to his commercial flair, his technical judgment and his power of decision, he found himself twenty years later possessed of £120,000, so he decided to sell his share of the business and retire! Yet, as is proved by Hudson's example, it was not all successes, and failure was one of the fundamental conditions of a competitive system that knew no limits. Some of the most resounding crashes, such as the fall of Peto, the great engineer and builder, claimed public attention – the higher the rise, the harder the fall. But the majority of these dramas were played out in obscurity. Silence engulfed bankruptcy, the pitiless sanction of *laissez-faire* morality. Yet there were some voices raised to warn against the intoxication of success and the danger of materialism. The caustic criticism of Sydney Smith deploring the shopkeeping concept of national destiny ('the major object for which the Anglo-Saxon seems to have been created is the manufacture of calico') is echoed by the sombre warning of Matthew Arnold in *Culture and Anarchy*: 'Faith in machinery is . . . our besetting danger.'

The popular classes

Going down the scale we come to the 'lower orders'. There was to be found the mass of the population, since the lower orders made up about five-sixths of the country, in fact the whole of the world of labour. Here above all the contemporary vocabulary, with its variants and variations, unwittingly reveals the current concept of the social order. So, while some expressions fairly current before 1850 were in decline, such as 'the labouring classes' and, above all, 'the labouring poor', others like 'working people' had a more durable life. Among the workers themselves the term 'working men' acquired great favour, but it was 'working classes' that was more and more generally adopted. However the word especially favoured by the 'upper classes' for forty years after the mid-century was 'artisans', doubtless because of its spurious suggestion of independence and respectability (though, curiously enough, it was a term more usually applied to wage-earners than to the self-employed in the strict sense of the word). In manufacturing districts they continued to use a more expressive word to designate proletarians who survived solely by their own muscle. They called them 'hands'.

In the course of this period the 'social question', the working-class movement and, in a general way, the whole nature of the world of labour were dominated by four great problems, which, either separately or together, have given rise to lively debate:

1 Do the economic structures in England at the time, and the composition of the world of labour permit us to include the latter under the generic term of 'proletariat'? Or would the traditional but more composite label 'the people' be more appropriate?
2 Did the working class, in the strict sense of the word, have a basic unity arising out of common characteristics, or did its various components make it break up into heterogeneous, not to say antagonistic elements?
3 Did the evolution of the standard of living tend towards pauperization or progress?
4 Was there in the third quarter of the century a process of *embourgeoisement*, involving a surrender to bourgeois values and capitalist order?

One can thus see laid out behind these questions the whole problem of the labour aristocracy, its place in the social hierarchy and its role in the labour movement.

First of all we must avoid a mistaken idea about England in the middle of the nineteenth century. There was indeed economic advance, but we must not depict England as the almost exclusive domain of a large concentrated industry, for there was a hybrid mixture of archaism and modernism. Side by side with highly mechanized activities there continued to exist many sorts of pre-industrial production. This showed up in society by the presence of a mass of small independent producers, artisans, craftsmen, journeymen and home-workers, while subcontractors and piece-workers, far from having been eliminated by industrialization, found new outlets for their energies and occupations. Furthermore, work by hand was still rather more common than machine work – at the 1851 census Great Britain had more shoemakers than miners. In total, out of about 5 million workers in industry and transport the number of workers in factories and mechanized plants was less than 2 million. In addition, marketing in most of the artisan crafts was not separate from manufacture. The workshop was where objects were sold as well as made. Another major factor must also be borne in mind. Two large groups, numbering in 1851 half as many people as the workers in industry and transport, must be included in the working classes even though appearances seem to separate them from the industrial proletariat. They were the domestic servants (who were as numerous as all the textile workers put together, i.e. 1,300,000) and the agricultural workers who formed the rural proletariat – a category whose members were numerous but widely scattered.

Of course large-scale industry did make steady progress. In 1871 an official enquiry registered a significant growth in concentration: an average of 570 employees in shipbuilding, 209 in iron and steel, 180 in cotton-spinning and 71 in hosiery. In effect, in textiles the dying domestic system was giving way to the factory system, and most of the hand-loom weavers and stockingers disappeared at the same time as Chartism. On the other hand there was a rapid increase in the number of miners, celebrated in song by Auguste Barbier, a minor Romantic poet:

> We are the miners of rich England;
> We live like moles six hundred feet underground . . .[31]

There were 216,000 miners in 1851 whereas there were 495,000 in 1881. Nevertheless, even where the growth of modern technology was most rapid, i.e. in metals and engineering, the small workshops continued to prosper, notably in the Sheffield and Birmingham areas. Highly specialized, they were perfectly suited to the needs of variegated production, working often to special orders, and continued to exist until after the First World War. The result was that in 1871, 600,000 metal workers were found to be scattered in 18,000 establishments. Another example was the building industry (450,000 workers in 1851), a trade that always resisted concentration and mechanization most vigorously. Traditional techniques and labour relations were always the rule in that trade. Very small employers or jobbers working on single sites always outnumbered the large builders. It is true that in the building trade, as in many other branches of activity like furniture, woodwork and footwear, only a very small capital, just a few pounds of savings, was necessary to try one's luck and set up on one's own. In addition, subcontracting was common, which favoured small, independent businesses. Home-workers managed here and there to preserve their autonomy, while sweat-shops abounded. The latter did their damage particularly in the clothing industry, especially tailoring, and the fashion business, where the female workforce increased all the time (two-thirds in 1881 as opposed to less than half in 1851). Finally, in the 'lower orders' there existed both in expanding as well as in sleepy traditional cities a motley crowd of people living from a multitude of occupations. Some worked on their own in transport and commerce (carmen, draymen, milkmen, costermongers, etc.), others did small jobs on the streets, either permanent or casual (sweepers, chimneysweeps, pedlars, street musicians, etc.) while others preferred to seek adventure as soldiers or sailors. . . .

The employment and business picture which emerges is a vast mosaic of activity in which a complex network of hierarchies constantly renewed itself as new techniques and new methods of production developed. The modern sectors of high concentration alternated with others in which tradition, combining with a desire for independence, tried to resist with varying success the encroachments of capital and big business. Our own conclusion is that the lumping together under the heading of 'proletariat' of such varied social groups as factory hands, artisans and craftsmen, small-scale employers, tradesmen, subcontractors, farm labourers and domestic servants, leads to an excessive simplification which in the end is hardly illuminating. Doubtless all these categories had certain things in common: the same dependence on the owners of capital, the same in-security, the same low incomes; but they differed so much in other aspects – way of life, relation with their employers, leisure activities, culture, family life, neighbourhood relations, religious beliefs – that one would do better to combine them in a larger ensemble with a genuine collective consciousness, that is as the 'popular classes'. In reality, while a working-class consciousness was gradually coming into being (particu-larly in the old trades and in large-scale mechanized industry) the 'popu-lar' consciousness, older and better represented, remained the more solidly rooted. It was reinforced by neighbourhood solidarity, the actual day-to-day experience of people in towns and villages, and drew nourishment from the political traditions of the world of labour. For the dominant ideology among working people, i.e. radicalism, always wanted to unite the forces of the 'common people' in the fight against exploiters and parasites. Those 'common people' were wage-earners, artisans, trades people, small entrepreneurs and progressive elements in the middle classes. Hence the working-class consciousness remained above all a democratic consciousness, that was more political than economic and was imbued with myriad characteristics of the popular soul.

If one now considers the internal structure of the working class, one fundamental fact jumps to the eye – the separation of workers into two levels, distinguished by their skill, their incomes and their status. At the upper level of the hierarchy were to be found the 'skilled workers' who had gone through a long apprenticeship. They occupied a key position in production because of their technical know-how. They were imbued with the dignity that goes with a trade and its tools. As they controlled entry into their trades at close quarters, they were in a position to exert continuous pressure on their employers both by invoking working practices and by the formation of associations. They were indeed the key element in the formation of the trade unions. At the lower level, the mass of unskilled workers formed a vast 'reserve army' of labour, taken on as circumstances demanded, either to back up the skilled workers or to take up activities requiring physical strength (e.g. as navvies or dockers) or simply the presence of a man paid at a cheap rate. However, side by side with the commonest types of economic activity where there was this straight divide between skilled and unskilled, there were others like the textile and clothing trades, mining and food industry where an intermediate category developed – the 'semi-skilled' workers who were generally put in charge of a machine. There were many women in this group. This occupational mix cannot be simply explained by the coexistence of ancient artisan structures and the effects of the first Industrial Revolution. It was essentially the result of techniques of production that prevailed right up to the First World War. Hence one finds an organization of work which varied very little and where there was a strict and relatively stable definition of tasks and rewards.

However, the technical divide between skilled and unskilled workers quickly became a social and psychological divide. From one universe to the other, said Mayhew, 'the moral and intellectual change is so great that it seems as if we were in a new land and among another race'.[32] Thomas Wright, 'the journeyman engineer', author of several books on the world of labour, speaks of the 'gulf' between the craftsman and the labourer, resulting in an attitude of superiority hardly favourable to proletarian solidarity: 'While the former resents the spirit in which he believes the followers of "genteel occupations" look down on him, he in his turn looks down upon the labourer. The artisan creed with regard to labourers is that the latter are an inferior class, and that they should be made to know and kept in their place.'[33] The scales of pay show up these distinctions perfectly. Not only was the gap between wage groups considerable (an unskilled worker earned hardly half what was earned by a skilled worker, a semi-skilled worker two-thirds) but the differential tended to become more pronounced between 1850 and 1890. Dudley Baxter has calculated that in 1867 one-seventh of the workers took up one-quarter of the total remuneration. The rift was no less great in the realms of culture and organization. A skilled worker who earned £80–£90 a year (as compared with an unskilled worker who earned £40–£50) was in a position to get some education, to read a paper regularly, to join a Friendly Society, all of which would appear unattainable to a labourer. Indeed for some observers the definition of an unskilled worker was one who does not belong to a trade union. So how easy it was for the worker elevated by his respectable status and by the way he was treated by his employer to make his superiority felt! And as for the top layer of foremen, overseers and gangmasters (3–4 per cent of the workforce in industry) who bordered on the lower middle class. . . .

To reckon up the size of the various categories of the labour hierarchy, one can estimate that the proportions were roughly 15 per cent for highly skilled workers, 45 per cent for unskilled workers and 40 per cent for the intermediate zones (starting with average qualifications and descending gradually to the modest specialization of the semi-skilled). It was the first of the three strata which essentially formed the 'labour aristocracy', or about one-eighth of the workforce in industry. It was undoubtedly a privileged category and one whose role has been the cause of much spilling of ink. Its representatives were above all to be found in the engineering industries, in building, in traditional crafts, and occasionally in textile plants, in mining, in the chemical industry and transport. One of the major contradictions of the 'labour aristocracy' was that professionally and socially they were careful to distinguish themselves from the other workers, while politically they tended to present themselves as the spokesmen of the assembled world of labour.

In view of all this, can one say that there was *one* working class, or was there simply a juxtaposition of various strata, bordering on one another but autonomous? The problem is obviously to gauge the depths reached by these divisions. For some historians working-class solidarity survived all the horizontal divisions; so according to Hobsbawm there was already a proper proletariat in England around 1840–50. On the contrary, says Pelling, a homogeneous working class did not appear until the end of the nineteenth century. Others have proposed linking the upper working to the lower middle class and separating it from the other workers. A contemporary observer as well informed as Frederic Harrison, the positivist philosopher, gave a mixed judgment. He was rightly insistent on the crucial role of the barrier which separated skilled workmen from unskilled labour. It is our opinion, however, that he was making a more profound analysis of the forces at work in English society when he wrote that the real breach in the class hierarchy occurred 'between the lowest of the propertied classes and the highest of the non-propertied classes'.[34] By that distinction the world of the manual workers finds a fundamental unity of which one tends to lose sight in a detailed study of its complicated internal hierarchy.

The picture of working-class conditions has so often been painted that it may seem superfluous to dwell on it. Let us just recall some essential traits. First of all, the long hours of work. The Factory Acts of 1847–50 limited the working week to 60 hours, but this applied only to the textile industry, and the average for the majority settled around 64 hours. The general rule was that in factories work went on from 6 am to 6 pm, and in shops from 8 am to 8 pm with 1½ hours off for meals, at least until 1874 when the principle of the 56½-hour week (or 10-hour day) was adopted. After 1850 the Saturday half-day became the general rule, work stopping on Saturday at 2 pm. The move which started around 1871–2 for a 9-hour day was successful in the metal and building industries. On the other hand working-class housing was often cramped, overcrowded and unhealthy; discomfort, promiscuity and brutality had to be endured. Above all the life of the working man was entirely dominated by a deep feeling of insecurity, so much was he at the mercy of the market and its cycle. Each worker found employment according to the fluctuating demands for labour. A crisis, a fall in demand, a bankruptcy were enough to plunge whole districts into unemployment and so into severe distress. For example, right in the middle of 'Victorian prosperity', the cotton famine in Lancashire at the time of the American Civil War, or the slump of 1867–8 gave rise to periods of appalling suffering. And what about the sombre year 1879, the worst of the half-century? Without social security of any sort, working-class families were haunted by the possibility of a disaster of some kind – an accident, an illness or some technological innovation. The fact was that daily life was so precarious (in normal times one just about 'managed') that the slightest mishap dragged a family swiftly and surely down the slippery slope. A fall or two, and one found oneself in the abyss of misery.

In the matter of wages the employers largely followed the teaching of the classical economists, i.e. remuneration was pitched at the lowest level consistent with the survival of the worker and his family. On average, a working-class household devoted 60 per cent of its budget to food, 20 per cent to housing (consisting of rent, heating and light) and 10 per cent to clothing. So there remained just 10 per cent for all its other needs – or 2 shillings a week for a worker earning £1 a week, a very usual wage. An average family budget amounted to 30 shillings a week or about £75 a year. In fact, taking account of differentials, the real income was on average £85–£90 for a skilled household, £70 for a semi-skilled and £45–£50 for an unskilled. Consequently one found in working-class districts one shop that was always flourishing, the pawnbroker's. Every Monday housewives came and deposited clothes, trinkets or household utensils, and then redeemed them the following Saturday after pay-day. In Liverpool 60 per cent of the objects pawned were worth less than 5 shillings. The labouring classes in their physique and health showed all the effects of malnutrition and bad hygiene. The average height of poor boys between 11 and 12 years old in industrial schools was 12 cm less than that of rich boys in public schools.

However what perhaps more than anything else made for the desperation and the resignation of the lower classes was the monotony, the brutality, the feeling that it was impossible to get out of this prison. The lucky people were those who could look upon inequality as simply the normal order of things – for then everyone had to resign himself to it. 'The lot of eating, drinking, working and dying must ever be the sum of human life among the masses of a large portion of the human family', had declared Sir James Graham, Peel's 'second self' in the House of Commons.[35] These views were so widespread as to be commonplace, even in the lower classes, where many decided to put up with their lot.

This is the proletarian existence that Dickens immortalized in *Hard Times* (1854) with his description of Coketown, archetype of the industrial city, a dump of grey ugliness and never-ending dullness, where the oppressive gloom left no room for hope:

> It was a town of machinery and tall chimneys, out of which interminable serpents of smoke trailed themselves for ever and ever, and never got uncoiled. It had a black canal in it, and a river that ran purple with ill-smelling dye, and vast piles of building full of windows where there was a rattling and a trembling all day long, and where the piston of the steam-engine worked monotonously up and down, like the head of an elephant in a state of melancholy madness. It contained several large streets still more like one another, inhabited by people equally like one another, who all went in and out at the same hours, with the same sound on the same pavements, to do the same work, and to whom every day was the same as yesterday and tomorrow, and every year the counterpart of the last and the next.

There was another working-class category, at the opposite end to this uniformity, the servants, who made up one-eighth of the occupied population in 1881, 90 per cent of them women. Their lot varied considerably. Some of them were well treated and became attached to the family they worked for; but for many others the position was hardly enviable. They were for the most part young girls, sometimes very young, often badly paid and overworked. They had to get up early, light fires, clean, scrub, and be scolded without flinching. There was little time off, strict supervision, and no 'followers'. . . .

As for farmworkers, they were widely scattered and had difficulty in establishing a common consciousness. Their condition depended largely on the way they were individually treated by farmers and landlords. Many lived in wretched cottages with primitive sanitation. Sweating away for a meagre wage, this agricultural proletariat, without a voice and without rights, having no vote and hardly any education for lack of schools, led a comfortless existence in a state of submission and dependence, but their grievances were mounting up. Joseph Arch, a labourer and Methodist lay preacher with a bold and obstinate character, launched the National Agricultural Labourers Union in 1872, which led in a few months to a sudden burst of union activity.

However, in this matter of working-class conditions, the important things to discover are the development trends. In which direction were social conditions moving? Were they improving? Pessimistic ideas on working-class pauperization were countered by a view (commonly held by contemporaries) that postulated a national progress in which the working class got its fair share. The advocates of this theory point out the rise in wages, the growth in food consumption and savings bank deposits, the advance of provident and temperance societies, the development of reading and education – all sure signs of improvement in material well-being. From this sprang the familiar picture of the solid workman, well turned-out, wearing a tie and sporting a gold watch in his waistcoat, enjoying his roast beef and his daily pint of beer, and able to take an occasional day off at the seaside.

Although this picture has some elements of truth, all this optimism is a bit suspect and may have resulted from a deliberate desire, in an age of euphoria and self-confidence, to look at things through rose-coloured spectacles. Isn't it always comforting to convince oneself that one is not the only person getting rich? So three considerations must be taken into account which considerably modify the traditional views. Firstly in relation to the standard of living, studies on the movement of real wages show, despite some disagreement among statisticians, that incomes hardly moved at all during the 1850s. They only started to rise around 1863, and for ten years there was indeed a phase of rapid growth, so much so that a workman in stable employment (an indispensable condition) saw his purchasing power rise by 20–30 per cent in the years between 1855 and 1875. In the second place there were differences between categories of employees, and these calculations applied above all to the top layer of the workforce. In fact skilled workers, taking advantage of their relative scarcity and their ability to use the union weapon which was mainly their preserve, succeeded in raising the price of their labour, even though they remained vulnerable to the changes and chances of their situation. A period of slump could easily alter the upward tendency. On the other hand, for the unskilled workers improvement seems to have been less obvious, if it existed at all. For instance recent studies carried out on social conditions in Lancashire tend to show that the lot of the unskilled and semi-skilled hardly changed at all. Where there was some advance, it appears to have been limited, patchy and fragile, and many sectors of society were virtually unaffected. Finally on the national scene, figures on the distribution of incomes show that the workers drew less profit from the general increase in riches than the well-off. According to Bowley, the proportion of wages in the national income dropped between 1860 and 1880 from 47 to 42 per cent – a figure that was also put forward by *The Economist* of the time.[36] In other words, the revenue from capital in the form of dividends and profits took a greater share than ever before, up to 1880. After that the opposite occurred up to the end of the century.

These reservations make the picture much less favourable for the workers than a partisan optimism liked to make out. It is certainly wrong to talk about pauperization, but neither can one conclude that there was a general unbroken improvement for the workers, corresponding to the boom in the economy. On the other hand it is true to say that the lower classes benefited indirectly from general improvement. Geoffrey Best has rightly pointed out the growing proportion of better paid jobs for qualified operatives, the long-term reduction in the length of the working week, and the progress of education.[37] One could add the establishment of fixed holidays by the Bank Holiday Act of 1871, the reduction in the adulteration of food in shops, and even more the development of urban facilities, of hygiene, of libraries and Sunday schools. Finally the very constraints of puritanism and respectability played a positive role in fighting drunkenness and insisting on more cleanliness, if only to seem like 'the best people'. Certainly a more moralizing and uniform culture was imposing itself compared with the robust old forms of popular culture, but it was better adapted to an industrial civilization. However the lowest ranks of the proletariat did not on the whole partake of this progress, and they remained chained to their degradation. For it was necessary to have a level of culture and a standard of living, which the poor were denied, to profit from these improvements. The main resources for the poor were the often humiliating gifts of private charity. Hundreds of thousands of pounds were distributed every month by charitable organizations in the form of cash, soup kitchens, clothes, etc., to those who were slightingly called the 'residuum' or the 'undeserving poor', as opposed to the 'deserving poor'. On the other hand there was also the Poor Law which enabled the indigent to pay the price of their poverty in grim workhouses, even if the degree of inhumanity did vary from one establishment to another. It is estimated that the Charities of London, i.e. the combined charitable foundations of the capital, paid out £2,440,000 during the course of 1861, while the Poor Law expenditure in the metropolitan area only amounted to £1,425,000 for an average year.[38] So, wading through this mass of rejected and marginal humanity – tramps, unemployed, casual labourers, bankrupts, down-and-outs, beggars, Irish immigrants who were laughed at and despised, discharged prisoners walking the pavements – one arrived at the edge of the under-world.

Unionism and social integration

Ever since the Webbs used the expression 'new-model' unionism to describe the labour movement in the years 1851–75, the latter has usually been interpreted as a reaction against the violent and semi-revolutionary claims of the preceding period. Instead of boundless hopes there now reigned, according to this thesis, a spirit of moderation and prudence, based on tactics that were realist and efficient. From this arose a unionism that was 'respectful and respectable', accepting the moral values preached by the bourgeoisie with a view to improving the lot of the workers. The watchwords were work, welfare and individualism. In brief, they were 'reasonable' trade unionists, preferring fruitful class collaboration to sterile and harmful class struggle. The credit for this change of climate would accrue mainly to the labour aristocracy who knew how to improve its standard of living, acquire its education and get a taste for self-help, all at the same time. 'In truth during the last quarter of the century', wrote the very orthodox economist Leone Levi, 'the higher strata of the labouring classes have exercised an elevating influence over every branch of British labour.'[39] And in 1869 the Comte de Paris devoted a book to *Les Associations Ouvrières en Angleterre* where he commended the seriousness and restraint of the British workers, so different from their French comrades who were always ready to adopt revolutionary ideas. If there was such a feeling of reassurance in the 'upper classes', isn't this just a sure proof that a process of material and psychological integration was at work in the world of labour, almost amounting to an absorption into the middle class?

In fact one can seriously question whether the break after 1850 was so complete and whether the labour movement did turn over a new leaf. In particular, was trade unionism so very different after the formation of the Amalgamated Society of Engineers in 1851, usually considered the point of departure of the 'new model'? There is no doubt that some major ambitions for labour emancipation were modified. But shouldn't one distinguish between appearance and reality? Yet the supporters of the traditional interpretation, firmly entrenched in their positions, have an impressive array of facts to support their thesis.

Firstly, one cannot deny that little remained of the two great forces which had animated the labour movement in the second quarter of the century – Owenian and cooperative socialism on the one hand, Chartism on the other. Chartist agitation certainly did not die out with the year 1848, as has often been said, but even where it did retain a certain vitality for another ten years or so, it was limited to scattered groups, a mere remnant floating on the ebb-tide of great aspirations. As for socialist ideas they underwent an almost total eclipse, except in the watered-down form of Christian socialism, and even so they were confined to a few sectors of the middle class. Avoiding heroic dreams and visionary utopias, the labour movement now advanced with determination and pragmatism in three directions. The activities to which they gave priority were the cooperative movement, the Friendly Societies, and trade unionism.

In the wake of the Equitable Pioneers of Rochdale (1844) the cooperatives multiplied rapidly. In 1872 there were 927 branches and 300,000 members, and their turnover was nearly £10 million. But the spirit of the cooperators had none of the messianic fervour of yesteryear. It had become a matter of shopkeeping, accountancy and individualism. There was no question, as the journal *The Cooperator* made clear, of putting an end to the inequalities of society – they simply wanted to reduce the exploitation of the workers. The president of the movement maintained that cooperation aimed at uniting 'the means, the energies, and the talent of all for the benefit of each by a common bond, that of self-interest.'

Yet idealism had not disappeared, it was simply the values that had changed. Instead of thinking of overthrowing the structures of society, the members of the cooperative movement accepted them as they were, so long as they could gradually and patiently improve them. 'We have seen enough of the Utopian ridiculous mummery of socialism. . . . We don't want it. . . . Let Co-operation inculcate no other spirit but gratitude to God, loyalty to our Sovereign, love to our country and good will to mankind.'[40]

The Friendly Societies on their side made good progress. They were not in fact a new phenomenon, indeed they were one of the oldest labour institutions. By 1815 they had already several hundred thousand members, and by 1850 probably a million and a half. In 1872 their total was 4 million, i.e. four times as many members as the trade unions and twelve times as many as the cooperative societies.[41] Born in a spirit of mutual help and given resounding names (Ancient Order of Foresters, Oddfellows, Druids, etc.), the Friendly Societies catered primarily for protection against the two great disasters of a worker's life, accident and illness. They also arose out of a desire to ensure the worker and his family a decent burial rather than the disgrace of a pauper's funeral, and to soften the effects of unemployment by paying compensation for loss of work. So it was a miniature social security system, entirely private and voluntary, founded on a sense of solidarity and a desire to escape the ignominious Poor Law by preserving personal independence. In the Friendly Societies one helped and was helped by one's friends within the working class.

As for trade unionism, which had come out into the light of day after the abolition of the Combination Laws in 1824–5, its progress showed ups and downs. The forward movement of the unions picked up after 1843–5 with its membership apparently exceeding 100,000, but the number of members, drawn almost exclusively from the skilled-worker class, increased very slowly. In 1868, when the Trades Union Congress was formed, the total was only around 250,000. Then a sudden jump occurred. In the space of five years the numbers rose to 735,000, only to fall, under the effect of the depression of 1875–80, to between 500,000 and 600,000. This unionism had certain original characteristics. Firstly it was above all a craft unionism which, within the workshop, defended workers' interests actively and stubbornly, concentrating chiefly on the defence of skill and wages, and having recourse, as circumstances required, to collective bargaining, arbitration or strike action. It was also a unionism with an educational purpose. It was the union's job to help members educate themselves, develop their abilities and thereby raise themselves as individuals. Thirdly the union movement was strongly political. Parallel to the economic struggle waged against the employer, labour was active in the sphere of government. One can distinguish three successive phases. From 1861 to 1867 there were the campaigns for universal suffrage, ending in the electoral reform of 1867. From 1867 to 1875 there was the agitation for the Labour Laws, which guaranteed union rights, freedom to picket, etc. After 1875 there was the official agreement between the unions and the Liberal Party, the 'Lib-Lab alliance'. In addition, throughout this period, internationalism was evidently flourishing, as shown by the campaigns of sympathy for democratic movements and national emancipation in Europe, or in the framework of the First International where the trade unions played an important role from 1864 to 1871.

Working-class action thus inclined towards social and political democratization, which conformed to the radical tradition inherited from the popular struggles of the seventeenth and eighteenth centuries and influenced by Jacobinism. But it suffered from a contradiction, albeit not clearly perceived, between an individualist ideology of the rights of man and the common people, which led to a largely political fight against the privileges of the power-holders, and a strategy of social struggle derived from the conflicting interests of wage-earners and capitalists, which ended in an economic fight against the privileges of the rich. Between the two terms of this dialectic – political struggle or proletarian struggle – the balance inclined at once towards the former. Furthermore, for radicals a class society was always considered inevitable. The aim was not to abolish classes but to guarantee to each individual the exercise of his rights and develop a society where each would occupy the place he deserved. This was the ambition that George Howell, one of the most representative leaders of the labour movement, expressed in the following terms: 'I have never been, and never shall be, an advocate for merely changing our masters. I want neither aristocratic rule, nor the rule of the middle classes, nor the rule of the working classes. I want a government of the entire people – where wealth and intellect will have its fair share of power – no more.'[42]

Finally in accord with the times, unionism was imbued with the spirit of morality. Side by side with firm solidarity and loyalty – the very stuff of collective action – the trade unionist cultivated the virtues of temperance, thrift and discipline. They had a horror of anything that reeked of the tavern. Puritanism acted as a basic ingredient of respectability. 'Working-class politics became less of a "knife and fork" and more of a "collar and tie" question.'[43] Indeed optimism joined up with idealism in a rather curious way. 'Three great forces for the improvement of mankind', asserted John Mitchell, 'are religion, temperance and co-operation; and, as a commercial force, supported and sustained by the other two, co-operation is the grandest, noblest, and most likely to be successful in the redemption of the industrial classes'.[44]

When facing all these arguments, must one accept as proven the thesis that the labour world was absorbed psychologically into the universe of the triumphant bourgeoisie? The abandonment of all revolutionary aims, the modest claims, the acceptance of middle-class ideals in their radical-democratic version, are all these undeniable traits decisive, and above all are they enough to reduce the labour movement to the dimensions of a narrow and pragmatic attitude, a more or less bastard version of socialism, after the bold quest for freedom of Chartism and before the birth of the Labour Party?

Whatever judgment one finally makes on the direction taken by labour and its 'rallying round' to the principles of capitalism (some would talk of 'contamination'), one point certainly stands out with which everyone agrees – the key role of the labour aristocracy. That is why the Conservative school of historical writing has credited this class with having avoided revolutionary and utopian shibboleths to concentrate on an historic task of the first importance – laying the foundations for legal, peaceful and constructive action on the part of the trade unions. Thanks to this move the workers were said to have shown their capacity for organization and to have hammered out practical, flexible and varied procedures for negotiation with employers and for pressure on the State. The solid common sense of people with their feet on the ground was said to have prevailed over disorderly thrusts and inflammatory declarations couched in the language of revolution. Conversely, the Marxist school of historiography has made the labour aristocracy responsible for the cessation (at least temporary) of the struggle against capitalism, accusing it of letting itself be corrupted by the crumbs from excess(ive) profits which their privileged position allowed them to pick up. Hence sprang connivance in the process of working-class exploitation, and an alienation brought about by the doctrines of the bourgeoisie.

We think in fact that it would be reasonable to modify these traditional views by introducing the following considerations. Firstly, the labour aristocracy did not deserve either this special credit or this special blame. Its cental role sprang from the actual organization of the economic system. In a society relying on directly productive work, it is the skilled operative, holding a key position in the productive circuit and in addition being relatively privileged by income and education, who is of necessity in the best position to oppose the capitalist. It was absolutely natural that he should assume the leadership in union action, and this arose logically out of the organization of industry. It was already true at the birth of trade unionism and Chartism, and it was no less true in the rest of Europe, starting with France. Some of the most intrepid of the working-class leaders were recruited from the labour aristocracy.

Secondly one must take into account the climate of events in which the workers' struggle took place. After the stormy 1815–48 period, during which hopes of a millenium could reckon on the collapse of a tottering economic system and of the old privileged class, there was no longer any question of basking in the same illusions during the third quarter of the nineteenth century when capitalism and *laissez-faire* were triumphant. As it was impossible to envisage an overthrow of the social system, labour strategy had to adapt itself realistically and effectively. Certainly the calculation was not very conscious, but working-class energies were channelled by taking note of the facts. Instead of wanting to tilt against windmills in a manner that was chivalrous but doomed to failure, it was better patiently to adopt the tactic of partial progress. Obviously there was a danger of falling from the romanticism of a Don Quixote to the bourgeois prose of a Sancho Panza, but what of it?

However the thesis of the *embourgeoisement* of the labour movement does come up against several major objections. Firstly, far from religiously accepting the laws of classical economics as has been maintained, the leading unionists never stopped opposing several of these tenets – among others the conception of labour as a commodity, the theory of wages, the principle of an identity of interests between employers and employees. It is true that one can cite a number of trade unionists' declarations criticizing class antagonism and strikes, and preaching arbitration and conciliation in their place. But the labour movement always continued to proclaim, as basic requirements, the right to work, the right to a decent standard of living, and 'a fair day's wage for a fair day's work' –

requirements that all contradicted liberal orthodoxy. Furthermore, the trade unionists always clung to two principles as essential for the advance of working-class interests: universal suffrage as a decisive weapon to ensure a hearing at the State level, and, when necessary, recourse to strike action as the only means of making workers' pressure irresistible. Even Howell, a symbol of the 'Lib-Lab' alliance and a man of peace, recognized that industrial conflicts were inevitable and that strikes 'appear to be an essential part of the economy of capital and labour, and the natural and inevitable outcome of the relationship now subsisting between employers and employed'.[45] And, in fact, the number of strikes did not diminish during the period 1850–80.

In the third place (and this is no doubt the most important factor of all) the majority of organized workers preserved a class consciousness and cultural autonomy which prevented them from toeing the dominant bourgeois line. All the ideological pressure of the governing classes did not succeed in squeezing out certain areas of popular culture. In that respect even the most tranquil working-class institutions such as the Friendly Societies and the Cooperative Societies stimulated a sense of class solidarity by encouraging a spirit of friendship and sociability among equals. A sort of conviviality brought together these men who recognized themselves as belonging to the same world and the same *milieu*. In addition, the violence of certain social conflicts (often provoked by lock-outs deliberately planned by managements) and the openly advertised desire of many employers to 'break' the trade unions would have been enough to cement a class front which never disappeared, but was continually revived during struggles stubbornly fought.

Finally, at the beginning of the 1870s the flare-up of trade-union activity completely transcended the framework of craft organization and reflected the awakening of the unskilled, who suddenly stirred and organized themselves. We have already mentioned the farmworkers' awakening. Now it embraced likewise the dockers, the gasworkers, the railwaymen, the seamen, etc. Undoubtedly the cyclical depression which descended on England from 1874 onwards sharply broke the impetus. However it is right to see in these signs of working-class militancy and pugnacity (and in this case it was an upsurge of the underprivileged, up to now the most passive section) a proof that they did not espouse, as much as has been asserted, the principles of deference and social peace. One should beware of being the prisoner of appearances. The sententious outlook of the working class, the stovepipe hat adopted as a symbol of respectability, the pedantic stiffness of people who seemed to have swallowed a petit-bourgeois umbrella, should not blind us to the reality, behind these masks, of working-class independence and fighting spirit.

Only all this was expressed in the optimistic language of the day, which hid out of sight the great collective ambitions, and considered that the cumulative progress of individuals would lead to communal progress, that is to say the salvation of the working classes.

3 Power and consensus

The social dynamic

Up to this point our perspective has consisted in analysing social structures, i.e. the hierarchical organization of British society with its complex stratification. We must now bring in a new dimension by studying the social dynamic, which is an expression of social trends and of the play of overall social forces. This approach should help to clarify inter-class relations as well as the struggles and confrontations between social groups, and to determine what was the real degree of social mobility in Victorian times. This will also lead us to ask questions about the distribution of wealth and power, the interplay of ideologies and beliefs, the loyalty to the existing social order and the willingness to change it.

After a long period of agitation and upheaval, mid-Victorian England presented a rare spectacle – a state of equilibrium. Not an equilibrium resulting from stagnation and archaic routines, as in the pre-industrial world, but an equilibrium achieved in the face of the rapid movements of a country in full growth. One fact is obvious, and that is the stability of the society and its power structure, a system strengthened by the sanction accorded both to the hierarchy of the classes and to the system of government. Its success cannot be denied, and even if the balance was considered precarious, it lasted for the whole third quarter of the century. During these years the paradox of England was that she was a society at the same time unequal and homogeneous. At the basis of the inequality there were of course the vast class differences, but, more important still, there was the fact that everybody accepted the hierarchy as natural and even necessary. At the basis of the homogeneity there was a consensus. One communed in the same beliefs and one adhered to the same fundamental values.

It is possible to represent quantitatively the comparative strength of the social components. Indeed, thanks to the calculations of the statistician Dudley Baxter, we have at our disposal for the year 1867 some fairly precise figures relating to the division of wealth. From this data there emerges with remarkable neatness the outline of a perfect social pyramid. The small handful of large fortunes are so well contrasted with the general mass of incomes that Baxter has been pleased to compare the structure to the peak of Teneriffe 'with its low long base of labouring population, with its uplands of the middle class, and with its towering peaks and summits of those with princely incomes.'[1]

Statistics relating to housing in 1862 give exact confirmation to this picture of a society that was extraordinarily inegalitarian: 0.2 per cent of the population paid more than £200 in rent, 0.8 per cent paid between £100 and £200, 11.5 per cent paid between £20 and £100, and 87.5 per cent less than £20.[2]

As for income from land, according to the calculations of Léonce de Lavergne, confirmed a little later by English economists, the landlords, who made up less than 1 per cent of the rural population, received two-fifths of the total in the form of rent; the tenant farmers (or one-sixth of the population) gathered in about a quarter; and the proletariat of agricultural labourers (about 85 per cent of the rural total) received only 35 per cent.[3]

The movements within society only aggravated this unfair division of wealth. For the important factor was not only that the distance between classes tended to widen rather than narrow. It is of course beyond doubt that the general standard of living did rise. Only, in spite of all the reassuring statements made by the professional optimists, the rich got richer with greater speed than the poor got less poor. Furthermore, within each of the three social classes, it was the most privileged elements that consolidated their wealth and their power. The result was that the whole social ladder grew longer and longer because the gaps within the classes grew at the same time as the gaps between the classes. The process which had been at work since the beginning of the century reached its peak between 1850 and 1880, after which there was a lull. This was a fine success for *laissez-faire* – the apotheosis of 'each for himself' and free competition. What was so surprising about the triumph of the strongest, since the guiding principle of a liberal society was that wealth bred wealth? In effect it was those who enjoyed the advantages of money, prestige and culture, or even those who possessed a morsel of power thanks to their place in the production cycle, who were in a position to profit from the opportunities that were offered, at whatever level of society they were – great patricians, landowners, captains of industry, or simple members of the labour aristocracy. All this operated to the detriment of the less favoured at all levels – the small-time squires, the lower middle class, the unskilled workers.

Was England revolution-proof?

Many English people, confronted with social contrasts of such dimensions and such brutality, imagined that an explosion was bound to result from these tensions. Hence, between 1815 and 1848, the widespread alarm at the idea of threatening revolution, so much panic over the dangers from the 'mob' . . . Indeed on several occasions revolutionary rumblings shook the whole social edifice. In 1844, Engels in *The Condition of the Working Class in England* prophesied with assurance: 'The Revolution must come'.[4] And yet revolution did not break out. England, after escaping it in 1830–2, escaped it again in 1848. Once more in 1867, popular agitation for the right to vote remained faithful to legal methods; and in 1886–7, the great turn-outs of the unemployed in the streets were more like ragged processions than organized revolutionary demonstrations. So during the whole of the nineteenth century, the country experienced no Commune, no barricades, no rivers of blood, no lasting hatreds. But, even if civil law and order won the day, one should not imagine that all was idyllic. The toughness of the ruling class, the bitterness of the social struggle, the repressive brutality of the penal system – these were all solid realities. The peace of the social scene should not lead us to underestimate class antagonisms and the intensity of the political and religious struggles, not to mention the Irish question whose battle-lines extended even to the shores of England.

However, the Establishment firmly held its ground. The English proletariat never rose in rebellion. Society worked out its mutations without upheavals or violence. Hence the questions: might England be resistant to revolutions? On what bases did the social balance of the country rest? What was the secret of constitutional stability in Britain? All these questions fascinated men of that time. In their turn historians have tried to pierce the mystery. Answers are indeed legion. From amid the flood of theories, all quite ingenious (which does not mean that they are convincing), let us pick out the main currents.

One explanation is founded in history, and Macaulay appointed himself its spokesman. If England knew no revolution in the nineteenth century, it was because she had carried out her own revolution in the seventeenth century. Indeed, once absolutism was overthrown and the principle of a society open to talents was recognized, representative government could take off and institutions could from the start assist the growth of English liberties. This blocked all recourse to insurrection and the use of force. Behind this eminently Whig interpretation one has no difficulty in descrying an apology for liberal parliamentarianism. English stability was simply attributable to the fact that England had invented a *via media*, based on moderation, between the two abominations that ran riot on the Continent – on the one hand military and police tyranny, on the other red republicanism. As Macaulay wrote, the country lived 'sheltered from the taint both of despotism and of democratic licence'.

A second explanation, psychological this time, alludes to the national temperament. In this theory it is the realism, the good sense, the practical and rational spirit of the islanders which has enabled them to avoid the pitfalls of revolutionary romanticism and messianic incantations. This is how the voice of reason, which is the golden mean, triumphed. 'We belong', exulted *The Economist* in April 1848,

> to a race which, if it cannot boast the flowing fancy of one of its neighbours [the Irish] nor the brilliant *esprit* of the other [the French], has an ample compensation in the solid, slow, reflective, phlegmatic temperament which has saved us from so many errors, spared us so many experiments and purchased for us so many real, though uncomplete and unsystematic blessings.

Obviously the argument is a shallow one, but it was taken up at a more profound analytical level by Bagehot, when he enunciated in his *English Constitution* his famous theory of 'deference'. According to Bagehot, England is the archetype of the deferential nation. The people have the wisdom to put their trust in an élite, and it is by common consent that some give orders while others obey. Thus stability has been perfectly preserved. This analysis of English political behaviour was indirectly confirmed by Taine (who in his *Notes on England* repeatedly insisted on the spirit of acceptance and submission) and by John Stuart Mill. Bagehot saw in this attitude of respect a fundamental political virtue, but Mill took the opposite view, deploring this disastrous tendency to deference and preferring the attribute of dignity: 'The English', he wrote to Mazzini,

> of all ranks and class, are at bottom, in all their feelings, aristocrats. They have some conception of liberty, and set some value on it, but the very idea of equality is strange and offensive to them. They do not dislike to have many people above them as long as they have some below them. And therefore they have never sympathized and in their present state of mind will never sympathize with any really democratic or republican party in other countries.[5]

A third group of interpretations lies in the political sphere. The key to national continuity has sometimes been sought in the typically British art of compromise; and then again it has been seen as the product of the ruling class's political genius. In particular, historians have credited the power élite with both remarkable sagacity and outstanding ability. At every major crisis this élite seem to have succeeded in avoiding disaster by making the necessary concessions in the nick of time. For example (the argument goes) first in 1832 the Conservatives consented to a political reform in order to save their economic privileges; then in 1846 they made economic concessions in order to protect their political privileges; then in 1867 they knew how to sacrifice part of their political influence so as to safeguard their social position. Each time they managed not only to avoid an explosion and guide events towards reform, but also to maintain their grip on the State and society. So the absence of revolution was attributed to the enlightened conservatism of a governing class that was endlessly resourceful and always capable of finding new ways of protecting itself. It was the triumph of a class that was a master of elastic defence and always knew how skilfully to combine partial concessions, delaying tactics and exploitation of its adversary's weaknesses, so as to safeguard the essential part of its power.

Elie Halévy, while admitting the solid foundations of this argument, put forward on his side a socio-economic interpretation that went much deeper and had the great merit of linking political and social life to the movement of ideas and religious beliefs. After having seen in Methodism the decisive factor which spared England a Jacobin revolution at the end of the eighteenth century, Halévy thought that he had found in the development of the middle classes and in political liberalism, which harmonized naturally with the spirit of Protestantism, the main reason for the absence of revolution in the nineteenth century. In particular he thought it was the 'Revolution of 1846', when free trade was imposed by the bourgeoisie, that took away all grounds for an English 1848. According to Halévy, the constant reinforcement of the middle classes was the main explanation of the social and political stability, firstly because these classes developed a spirit of liberty out of their own ideas and beliefs, and above all because economic factors were added to these moral and religious ones. The presence of a middle class conscious of its power eased the gaps in wealth and living standards, and opposed extremist policies and attitudes by its centrist position. Between the enormous wealth of the aristocracy and the misery of the popular masses spread 'l'intervalle immense qui est rempli par l'immensité des classes moyennes' (the vast gap that was filled by the immensity of the middle classes).[6] However Halévy's thesis does come up against serious objections. First of all, France too had a developed middle class, large in numbers and attached to liberal ideas, while the industrial proletariat was far smaller than across the Channel – which did not prevent France from setting up a record for revolutions. Furthermore the English aristocracy had kept much more solidly entrenched positions than Halévy appears to have thought. Finally, religious influences, especially Methodism, did not play such an anodyne role as has been made out, nor did it constitute a barrier against revolution more than in other countries.

Let us admit then that none of these explanations seem to be really satisfactory. While most of them in different ways cast light on the problem, none of them carry total conviction. In our opinion the equilibrium of English society is decisively explained by the conjunction of three factors: first and foremost the triangular class system, then the weakness of the revolutionary ideology, and finally, after 1850, the existence of a consensus leading to an integrated society.

British society with its division into three classes presented a vertical structure controlled by a strict hierarchy, but at the same time its triple structure gave rise to a triangular play of forces in which sometimes two partners opposed each other, and at other times two partners joined together against the third. The result was that an equilibrium tended to result from pressures that balanced each other, for the system offered a multiplicity of combinations and led to fluid alliances that were easy to terminate, either partially or entirely. Furthermore it was as hard for one class alone to dominate the other two as it was to overthrow their power. Reaction and revolution, or, if you prefer, tyranny and subversion, were thus made equally difficult. The equilibrium brought about by these many tensions might appear fragile (and this was certainly the case in the first half of the century), but it did prove effective and lasting.

It is true one cannot regard the three forces in the triangle as equivalent. There was social inequality in the tripartite structure, and therefore top-dogs and underdogs. One thing that was clearly shown up by Chartism was the weakness of the labour world as well as the strength of the ruling classes. However one of the characteristics of English society was that, very early on, the numerical force of the proletariat obliged the ruling classes to take note of its existence. This was accentuated by the early rise of the labour movement, which through its organization gave undeniable influence to the workers in their triple role of political force, social partners and consumers.

In the course of the years 1830–40 the desperate search for this point of balance in the midst of crises led to every variation of alliance between the forces of the triangle (themselves subject to changes of political and religious support). The groupings chopped and changed, varying according to the tactical objective. Bourgeoisie and labouring classes combined against the aristocracy over the Reform Bill, while there was a common front of aristocrats and working men against the manufacturing bourgeoisie in the Factory Movement. In the face of Chartism, the middle classes and the landlords found themselves on the same side to defend law and order against the revolt of the workers. On the other hand they fought each other fiercely in the Corn Laws controversy. The situation changed noticeably from the mid-century onwards as the result of new groupings which strengthened the long-term balance. On the one hand, as Peel had anticipated when he supported free trade, there was a *rapprochement* between the aristocracy and the bourgeoisie with a view to their sharing power. The process that had been fermenting for years – towards a bicephalous society – had come to a head, that is to say that the alliance between the aristocracy of land and birth and the aristocracy of money and ability had frankly arrived, and it was an arrangement that guaranteed more than a quarter of a century of stability. In this sense one might say that the 'Revolution of 1846' did not so much prevent revolution in 1848, as Halévy thought, as seal an alliance between the two divisions of the ruling class. One must see in this semi-economic, semi-political compromise one of the keys of mid-Victorianism. In some ways the situation was to continue right up to 1914. So it was on an enduring basis that the British lion became a lion with two heads – at least until the day when a third head, proletarian this time, would begin to show its profile in the last years of the century.

After 1848 radicalism successfully resumed its traditional strategy of allying the advanced bourgeoisie to the working-class forces, as in 1816–19 and 1830–2. It was this alliance that Chartism had broken into and rendered ineffective by preferring to conduct a purely working-class struggle. Conversely, after 1850 the tactic of setting class against class was rejected, and one sees in all the political and social campaigns (electoral reform, elementary education, labour legislation) workers and members of the middle class marching hand in hand under the radical banner, the *entente* reaching its culminating point in the 'Lib-Lab alliance' during the 1870s. The cumulative effect of these various forms of class collaboration was that social antagonisms, which had predominated in the first half of the century, began to die down. In their place grew up a social climate that was more peaceful, reflecting the stability of a society whose interests were orderly evolution, reform and political consensus.

Another factor that made for equilibrium was the absence of revolutionary spirit. Here again one notices a striking difference between the pre-1850 and the post-1850 periods. In the first half of the century there was a search for a revolutionary ideology, hesitating between a French-type Jacobinism, a utopian communism and a Chartism that claimed basic rights for the workers. By contrast in the third quarter of the century, while Chartism was in its death-throes and pure socialism was fading out, there was no general questioning of the social order. On the doctrinal plane there was no successor. The anti-capitalist and anti-bourgeois ideologies which flourished among the revolutionary refugees in London were not attractive to the English. The most they did in *avant-garde* circles was to sympathize with the exiles for being victims of persecution, but they went no further than that. Karl Marx lived in London for thirty-five years almost unknown; at his death it was *The Times* correspondent in Paris who cabled the news to his paper in London! The model to which working-class circles aspired was a progressive democracy which gave scope to the individual. All the effort in popular campaigns was turned towards the peaceful acquisition of the franchise and universal education, towards social and humanitarian reform. Absolute priority was given to political and parliamentary democracy. When in 1867 a section of the workers won the right to vote, an increased legitimacy was thereby conferred on the established powers because from then onwards it derived from a semi-democratic suffrage. All recourse to violence was outlawed, witness the Sheffield outrages perpetrated by a few enraged workmen. To preach subversion was also badly viewed, hence the embarrasment of the advanced radicals when they had to react to the events of the Paris Commune. Nor was the heart on the side of revolution any more than the mind. There was no revolutionary enthusiasm, no romantic nostalgia that came to bathe the idea of insurrection in a strange mysterious glow. On the contrary, everyone united in their praise of the virtues of civil peace. There was no smell of powder or barricades in the streets, the pavement was there simply for walking on. Revolution was absolutely alien to the general mentality – only good for those who did not enjoy English-style liberties. On English soil reigned order and peace.

Finally since the middle of the century there existed a broad consensus on the ultimate aims of society. It was a consensus that strengthened cohesion and helped social integration. Among the common values which held the members of the social body together were the cult of self-help, attachment to the monarchy (Bagehot underlined the mystical function of the sovereign's person), a patriotism that drew people together in a communal emotion, the acknowledgement of the great principles of Christianity (at least in their moral form) and, last but not least, the acceptance of the hierarchic principle and of social inequality. Consequently the legitimacy of political power and social order did not derive so much from above, from some royal or aristocratic authority, but from *below*, thanks to the general consensus. The perpetuation of a liberal and inegalitarian society became an objective that was accepted by all. In face of the silence of the poor and the passivity of the workers, it was Cobden and not Marx who in his astonishment and indignation preached revolt: 'I wonder the working people are so quiet under the taunts and insults offered them. Have they no Spartacus among them to head a revolt of the slave class against their political tormentors?'[7]

It was no doubt the spectacle of this resignation that led Engels at this time to dub England 'the most bourgeois of all nations', and to accuse the English proletariat of becoming more and more middle-class.[8] In any case the integration of the working classes into the *laissez-faire* society, although not total, was sufficiently advanced after 1850 for there to be no revolutionary alternative, indeed for there to be no alternative to the political see-saw of Whigs and Tories.

The individual and the State: liberalism triumphant

England, land of liberty! The commonplace might well be repeated on every occasion and in different tones of voice, but the truth of it was clear for all to see. Everyone experienced it every day in the thousand and one aspects of public life. For at every level of society liberty was no abstract concept. It was first and foremost a concrete reality, lived by all. Far from being the product of clever indoctrination, it was consistent with a deep-felt sentiment which arose out of history and everyday practice, in spite of the heavy economic constraints that weighed on individuals. The 'free-born Englishman' did not need persuading that he was born free.

Indeed he only had to glance across the Channel – the comparison with European nations where authoritarian regimes flourished was instructive. Over there despotism and the police reigned supreme. In his own country the Englishman considered that fundamental liberties had long since been established. Furthermore important progress had just been registered by the elimination of old restrictive barriers. Religious discrimination had diminished; the right to associate and the liberty of the press had become realities. These victories affected everyone, the humble as well as the powerful. Of course, in the eyes of democrats, the battle for emancipation was far from finished. What John Stuart Mill called the great historic struggle between Liberty and Authority continued. But many associated themselves with the cry of triumph uttered by *The Spectator* in 1851: 'The half-century has changed the aspect of society: where all was Tory suppression at the beginning, all is thrown open now. We have gained freedom, political, religious and commercial.'[9]

It is true that sometimes the understandable feeling of pride turned to complacency, and even priggishness. An example was Roebuck's boast, brutally taken apart by Matthew Arnold in *Culture and Anarchy:* 'I look around me and ask what is the state of England? Is not every man able to say what he likes? I ask you whether in the world over, or in past history, there is anything like it?'[10] In the mouth of a radical it was certainly making light of the exploitation of the multitudes, whether on British soil or across the Empire. But the fact remained that England was the incarnation of liberalism, and what is more a liberalism linked to Protestantism. In comparison with other countries (with the possible exception of the United States) she acclimatized it in such an original manner that the islanders ended up by regarding England as the historic repository of Liberty, much as the French considered themselves the guardians of the Rights of Man.

This triumphant liberalism was made up of three components: the practice of liberty and tolerance, a philosophy of individualism, and a theory of State that was a hybrid of *laissez-faire* and rational interventionism.

For the English *liberty* meant above all the enjoyment of *liberties*, above all personal liberties. These consisted of the free use of one's body *(Habeas Corpus)* and its movements, the safety of one's person and the free enjoyment of one's property. There was no arbitrary arrest or imprisonment without trial, the accused being presumed innocent and tried by a jury – these were the fundamental guarantees already admired by Montesquieu and Voltaire. Their practice had entered common law at the same time as it had become standard behaviour. One could easily show that these rights benefited most of all the people who were well-off and respectable. It was inadvisable for the outcasts of fortune or for those belonging to the 'dangerous classes' to fall foul of the penal code. However the law was the law, and the poorest had the benefit of guarantees as much as anyone else. In a country where the whole tradition consisted of fighting against the excesses of arbitrary oppression and defending the individual against the tyranny of power, protection was spread wide enough for everyone to have their share. At the same time public opinion, as it had developed by age-old tradition, built up a spirit of resistance to all that threatened fundamental liberties. In addition, wasn't one of the characteristics of the liberal conscience to protest on principle against illegality and injustice, wherever they occurred? In view of all this, to talk contemptuously of a purely 'formal' liberty in nineteenth-century England smacks of unsound pleading, and the charge need not detain us. The large number of exiled refugees on British soil would tell another story. From Guernsey Victor Hugo exclaimed about England: 'Comme terre illustre et libre je l'admire et comme asile je l'aime' (As a land that is illustrious and free I admire her and as a refuge I love her).[11] At the congress of the First International at Basel in 1869, one of the most prominent trade-union leaders, Applegarth, explained proudly to his continental fellow-workers: 'Fortunately we in England have no need to creep into holes and corners lest a policeman should see us, but can meet in open daylight and organize ourselves, and treat of any questions which affect us without fear.'[12] The fact was that to civil liberties were added political liberties (the right of assembly and association, freedom of speech and demonstration, the right of petition, freedom of the press – the black spot being the franchise, though after 1867 political representation was granted to workers in boroughs) as well as economic liberties (freedom of trade and of work, etc.). Above all, the prevailing outlook ensured that these liberties were living realities, and not merely paper rights. They were supported by a taste for independence, a horror of slavery and tyranny, and a sensitive consciousness of the rights of each citizen.

Similarly, tolerance was gradually established after a long historical process. It was the result of a double advance, sociological and religious. As far as social relations were concerned, tolerance was a necessity in a violent and quarrelsome society, just as sport supplied a sublimation of natural destructive energies by transforming them into organized games. It was a way of putting an end to disputes and savage feuds that might lead to destruction and blood. Hence the ideal that had prevailed since the eighteenth century: a civilized society can be judged by the respect accorded to others, their personalities, their ideas and their habits.

In another important sphere the break-up of religious unity made England a battleground in which not only did the three great versions of Christianity – Anglicanism, Calvinism and Roman Catholicism – vie with each other, but there also flourished a multitude of schisms and divisions. There was a multiplication of sects, and each successive 'revival' added new lines of demarcation. Theological battles never ceased to rage, especially within the established Church. Before this bewildering patchwork, wisdom counselled mutual acceptance of different Churches, each with its own orthodoxy, its own creed and peculiarities. Hence the necessity of coexistence, grafted onto the requirements of national unity, imposed a *modus vivendi* which the country more or less accepted after several scuffles. However, what was originally accepted under the pressure of events quickly became idealized, and tolerance was elevated to the status of a virtue. It was secularized, turned into an ideology and applied to all sections of life, both private and public. So on the religious and civil plane everyone found that his freedom of belief, of personal choice and lifestyle was generally accepted. There were a good many dark areas still remaining in the middle of the nineteenth century. Peace could hardly be said to reign between religious denominations. Virulent anti-Catholicism, bitter quarrels between Nonconformists and Anglicans, furious battles over the application of science to the origins of men and to biblical texts, all these frictions revealed both a passionate search for truth and salvation, as well as deep prejudice and intolerance. One should also add the considerable weight of orthodox conformity. Nevertheless tolerance, once implanted, and whatever its limitations might be, was one of England's major contributions to European civilization.

From the philosophical point of view, we find at the basis of the individualism which prevailed the principle of free choice, a basic value in the eyes of the Victorians. The 'horizontalist' philosophy of the Liberals – as opposed to the Tory conception inherited from medieval Christianity, for whom society was an organic unit with a vertical hierarchy – was itself founded on two principles:

1. A society was only the sum of the individuals of whom it consisted.
2. Everything which favoured the interests of the individual was of benefit to the collectivity, as there was correspondence and not contradiction between individual interest and general interest.

In his *Social Statics* (1851) Herbert Spencer picked out what he called 'the law of equal liberty' and asserted that, from the moment it operated, social equilibrium became apparent. So everything depended on the individual, his will and his capacities. As John Stuart Mill wrote at the end of his book *On Liberty* (1859): 'The worth of a State, in the long run, is the worth of the individuals composing it.' That is why the Victorians exalted the spirit of independence and self-reliance, opposing it to paternalism which, under the guise of protection, treated people like children. With energy, courage and perseverance an active and gifted individual could reach the top, and everyone would profit from his success. Take the case of Stanley the explorer, readily quoted as an example. He was an illegitimate child, brought up in a sordid Welsh workhouse who first made his way in journalism in the United States before discovering vast territories in Africa. So freedom of initiative and social mobility joined forces. This is what made John Stuart Mill, a champion, if ever there was one, of optimistic individualism, write: 'Human beings are no longer born to their place in life . . . but are free to employ their faculties . . . to achieve the lot which may appear to them most desirable.'[13] (The amusing thing is that these statements occur at the beginning of a work denouncing the subordination of women in society.)

There followed a conception of the State that was at first restrictive. Relying on the 'March of Intellect', Benthamite utilitarianism and the classical economy sank so deep into men's minds that their outlooks became saturated with them. They maintained that, instead of counting on the government which always tended to tyrannize because its activity consisted in passing laws and regulating people, the individual ought to depend only on himself, in the pride of his freedom and independence. That is why Dicey, advocate of unlimited individualism, was so alarmed by the development of State intervention after 1870. And this explains his nostalgia for the mid-Victorian period when there prevailed 'the faith of the best Englishmen in individual energy and in the wisdom of leaving every one free to pursue his own course of action, so long as he did not trench upon the like liberty or the rights of his fellows.'[14] All the supporters of individualism were indeed convinced that a clearly defined line of demarcation separated the sphere of the individual – the area of liberty and initiative – from the sphere of the State – the centre of constraint and oppression. Against the many dangers that arose out of Leviathan, recourse was had to decentralization, self-government, voluntary organization, the action of intermediate bodies (through gentry, clergy, the professions, local associations, etc.) and above all to the free expression of individuality.

However the individualism of *laissez-faire*, supported naturally by the Protestant spirit of free enquiry, was a long way from resulting, as has been claimed, in the abdication of the State. Even at the time of its greatest retreat under the pervading influence of liberalism, the English State was never a skeleton and its power remained considerable. Why indeed should the governing classes have let slip such a privileged engine of power? In truth the liberal State was never restricted to its simple policing role. Utilitarianism, inasmuch as it wanted to make liberty and reason reign in the place of privilege and favouritism, displayed a will to centralize, so that government could put an end to muddle and waste by installing the rational rule of law, and guarantee the greatest happiness to the greatest number – a factor that was underlined in Halévy's analysis. In other ways the power of the State was constantly making itself felt by positive action. It was influential in the legislation which gradually regulated factory work (the Factory Acts), public health, education (the Education Act of 1870), the police, the prison system and government administration. The organization of a modern Civil Service dates from the reform of 1855, which substituted merit for patronage. Although it strikes us as excessive and untenable to look for the origins of the Welfare State in the Victorian era, as has been argued, we should certainly emphasize that at no moment, even at the zenith of liberalism, did the State surrender its rights or its power.

A Christian land

Everyone would agree that religion exercised a capital influence on the life of England in the nineteenth century. The real problem is to know what religion we are talking about, and in what depth Christianity was rooted beyond the outward conformity and the abundant evidence of religious feeling. To clarify the debate it would be a good idea to distinguish three aspects of religious life. At one level, the personal one, religion is made up of a quest for truth and salvation. This is the area of the individual's personal relations with God (Newman's 'My Creator and myself') and, from that point of view, many people in Victorian England aspired sincerely to a rich interior life, an ardent piety with surges of faith inspired by great religious leaders. At a second level, that of the organized Churches, Christianity was an institution and religion a social force, providing a framework for strong public influence. This process reached a point where, although some spoke of 'infidelity' or 'leakage' (what we call today 'de-christianization'), very few people denied all religious ties and did not belong, at least nominally, to a Church or a sect. Finally, at a level which transcended sectarian boundaries, the heritage of Christianity dominated the population, *undenominationally* you might say. Even when there remained no definite belief, a religious substratum persisted, influencing morality and social relationships, even in their humblest detail. To take only one example, nineteenth-century England is totally incomprehensible if one does not take into account the power of the Bible and its constant presence in men's hearts. For it was 'Holy Writ', supreme textbook of all education, sacred and profane, that initiated English boys and girls in their earliest youth both to culture and to the Christian faith. Bible pictures, Bible language (in the beautiful Authorized Version of the seventeenth century), Bible quotations made up a mental landscape in the middle of which Bible characters walked about, as familiar as the inhabitants of the next street or the next village.

The official character of religion, both in public and private life, was not only made obvious by the existence of an established Church, and a Queen in whose person were combined the functions of temporal power and those of 'Head of the Church of England' and 'Defender of the Faith'. A thousand details constantly reminded people that England was a Christian country. In 1867, in connection with a matter of secularist propaganda, a court decision (Cowan *v*. Milbourn) repeated the principle whereby Christianity was 'part and parcel of the law of the land'.[15] The last discriminations against Jews were only abolished in 1858. Before that they could not sit in Parliament, and so Lionel de Rothschild, when he had been elected to the House of Commons in 1847, was not able to take up his seat. Until 1871 it was impossible to teach at Oxford or Cambridge if one had not signed a declaration of loyalty to the Thirty-Nine Articles. In 1880, the radical Bradlaugh, noisy organizer of campaigns in support of atheism, was elected to Parliament, but as he refused to take the oath on the Bible, he was not admitted to take his seat, and only in 1886 was the rule relaxed so that he could sit as a Member. One can of course see in all this the obvious signs of a narrow bigotry, but there was more to it than that. Firstly there was the notion that the duty of the State was to support the Church of Christ. Gladstone, for example, was a champion of the alliance of the temporal and the spiritual all his life, and Erastianism maintained a strong impact. Then there was the conviction that Christianity constituted the moral cement of the country. Besides, the idea of God's will and the basic principles of Christian morality were so generally accepted that they numbered among the current truths, side by side with the necessity of thrift, freedom of enterprise and the virtues of self-reliance and manliness.

However, although Christianity acted as a common denominator, it was itself split into numerous tendencies and rival sects. To the three main divisions dating from the Reformation – Anglicanism, Dissent and 'Papism' – were added new schisms and 'revivals' in the eighteenth and nineteenth centuries. Denominations, chapels, groups and communities proliferated to infinity. The mid-Victorian era saw the biggest explosion of Protestantism. The Church of England, while it kept its privileged position and the advantages attaching to a national institution, accounted for only half the country as was shown by the religious census of 1851. In spite of sociological handicaps and in a desperate move to keep in contact with the masses, the Church of England embarked on a considerable effort of evangelization through its 'Low Church' and its 'High Church' wings. Many parishes were created in expanding towns and many new churches were built. To this end £1.5 million were spent in the diocese of Manchester alone between 1840 and 1876.[16] Substantial resources were also devoted to schools, charitable institutions, missions and parish life.

On their side the Nonconformists, whose advance had been so notable since the last years of the eighteenth century, continued to make progress. One could even describe the second half of the nineteenth century as the golden age of Nonconformism. On the legal plane their long fight for emancipation and equality bore fruit. One by one their claims over church rates, the right to be buried in public cemeteries, and entrance to universities were granted; but there was one black spot, the education question, an area of fierce struggles with the established Church, especially as before 1870 the latter ran nine out of every ten primary schools. In the matter of numbers the Methodist persuasion, itself divided into various groups, was by far the most important. In fact the Methodists made up the largest religious group in the country after the Anglicans, representing half the total of Nonconformists. Unlike Methodism, which had a large working-class following, especially in the Primitive Methodist branch, the other two most important Free Church groups, the Congregationalists and the Baptists, found the majority of their recruits in the middle classes. Certain sects, although small in numbers like the Quakers (about 20,000), exercised considerable influence on the economic, social and intellectual life of the country.

As for the Roman Catholics, their revival was spectacular. In the eighteenth century they had looked as if they were dying out, for in 1767, according to J. A. Lesourd's calculations, there were only 72,000 Roman

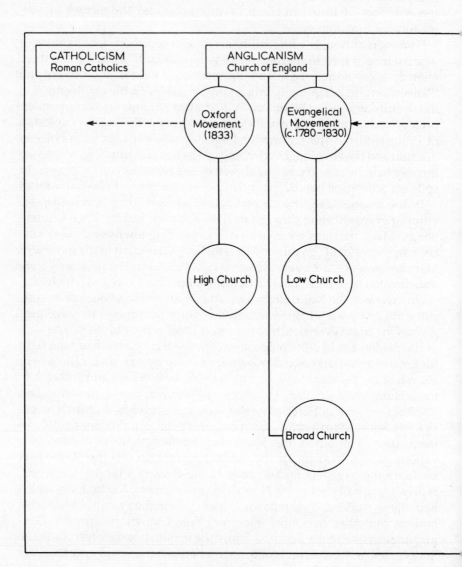

Figure 1. Churches and sects in England

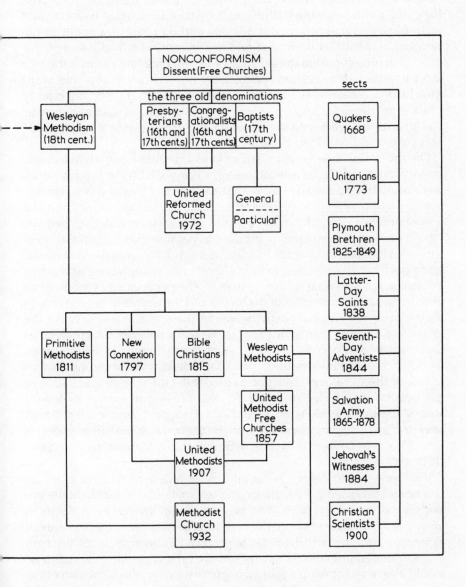

Catholics in England and Wales. The number had gone up to 120,000 by 1800, and in 1851, largely because of the Irish immigration, it reached nearly 900,000. At that date the Roman Catholics, who had recovered their civil rights since the Catholic Relief Act of 1829, again had a regular ecclesiastical organization with bishops and dioceses as a result of the restoration of the hierarchy in 1850. The converts from the Oxford Movement also brought them the prestige of intelligence and culture, the two most sensational conversions being those of Newman in 1845 and Manning in 1851. There were 826 Roman Catholic priests in 1851, but twenty years later this number had doubled. Slowly Roman Catholicism was working its way back into the life of the country, despite the violence of anti-papist and anti-Irish prejudices.

On the social side religion in England presented two characteristic traits. First of all the 'sandwich' image. The positions of the Churches were compared to a sandwich, with the Church of England corresponding to the top and bottom slices of society, i.e. the aristocracy and the 'lower orders', while the interior of the sandwich consisted of middle-class Nonconformists. One might note in passing that Roman Catholicism, with its small aristocratic fringe and its proletarian basis, took up the same position as Anglicanism in the sandwich, being strong at the two extremities of the social ladder. However, the penetration of Methodism into the working-class areas of the towns and the country, and conversely the extension of Anglican activity among the middle classes, make the image less accurate than in the past. It was really only the rural proletariat that remained in part loyal to the established Church, while the urban working class slid into indifference. That indeed was the second characteristic of the sociology of religion in England – the de-christianization of the people. It was clear that the practice of religion was at its lowest among the town workers of the industrial regions. On the map drawn after the 1851 census there is clear evidence of the small number of churchgoers in London as well as in Birmingham, Manchester and Newcastle (see Map 4).

If we now try to define the dominant emphasis of religion as it was taught and practised in English society, we are bound to highlight the importance of moral restraint. Whatever were the differences in doctrine, liturgy or spirituality between the various Christian sects, there prevailed a common influence which tended to protect the atmosphere of Christianity. An 'undenominational' portrait of a Christian in the years 1850–80 would above all show up a moralizing Christianity. This Christian ethic, mixed too with a strong dose of stoicism, put the accent on will-power, manly qualities and the domination of the instincts. From this came the commendation of temperance and above all chastity. The sin of the flesh, that was the supreme vice. Puritanism reached an unprecedented degree

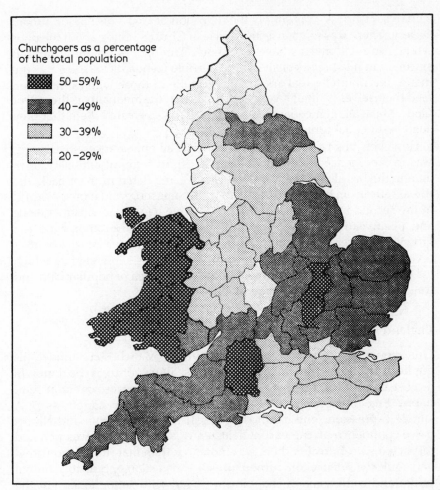

Map 4. Religious practice in England and Wales, 1851[17]

of rigidity, to the point of becoming obsessional, leaving the field open to the hypocrisy of countless Mrs Grundys. In the second place Christianity showed itself both introspective with endless questioning of one's sins, and also inclined towards action. God blessed the bold, and success in business was a sign of divine favour. One could almost equate one's bank account with one's place in heaven. At the same time, the bourgeois spirit was solidly entrenched in all the religious sects. It was as if the Gospel and respectability went naturally hand in hand (Chesterton was to talk amusingly of 'God in a top hat'). Finally this Christianity was a profoundly inegalitarian Christianity, for which the social hierarchy, far from being a sign of selfishness, was simply the reflection of God's design for human society. There was much use and abuse of Christ's saying about the poor whom 'you will always have with you'. Trollope, questioning himself sincerely in his *Autobiography* on the 'terrible inequalities we see . . . the inane, the unintellectual and frostbound life of those who cannot even feed themselves by their sweat' concludes that the inequality is the will of God. 'Make all men equal today and God has so created them that they shall be unequal tomorrow.'[18]

However, this religion, which seemed to all appearances so assured, was in fact menaced, and this was felt. Apart from an anti-clericalism among the people that was very much alive and dated from far back, the threat came from two forces that were to become more and more powerful in the second half of the century. On the one hand rationalism, science and positivism which were in full spate; and on the other hand the growing indifference among the masses. The religious census of 1851 revealed an alarming number of people who practised no religion, which led the more clear-headed to wonder what remained of popular faith and true religion behind the façade of Christianity.

England *über alles*

One evening in 1853, a cotton manufacturer in Manchester confided his euphoria to his diary in the following terms: 'Our country is, no doubt, in a most happy and prosperous state. Free trade, peace, freedom. Oh, happy England! Mayest thou know and deserve thy happiness.'[19] A simple expression, one might say, of satisfaction, of pride and almost naïve confidence on the part of a citizen of a country that was rich and respected. . . . In reality there was more to it than that. It is obvious that very quickly satisfaction turned to self-satisfaction, pride to national pride, and confidence to chauvinism tinged with xenophobia. For the optimism which reigned generally, and was evident to all, took root in ground that was particularly receptive to emotional feeling – patriotism. This sentiment became an antidote to the many confrontations and splits in society, so that instincts of solidarity and aggression combined to cement all classes in a solid unity. The prevalent nationalism helped everyone to combine and work together. People were comforted by it and revelled in it, if only to disparage the foreigner, the one who was not a member of the chosen people. 'The Englishman has such an idea of his superiority in all things', noted Hector Malot in 1862,

> that his pride cannot understand how the matter could even be worth
> discussing. For him this superiority is like the light of the sun, and
> those who are not used to its brilliance must be dazzled – no more, no

less. The proof of this superiority, they say naïvely, is that we carry our way of life all over the world, and we impose it on the people we encounter, without ever letting ourselves be affected by their customs.[20]

By constant repetition of 'first in the world' and 'best in the world', how could the English not be convinced in their heart of hearts of their superiority over other people? How could they not conclude that they belonged to a chosen race? Brought up on the Old Testament, they naturally associated the destiny of their nation with that of the people of the Bible, treading with assurance the path traced out by God. Or, strong in their classical culture, they might prefer to take their inspiration from the majestic example of Rome and her empire. The peace-loving Shaftesbury maintained that the safety of the English people was a special concern of Providence, and Carlyle described two grandiose missions assigned by history to the British people: 'Huge looming the grand industrial task of conquering some half or more of this terraqueous planet for the use of man; then secondly, the grand constitutional task of sharing in some pacific endurable manner, the fruit of said conquest.'[21]

What bold assurance to feel the blessing of heaven upon one! What a comfort to know that one was labouring under the benevolent eye of the All Highest! One began to wonder if God might not have become English. . . . From this point of view a sacred egoism did not only seem justified, it became a positive duty. Some people, adapting the arrogant formula of the citizens of the Most Serene Republic, *'primo Veneziani, poi Cristiani'*, proclaimed fearlessly: 'Let us first be Englishmen, and then. . . .'

A thousand factors, important or trivial, encouraged the British in this sense of superiority. First of all there was the quiet conviction of being the centre of the world. Industrialism, Protestantism, liberalism, the three great forces of the age, and doubtless the keys to the future – England was the incarnation of them all. There was the *Pax Britannica*, a striking demonstration of naval and diplomatic supremacy. In geography it was by reference to the Greenwich meridian that every country on earth measured its longitude. Philately offered another symbol – England was the only country in the world that put no name on its stamps, the head of Victoria was enough. 'We are a rich people, powerful, intelligent, religious. . . . Our spirit governs the universe' cried the *Illustrated London News*, and the same journal on another occasion developed the idea that the English, 'the harbingers of civilization', were necessary to the world. Everywhere 'we have left our beneficial mark. All the regions of the globe feel our physical, moral and intellectual presence. . . . They could not live without us.'[22]

What is obviously at the basis of this 'Anglocentrism' is the insular spirit. 'Every Englishman is an island', said Novalis. But the high point of insularity was reached in the course of the nineteenth century and was to persist intact up to 1914. Indeed the sea gave the British a double feeling of security and superiority. The islanders felt protected by the expanses of water which both linked them to every point in the planet and isolated them. At the same time they governed the oceans as if they were their own property, according to the old adage: 'The Ocean has but one master.' Their immunity from attack was thus assured, for who could threaten the national territory? What is more, as naval supremacy was not localized like land power, and as the Royal Navy was in a position to appear any time at any point on the globe, the nation had the impression of enjoying a sort of universal sovereignty.

This picture of a confident country, formidable and ready to defend herself, extended even to physical appearances. It was at this time that the model of the typical Englishman became current: large, ruddy, solidly built, with his muscles kept in good trim by games and sport. As for character, the English won a reputation for being cold, phlegmatic, undemonstrative but at the same time energetic, tenacious and calculating. The caricatures of John Bull, drawn by the English themselves, showed an enviably solid frame, stout fists and threatening jaws. With his bulldog appearance John Bull was pictured clad in strong boots, a stout stick in his hand, full of good sense but not to be argued with, being perfectly capable of matching up to the toughest adversary. In relations with foreign countries the will to power did not shrink from brutality and insolence. It is enough to listen to Palmerston propounding without equivocation the principles of strong-arm politics:

> These half-civilized governments such as those of China, Portugal, Spanish America, all require addressing every eight or ten years to keep them in order. Their minds are too shallow to receive an impression that will last longer than some such period and warning is of little use. They care little for words and they must not only see the stick but actually feel it on their shoulders before they yield.[23]

In a country convinced of its own superiority, cultural supremacy of course marched side by side with economic and political supremacy. For example the historian Buckle, whose *History of Civilization in England* (1857–61) was widely read, maintained that all the civilizations of the world were so many deviations from the norm embodied in British civilization. The commentaries of outraged foreign visitors on these countless displays of nationalism showed a fine consistency. Jules Vallès, doubly bruised as patriot and exile by this unbending pride ('the meanest clerk, even the lowliest lackey seems to have swallowed Wellington's sword'), vented his wrath at this almost morbid patriotism', this 'fierce love of the flag' that was given full rein. However he did recognize that English pride acted as a powerful stimulus to national greatness. 'They have for foreigners', he admits in tones that are at the same time exasperated and admiring, 'an infinite pity, deep and wide as the Ocean. They gaze at the whole world from the tops of their high masts and, seeing their colours floating under every sky, they spit their disdain on all who question or criticize them.'[24]

II The Old World Resists: 1880–1914

4 The crisis of Victorian values

The great climacteric: appearance and reality?

Was there a decline after 1870 in the British economy? Did growth slow down, and prosperity come to a halt? So many reputable historians have proclaimed that with the 'great depression' (1873–96) England entered an era of sloth and stagnation, even of retreat, that the claim has almost been promoted to a dogma. After the zenith of the mid-century the Victorian star is said to have followed a downward course towards the 'Edwardian twilight' before sinking into the troubled waters of the two World Wars. According to this thesis, which has become classic, the serious difficulties that beset the nation condemned it to a general decline in efficiency. In short, the late-Victorian climacteric marked the fateful turning-point between the crushing superiority of the nineteenth century and the slow foundering of the twentieth century.

At first sight, even if the actual notion of a 'great depression' has been seriously dented by recent studies and at last reduced to fairly modest proportions, the supporters of the structural decline thesis do have a large range of arguments at their command. Some have put forward the faulty mechanism of the economy, industrial growth hampered by inadequate interior demand and stagnant production, inadequate functioning of the capital market leading to excessive investment abroad and too little investment at home. Others have insisted on psycho-sociological factors: a decline in entrepreneurship and even an exhaustion of national energy.

It has been said that, at the head of businesses, generations of 'heirs' succeeded generations of 'pioneers', characters less hardened, less inventive, less aggressive, less hard-working and more concerned to enjoy their possessions. So the *'rentier'* spirit gradually took over from the 'producer' spirit. Technical reasons have also been invoked – ageing machinery, indifference to new technology, lack of scientific spirit, of rationalization, and of professional training.

In a more general way the early start of British industry has been brought into the argument. The country, according to this theory, reached a point where she became a victim of her own brilliant past, for her advance on her rivals, advantageous for so long, eventually worked against her. Routine took over, growth slowed down for lack of innovation, and stagnation set in, prefiguring the difficulties of the inter-war years. Hence, in the closing years of the nineteenth century, one finds England's position in the world weakening, and also some worried introspection, which showed a crisis of confidence about the nation's future.

Yet these pessimistic views, although widely accepted, do deserve careful examination. One cannot gainsay that they derive from a proven fact: England was no longer in a position of supremacy now that the world economy had many centres. In the last quarter of the nineteenth century, as other powers became industrialized, the near-monopoly in industry and commerce, which England had hitherto enjoyed, gradually disappeared. Powerful rivals appeared in the world's markets, particularly Germany and the United States. But did this process, which was after all inescapable, necessarily portend disaster for England? In a healthy economy, would the loss of a monopoly, which was caused by special factors and was bound to be temporary, necessarily bring in its train a halt in growth and the accumulation of capital?

If one examines the statistics relating to the results achieved by the national economy, one is bound to conclude that they do not support the gloomy view. Although it cannot be denied that in 1913 England only supplied 14 per cent of the world's industrial production instead of 32 per cent as in 1870, the increase in the national income during roughly the same period continued to be spectacular. The total (in constant prices) advanced from £932 million in 1880 to £2,021 million in 1913, a rise from £27 to £44 per inhabitant.[1] The annual growth rate (2.3 per cent on average) was on the same scale as a half-century before, a period of undoubted expansion. Another sign of good health was that in the period 1880–1910 the gross national product increased by 80 per cent. In 1914 England still accounted for 25 per cent of world trade in manufactured goods against 37 per cent in 1883.[2] On this point one might add that her share of world trade had declined much less than her share in world production. As for her fleet it remained by far the largest in the world. On the eve of the First World War total British investment overseas reached the fantastic sum of £4,000 million, or about half the domestic stock capital, and one-fifth of all the capital in the world. These investments brought in £200 million a year to their owners, or the equivalent of the whole French national budget! Surely these were signs of flourishing capitalism and prosperous capitalists. . . .

However there were not only overall indicators of economic activity to contradict the traditional gloomy view. A whole series of researches undertaken by economic historians in England and the United States have seriously shaken the idea of a decline in the British economy. It is unnecessary for us to go into the details of the technical arguments, but it has been shown that the flexibility of the capital market, the rate of saving, the judicious choice of investments, the diversification of the output, the recourse to new techniques and even more to new products, far from resulting in the weaknesses usually criticized (e.g. wastage in home consumption, excessive and unprofitable investment abroad) allowed favourable comparisons with Germany and the United States, even where productivity was concerned.[3] The traditional areas of British superiority, such as textiles, coal, shipbuilding, were not the only ones where the country continued to hold her own. It was equally true of the growth sectors of the 'second industrial revolution': machine-tools, chemicals and electrical goods. In armaments and public works English firms were renowned throughout the world, and in the years before 1914 the motor-car industry, which had started slowly, caught up thanks to a very rapid advance.

If one turns to entrepreneurship, one is bound to admit that some managers tended to rest on their laurels, but others were at least the equals of their foreign rivals in initiative and drive. One has only to recall the names of Lever and Mond for chemicals, Boots for pharmaceuticals, Courtauld for artificial textiles, W. H. Smith for the retail of books and newspapers, Harrods, Whiteley and Lewis ('the People's Friend') for big retail stores.

As for the theory making the early industrial 'take-off' the reason for England's troubles, it rests on woolly reasoning and unsound generalizations. Why should a dynamic economy be the prisoner of its past and, what is more, incapable of finding in itself the resources necessary for its renewal? Besides, if there were some ineluctable law at work, how could the United States have maintained their supremacy up to today when it is already three-quarters of a century old?

That is why we come to the conclusion that the British economy was in less bad a shape than some have averred. Even if her health was not as radiant as it had been in the past, it is quite wrong to imagine her stricken

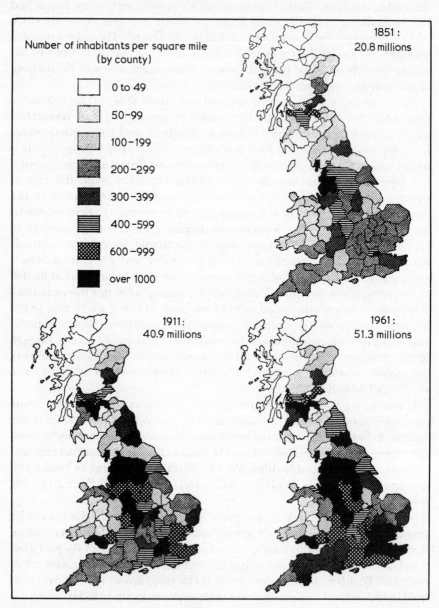

Map 5. Distribution of the population in Britain, 1851–1961

with serious anaemia. In spite of certain setbacks the national economy remained essentially prosperous up to the First World War.

Laissez-faire challenged

The actual impressions of contemporaries were, however, far from matching the findings of modern research analyses and statistics. The people of the time, as always, were particularly influenced by the short term, so the pessimists outnumbered the optimists by far. That is why there was so much divergence between objective developments and the way they were perceived by the community. Once again the actual and the psychological did not correspond.

In the last twenty years of the century a crisis of confidence shattered nearly all the old certainties – a state of mind that continued even after prosperity seemed to have returned with the new century and the period up to the outbreak of war in 1914. This was firstly because the cyclic depressions were very grim. The ones that struck the country in 1879, 1885, 1894, and 1904 were extremely severe. With their usual train of suffering they condemned their victims to the humiliating Poor Law, to emigration and indigence.

Furthermore, public opinion was wracked by chronic anxieties, which were widely ventilated, if only because during the 1880s the governing classes, who dominated the news media, themselves felt the effects of these recessions quite severely. For the aristocracy there was a sharp reduction of income from land. For the bourgeoisie, the entrepreneur as well as the shareholders, there was a drop in profits and dividends. There were attempts to find the causes and remedies for the ailment, as witness the large number of Royal Commissions of Inquiry on trade and industry, on the monetary system, on agriculture. . . . One might say that although the economic reality of the 'great depression' might well be disputed, there was no doubt about its psychological reality.

In this climate of uncertainty, the prosperous were having their peace of mind shaken by other causes for anxiety. There were peaks of unemployment and waves of working-class despair arising out of poverty and sometimes leading to outbreaks of violence; and to these were added the most alarming revelations in the press about the living conditions of the proletariat. Was England once again, people wondered, going to face the spectre of popular revolt? Was King Mob going to bring the triumph of disorder and sedition, as in some vulgar continental country? Certainly the 'condition of England' was being discussed in tones that had not been heard since the days of Chartism. The processions of unemployed marching down the streets of the capital and occupying the West End stirred feelings of alarm in some citizens and bad consciences in others.

This questioning of liberal orthodoxy, once it had got under way, did not die down even when the economic situation improved a few years later. On the eve of the First World War, at the time of 'labour unrest', the great strikes revived fears of revolution at a time when the rich were enjoying a period of great ease and prosperity. In fact the breakdown of the Victorian credo did not derive solely from changes in the international economy and class relationships. It was just as much caused by new theories on the organization of society and by the various philosophical, literary and aesthetic movements of the time. In the latter field, as early as 1875–80, a first generation of moderates like Matthew Arnold, T. H. Green and Meredith, and revolutionaries like William Morris began to undermine the basis of the liberal consensus. Then, in the last years of the century, there succeeded to this generation of critics a generation of rebels like Bernard Shaw, Oscar Wilde, H. G. Wells and their disciples.

In fact the questioning of standard values arose out of a double crisis. There was a moral crisis connected with the discovery of suffering and injustice, which tortured men's consciences and shook the serenity of the classical economy's supporters. There was also an intellectual crisis which led people to call in question the very foundations of liberalism, namely competition, individualism, and even the notion of progress. This double crisis touched above all the ruling classes, who had been so sure of themselves up to then and so proud of the Victorian gospel. So disquiet began to spread through society, as the dominant cultural model began to be disputed and discredited.

The shadow of poverty, and even more the sight of the poor, who were once thought to have been dealt with by a combination of a prosperous economy and charity, had a powerful effect on men's consciences and sensibilities. This important change of outlook came about in two ways. Sometimes what were now called 'the poor' (a mixture of the 'labouring classes' and the 'dangerous classes') irrupted into the view of the well-to-do. Indeed some of the latter went voluntarily to look for them, and it became fashionable to 'go slumming'. Sometimes it was an array of reports and inquiries, the scientific rubbing shoulders with the sensational in a strange partnership. Indeed it was from this period that dated the first great surveys of the pioneers of sociology. They revealed the staggering dimensions of the plight of the poor, which had in the past been concealed by so much reassuring talk. And those who conducted these inquiries on the ground were far from being revolutionary firebrands. On the contrary, they were respected figures of industrial society. One of them was a great shipowner, Charles Booth, who discovered in 1887–90 that out of 4,200,000 Londoners there were 1,300,000 living in poverty. There was Rowntree, a leading chocolate manufacturer and a Quaker with a conscience, who in 1899 found that in York, a typical medium-sized town, much the same proportion of poor people (28 per cent) could not make ends meet or manage to lead a decent existence. Nor was anyone able to refute these statistics. At the same time another more famous Booth, 'General' William Booth, founder of the Salvation Army, published a book, *In Darkest England* (1890), which created a sensation with its title parodying the explorer Stanley's best-seller. His thesis was that England, under the label of a 'civilized' and 'Christian' country, concealed in its depths as much misery and degradation as Central Africa with all its pagan savagery. Those who belonged to the category of the oppressed, the 'submerged tenth' as they were called, were in a state of spiritual as well as material perdition: 'what is the use of the gospel of Thrift to a man who has had nothing to eat yesterday, and has not three pence today to pay for his lodging to-night?'[4]

Obviously those who were seized with 'social remorse' asked themselves: 'What are the remedies? How are we to reform such a pitiful and scandalous state of affairs?' Views differed on this matter, the bold grew vague, and many expressions of indignation died away. However, even though the solutions put forward by such reformers as General Booth (e.g. the eternal 'back to the land' in the form of agricultural colonies, kinds of autonomous cooperatives) were utterly inadequate, and even though Booth attacked, like so many of his clerical and philanthropic colleagues, the 'dangerous utopias' of socialism, he did stir men's consciences by his onslaught on the monstrous indifference of a heartless society, and open their eyes to inequalities that were felt to be deeply unjust. This was particularly true among the professions, the intellectual world and the clergy. Young people of the middle classes, pricked by their consciences, did an about-turn. Feelings of guilt led to a real conversion for some, as was vividly described in the memoirs of Beatrice Webb. Others turned to the workers, like Arnold Toynbee who in 1883 cried out pathetically:

We, the middle classes, have neglected you; instead of justice we have offered you charity, and instead of sympathy we have offered you hard and unreal advice; but I think we are changing . . . You have to forgive us, for we have wronged you; we have sinned against you grievously, not always knowingly, but if you will forgive us, we will serve you, we will devote our lives to your services.[5]

Such words certainly contradicted mid-Victorian complacency. Nevertheless it still remained for the privileged to go beyond fine phrases and worthy sentiments. Deep-seated fears, which they dared not confess, mingled with bursts of generosity, and the ones who in their reforming zeal gave up the comforts of respectability and patronage were not numerous. Only a minority dared to 'go over to the barbarians', that is to say become socialists and fight at the workers' sides. Yet similar currents of feeling affected the young at the old universities. At Oxford and Cambridge students listened to the call to justice and charity, and decided to go and live among the poor in the squalid parts of London's East End. The basic idea of these University Settlements was to start centres of culture and human warmth among the most destitute citizens. To 'go to the people', to 'educate the people', to bring them light, restore their dignity, help them to earn their bread, so as one day to bring them back to moral living and perhaps even re-christianize them – those were the ambitious goals of the Settlements where a generous impulse to liberate their fellow men blended with paternalism and preaching.

However it was probably on the theoretical plane that liberalism found itself most strongly attacked. In fact its assumptions were submitted to a double critical assault. First of all there was more and more interest in the distribution of wealth, whereas hitherto the accent had been on production. Events over a century had presented *laissez-faire* in a favourable light as there had been a spectacular increase in material goods, but now its deficiencies on the distribution side were being shown up. How could one regard an economic system as efficient when it not only perpetuated excessive inequalities between rich and poor, but also was incapable of guaranteeing a decent standard of living to the mass of the population? What was the use of brilliant progress if all the wealth so created only profited a handful of already well-endowed plutocrats, while most of the population lacked basic necessities and lived lives of extreme privation? When one reads the words of an economist in 1884 reporting from official documents that 'in the wealthiest nation of the world almost every twentieth citizen is a pauper', that 'according to Poor Law reports, one-fifth of the community is insufficiently clad', that 'the great proportion of our population lead a life of monotony and incessant toil with no respect in old age but penury and parochial support', and that 'one third, if not indeed one half, of the families of the country are huddled, six in a room, in a way quite incompatible with the elementary claims of decency, health or morality', one would think that one was reading a denunciation of the evils of capitalism by some socialist propagandist. In fact it was in a Conservative review that these arguments were so amply developed and by an economist who was an enemy of socialism![6]

However the criticism of economic liberalism did not stop there. Not only did the system fail to match resources to population and balance the production and distribution of wealth, but what is worse it gave rise to wastage in the labour market that was as irrational economically as it was harmful on the human level. Here in effect was a system which, instead of furnishing regular work to those who needed it, condemned hundreds of thousands to underemployment. The curse of unemployment! Scarcely a day passed that did not remind a troubled public opinion of its existence.

One might note at this point that the noun 'unemployed' and the word 'unemployment' made their first appearances in the Oxford English Dictionary in 1882 and 1888 respectively.

By the same token the long-vaunted merits of competition became suspect. Wasn't it just this unlimited competition that led inexorably to the crushing of the feeble? Where people used to gorge themselves on Social Darwinism, applying, after Spencer, the 'struggle for life' notion to business so as to justify the selection of the stronger and the disappearance of the less able, opinion now went abruptly into reverse. It was seen that such arguments for a hierarchy, quoting 'natural law', resulted in unfairness. All these discoveries dealt severe blows to *laissez-faire*.

There was a parallel change of view on the other great question of the day, pauperism and its causes. Up to then there had been the constant refrain, based on the teachings of the classical economists, that each person in society met with the fate he deserved. Now it was precisely this subordination of economic to moral considerations that was put in question. The prime explanation of poverty (the argument now ran) must not be sought in the personal failings of the individual as orthodox individualism asserted, but in the disorder of the markets and their corollary, an unjust society. It was a bold assertion, even scandalous, but was corroborated by the facts patiently revealed by the social surveys. An important discovery, and for many a revelation. What were the causes of poverty? They did not reside, as had been thought, in laziness, improvidence, drink, promiscuousness and vice among the 'lower classes'. Poverty resulted above all from the malfunctioning of an industrial system which did not assure workers either regular employment or decent wages. It only too often condemned the man to forced idleness, the woman to prostitution and the child to the slums. Consequently the key to balanced happiness must be sought in the economic order rather than in individual morality. Instead of a moral debate with a subjective and individualistic ethos, there were now ideas abroad that blamed the structures. It was now up to society to take the welfare of its members in hand by making the necessary changes.

What a long road had been travelled since the middle of the century! What a reversal of ideas! In the old days optimism reigned supreme, carried along by that fine utilitarian confidence in 'the March of Intellect'. It was the time when the Crystal Palace was the symbol of economic success, material progress and the mastery of man over the machine; when Thomas Arnold saluted ecstatically the advent of the railway, thinking that he had seen signs that 'feudalism had disappeared for ever'. Now here was his son, the great Matthew Arnold, being the first to denounce the mechanical and joyless existence of the inhabitants of large towns, the hollowness of a progress that had brought with it only materialism and philistinism. In a sarcastic observation which has an astonishingly modern ring he asserted, a century ahead of our time, that for the bourgeois of his day it was the acme of civilization that trains ran every quarter of an hour between Islington and Camberwell, and that there were twelve deliveries of post a day between the same districts. But what was the good of all that if it only enabled people to pass from a dull and limited life in Islington to an equally dull and insipid life in Camber-well and if the letters only proved that the writers had nothing to say to each other?[7]

Pessimism and anxiety became the rule. The men of the late-Victorian and Edwardian generations freely admitted that they were 'in the dark' and that 'the unknown' surrounded them. And yet, someone will say, wasn't this the moment when imperialism was at its most successful? How could so many conquests by the Anglo-Saxon race fail to restore the nation's optimism? In fact questionings and uncertainties still persisted. One finds them right up to the great *Recessional* of Rudyard Kipling written for the 1897 Jubilee. Some hoped to exorcize their fears for the future by repeated self-disparagement, as in that masterpiece of economic masochism, the celebrated pamphlet *Made in Germany* which appeared in 1896, or by imagining some impending apocalypse. 'We are uncertain whether civilization is about to blossom into flower or wither in a ruined tangle of dead leaves and faded gold.'[8] However most thinking people chose the way of lucid thought, without illusion or pretence. It was this determination to see clearly, so as to arrive at a rational view of the world, away from traditional taboos, that was perfectly expressed by the economist J. A. Hobson when he wrote in *The Crisis of Liberalism* (1909) that more and more people were 'possessed by the duty and the desire to put the very questions which their parents felt shocking, and to insist upon plain intelligible answers.'[9]

So the intellectual foundations of *laissez-faire* were beginning to totter, even though the doctrine retained a great number of adherents. It would indeed be entirely wrong to underestimate the imprint of economic individualism, whose influence on the public mind can be traced up to our own times. Yet new ideological currents were infiltrating through all the cracks in the liberal edifice. They all led to a redefinition of the relationship between the State and the individual. They all carried Eng-land towards a restoration of the functions and the power of the State, either in the limited framework of interventionism (the radical way) or by advocating nationalization and collective management (the socialist way). So one sees why an ultra-individualist like Dicey did not hesitate to name 1870 as the last year of English liberalism, for he saw it as the beginning of Moloch State's takeover of public life. With more subtlety Elie Halévy decided to put later, in the last years of the century, the decisive turning-point of modern England, i.e. the decline of liberal individualism inspired by Protestantism and the advent of a Prussian and bureaucratic conception of the State. Indeed he foresaw it as a dangerous prelude to the 'era of tyrannies'.

In practice, the radicalism, rejuvenated and refreshed, which governed England from 1906 to 1914, took upon itself the mission of combining the virtues of individualism and private enterprise with the government intervention necessary to correct abuses and protect the rights of the weakest. This was a difficult gamble, and while political democracy gained from it, capitalism was hardly inconvenienced. As for socialism, another gainer from the crisis of classical liberalism, it usually emerged as the winner of ideological encounters. This was firstly because it brought an answer to the age's double yearning for rationalism and justice. Secondly, within a few years, it succeeded in capturing the attention and sometimes the support of the intelligentsia. One might even describe the period as the golden age of English socialism. After the 1914 war, Labour's progress was electoral and political, but the doctrinal inspiration dried up; whereas between 1880 and 1914 the current of socialism was in full spate. There was Marxist socialism, with the Social-Democratic Federation, founded in 1884, as its main support; there was Fabian socialism, the Fabian Society having also been founded in 1884; and there was religious socialism, as the Christian socialism of 1848 had a vigorous revival at the end of the century. On the labour side there was the Independent Labour Party, created in 1893, which acted as a link between the advanced wing of trade unionism and the elements of the middle class won over to the liberation of the workers; and there was revolutionary 'syndicalism' whose forceful thrusts began in 1910.

Traditional beliefs and new modes of behaviour

Should one take Virginia Woolf literally when she claimed that 'in or about December 1910 human character changed'. For in that year, according to her, 'all human relations have shifted – those between masters and servants, husbands and wives, parents and children. And when human relations change there is at the same time a change in religion, conduct, politics and literature.'[10] Of course it was a case of the contemporary observer's imagination wanting at all costs to assign a date to the changes in civilization unrolling before her eyes. But equally there was a profound intuition at work. Hers was a mind seeking to penetrate the tendencies of her own times, to take their measure and fix landmarks. It is true that the dawn of the new century brought so many changes in material existence, in manners and in mental outlook that the old society was stirred by a thousand new ideas and ambitions. Cheap newspapers, cycles and motor cars, mass leisure for the first time, changes in dress fashion, *fin de siècle* aestheticism, 'Edwardian' decor, how could all these innovations fail to make people feel that they were entering a new world? – even though there still remained the vast weight of inertia in a society where tradition was credited as a major virtue, and where new ideas came up against formidable obstacles. 'In England', remarked Sidney Webb wittily, 'there are three stages through which every notion has to pass: 1. It is impossible; 2. It is against the Bible; 3. We knew it before.'[11]

However, once the size of the change has been underlined, rather than taking a bird's eye view of the many manifestations of the 'new spirit', we prefer to concentrate our analysis on two sectors: religion and the family. These are special areas that control social conduct at a deep level, but they are hard to penetrate in spite of much research, for they are sealed up by secrets buried in individual consciences or in the collective unconscious. Nevertheless two pieces of evidence jump to the eye – the retreat of religious faith and the drop in the birth-rate. It is this decisive change in behaviour, making a complete break with the habits of centuries, that we must study here.

We have already seen to what degree England was a Christian country and how its history and outlook were conditioned by the various religious sects. Whether he liked it or not, every Englishman was moulded by Christianity to the depths of his being. Of course one must not idealize the situation. The existence of active centres of free thought, the de-christianization of the common people, the more or less open resistance to the established Church's continuous presence were obvious and long-standing facts whose origins went back beyond the mid-century. The new development at the end of the Victorian period and even more in the first years of the twentieth century was the gradual disruption of the traditional balance between religion and society. This retreat took three forms. First of all there was the retreat of the Churches as institutions directing and controlling everybody's life. In fact the Christian world began to disappear. In the world that succeeded it the profane and the sacred coexisted in peace, but without the former being, as before, subordinate to the latter. Secondly faith, insofar as it was a personal belief and a source of interior life, tended to become a minority phenomenon because of the gradual decline of traditional Christianity. The latter faded away and was replaced by smaller religious communities that were far less numerous but generally more convinced and fervent. Finally, as Christianity exercised less and less social influence, religion gradually lost its important role as a cohesive force in the community.

One can see clearly that there was a process at work going far beyond the ritual lamentations over the disintegrating effect of rationalism, the vogue of science, the irruption of hedonism and materialism, and the taste for comfort and leisure pursuits. Undoubtedly all these factors counted, but should we call them causes or merely contributors to a process?

In this general decline it was obviously the Church of England that was most affected. Her position as the official Church probably did her more harm than good in her efforts to spread the Gospel and carry out good works. The churches were half empty, and the recruitment of clergy was not without difficulty, all the more because the livings were affected by the agricultural crisis. In the country the vicarage was no better-off than the manor. The situation in the towns, where enormous efforts had been made to establish new parishes, settled down more or less. The distribution of charity and the festive character of religious ceremonies helped to keep congregations in existence round the clergyman. However, on the eve of the First World War, the total number of Easter communicants was only 2.2 million, or 10 per cent of the population over 15 years old. The situation was not much better on the Nonconformist side. After the peak years 1870–80, a slow decline in attendance at the chapels took place. A loss of vitality, the disappearance of the old urban congregations as the middle classes moved to the suburbs, the weakening of the Liberal party, the scarcity of ministers – all these debilitating factors were outweighed by the efforts towards re-union made by various sects.

Another disturbing symptom for the Protestants was that no more 'revivals' occurred after the middle of the nineteenth century. The Oxford Movement was the last of the great religious awakenings. One could hardly consider ritualism, salvationism (the Salvation Army dated from 1865–78) or, in the Methodist Church, the Forward Movement, as anything but pale successors. There were other small but revealing signs of changes in religious attitudes. Family prayers in the morning, with the children and servants present, were gradually discontinued with the aristocracy showing the way. There was less observance of Sunday. For example the National Sunday League organized railway excursions at low prices; and in 1896 a law authorized the Sunday opening of museums, to the great outrage of the traditionalists. Still the famous English sabbath justly maintained its reputation as an austere day which was only cheered a little for the working classes by the pub and the Sunday roast-beef.

All the statistics on religious practice agree in showing up the indifference of a large proportion of the people. This holds true even when one takes into account the uncertainty of the criteria of church membership that reflected the bourgeoisie's and clergy's view of religion. For instance in Sheffield an inquiry carried out in 1881 fully bore out the conclusions of the religious census of 1851 – only one out of three who could and should have been practising Christians attended church. In London a survey conducted by the *Daily News* in 1903 arrived at a similar result: churchgoers amounted to between one-fifth and one-sixth of the total population. On the eve of the war, only three marriages out of four were celebrated in church in England and Wales. In Scotland, on the other hand, the proportion of religious marriages was still about nine out of ten.[13] The only denomination to increase their numbers were the Roman Catholics. In 1900 there were about 2 million in Great Britain, of whom more than 400,000 were in Scotland; and in 1914 they formed 5 per cent of the population in England and 11 per cent in Scotland. By comparison the Methodists numbered 750,000; the Baptists and Congregationalists oscillated around 400,000 members each; and the total number of Presbyterians came to 1.2 million, nearly all concentrated in Scotland.[14] As for the Church of England statistics, they varied in the proportion of seven to one, depending on whether one counted all the nominal members of the Church of England or only the Easter communicants. Finally, if one lays on one side Roman Catholicism (which was on the increase) and positively declared atheism (which was very rare) on the other, it was indifferentism which was becoming more and more common. Behind a façade of religious institutions and traditional customs, England was becoming secularized, in the personal as well as in the public sphere; but there still remained, even among the indifferent, a sense of the sacred and puritan

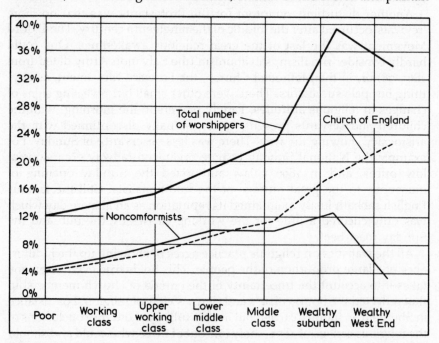

Figure 2. Church attendance among adults by social class in London at the beginning of the twentieth century[12]

morality. Above all there was everpresent an undenominational religious outlook.

At the same time an important turning-point was reached in family life – the start of voluntary birth-control. The practice itself was not new. What was new was its practice on a vast scale. One can fix the date exactly; it started some time around 1875–80 and in a few years reached massive proportions, changing the whole demographic face of England. Just as the French had done a few decades earlier and as other European nations would soon do, the English broke with ancestral habits and adopted new modes of behaviour in human reproduction. These led not only to a change of attitude towards children, but also to a new conception of the family and life in general.

We must distinguish here two aspects of this upset of traditional ways. First of all simple facts, and here the picture is as clear as daylight. Then there is the interpretation of these facts, and we start to stumble in the dark. We will begin by letting the figures speak for themselves. They describe a curve of extreme simplicity on the demographic graph. Firstly the birth-rate, which had been nearly stable for half a century at around 35 per '000, diminished from 1875–80, then dived steeply to end up at 24 per '000, in the years just before 1914. Secondly, the net reproduction rate naturally followed the same pattern, i.e. having wavered between 1.4 and 1.5 between 1851 and 1871, it fell in 1911 to 1.1, only just achieving replacement between generations. The third criterion, which was even more revealing, was the number of children per family. Around 1870 it was 6; in 1890–9 it dropped to 4.3, and in 1915 it was no more than 2.3.

It was an extraordinary decline in fertility, and a very sudden one too, concentrated into a very short time. The transformation occurred within thirty years, or a generation. How does one explain a mutation of this magnitude? It is worth noting that, although the drop in the birth-rate affected all classes eventually, it started with the ruling classes. It was the bourgeoisie, and in particular the professions who started the trend, whereas the tendency was less striking and certainly slower to develop among urban manual workers and agricultural labourers. In fact recent demographic research has shown that the process had already started in certain groups at the beginning of the nineteenth century, in the aristocracy for example. Average figures should not mask the differences that existed between social classes. The differences are glaring when one starts to calculate fertility by socio-economic groups, the proportion approaching two to one. For couples married in the period 1890–9 the average number of children per family in the professions was 2.80, among the salaried employees (white-collar workers) 3.04, among the manual wage-earners 4.85, and among the labourers 5.11. For couples married in

1914 the figures had everywhere diminished but the proportions were much the same:

Professional	2.05
Salaried employees	1.95
Manual wage-earners	3.24
Labourers	4.09[15]

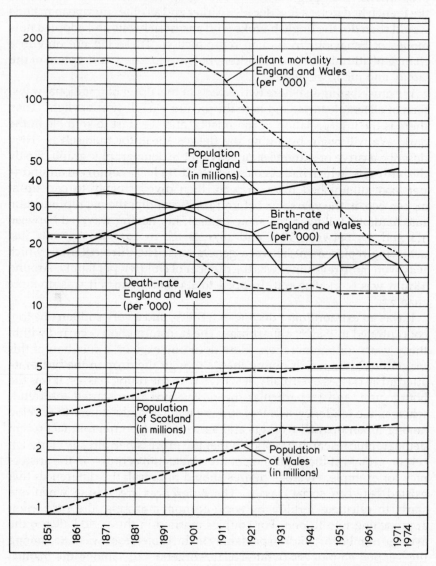

Figure 3. Populations trends in Great Britain from the mid-nineteenth century

As a result of these statistics eugenics started to flourish as a theory under the pretext of preventing the increase of unhealthy stock and improving the biological and mental quality of the race – so widespread was the fear of seeing England deprived of its élite and becoming a country dominated numerically by the degenerate and alcoholic 'lower classes'.

So one point is established, that the spread of new methods of birth-control through English society started from the top. It was the upper classes who were the first to restrain their fertility. It was their example and the pressure of the cultural model embodied by them that gradually imposed a norm of one or two children per family. But if one searches more closely for the motivations of a transformation that was so funda-mental, one comes up against problems with no clear answer, so that one has to guess rather than offer clear-cut replies. Would one support, for example, Bagehot and Spencer by saying that the diversification of leisure and pastimes diminished the role of sexuality and so reduced procrea-tion?[16] Shouldn't one rather invoke material considerations, improved living standards, the desire for more comfort, the fears of the bourgeoisie in face of the 'great depression' and the uncertainties of the future – all factors which would lead to the limiting of numbers so as to draw more profit from existing resources? Oughtn't one also to adduce the new ideas about children's futures, the wider ambitions of parents for their off-spring, the worries about education and, above all, about 'getting on'? All these trends required that care be concentrated on smaller numbers so as to ensure success in the race for promotion, especially as social mobility, although loudly proclaimed, was in fact fairly limited. Similarly, did the progress of education and labour legislation have its effect, delaying entry into the world of production, while the cost of bringing up children tended to rise? How can one measure the fading of that age-old fatalism, which meant that all children were accepted passively as 'sent by God'? And what was the impact of a neo-Malthusianism (heralded by the resounding Bradlaugh-Besant case in 1877) which preached birth-control in the name of the struggle against poverty and overpopulation? All these factors certainly played their part. But were they decisive?

On the other hand we must reject two explanations often advanced, on the grounds that they affected the situation only much later. It is undeni-able that the factors involved accelerated the process at a later stage, but they did not have much effect at the beginning. The first was women's desire for emancipation. The desire to be freed from the slavery of mater-nity was indeed felt, but it always held a secondary place in that period, as the works of J. and O. Banks have shown. Furthermore feminist aspira-tions only began to be a force after 1900. The other explanation was the spread of contraceptive techniques. In spite of progress in the manufacture of contraceptives and spermicides, the methods used remained extremely rudimentary. The fall in the birth-rate was above all attributable to *coitus interruptus*, while the more refined methods of contraception were the preserve of a small minority even among the educated classes. It followed that birth-control remained for some time a male prerogative.

One last point remains to be emphasized, which does not seem to have had enough attention. Parallel with the drop in the birth-rate, a continuous and very marked drop in the death-rate was evident in the last quarter of the nineteenth century. This had been very stable from 1850 to 1875 at around 22 per '000, but it decreased steadily after that period to arrive at 14 per '000 in 1901–13. This change was due to two main causes: improvement in nutrition and progress in hygiene. On the other hand, infant mortality played no part in this decline, except right at the end of the period, for it remained at the constant and very high level of 15 per '000 right up to 1900. As the adult mortality declined, the difference between births and deaths remained constant, even though fertility diminished. As natural growth, and so the future of the nation, seemed assured, why shouldn't families from now onwards indulge their new ambitions and control their fertility, a policy which seemed to guarantee a better life for all, both parents and children? Such a new demographic regulating system would explain how the transmission of life became dependent on the new mechanism of voluntary fertility instead of on the age-old drive of biological fertility.

Women make themselves heard

A new figure, presaging far greater upheavals, entered on the scene in the *fin de siècle* atmosphere when 'art nouveau', 'the new theatre' and 'the new realism' were making headway – 'the new woman'. Appearing soon after 1880, she dominated the 1890s and then consolidated her advance during the whole of the Edwardian period. She objected to the traditional balance of the sexes in terms that were sometimes moderate and more often radical, and she demanded a new definition of the sex roles. It was the beginning of the feminine revolt against the traditional order, the first steps on the long road to emancipation which has continued up to our own time. It was the harbinger of the 'sexual revolution' of the twentieth century.

Not that the struggle against 'sexism' had to wait for the end of the Victorian era to take shape. There had been a number of forerunners like Mary Wollstonecraft, the first of them all (*A Vindication of the Rights of Women*, 1792) and Barbara (Leigh Smith) Bodichon (*A Brief Summary of the Most Important Laws Concerning Women*, 1855). There were male champions of the equality of the sexes such as the socialist William Thompson (*Appeal of One Half of the Human Race*, 1825) and John Stuart Mill (*The Subjection of Women*, 1869). But they were voices crying in the wilderness, if one excludes certain isolated circles of convinced supporters. There were some remarkable individuals, victims of the inferiority of their sex, such as Harriet Martineau, Jane Carlyle, Harriet Taylor, Florence Nightingale etc., who had risen in protest against the oppressive tyranny under which they were suffering. In spite of all this it was not until the last quarter of the century that these feminist ideas gained ground and spread widely, thanks to some sudden publicity. Isolated efforts began to be coordinated and a real movement was born. In the face of enormous resistance it reached wider circles after 1900 in the upper and middle classes, and even in part of the working class.

Two traits of English feminism were apparent in this first phase of the struggle. Firstly its origin was bourgeois. It was amongst the privileged that the first stirrings were felt. As Viola Klein put it, feminism did not start in the factories, nor down the mines, but in middle-class Victorian drawing-rooms. At the start there was the activity of small intellectual groups with literary or political leanings, sometimes radical and sometimes socialist. In the next stage, as the battle was joined, a split began to appear between the moderates and the extremists. The latter inclined to total emancipation, including sexual liberty, while the former demanded first of all civil and political rights, without in the least putting in question the foundations of traditional morality. It was this second current of opinion that dominated English feminism in our period, showing the preponderance of the middle classes who were guided by a strict puritanism, by principles of duty and discipline, family loyalty, and a respectability imbued with the influence of religion. So the Rev. Hugh Price Hughes, the 'conscience of Wesleyanism', could congratulate himself in the first years of the twentieth century that the strictness of Protestantism had imprinted on British feminism a moral austerity that would protect it against the more dangerous aspects of Continental feminism . . . .[17]

To understand the revolt of the feminist *avant-garde* against the male order we must first of all give a brief sketch of the position of women in England during the second half of the nineteenth century, as well as examine the predominance of inegalitarian beliefs still held by the general public. We can then arrive at the methods, aims and progress of the fight for emancipation.

The feminine condition in the Victorian age derived from the existence of two superimposed structures – the ancient patriarchal regime and the modern bourgeois regime. Traditionally relations between the sexes were governed by a fundamental principle, the subordination of woman to man. This was the deep-rooted heritage of the age-old division of production and reproduction. The model to which social pressure made people conform or be ostracized, reflected the values and mandates of classic patriarchal societies, i.e. the authority of husband over wife, father over children, brother over sister, was automatic. The Victorian bourgeoisie skilfully took up this rural model and adapted it to an urban and industrial society. It even enriched, refined and, one might say, 'sublimated' it. At base there was of course the division of roles and masculine superiority. The break-up of old communal ties, the triumph of individualism and the commercial economy, and the substitution of an exchange value for a utility value reinforced man's superiority in the family and in society. The woman, on the other hand, found herself exalted and put down at the same time, while moral and religious considerations were subtly blended with economic needs. At the same time the model could also be laid down for the whole of society. Accordingly the 'lower' classes, already conditioned by ancestral habits of inequality, could follow painlessly the example coming down to them from the 'upper' classes.

So the key position held by property in the capitalist social system gave privileges to the man as sole owner of productive capital, of the business and the know-how, or even simply the strength, to work. Hence the cult of 'virile' qualities – creative energy, endurance, spirit of conquest and adventure, capacity for invention, taste for the rational and speculative intelligence. It was up to the man, a being made for action and command, to protect the woman – frail flower, feeble creature, born to submission and devotion. The one and only feminine vocation was maternity and the home. To serve and obey, that was her duty. But the woman, while still the victim of proprietary rights, also found herself by some compensation mechanism raised high, idealized and transformed into an ethereal being. Her dependence and her physical weakness were exalted. Coventry Patmore proclaimed her 'the angel in the house'. Worshipped everywhere as 'the priestess of the hearth', she was venerated as inspirer and counsellor, while at the same time she was the personification of innocence and purity. Halfway between doll and Roman matron she was, it was said, above all the civilizing force of the universe. For she was not only the one who gave birth, who brought up, who adorned. She was also the source of human warmth, tenderness, domestic peace, indeed of peace itself.

> 'Man for the field, woman for the hearth,
> Man for the sword and for the needle she:
> Man with the head and woman with the heart,
> Man to command and woman to obey',

said the father in Tennyson's poem, *The Princess*.[18] And to the question of how to define femininity Ruskin replied: 'The man's work for his own home is to secure its maintenance, progress and defence; the woman's to secure its order, comfort, and loveliness.'[19] In this connection no one has pushed the sanctification of the feminine further than the Pre-Raphaelites, whose ethereal creatures resemble messengers of the absolute. The more woman's dependence was emphasized by the rules of the social and financial code, the more this spiritualizing process developed. The expression 'sacred womanhood' became a sort of dogma only equalled by the dogma of the family. Anything that might constitute a source of temptation was speedily relegated to the animal depths. For of course the unequal share-out found extra justification in a religious context. Masculine superiority had long been integrated into Christian doctrine and the evangelical movement gave it a new vitality. All the great Biblical texts were invoked for its support from Genesis to the famous Pauline precepts. Furthermore, the attitude of the agnostics was no different: Chesterton was absolutely right when he underlined the fact that the mid-Victorian generation was the first to promote 'the cult of the home without the altar'.[20] There was no exception to the female vocation, and 'Home, Sweet Home' was the only refrain.

A few women managed to emerge from obscurity and impose themselves in public life, exciting admiration like Florence Nightingale or provoking scandal like George Eliot, but the mass lived out their anonymous existence, prisoners of a universe that was dominated by man. Of course one can cite a certain number of writers, from Mrs Gaskell to Mrs Humphry Ward (it had even been said that the novel was the special preserve of women), a few philanthropists such as the Baroness Burdett-Coutts with her vast wealth and Octavia Hill whose rigid charity was devoted to providing decent housing for workers, and certain militant figures in great social and political causes, such as Josephine Butler, tireless in her fight against prostitution, Annie Besant, apostle of birth-control and socialism, and Eleanor Marx-Aveling, passionate and tragic revolutionary. But the total roll of such figures is small.

One might say nowadays that this was a proof of profound alienation. Others would add that it was a sign of masculine oppression without restraint. Alienation there certainly was, and women's acceptance of their inferior status, which was evident to all, gives the best proof of it. On the other hand, the historian must have reservations about the idea of oppression. There are subtle differences here and one must make distinctions. Objectively speaking, there was of course oppression as long as there was both domination and alienation. Subjectively the situation was rather different. For women did not look upon their condition as an intolerable surrender to man. Because of age-old prejudices, and the Victorian sublimation of the 'feminine soul', women were far from revolting against the lot reserved for them, and indeed accepted it as normal and dictated by Providence. In this situation it would be risky to equate alienation with unhappiness. Certainly the social code in all its rigour plunged a number of women into frustration and despair and even neurasthenia, but many others were perfectly at ease, happy and fulfilled in their own setting, narrow though it might be, without feeling themselves victims of 'male chauvinism'. That was what made the struggle of the feminists so hard; for, in addition to the instincts of domination and the prejudices of men, they had to cope with the passivity and resignation of their own sex.

Furthermore, even among those who did not give in and those who were victims of laws which denied women the most elementary rights, respect for conventions dating from a distant past was slow to die. Listen for example to Caroline Norton, poet, woman of letters, grand-daughter of Sheridan, Meredith's model for a character in *Diana of the Crossways*, a woman of independent spirit and behaviour, who had to fight a legal battle to prevent her husband (from whom she was separated) from laying his hands on the money she earned by her pen: 'As for me (and there are millions of us) I believe in the natural superiority of the man as I do in the existence of a God. The natural position of a woman is inferiority to a man, that is a thing of God's appointing, not of man's devising.'[21]

If we now turn to the working classes, the situation is not very different. Male pre-eminence was the rule, without argument but also without pretence, as there was no recourse to bourgeois sublimations. The whole teaching of the Christian Churches acted as a backcloth to the spiritual justification of inequality. Marriage and maternity, that was the natural destiny of woman. As for the women who worked (only a fraction of them were married) they were divided into three more or less equal groups. The first third were employed in industry as workers in mechanized factories, especially textile factories, or in small workshops. The second group were domestic servants, a feminine occupation above all others (nine out of ten servants were women), whose greatest numerical strength was reached in 1880–1900. As the very symbol of dependence, domestic service was regarded as a servile activity. Finally the third category occupied a position midway between the subordinate position of wage-earner and the slave position of the servant. These were the home workers, more particularly in the garment trade, who had to submit to the pitiless law of the sweating system. So on every side the picture was a sombre one – low wages (always far below men's wages, generally half), repetitive work without responsibility, poor qualifications, and productivity reduced by the addition of household tasks to their gainful occupation. At every level of work, in town as well as country, the economic exploitation of women aggravated the social inferiority of their sex.

Yet it was the Industrial Revolution much more than the diffusion of liberal ideas which brought about the transformation of the feminine condition. It was the Industrial Revolution which in the long run set up the foundations of emancipation by breaking the patriarchal pattern of work in the home. It undermined the traditional idea of the woman as having a horizon that was limited to the family group, by drawing her into the larger world outside. Industrial capitalism, by multiplying the docile and underpaid workforce of women, gave a recognized value to the professional labour of each woman, which became remuneration negotiable on the open market and an eventual guarantee of independence. Of course the effects of this economic transformation took a long time to make themselves felt, even though England in this sphere as well was in advance of other countries, but in the last third of the nineteenth century the change had undoubtedly taken place. It also coincided with a change of opinion in the country. New ideas on the capacities, rights and roles of women were making themselves felt. Indeed shouldn't the notions of liberty and equality energetically propagated by the male sex apply equally to the other sex? The struggle for emancipation was born, and it grew year by year up to 1914. Its strength derived from the fact that it combined from now onwards economic factors (which tended to project the woman out of the home into wider spheres) and intellectual pressures (resulting from the growing success of feminist theories and sentiments).

The demands of the movement took four different forms. Emancipation sought, either in turn or simultaneously, goals that were legal, educational, political and sexual. In civil rights the first important change came in 1857 with the Matrimonial Causes Act. In authorizing divorce (albeit with numerous restrictions) the law aimed in theory at liberating the woman who found herself the prisoner of an imposed situation. But the cost and complications of the procedure limited its application to the wealthy classes. Besides, the measure directly reflected the inequitable concept of the 'double standard'. For the husband it was enough to show evidence of the wife's adultery to obtain a divorce, but the opposite was not the case. The adultery of the husband was not enough for the wife, who had to show that it was aggravated by other wrongs, such as desertion, cruelty, etc. Indeed half a century later there were only one thousand dissolutions of marriage in the whole of Great Britain, or 0.2 per cent of all marriages. Here is proof that divorce remained a facility for the privileged. Equality between spouses only came in 1923, and divorce became available for everyone only in 1949 thanks to Legal Aid. In the matter of property the law emphasized the inequality even more clearly, for English matrimonial law stipulated that through marriage the husband become the owner of all the property, even the real estate, of his wife. As John Stuart Mill wrote, outraged by this denial of justice, 'whatever is hers is his, but the parallel inference is never drawn that whatever is his is hers'. And he added, 'I am far from pretending that wives are in general no better treated than slaves; but no slave is a slave to the same lengths, and in so full a sense of the word, as a wife is'.[22] On this point a decisive reform was accomplished by two laws, the Married Woman's Property Act of 1870, and above all that of 1882. By these measures the wife saw herself regaining full possession of her property, whether it was property acquired before marriage or after. So legal guardianship by the husband was replaced by the separation of property. An anecdote will illustrate the state of mind common at the time. While campaigning in East Anglia in favour of reform, Millicent Garrett Fawcett, pioneer feminist and suffragist, was given the following reply by a farmer: 'Am I to understand you, ma'am, that if this Bill passes, and my wife have a matter of a hundred pound left to her, I should have to ask her for it?'[23] There was another step forward in the legal status of women. From 1884 onwards a wife was not liable for prison if she refused to return to the conjugal home, and soon afterwards legislation removed from the husband the right to confine her in the event of such behaviour. So the wife ceased to be the property of her husband.

In the sphere of education, there were two important innovations between 1850 and 1880 – the start of secondary education for girls by the foundation of several boarding and day schools, and the entry of girls to universities. These were advances of considerable importance, even though this type of education was reserved for young ladies of the bourgeoisie. By the end of the century the results began to have their full effect. Instead of having their horizons bounded by drawing-room and needlework, daughters of good families pursued their studies, went to Oxford and Cambridge, travelled, rode bicycles, played tennis and took up eurhythmics. Some launched out into the professions, into medicine (there were 25 women doctors in 1881, and 477 in 1911), journalism and above all teaching. There were 70,000 women teachers in 1851 and 172, 000 in 1901.[24] Others became nurses, dentists, librarians. . . . Yet many barriers continued to exist. Up to the First World War whole professions, e.g. the Bar, the Stock Exchange and Parliament, remained closed to women. As for public service, the female sex was well represented, but had to be content with lowly jobs. The general picture was only moderately satisfactory. Progress was slow, obstacles were numerous, and equality seemed a long way off indeed.

It was really in the political sector that the activity was most spectacular and claimed the most public attention in the ten years before the war. Not that there had been any lack of effort before that time. The first association for female suffrage had been formed in 1867, the National Society for Women's Suffrage, and for years well-behaved feminists had patiently demanded the extension of the right to vote to the second sex by holding meetings and writing articles. At the local government level, English women had early on won the right to be electors provided that they were unmarried or widows. (No married woman who was entitled to a vote since she was supposed to be represented by her husband.) Thus since 1834 women had been able to elect Poor Law Guardians. In 1869 they were given the right of electing members to municipal councils in certain towns, and this right was extended to county councils in 1888 and to district councils in 1894. Finally in 1870 they were able to elect members to school boards. But after all it was simply conceding to women the right to concern themselves with welfare, education and hygiene, for which their domestic tradition fitted them without much trouble! When questions of high politics such as law-making, diplomacy and finance were at issue, a different view was taken. These questions were always matters for men, and their preserves were jealously guarded.

All this explains the foundation in 1903 of a new-style feminist organization, the Women's Social and Political Union (WSPU), directed by Mrs Pankhurst and her two daughters. This time there was no more question of confining themselves to peaceful propaganda and waiting for the day when men would agree to grant political rights to women. For the 'suffragettes', the derisive name given to the militants of the WSPU, what counted was to win these rights by organizing a noisy and determined pressure group, ready if necessary to agitate in the streets. So the chosen weapon was publicity, and the tactics were those of a pushful minority. Interruptions of meetings, delegations and demonstrations in public, and soon hunger strikes, succeeded one another with no respite for the authorities. The Liberal leader, Campbell-Bannerman, advised them, 'Harass us and be patient!', but they only obeyed the first half of the advice! Braving jibes, blows and prison because for them 'the cause' deserved every sacrifice, the little phalanx of militants, ranged behind Mrs Pankhurst, managed in a short time to bring the debate on civil equality for women to the centre of the public stage. However, as no legislation came to pass in spite of the growing support of public opinion and as the cry 'Votes for Women' came up against masculine inertia exemplified by the dilatory and contemptuous attitudes of politicians, the women's suffrage movement split in two. The more determined minority plunged into violence and martyrdom in order to wrest a decision. In fact the contrary result was achieved. The suffragettes lost part of their support by going over to illegal methods. During 1912–14 their base, which had always been almost exclusively bourgeois, narrowed and finally, despite the devotion and obstinacy of the pioneers, they had to wait for the pressure of war, which gave women new roles, to obtain the franchise in 1918.

The final battleground was the struggle for sexual emancipation. While the 'new woman' was triumphing in the works of Meredith, Gissing, Shaw, Wells and Ibsen, she was also making headway in real life. Conscious feminists like Sue Bridehead in *Jude the Obscure* or Ann Veronica or again the heroine of Grant Allen's symbolically titled novel *The Woman Who Did* found imitators or, on the contrary, were inspired by actual cases. Here however we must make a distinction, for the struggle had two aspects. Sometimes the accent was placed on an individual ethical claim demanding for each woman the right to live according to her own rules, instead of being ostracized the moment she flouted the conventions. Sometimes the movement was wider, affirming the autonomy of the second sex – a kind of quest for identity and independence all at the same time. In the case of the former two currents met from the two extremities of the social scene, the drawing-rooms of the bourgeoisie and the ranks of the socialists and anarchists. Rebelling against the puritan morals prevailing among the majority of 'respectable' feminists (('Votes for Women and Chastity for Men', proclaimed Christabel Pankhurst in 1914), these 'emancipated' feminists rejected the notion of the equality of the sexes which would lead to virtue being obligatory for all. Criticizing conformity and bourgeois legalism, and particularly marriage, they called for spontaneity of feeling, for the right to dispose of one's body and choose one's partner as one wished. It was a new conception which exalted 'free love' as the only real fulfilment of equality. Other feminists aimed higher. For them 'free' morals were not enough to abolish slavery. They had to upset the primacy of the male sex in the universe by dislodging men from their monopolies – witness what one suffragette said to another: 'Trust in God – *She* will help you!' Hence some battles in the sex war. Nevertheless for most militant women the major objective remained to place women everywhere on an equal footing with men and to give them full possession of their rights.

5 *From oligarchy to democracy?*

The aristocracy on the defensive

After 1880 the social scene was dominated by two major forces – the bourgeois ascendancy and the thrust of labour. As a result of the former phenomenon there was a shift in the balance of power at the top. From the latter change came a modification in the power structure of society, because of the new relationship between the workers and the governing class. This transformation was in fact slow, and one should not exaggerate its extent, but it was real and above all full of consequence for the future.

Let us start with the case of the rich and powerful. Here the contrast between the two panels of the diptych is striking. On one side an aristocracy on the verge of decline, taking up a defensive position almost all along the line; on the other a bourgeoisie consolidating its advance and gaining position and positions. England did not cease to be attached to its nobility (name and lineage counted for more than in other countries) but every day it became more and more a middle-class country. Even feudal power and the prestige of monarchy found it difficult to resist this insidious penetration of bourgeois power, which took so many forms. It is enough to take Queen Victoria as an example. The greatest compliment that her faithful minister Lord Salisbury, the archetypal old-style patrician, found to pay her at her death was to have been a perfect representative of the middle classes and to have understood them admirably![1]

Certainly lords and squires continued to enjoy advantages arising from their situation; but while the aristocracy appeared to preserve its eminence – its rank in the State, its prestige, its luxurious way of life – in fact it was losing its pre-eminence once for all. It was menaced from two sides, by money and power. For land, which had been the ancestral source of their wealth, declined in value, and in the State sector the institutions and the top posts in the government were passing out of the influence of the aristocracy.

First of all, the land. After the lush years of mid-Victorian prosperity the English countryside passed through hard times in the last twenty years of the century. Two consequences of this were a rude blow inflicted on the fortunes of the nobility and a crisis in the whole of rural society. The fact was that between 1874 and 1896 agriculture endured a series of almost uninterrupted catastrophes (disastrous weather, animal diseases, bad harvests) and, worst of all, economic difficulties arising out of competition from new countries and the drop in world prices. In a few years the price of wheat fell by half, and income from real estate was badly affected. Between the periods 1874–8 and 1894–8 rents dropped on average by 25 per cent, although after 1896 they did stabilize and even rise a little before the 1914 war. At the same time the position of agriculture in the national economy never ceased to decline. The number of people actively engaged in agriculture was always on the wane, falling from 2 million in 1851 to 1.4 million in 1901. In 1911 its proportion to the total occupied population had dropped to 8 per cent, as compared with 22 per cent in 1851.[2] Another even more serious sign of the weakening of landowners was that the price of land was going down, and this had psychological as well as economic effects. The possession of land seemed less attractive because it did not procure as much influence as before. As an Oscar Wilde character said in *The Importance of Being Earnest* (1895): 'Land has ceased to be either a profit or a pleasure'. One must also bear in mind that urban life was becoming the rule, while life in the country seemed to be the exception. The town was now the prevalent model. Was the prestige of money about to eclipse the prestige of land? One sees doubt and anxiety creeping in at the manor as well as on the farm. Must one then conclude that aristocratic capital was breaking up? Or was the world of the nobility really more stricken psychologically than financially?

Two important corrections must be made here. The first concerns landed wealth. People have tended to overestimate the effects of the agricultural depression in this area. Ruin certainly did occur, and a number of farmers went bankrupt. But many managed to adapt their methods to market conditions, and prepared a bright future for themselves. More exact studies of agrarian history conducted at the regional level have shown up a great difference in performance. Those who suffered most were the wheat growers, especially when they combined wheat with raising sheep. Certain pastoral regions on the other hand did extremely well. For instance, although it is true that the *average* fall in rent was 25 per cent, there was a great difference between the cereal plains of East Anglia and the south, where it reached 40 per cent, and the north and west where it was only 12 per cent. One should therefore distinguish between three types of cultivation. First of all there were the farms that went in exclusively for cereals, and they were the ones who were pitilessly hit by the slump. Then there were stock farming regions, which had mixed fortunes, for where the farmers managed to lower their costs and adapt to the soil and the markets, they succeeded in surmounting difficult conditions. Finally there were the sectors which catered for the ever-growing demands of urban consumption (dairy farming, market gardening and fruit-growing) and these got on very well indeed. The way English farmers reorganized themselves on the eve of the First World War reminds one inevitably of Caesar's remark on the ancient Britons: *'lacte et carne vivunt'*. So on the whole it would be a grave error to believe in an impoverishment of the aristocracy. Not only did real property incomes fare better than has been said, but the style of living in country houses did not deteriorate as one might think. Either the landowners managed to trim the costs of running their estates or they made up with revenue from other sources. The agricultural labourers on their side, considerably reduced in numbers by the flight from the countryside, enjoyed a notable improvement in their conditions.

In the second place, the fortunes of the aristocracy survived by diversifying. It is well known that for a long time the landed interest had participated in the leap forward of commerce and banking. Peers and plain squires were on the boards of railway companies, and now they were breaking into the City. They were sometimes appointed directors for their money and sometimes for the glamour of their names. They invested in government stock and foreign loans, and some of them found in town rents and property speculation ample compensation for their reduced farm lettings. 'Land is no longer an enviable possession unless it is coupled with a good income from other sources', sighed a Kentish landlord towards the end of the century,[3] but the lifestyle of the upper classes, which was generally very comfortable among the gentry and often luxurious in the upper ranks of the aristocracy, leads one to believe that secondary revenues were not inconsiderable.

However, when one speaks of the Edwardian aristocracy, is one still speaking of the same aristocracy as before? In other words, wasn't penetration by the upper middle class drastically changing the character of the old landed families? The fact is that two tendencies, opposite but com-

plementary, were at work, which led to a convergence, and even sometimes to a confusion of the aristocracy of blood and the plutocracy of trade
and manufacture. On the one hand the nobility, by venturing unreser-
vedly into the world of business, was running the risk of contaminating
its patrician spirit by contact with the bourgeois mentality. On the other
hand, as the wealth of the middle classes expanded, an ever-increasing
number of parvenus penetrated (by ennoblement, by marriage, etc.) into
the magic circle of the aristocracy that had been so jealously guarded in
former times.

While the old rural England survived, the predominance of the nobility, such as prevailed in the eighteenth century or even in the first
seventy-five years of the nineteenth century, continued its natural existence. But it was too much part and parcel of the rural world to survive the
basic redistribution of wealth and power which followed the arrival of
industrial capitalism and urbanization. The day that these two
phenomena came to dominate the life of the country, when agriculture's
share in the gross national product fell from 20 per cent around 1850 to 6
per cent around 1900, how could the aristocracy continue to spread its
influence except by dabbling more and more in urban activities, commerce and manufacturing? Its members were of course liable to be
infected by the commercial or bourgeois ethos and they risked tainting
their true nature, which had been handed down to them from the feudal
past. Not that they abandoned their manor-houses – on the contrary, the
arrival of the motor-car allowed them to live more easily on their estates
and more economically while they pursued their business in town. The
demands of patronage also continued to receive attention, but as revenue
decreased, so did preoccupations of this kind. Some people were repelled
by the sight of the aristocratic spirit dabbling in commercialism;
Gladstone, for example, deplored the growing number of 'hybrids', half
business men, half country gentlemen, titled people who unashamedly
'give their names to speculations which they neither understand nor
examine, as Directors or Trustees'.[4]

The second aspect of *embourgeoisement* was the penetration of the aristocracy by businessmen. In this respect the end of the nineteenth century
marked a turning-point whose date can be precisely fixed.[5] Up to around
1885, despite the relative mobility of English society, the peerage
remained well protected against the intrusion of parvenus, and the barriers separating the world of titles from the world of business continued to
function efficiently.

Between 1832 and 1885 there had been only 166 promotions to the
peerage, a slow rate that avoided any danger of dilution. Above all,
three-quarters of those who were raised to the peerage were politicians,
generally Members of Parliament, and nearly all belonged to the gentry.

Indeed you could count on your fingers the representatives of business who had acceded to the hereditary nobility. Banking was the first to score with Baring in 1835, but the ennoblement of an industrialist had to wait until 1856 when the cotton-spinner Strutt became Lord Belper. Twenty to thirty more years elapsed before it was the turn of two ironmasters, then of two brewers, Guinness and Bass, and finally that of the Prince of Finance, Nathan Rothschild, in 1885. The 'plebeian aristocracy' which Disraeli thought he could see making its entry with the Reform Act of 1832 was a myth, as it only appeared on the scene after 1885. Then the process accelerated. Paradoxically it was in the time of the Marquis of Salisbury that the bourgeoisie entered the peerage in large numbers. Some people looked on their arrival as new blood; others maintained that it was a prostitution of honours.

Between 1886 and 1914 about 200 peers were created, and one can now talk about the arrival of industrial England in the House of Lords. The majority of promotions continued to be the reward for services rendered to the State in politics, the army, diplomacy and the Empire, but a third of them went to businessmen – manufacturers like Armstrong the munitions magnate, or Lord Ashton who was nicknamed 'Lord Linoleum', shipbuilders like Pirrie of Harland and Wolff in Belfast, merchants and bankers, not to mention 'press barons' who became plain barons, such as Northcliffe and Rothermere. In the face of this flood it was rumoured that the sale of honours was practised in order to fill the coffers of the party in power. . . . At the same time other alliances sped the growing merger of feudalism and plutocracy. First of all marriages: daughters of businessmen, American heiresses and even actresses were accepted. After having for years jealously guarded its integrity, here was the aristocracy linking itself to bourgeois trades and mercantile preoccupations. At political and society parties, statesmen of middle-class origins such as Chamberlain, Asquith and Haldane rubbed shoulders with politicians who boasted of grand names like Cecil, Churchill, Rosebery, Balfour and Curzon. A sign of the times was when Asquith became Prime Minister in 1908. He was the first head of government who did not belong to a landed family, if one excepts Disraeli (who was always an exception). When Bonar Law became head of the Conservative Party in 1911, he was the first Tory leader to spring from middle-class industrial origins.

New faces to be seen in politics, retreat of aristocratic influence in public affairs – on every side a transfer of political power is evident in favour of the middle class. Here, too, noblemen and landlords were on the defensive. In the 1865 House of Commons the landed interest took up three-quarters of the seats, 31 per cent of the members belonged to the higher aristocracy and 45 per cent to the gentry, a proportion which had not greatly changed since the eighteenth century.* By 1910 the number of landlords had dropped to one-seventh of the House. The development was no less striking in the social structure of the Cabinet, the turning-point being in the last years of the century, in Salisbury's time to be precise. Not that the old leader deliberately sought this change, but he had to bow to circumstances. While from 1880 to 1895 the Cabinet contained 47 aristocrats and 30 bourgeois, between 1895 and 1905 the numbers were 17 and 21 respectively, and between 1905 and 1914 they were 13 and 23.[6]

The gradual reduction of the landed interest's power was not only to be found at Westminster. It was evident at the local as well as the national level. There could be no denying that along all the avenues of power the middle-class battalions were pressing forward while the aristocracy was retreating. In the short term the reforms, under the cover of democratization, were of more advantage to the talented than to the popular classes. Among the measures which conspired to diminish the influence of the aristocracy in the country one can cite the electoral laws: the Ballot Act of 1872 (which put an end to pressures from landlords), the Corrupt and Illegal Practices Act of 1883, and the third Reform Act of 1884–5 (which gave voting rights to agricultural labourers). There was the reform of local government in 1888 which in each county replaced the old aristocratic institutions by elected councils – a reform that was extended in 1894 to all rural districts. There was the Ground Game Act of 1880 which suppressed the game monopoly by allowing everyone to kill rabbits and hares on their own land. In the Civil Service and the Army the reforms carried out between 1855 and 1875 (recruitment by examination for the Civil Service and the abolition of the purchase of commissions for officers) gradually put an end to patronage and nepotism. Merit became more important than social rank, and competence than birth. Another factor in the retreat of the aristocracy was the transformation after 1875–80 of the political parties into great organized machines. This made it much more difficult for a small oligarchy of peers and squires to control the party, as it did in the good old days. This was particularly true of the Liberal Party, which escaped from the traditional Whig dynasties by becoming more radical itself. Even among the Tories, when they were obliged to imitate their adversaries in setting up local organizations in each constituency, the old landed families had difficulty in preserving their influence in spite of some rearguard actions which tried to manipulate the levers of democratic society. One such attempt was the Primrose League which sought

*In 1761 at least 50 per cent of Members of The House of Commons belonged to families of the peerage or the baronetage. For 1865 the figure was still over one-third. One can see that events belied the withering prophecy of the Duke of Wellington on the 1832 Reform Bill: 'The Reform Bill would make the House of Commons unfit for gentlemen to sit in.'

to encourage a code of chivalry right down to the lower middle class. But, in order to succeed, they would have to have been more calculating and less prejudiced. One could see it all happening in the fierce battle fought in 1909–11 over the House of Lords. Having allowed themselves to be clumsily caught in the dilemma 'Peers versus People' the Members of House not only endured a decisive restriction of their powers with the passing of the Parliament Act of 1911 which made the House of Lords simply a chamber of record, but they also forfeited their right to the respect of a section of public opinion. 'As long as the dukes were contented', commented Lloyd George savagely, 'to be mere idols on their pedestals, preserving that stately silence which became their rank and their intelligence all went well, and the average British citizen rather looked up to them . . .', but they made the mistake of stepping off their perches.[7]

One would be wrong to take this crushing observation too literally. Wasn't Lloyd George the first to increase the creation of peers as soon as he became Prime Minister? And didn't he in the end accept a peerage for himself? The fact was that the aristocracy still held some trump cards. It is true that it had to give up its monopoly of honours and share power and prestige with others, but the feeling of innate superiority was still there, and every day there was evidence that their importance was still recognized. For instance a shrewd observer like Elie Halévy, on one of his first stays in England at the end of the century, was struck by the profoundly aristocratic character of English society, so different from the republican Establishment which he frequented in France. In the same way Taine thirty or forty years earlier had been intrigued by the persistence of the 'feudal' spirit in the midst of bourgeois liberalism. As late as 1911 patrician haughtiness emerged in a novel by Mrs Humphry Ward, *Lady Connie*, where 'our feudal lords and superiors' are depicted in the persons of Douglas Falloden and his father, Sir Arthur. One is told straight out that they 'have a right to the services of those beneath them; and everybody is beneath them – especially women, and foreigners, and artists, and people who don't shoot or hunt'.

Finally, in addition to receiving the respect and deference accorded to country gentlemen, the old landed society held its own by its style of living. The more it lost on the political plane, the more it sought to shine on the social plane. It must be said that its gift for display continued unrivalled, and its splendour, supported by its ancient lineage, easily excelled the vulgar luxury of the new-rich. The nobility kept its head high thanks to its society occasions, its balls and the Turf. Up to 1914 the splendid London town houses – Grosvenor, Dorchester, Londonderry, Devonshire, Apsley, Bridgewater, Holland and so on – shone with a thousand lights; and one could multiply the examples of opulence. The

Marquis of Bute, at his death in 1901, left a fortune of nearly £2 million.[8]
The Marquis of Ripon, according to his friend the Duke of Portland, kept a
strict enough count of his shooting bag to calculate that between 1867 and
1900 he killed a total of 142,343 pheasants, 97,579 partridges, 56,460
grouse, 29,858 rabbits and 27,687 hares, not to mention 2 rhinoceroses, 11
tigers and 12 buffaloes![9] At Blenheim Palace, the patrician magnificence of
the Marlboroughs kept a squad of footmen, all chosen for their height and
dressed in the ducal livery – maroon coat and breeches, waistcoat with
silver trimmings, silk stockings, shoes with silver buckles, powdered
wigs. . . . While the heads of titled families paraded at Court, the
younger sons continued to staff certain Departments of State, in first
place the Diplomatic Service ('the outdoor relief of the British aristocracy',
according to John Bright's jibe) and the Royal Navy, not to mention the
Army and the Church. As in the past, the law of primogeniture ensured a
spirit of initiative and dynamism among the younger sons of noble
families. All things considered, the aristocracy still retained some worth-
while remnants of power, even if it was now on the defensive.

The awakening of Caliban

We saw earlier how in the mid-Victorian calm the very liberal and peace-
loving Cobden showed surprise at the apparent passivity of the workers
and almost cried out for the rebellion of a Spartacus.[10] Indeed why was
there such a spirit of acceptance and even resignation? Why such an
absence of revolt? This self-same question was posed by the founders of
scientific socialism who had taken refuge in London. While Engels in a
letter to Marx in 1858 had complained, 'The English proletariat is actually
becoming more and more bourgeois', twenty years later, Marx echoed the
feeling when he spoke of the growing 'demoralization' of the working
class.[11] Yet it only took a few years for the labour *avant-garde* around
1880 to adopt an attitude of challenge, both theoretical and practical, to
existing society. How can one explain such a change? What were the
reasons for this awakening of the labour world, and what forms did it
take?

First of all we must insist on a point that is too often ignored – the
subjugation of the working class was less advanced than has been made
out. True, Victorian society had succeeded in transforming its three-part
division into a dyarchy of aristocracy and bourgeoisie, working in harness
since the mid-century so as to assure themselves of control of the country.
Furthermore those who had set up this two-headed system had been
clever enough to try to integrate the third element in the social structure,
the working class, so as to turn it away from violence and convert it to
their beliefs. This tactic was far more astute than its equivalent in France,

where violence was rampant and where the centre of gravity of society – the bourgeois-peasant alliance versus the workers – depended as much on force, from June 1848 up to the Commune, as on universal suffrage. Yet in England this attempt at integration only half succeeded, for large sectors of labour kept aloof, either involuntarily because of a cultural barrier to middle-class penetration, or consciously, by a deliberate resistance to the seduction of crumbs from the rich man's table.

In addition, integration was only possible on two conditions: a hopeful climate of expansion and prosperity, and a bourgeois atmosphere that was contented and self-confident. When after 1880 these two preconditions faltered (for they were replaced by economic uncertainties and feelings of guilt on the part of the ruling classes), the chances of working-class autonomy much improved.

Finally one must take account of other factors that were favourable to a revival of the workers' struggle. There was the strength of numbers, for the numerical increase, notably in the trades that were unskilled but labour-intensive, e.g. transport, gave the workers a feeling of effectiveness. There was also a return to ideology, a tool both of analysis and action, whereas the immediate post-1848 period had been a dead season for socialist utopias and had left the field open to a pragmatic individualism that was fragmented and lacking in an overall view. Furthermore the labour movement benefited from its alliance with the 'advanced' elements of the middle class. This was no new thing, but now the understanding no longer operated under the aegis of the old radicalism but under the banner of socialism, and in a conceptual framework where economics took precedence over politics.

So working-class resistance broke its old shackles and deployed its forces in several directions. Sometimes it chose a trade-union approach and worked out a new anti-capitalist tactic – this was 'the new unionism'. Sometimes it preferred a political approach and rediscovered the path of ideological combat – this was the renaissance of socialism.

In spite of everything one should not minimize the impact of mid-Victorian integration, even though it was incomplete and transitory. There is no doubt that it has profoundly influenced British society right up to our own times by providing a code of conduct that is accepted by all. The resulting consensus included an emphasis upon personal respectability (tinged with puritanism), a predilection for democratic and parliamentary methods (renouncing indiscipline and bursts of violence of a Chartist or Jacobin type), and the adoption of many of the ideals of the ruling classes. Other factors that made for cohesion were the educational system, a common feeling for the monarchy, a touchy patriotism, and frequently an imperialist spirit in full flood. Resistance to integration, on the other hand, was to be found where class consciousness, everywhere powerful, could draw support from regional or national loyalties, especially in the Celtic fringe.

The labour revival at the end of the century, by questioning the inferior status of workers both in society and politics, gave rise to two parallel series of struggles. On the industrial side there were stirrings and conflicts at the shop-floor level. On the political side there was a demand that the working class should have some access to power, first of all in Parliament and eventually in the government. But here was a fundamental split arising out of the existence of the two schools of thought which divided labour strategy. For the majority the supreme instrument for political as well as industrial success was the trade union. Its role was to assure workers' representation in the Commons and at the same time to harry employers ceaselessly, especially by collective bargaining, so as to consolidate gains and achieve new ones. One might add that another function of the trade union was to act as a cultural leaven and help to educate the workers. On the other hand, for a minority that was more guided by ideology, whether of a Marxist or a Fabian kind, the future belonged to political action. This would involve either the foundation of a revolutionary working-class party (which was the Marxist position of Hyndman's Social-Democratic Federation) or the seizing of key positions in parties and institutions that already existed, as much at the municipal as at the national level. The latter was the Fabian thesis of 'permeation', a form of 'agit-prop' preached by Sidney Webb and Bernard Shaw.

Whatever might be their theoretical differences of opinion on strategy, all factions agreed in the short term on the key demands which became the rallying-cries of the 'new unionism' from 1889 onwards. Besides the traditional claims of 'old unionism' (the development of collective bargaining, protection of wages and apprenticeship, guarantees against unemployment) these key demands, addressed to the State and seen by many as a prelude to the abolition of capitalism, were essentially the legal minimum wage and the compulsory 8-hour day. For the latter claim they even invoked historic precedents going back to the ninth century, because, according to legend, King Alfred the Great was the first to have divided the day into three equal parts – work, sleep and leisure! The moderate motto, 'A fair day's wage for a fair day's work', was replaced by the 'four eights' slogan which lasted up to the First World War: 'Eight hours work, eight hours play, eight hours sleep and eight bob a day.'[12]

What gave a special vigour to these claims, rising as they did from the depths of working-class experience, was the improvement which was taking place at the same time in the conditions of the workers. Although the basic results of *laissez-faire* – insecurity, subordination, a hand-to-mouth existence – had not changed, the standard of living rose. In a first phase it rose rapidly, for in the last quarter of a century it progressed from

30 to 40 per cent. This was the result of the unions' stiff resistance to attempts at wage reduction in spite of a fall in prices, but it was also the effect of strong labour offensives, as during the economic recovery of 1888–90. This ended in the important series of strikes that launched the 'new unionism'. On the other hand, after 1900 real wages stagnated, even declined, up to about 1910, in spite of a brilliant economic expansion. A feeling of frustration among the workers was the result, which gave rise to other forms of strife and helped to explain the labour unrest of the years 1910–14.

One is therefore justified in talking of 1880 as the end of the Victorian calm. What Burke contemptuously called the 'swinish multitude' was waking up. Caliban demanded his place in the sun. It was an attitude that carried the germ of Labour's rise and bred a new mentality. Just as one detects a change of outlook in parts of the governing and middle classes who felt uncomfortable in the face of dire poverty, the vanguard of labour, growing in strength, began to revolt against a system of inequality and injustice that condemned the worker to a grey and miserable existence, against the autocracy and arrogant paternalism of the 'masters' with their innate contempt for the 'lower classes'. It was not entirely a matter of ending caste prejudices, though weren't 'respectable' folk still convinced that getting drunk and beating their wives were the two main hobbies of the workers? It was a question of claiming a right to equality of respect and dignity.

Nevertheless, once the process started, the radicalization of the labour movement did not follow a straight course. It worked in successive phases, a style of progress peculiar to all proletarian action, great leaps forward, interspersed with periods of marking time or retreat. So between 1880 and 1914 one can distinguish three stages. The first runs from 1880 to 1892. It was a mixture of ideological renaissance, street demonstrations, union battles and a search for parliamentary representation for labour. The ideological renaissance sprang from a sudden outburst of a new socialist doctrine which transformed the intellectual horizon in a few years. It started with the introduction of Marxism into England by Hyndman in his book *England for All* (1881) and continued with the elaboration of Fabian theories (*Fabian Essays*, 1889). In addition, the severe slump of 1885–7 threw thousands of unemployed onto the streets and led to impressive public demonstrations. Bursting out of the poor quarters of London, howling mobs in rags, such as had not been seen since 1848, spread general alarm and added fuel to socialist propaganda. Up till then the bulk of the workers organized into trade unions had remained quiet under the discreet guidance of the 'old' unionism's moderate leaders, but from 1889 onwards the *avant-garde* with its revolutionary ideas now threw itself into militancy. It addressed itself to new categories of wage-earners who had remained apart from unionism, but had considerable potential for combat. In particular there were the transport workers who had twice in the past, in 1832–4 and 1871–4, tried to organize themselves, but without success. The signal for a push forward by the working class was given by the big dockers' strike in London during the summer of 1889. Unions of unskilled workers were formed all over the country. Between 1888 and 1891, thanks to the 'new unionism', the number of trade unionists doubled, rising from 800,000 to 1,500,000. Finally, the idea of labour representation in Parliament, which had first been mooted at the time of the 1867 Reform Act, gained ground in the labour movement. It made enough progress for an unknown Scottish miner, Keir Hardie, to stand as a candidate in 1888 in a three-cornered contest, and for the first workers' party with socialist leanings to be formed, in January 1893 under the name of Independent Labour Party or ILP.

In 1893 precisely, a second phase in the history of Labour began – a phase of organization and consolidation which led to a new advance, this time in the political sphere. The first event was a large-scale counter-offensive on the part of the employers. Faced with the emergence of a workers' front with vast ambitions running from the new unionism to the ILP, they decided to counter-attack. Their object was to cause a general retreat of the working-class movement by breaking up the young revolutionary trade unions, which they considered to be fragile. But there they made a grave miscalculation, for the move at once boomeranged. Seeing the employers threatening a general and legally backed repression of unionism, even the most moderate trade unions took fright and sprang to the defence of union freedom. The immediate result was the formation of the Labour Representation Committee, or LRC, the actual birth of the Labour Party, whose progress was swift enough to win 29 seats at the General Election of 1906. So by overreacting and striking too hard, the employers only increased the strength of the labour movement. The latter came out deliberately in favour of a parliamentary party as an instrument of pressure on the government and a means of winning more power. But in order to overthrow capitalism and impose a socialist and egalitarian management of the country, even advanced Labour from now onwards confined its activities to winning votes, which meant accepting the rules of the parliamentary game invented by bourgeois democracy. This was an historic choice with immense consequences. Yet although the political strategy did overtake the industrial strategy, it was no substitute since the Labour Party was in fact controlled by the unions much more than by the socialist elements, e.g. the ILP and the Fabians, etc. And, as Pelling has emphasized, the unions, like the rank-and-file workers, were not great ones for socialism.

Here we arrive at the third phase, the rise of syndicalism in the years

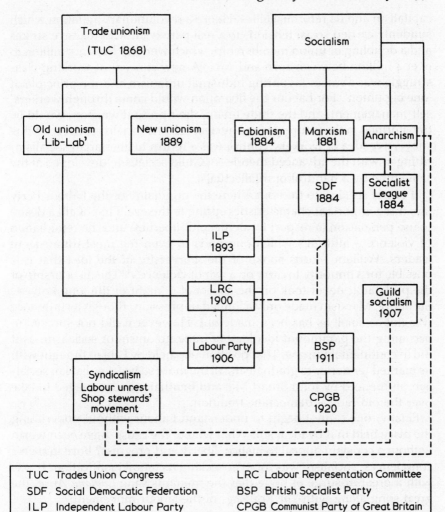

Figure 4. The components of the Labour movement: trade unions, socialist doctrines, parliamentary party

1910–14. Everything contributed to this great labour unrest – the flaccid debates in the cosy atmosphere of Westminster, the impotence of a Labour Party that had broken the old 'Lib-Lab' compromise of the 1870s only to lock itself into a new alliance with the Liberal Party, the mediocrity of the party leaders and in general the contrast between the rapid enrichment of the privileged, who flaunted their wealth, and the shrinking of workers' incomes. That is why a handful of militant syndicalists attracted the support of many wage-earners by an uncompromising opposition to capitalism and its reformist allies. Hence a revolutionary agitation which suddenly carried social tensions to a real paroxysm with massive strikes and a doubling of union membership, which went up from 2.5 million to over 4 million between 1910 and 1914. A new concept of working-class struggle was abroad, favouring industrial unionism and the principle of 'one big union'. For Labour the liberation would come through workers' self-management, and the trade union, their present weapon, would be transformed in the future into the nuclear cell of a socialist society. So this subversive idea of workers' control was a return to libertarian socialism, fitting in with the advanced theories of Guild socialism, developed at the same time by a handful of intellectuals.

If one is seeking to find out where the originality of the Labour Party lay, three important characteristics spring to the eye. First of all, a desire to use persuasion, a respect for democratic liberties, and the repudiation of violence – attitudes which one finds in even the most intransigent leaders. William Morris spoke of the 'perversity of the idea that it is possible for a minority to carry on a war of violence'.[13] The dictatorship of the proletariat never took on the aspect of a 'night of the long knives'. Secondly, Marxism made only a limited impression, though its influence was not as small as has been made out. However it did not succeed in becoming the paramount ideology of trade unionism or socialism, as it did in continental Europe. That position was held by Fabian thought with its marked tendency to gradualism, all the more so because Fabian social- ism, influenced by John Stuart Mill and Bentham, had managed to take over the old radical democratic tradition.

Finally, one cannot begin to understand Labour without underlining the place held in it by idealism. What would 'the cause' have been worth without a constant appeal to justice, liberty and progress? Born in men's consciences, socialism was for ever seeking its moral justification. It was with a great upsurge of hope that the militants sang *England Arise*, the great song along with *The Red Flag*, of the labour movement:

> England, arise! The long, long night is over,
> Faint in the East behold the dawn appear;
> Out of your evil dream of toil and sorrow –
> Arise, oh England, for the day is here.

However if one is to talk of mystical force, one must define the term. Even if Labour was a profoundly religious movement in its origins, it was not, as has too often been suggested, because Wesley had replaced Marx. Socialism had taken the place of organized religion in the souls of many, though in others it had taken root by returning to Gospel principles. For the latter it was without doubt the fulfilment of Christianity, while for the others it was a counter-religion, in the same sense that it was an alternative to current society. But in the eyes of all it aspired to the liberation and flowering of the community, reconciling man with man. In that sense it was a socialism of harmony, rather than a socialism of the harmonium. It was a passionate search for the Holy Grail, a pursuit of truth, a salvation that was spiritual as well as temporal.

All in all, Labour carried a considerable emotional charge. Keir Hardie, contrasting the intellectual socialism of the economists with the day-to-day socialism of the militants, pointed out that for 99 per cent of the ILP members, socialism had the emotional strength of a great religious truth.[14]

Without a shadow of doubt it is at the middle level of the movement that one can best feel the millenarian fervour that carried all its hopes and all its creative energies. In a book of reminiscences a party worker of this kind described the state of mind which he shared with thousands of other pioneers:

> The driving force behind the attack on capitalism was not primarily political ambition nor economic distress, but moral indignation. Those who, like myself, were associated with its earliest phases, were not consciously moved by envy of the capitalist; they were the willing servants of a moral idealism, which aroused in them a devotion and a passion for service, such as had previously been associated only with purely religious movements. The compelling power of the Socialist appeal at that time was extraordinary; it held captive and placed its yoke upon young and old alike . . . It was this creative enthusiasm which gave to the early Socialist movement, and to the Labour Party which was its child, a freshness and a driving power such as Liberalism did not possess, and Toryism could not buy. The young Socialist advocates were not political adventurers; they were preachers filled with the Holy Ghost . . . Without money, social prestige, or political experience, and opposed by the united power of politicians and publicists of the land, they created by their enthusiasm and their faith an organized social force which, in less than two generations, broke the power of Liberalism . . . in the most solidly-based capitalist country in the world.[15]

The slow march of democracy

If one admits that Labour did make big strides, can one say that in 1914 the old world was on the point of crumbling and that bourgeois society was really in danger? In other words, was the old Liberal England, as Halévy and Dangerfield both tried to point out, seriously menaced by a 'workers' rebellion' made even more threatening by its simultaneity with the 'women's rebellion' and the 'Irish rebellion'? In short was the wave of democracy going to engulf everything, starting with parliamentary government itself? As it turned out, the old world fought back, as it had done before. Stubborn on the political front as well as in the sphere of social reform, it controlled and filtered the current of democratization. The cries of alarm at the audacities of the Liberal Government of 1906–14 (pretty mild though they were) should no more deceive us than the lamentations heard some thirty years before at the 'radicalization' of the party, when Queen Victoria described Gladstone as a 'madman' and scolded her ministers saying that Her Majesty 'cannot and will not be the Queen of a democratic monarchy'. Someone else would have to be found . . . [16]

For in the progress of democracy there were certainly two successive periods of advance. One occurred between 1870 and 1885. It was marked by a few measures of social legislation (the labour laws of 1871 and 1875 guaranteeing union rights and peaceful picketing, plus some timid moves in favour of public health and working-class housing) and also by educational development, especially in the field of primary education. But the main progress was made in the political domain. On the one hand there were the important reforms in the electoral system (introduction of the ballot in 1872, extension of the franchise and redistribution of seats in 1884–5, election of local authorities in 1888 and 1894), and on the other hand there was the reorganization and transformation of the political parties. These parties became powerful machines, now based on local branches, so bringing a new balance between the leadership and the rank-and-file. The local workers, whether voluntary or paid, could act and exert influence in a way that had not been possible before. At the same time improved discipline restrained the intrigues and patronage of high-ranking individuals. The result was that, under the double pressure of 'radical' Liberals and Tory 'democrats' (although the latter were often windbags and the former did not carry much weight) the two great parties had to admit new preoccupations. The Liberals were increasingly concerned with the labour question, while social reform and welfare became a *leitmotiv* among the Tories. Finally, democratization made headway at the local level. Self-government on the elective principle had up to then only existed for large towns (since 1835). This was extended to counties in 1888 and to all urban and rural districts in 1894. From then onwards elected representatives, instead of appointed bigwigs (though they were sometimes the same) managed the very large field of local affairs, including in particular, health, the police, sanitation and, after 1902, education.

The second wave of democratization coincided with the arrival of the Liberals to power and the active reforms carried out from 1906 to 1914 by the radical wing which dominated the government. This explains why the accent was now placed on social measures, while political reform remained in the background. Indeed among the many members of the middle classes who were doubtful about the value and effectiveness of classic liberalism, but nervous about the swelling ranks of Labour, radicalism seemed a middle way between the dusty old world of the squires and the messianic aspirations of emancipated labour as represented by the small socialist groups. In short it was a reassuring compromise, for radicalism preached intervention on the part of the State, but guaranteed order and free enterprise. Hence some reforming innovations which shocked the supporters of *laissez-faire*; but hence also some shrewd bourgeois moves calculated to foil left-wing plans for collectivization and thwart all their hopes of winning the support of the masses. So came into being the concept of social services, i.e. State organizations which assumed communal responsibility for rescuing people from misery and guaranteeing a minimum of welfare. It is within this political and intellectual framework, at once ambitious and limited, that we must view the torrent of legislation passed: the introduction of school meals for poor children (1906) and a school medical service (1907), two measures which challenged the hitherto sacred responsibility of the father of the family; the creation of a system of old-age pensions (1908), financed by the State and not by individual contributions; the introduction in 1911 of a wide scheme of social insurance against sickness and unemployment. Other reforms came into being which asserted the principle of the minimum wage, which established labour exchanges, and which controlled housing and town planning (1909).

However we should not delude ourselves about the extent of these reforms. There has been a tendency to equate them with State control or to talk of the advent of the Welfare State. They were only antidotes to *laissez-faire*. Democracy was far from flowing in full flood, either in the political or in the social sphere. In a country which looked like the model of a parliamentary democracy, just after the Reform Act of 1867, only one inhabitant in eleven of Great Britain had the right to vote. In 1913 the figure was still only one in five. Table 3 gives a clear idea of how slow was the spread of the franchise.

Furthermore the 'progressive' democracy of the radicals, though it was based on the principle of State intervention, only aimed to correct the mistakes and weaknesses of liberal society, and not to change its structures. It was basically a question of remedying the feebleness of the feeble, either by legislation or by financial grants, and placing certain limits on the immense power of the strong. It did happen in certain cases that public authorities took the place of private enterprise, in local services and public utilities for example. So, in 1913, four-fifths of the water, two-thirds of the electricity, two-fifths of the gas consumed in England were run municipally, and the same went for 80 per cent of the trams.[17] But these were limited areas – concessions to a pale 'municipal' or 'gas-

and-water' socialism in the Fabian style. Elsewhere, that is to say in 'normal' cases, there was no question of infringing either the liberty of the entrepreneur or the principle of the moral responsibility of each individual. One sees the principle at work when the Liberal Government refused to break with the traditional concept of the Poor Law as defined by the Benthamites in 1834. This was the touchstone. In the course of the great debate in the Royal Commission of 1905–9, while a left-wing minority supported the idea of a system of national assistance that was both humane and adapted to needs, the report of the majority, as adopted by the Liberal Cabinet, persisted in making the poor responsible for their poverty. It considered that pauperism was the fruit of idleness, vice, alcoholism, dirt and immorality. Poverty, it explained, gathered 'in your midst a vast army of people incapable of providing for their subsistence', and living in consequence on the taxpayer's money. As this was the case, the only defensible attitude remained dissuasion: to make assistance so unattractive that only the genuine poor would apply, while the idle would disappear of their own accord . . . So long as this remained the basic idea of a Poor Law, the old order of society certainly held fast.

One last question has to be answered. Who derived the most advantage from this slow march towards democracy? The middle classes or the working classes? As far as social reforms went, it was mainly the working classes, but where political reforms were concerned, it looks as if the bourgeoisie were the winners. Let us look at the forces at the level of

Table 3 Progress of the franchise in the UK, 1830–1930

Date of the electoral register	Registered electors as a percentage of the total population aged over 20 years	Comments
1831	5.0	1832 : first Reform Act
1832	7.1	
1864	9.0	1867 : second Reform Act
1868	16.4	
1883	18.0	1884–1885 : third Reform Act
1886	28.5	
1914	30.0	1918 : Representation of the People Act (universal male suffrage and the right to vote for women aged over 30 years)
1921	74.0	
1927	74.0	1928 : Equal Franchise Act (the right to vote for women from the age of 21)
1931	96.9	

political power and political institutions. In its external appearance the State, still dressed in its feudal trappings, continued on its course under the double guidance of aristocracy and bourgeoisie. But in fact it was less and less dualist because increasingly the aristocracy played a secondary role in politics. Certainly one would continue to see the aristocratic conductor on the box of the chariot of state, but it was the bourgeois coachman who held the reins, while the working horse trotted in front; and from time to time the crack of the whip was heard as a call to order. Even if the alliance of land and capital went merrily forward (in fact one sees a tendency for the owners of land and businesses to close ranks before the rise of 'Red socialism') it was the high peak of bourgeois power that was reached whether the members were recruited from the traditional middle class or from the *nouvelles couches* in full expansion. Politics, press, local government, administration, nearly all the avenues of power were occupied by the middle class.

In the last analysis, the very attacks launched by the radicals against privileges and monopolies served the interests of the controlling bourgeoisie, for these attacks were directed by preference against the traditional enemy – the noblemen and the landlords. When in his turn Lloyd George took up the old battle-cry – The cottage against the castle! The working multitude against the idle aristocrat! – he was accusing landed capital but he was careful not to attack financial capital. It was a strange paradox that these radical campaigns, which turned their rebellious feelings against the landowner in decline rather than against the capitalist, were very widely supported among the electorate for half a century. It was a blessing for the plutocrats to be thus spared and to see the aristocrats paying for democratization. The change in democratic tactics had to await the replacement, after the war, of the weakening radicals by the new Labour Party.

6 The splendour and squalor of a golden age

With an empire covering 12.5 million square miles, inhabited by 450 million people – a quarter of the human race – one might ask why England, having already appropriated the proud Spanish slogan 'the empire on which the sun never sets', did not also adapt to its own use the even prouder motto of the Austrian Habsburgs, AEIOU ('*Angliae est imperare orbi universo'*, England's destiny is to rule the world). Was not her empire, as Joseph Chamberlain proclaimed,' an empire such as no other empire in the world will ever be able to rival, in size, in population, in wealth, in diversity of resources'? One is more inclined to seek a comparison elsewhere – with the Roman empire. For one has to go back to the last days of Rome to find such widespread uniformity of government, institutions, language, even religion, all imposed on peoples so numerous and so disparate. What was there in common between a Newfoundland fisherman and a Ugandan tribal chief, between an Australian miner and a Boer farmer, a Bengali peasant and a New Zealand sheep farmer? Yet the *Imperium Britannicum* majestically affirmed the unity of its civilizing power:

> One life, one flag, one fleet, one Throne!

proclaimed Tennyson. One might even claim that in one sense Britain had the better of the Roman comparison as the propagator of the Christian faith, whose every territorial gain meant a setback for paganism. The missionaries who manned the frontier posts witnessed the edifying spectacle of the 'flag following the cross' – *'nova gesta Dei per Anglos'*.

The imperial idea, which reached its zenith between 1880 and 1914, was a strange compound of widely different ingredients: the will to power, the profit motive, national pride, Christian zeal, humanitarian feeling – an extraordinary mixture of cold calculation and passion, reason and sentiment, all combined in one irresistible thrust. Everything seemed to favour its onward surge. For action, there was the stimulus of international rivalry such as the 'scramble for Africa'; in the realm of ideas, there was the influence of intellectuals and propagandists, the evangelists of overseas expansion such as Dilke, the author of *Greater Britain* (1868), Seeley with *The Expansion of England* (1883), Froude with *Oceana* (1886), Kidd, who published his theories of race in *Social Evolution* (1894) and Kipling, whose *Seven Seas* (1896), *Recessional* (1897) and *The White Man's Burden* (1889) were read by tens of thousands.

Apart from the occasional candid reference to the markets open to exploitation (such as Stanley telling the cotton-spinners of the Manchester Chamber of Commerce that there were 40 million natives beyond the gateway of the Congo only waiting to be clothed) the language of imperialism abounded in idealistic statements. Less was said of trade than of duty and religion. The basic idea was quite simple: the English were a chosen race entrusted with a mission that was both human and divine, and which it was their duty to discharge. In 1894 Curzon dedicated a book 'to those who believe that the British Empire is, under Providence, the greatest instrument for good that the world has seen'.[1] At the same time Rosebery declared: 'We have to remember that it is part of our heritage to take care that the world, as far as it can be moulded by us, shall receive an English-speaking complexion, and not that of other nations.'[2] In other words every inch gained by the British flag meant the advance of civilization. In 1897 an article in *The Nineteenth Century* defined Great Britain's role in the following terms:

> To us – to us, and not to others, a certain definite duty has been assigned. To carry light and civilization in the dark places of the world; to touch the mind of Asia and of Africa with the ethical ideas of Europe; to give to thronging millions, who would otherwise never know peace or security, these first conditions of human advance: constructive endeavour such as this forms part of the function which it is ours to discharge.'[3]

The following year an eminent 'colonial', the Canadian Sir Wilfred Laurier, paid tribute to the mother country in language of unqualified fulsomeness:

Apart from the realm of letters and art – in which in my humble judgement France is her compeer and even her superior – in everything that makes a people great, in colonizing power, in trade and commerce, in all the higher arts of civilization, England not only excels all other nations of the modern world, but all nations in ancient history as well.[4]

After all these professions of faith two questions remain to be answered. Firstly, did imperialism reflect some deep feeling of the whole population? Secondly, to what extent were the outlook and behaviour of the British affected by thoughts of the world beyond the seas? For a clear answer to these questions one must distinguish between three strands of thought which are often confused: imperialism, expansionism and patriotism. These had very differing impacts on people. In our opinion imperialism was a phenomenon of limited appeal, expansionism was widespread and patriotism universal.

Imperialism was an intellectual concept calculated to appeal to the educated. Hence it found its adherents largely among the upper and middle classes – the shapers of public opinion. Conversely the jingoism of the masses has been grossly exaggerated. Even during the Boer War, at the high tide of imperialism, many of the working class and most country-folk remained uninfected by the colonial fever. The champions of 'Greater Britain' ran foul of a deeply rooted pacifism, mistrustful of foreign adventures, backed by the old liberal tradition of the 'little Englanders'. They were faced too with a well-considered suspicion of economic interests forwarded under the guise of colonial conquest, with visions of capitalists eager for gold, land and cheap labour. A further obstacle was simply the complete indifference of a large part of the population, for whom there was one all-important problem – how to get enough to eat, and not to end up in the workhouse. Nevertheless, here and there more pronounced imperialist feelings were to be found: in Birmingham, for example, where Chamberlain's influence was strong, and in cities like Liverpool and Glasgow, where reaction to a large Irish immigrant population took this form, and of course London, the capital of the Empire. Patriotic songs ('Soldiers of the Queen' or 'Sons of the Sea') were certainly all the rage in the music halls, and during Victoria's two jubilees the festive crowds always scrambled to see and cheer colonial troops and other symbols of Empire. But on the whole not too much importance should be attached to such demonstrations. When Engels commented in 1882 that the English working class was only too willing to share the benefits of the country's colonial monopoly, or when Lenin, twenty-five years later, spoke of the proletariat's 'colonial chauvinism', they were simply sneering at working-class leaders and not attempting serious sociological analysis.[5]

On the other hand patriotic pride, so evident even in the peaceful mid-Victorian era, was very pronounced, while the emotional ties that united the British Isles with their overseas possessions were deeply felt in the collective consciousness. One must not confuse this prickly nationalism which pervaded all classes of society with the spirit of imperialism, although they occasionally coincided. Jules Vallès noted with surprise how the feeling of social togetherness arising out of aggressive patriotism could make up for a lack of the most basic necessities: 'They are proud of being English; that's enough. Without a shirt on their backs they find consolation in seeing a scrap of bunting in the wind – a Union Jack; shoeless, they are happy to see the British lion with the globe beneath its paw.'[6] Pride of race, pride in British achievement at home and abroad was enough, without having recourse to abstract theory. Such theory did have its effect, but not as widely as has been made out. 'What should they know of England who only England know?' remarked Kipling, with a hint of arrogance. All the same, many of his compatriots, whose horizon was confined to England alone, might have replied that they were well aware of the nation's dynamic urge to expand, and full of feeling for their brethren abroad.

For three centuries the English had expended a prodigious amount of energy overseas. Emigration and journeyings to foreign parts had for long been part of the life of many families. The Royal Navy and the Merchant Navy, trading stations and missions, all combined to familiarize those who had never set foot abroad with the idea of distant lands. Sydney Smith said that the English had a peculiar genius for establishing garrisons 'on every rock in the ocean where a cormorant could perch'. What lay behind the strength of British expansion in the world, the irresistible drive towards *imperium*, was not the colourful and much trumpeted exploits of the great colonial pioneers, and even less the careful planning of governments and civil servants, but the patient, determined and effective work of hundreds of individuals in different walks of life in different parts of the globe – traders, prospectors, settlers, missionaries, engineers, doctors, the adventurous of every class and breed; in short, just that mass of obscure and enterprising expatriates that Kipling called 'the doers'. It was thanks to their energy, and strength of character, their will to succeed at all costs, and in the face of every sort of difficulty (fever, tropical heat and arctic cold, perils of all kinds) that the colonial Empire spread and consolidated itself. It was the sense of kinship with these often quite obscure pioneers that stirred the hearts of humble folk at home far more than abstract speechifying about the Empire, even though it was this talk that was recorded in the history books, which in their turn confirmed and diffused the imperial creed. Such were the reasons for the country's obsession with overseas expansion, meaning the possession and exploitation of the world's riches, and they gave rise to a thrusting and overbearing self-confidence. One need look no further than this, and a fervent nationalism, for the origins of the colonial obsession.

Inequality: opulence and deprivation

In a celebrated passage in *The Economic Consequences of the Peace*, John Maynard Keynes recalls with undisguised nostalgia the comfortable life led by the English before 1914:

> The greater part of the population, it is true, worked hard and lived at a low standard of comfort, yet were, to all appearances, reasonably contented with this lot. But escape was possible for any man of capacity or character at all exceeding the average, into the middle and upper classes, for whom life offered, at a low cost and with the least trouble, conveniences, comforts and amenities beyond the compass of the richest and most powerful monarchs of other ages. The inhabitant of London could order by telephone, sipping his morning tea in bed, the various products of the whole earth, in such quantity as he might see fit, and reasonably expect their early delivery on his doorstep; he could at the same time and by the same means adventure his wealth in the natural resources and new enterprises of any quarter of the world, and share without exertion or even trouble in their prospective fruits and advantages. . . . He could secure forthwith, if he wished it, cheap and comfortable means of transit to any country or climate without passport or other formality, could despatch his servant to the neighbouring office of a bank for such supply of the precious metal as might seem convenient, and could then proceed abroad to foreign quarters . . . and would consider himself greatly aggrieved and much surprised at the least interference. But, most important of all, he regarded this state of affairs as normal, certain and permanent, and any deviation from it as aberrant, scandalous and avoidable.[7]

Unrestricted travel, unimpeded circulation of gold and goods; domestic comfort and a life of ease; insular superiority in the imperial noonday: such is Keynes' picture of this golden age, symbolized and sustained by the prosperity of the City of London, the citadel of capital. An age of opulence, both coarse and refined.

An age of dash and glitter for the owners of capital. For this favoured group – gentlemen of leisure, captains of industry, merchants, shareholders, members of the professions, with well-invested capital – life was indeed good. All the more so because in the years preceding the war personal savings were accumulating very rapidly. In 1913, lumping together all forms of unearned income, rents, dividends, interest from State and private loans, they amounted to 35 per cent of all personal incomes, against 65 per cent for earned incomes. Firmly based in the City, this amounted to a money oligarchy that extended its tentacles all over the British Isles, down to the modest saver. At the heart of this plutocracy was the City of London, the centre of financial capitalism. As early as 1873 Bagehot could see in Lombard Street, the main artery of the London money market, 'by far the greatest combination of economic power and economic delicacy that the world has ever seen'. City magnates profited very greatly from their role as controllers of the movements of the world's economy. The City's position was thus unique. In the words of Joseph Chamberlain it had become 'the clearing house for the world'. Its heart-beats could be felt in the remotest corners of the earth. At the centre of a huge flow of gold, foreign exchange and commodities, London domi-nated the world market in all the main products of international trade, in bills of exchange and securities. In a world ruled by market forces, the City with its specialized institutions and its huge fund of information controlled the economic activities of the five continents. Financially sup-reme, and with the world's leading currency, the City dominated the machinery of the liberal economy, the free exchange of wealth. Through its management of the tools of free exchange – gold, skilled services, stocks and shares, the commodity markets – the City ensured England's privileged position in the world and enriched those privileged people who ran the system – a system that was to survive with difficulty the stress of war.

Hence the image of splendour left by the high society of the Edwardian period. Years of florid prosperity punctuated by festivities and recep-tions, balls and parties (the period has been arbitrarily characterized as 'the long garden party'). Glamour and ostentation against the opulent background of Edwardian fashion with its profusion of baroque shapes and rich materials – terra cottas, stained glass, mosaics, as well as stone and brick – in rooms festooned with ornate draperies, at tables groaning with food and drink (rarely has so much been eaten as in this period). The era set its mark on a generation, at least on those members of it who were able to enjoy what it had to offer in money, pleasure, travel in a carefree atmosphere of apparently unchecked progress. For those who had lived during this perpetual fireworks display, drifting from the London Season to the amusements of Paris, or from their charming country houses to Monte Carlo or Marienbad, there was no doubt a tendency after a devas-tating war to exaggerate the delights of pre-war existence. All the same, C. E. Montague, a Liberal journalist, well expressed a widely shared feeling in the words: 'Surely there never was any time in the life of the world when it was so good, in the way of obvious material comfort, to be alive and fairly well-to-do as it was before the war.'[8] The sombre character of later years was not the only cause of nostalgia. Even in the ordinary middle classes it came from the memory of the ease and varied amenities of a sheltered life, with steady technical progress, in times of peace. Physical comfort was enhanced by intangible pleasures: the clatter of horse-drawn vehicles, swarms of attentive servants, respectable church-going families bearing prayer-books in white-gloved hands. Such were the tranquil pictures of England before 1914 conjured up by the privileged.

One aspect of the attractions of wealth was the desire to cut a fine figure at all costs. Hence the self-advertisement through ostentatious display (the 'conspicuous consumption' described by Veblen in his *Theory of the Leisure Class*, published in 1899) and extravagant spending on blatantly materialistic enjoyments. The vulgarity of the newly-rich mingled with the refinements of inherited wealth. Beatrice Webb, describing a *soirée* in a millionaire's mansion at the beginning of the century, is irresistibly reminded of the Golden Calf. The sight of such a surfeit of flowers, ornaments, wine, food made her write in her diary: 'There might just as well have been a Goddess of Gold erected for overt worship – the impression of worship in thought, feeling and action could hardly have been stronger.'[9] On her side Lady Dorothy Nevill, the gilded scion of an ancient aristocratic family, complained that money had usurped the place formerly held by wit and good taste (and she might have added birth).[10] The motor-car had become a symbol of the new modes of ostentatious consumption. A luxury object, rarely put to any useful purpose, it served amid noise and dust only to impress the vulgar crowd in town and village (in 1913 there were but 106,000 in use). Mr Toad of *The Wind in the Willows* (first published in 1908) was a typical case. In sum, a frivolous, extravagant and thoughtless society. Witness an exchange of letters between the young Winston Churchill and his mother, the shallow and spendthrift Lady Randolph: Winston, commenting indulgently on the fact that his mother has just heedlessly spent £200 (three years' earnings for a working man) on an evening dress, enough to make quite a hole in her bank balance, ends by simply saying 'the pinch of the whole matter is we are damned poor'.[11]

One did not have to go far, as Churchill well knew, to find the real 'poor'. The majority of the population were not taken in by the ostentation of a small coterie. Life had changed very little for most English people since the mid-Victorian era. It was still a daily struggle for survival, harsh and perilous. Not far above the abyss of poverty in which dwelt the most wretched – the dregs, the chronic unemployed, the tramps and idlers, the perennial workhouse inmates, the beggars and cripples – lived the workers, themselves ever on the verge of pauperism. In the capital of the

Empire on which the sun never set, there was many a household on which it never rose.

The harshness of social inequality had its roots in history. The great void that separated rich and poor was enormously enhanced by the rigidity of social attitudes, to such a degree that the gulf between the 'respectable' favourite of fortune and the manual worker was as deep subjectively as it was in fact. It was based on an inflexible class system, of which there were constant reminders in daily life. In London, for instance, at the entrance to public baths one might read: 'Workmen's baths; cold, 1 penny; hot, 3 pence. Others; cold, 3 pence; hot, 6 pence.' One has only to read the novels of Galsworthy or E. M. Forster to realize the multifarious nature of class distinctions. They could be seen everywhere, in modes of life, clothing and culture. Even physically the differences were striking. On the eve of the First World War, Oxford and Cambridge undergraduates were on average 3.25 inches taller and 25 pounds heavier than the working-class youths from the industrial areas of the Midlands and Lancashire, who were to be conscripted into the army three years later. In the period 1900–10 children in state schools aged 13 weighed on average 6.5 pounds more than children working in factories eighty years earlier. But children of the same age at 'public' schools were 2 to 3 ins taller than the children of agricultural workers. By the outbreak of the Second World War the difference had been reduced by half.[12] The difference in mortality is the most striking. In 1911, infant mortality was 76.4 per thousand in the middle and upper classes; the average for wage-earners was 132.5 per thousand, while for manual workers it was 152 per thousand and for miners 160 per thousand.[13]

Riches and Poverty, Leo Chiozza Money's book, published in 1905, provided some startling facts on the distribution of wealth, confirmed by later statisticians such as Bowley. Dealing with incomes, he drew a line, which he called the 'equator', dividing the British national product into two equal halves. But one half was shared out among 39 million people, while the remaining 5.5 million (12 per cent of the population) shared the whole of the other half of the cake. Ownership of capital was even more disproportionate, since Money showed that 120,000 people (amounting with their families to one-seventh of the population) owned two-thirds of the national capital – a mere handful of individuals with a monopoly of wealth. Extending his research to inheritances (although one-third escaped all or some tax, either through clever financial arrangements, or by fraud) he calculated that the 650,000 poorer people who died each year left bequests totalling £30 million, while fortunes amounting to £260 million were left by the 30,000 well-to-do (of whom 26 alone left property worth the total of that left by the poorer section).[14]

The breakdown of class was roughly as follows: upper class 5 per cent, middle class 15 per cent, lower class 80 per cent. In 1911 the labour force comprised 15 million manual workers (craftsmen, factory hands, labourers, domestic servants, farmworkers, transport workers); the lower middle class included 1.2 million clerks and other office workers, an equal number of tradesmen and shopkeepers, and the greater part of a total of 600,000 employers. In the middle class were to be found the remainder of the employers, businessmen, some tens of thousands of farmers and 400,000 members of the professions, civil servants, directors and managers.

Within the workers' world there were still two levels. The craftsman was far above the ordinary labourer; 'comfortable', 'self-respecting', he earned twice as much. For the proportion of unskilled labour among wage-earners was far higher than it was to be twenty or thirty years later. They formed a large impoverished group suffering all the uncertainties of the labour market. But for wage-earners as a whole the age of Edwardian prosperity meant stagnation and a fall in their standard of living. Between 1900 and 1913 there was no increase in the amount of goods and services consumed by the masses (moreover in this period there was a burst of emigration, 2.5 million people leaving the shores of Great Britain) whereas among the privileged there was glaring evidence of increase in income and well-being. Thus class differences were accentuated. The rich grew richer; the poor stagnated.

To get an idea of popular consumption before 1914 one need only look at an average working-class budget. A typical family of five or six lived on 45 shillings a week (including any possible earnings of wife or children). Of this sum almost half was spent on food; that is 33 pounds of bread and flour, 15.5 pounds of potatoes, 9 pounds of meat and bacon, two pounds of butter and margarine, 5.5 pounds of sugar, a dozen eggs, 9 pints of milk, 0.5 pound of tea, hardly any fruit or vegetables, very little fish, coffee or chocolate. Housing costs (rent, heat, lighting) amounted to 7 or 8 shillings. Seventeen shillings was all that was left for clothing, repairs, beer and tobacco, travel insurance payments, outings and family amusements. In fact the smallest accident could be enough to tip a family over the poverty line. No wonder this was the age of the public house. Wasn't drink the easiest, the most universally accessible way to forget, to escape from grinding poverty, gloomy streets and squalid housing? Beer consumption, on the increase ever since the earliest days of Queen Victoria, reached a record figure at the end of the century – about 3 pints a day per adult male.

Class differences were nothing new. What was new was the increased and lively recognition of their scale and their injustice; and this is what gave social conflict, arising out of labour unrest, its bitter character on both sides of the fence.

Education and class

The historian is faced with three different ways of looking at the history of education in England and its integration into the social structure. One way is to look at its long-term evolution and show how the country moved from a period of wholly private initiative, prior to Forster's Education Act of 1870, to one of public provision. The latter policy, looming up at the turn of the century, has become the accepted way ever since the Second World War. Between these utterly opposed systems – private versus public, local institution versus centralized control, spontaneous versus planned – there has never been war to the death. Accomodation has always been the rule. In this dualism lies the originality of the British system. This is expressed by the co-existence of schools privately founded and funded, often of religious origin, whose uncontrolled growth ('administrative muddle', according to Adamson) reached its height at the end of the nineteenth century and necessitated reform from above, and alongside them schools open to all as a result of increasing State control and involvement in education. This involved the increasing control of education by the central government and resulted in the creation of the Board (later to be the Ministry) of Education in 1899 and three fundamental documents, the three great Education Acts: Forster's of 1870, establishing a system of primary education for all, Balfour's of 1902 and Butler's of 1944. Thus there were three stages: State assistance (1870–1902), State supervision (1902–44), State control (post–1944). The private sector, far from being swept away by successive reforms, managed to survive, though it had to accept partial integration. All this accounts for the complicated though infinitely adaptable structure of the whole system, as well as its comparative independence.

Another way of looking at the subject is to see the school as the battleground of the great religious controversies which shook the country from the mid-century onwards: Dissenters against the established Church, champions of secular as against religious education, Catholics against Protestants, Latitudinarians against Fundamentalists. Every shade of opinion, every cause was involved in the semi-political, semi-theological battle between Churches, sects, pressure groups, and political parties.

A third way of looking at the educational system is to study it in its relations with society as a whole, and the way it embodies the prevailing values of that society. It is on this aspect that we hope to shed a little light. For systems of education both reinforce the structure of society and mirror its features; but in England, more than elsewhere, they have been, and to some extent remain, a decisive cause of inequality.

The basic fact is that there was not just one single system. There were two, functioning independently side by side, but not communicating at all. One was for the élite, the other for the masses. The first was elaborate, expensive, richly endowed and intended for the children of the ruling class; these it received at a tender age in 'preparatory schools', then led them to that key institution the 'public school' where their character received its crucial stamp, then perhaps it led them to a university, probably one of the two oldest, Oxford or Cambridge. The other system, for ordinary children, was rudimentary, brief and free; it turned on the 'elementary' school and finished when the child went out to work at the end of his thirteenth year. This system included the 'Sunday schools', and some technical and higher primary schools. Thus two educational channels existed side by side quite independently, separated by water-tight barriers – a scholastic segregation that both typified and aggravated social segregation. Disraeli's 'Two Nations' remained, becoming (as education progressed) even more rigidly circumscribed and kept apart by an unbridgeable divide. Finally the very slight democratization induced by the spread of popular education in the last third of the nineteenth century was amply offset by the control exercised by the ruling class over the very structure of teaching. It was fruitless to enlarge the house of education if all the best rooms were to be reserved for the privileged, while the masses were relegated to the outhouses and basements. This was why, apart from a little diversification due to increased demand, education kept the same structure as developed between 1840 and 1870 right up to the end of the century, and in many aspects on until the inter-war period.

The public schools were the centre of élite education. Their popularity and their reputation were enormous. In the classic troika – primary ('preparatory school'), secondary ('public school'), higher education (university) – it was the second that really counted; for the public schools were the moulders of the nation's ruling and managing classes. The university was merely complementary, only necessary for those destined for careers in government and politics, the Church, Law and science. But to achieve or to keep one's place among the élite it was essential to have been at the right sort of school. After that one was accepted into the charmed circle, for one was stamped with an easily recognized mark of social superiority. These key centres in the social edifice have rightly been compared to Catholic seminaries. Future leaders were being prepared there for their life's work, and in this lay the originality of the public schools. They aimed at shaping character as well as brainpower, bodies as well as minds, team spirit as well as individuality. In phrases of memorable pride the Clarendon Commission of 1864 praised the merits of these establishments where specifically English qualities were being inculcated; and the same sort of language was being used fifty years later:

. . . their capacity to govern others and control themselves, their aptitude for combining freedom with order, their public spirit, their vigour and manliness of character, their strong but not slavish respect for public opinion, their love of healthy sports and exercise. These schools have been the chief nurseries of our statesmen; in them, and in schools modelled after them, men of all the various classes that make up English society, destined for every profession and career, have been brought up on a footing of social equality, and have contracted the most enduring friendships, and some of the ruling habits of their lives; and they have had the largest share in moulding the character of an English Gentleman.[15]

The public school system itself had its own pecking order. There were two tiers. At the top were the schools frequented by the upper classes – aristocracy, gentry, and upper middle class – shaping them to be the future heads of the Army, the Church of England, senior politicians and the flower of the professions. The majority of young men destined for such exalted futures went to nine great schools, the oldest and the smartest. This 'sacred nine', reformed by the Clarendon Commission (1861–4) comprised seven boarding schools: Winchester (founded in 1382, with the motto 'Manners Makyth Man'), Eton (1440), Westminster (1560), Charterhouse (1611), Harrow (1571), Rugby (1567), Shrewsbury (1552), and two day-schools, St Paul's (1509) and Merchant Taylors (1561).

Ranking below these was a very large number of other public schools. Usually of recent foundation, they were intended for the sons of the middle classes, from among whom would emerge top and middle-ranking administrators, lawyers and businessmen. There were three categories of such schools: (1) grammar (or endowed) schools, ancient foundations which had been modernized in the nineteenth century; (2) proprietary schools (private but non-profit-making, often owned by a collective body), founded after 1840 for middle-class boys and as a kind of riposte to the ancient aristocratic institutions; and (3) some private schools (belonging to individuals who ran them for profit). Among the better known of these public schools for the young of the middle classes (listed by the Taunton Commission of 1864–7) were Cheltenham (1841), Marlborough (1842), Rossall (1844), Radley (1847), Lancing (1848), Epsom (1853), Clifton (1862), Haileybury (1862) and Malvern (1865). Some were of Nonconformist origin, others specifically Anglican, such as Lancing and Marlborough (the latter specializing in taking sons of clergymen). The Roman Catholic schools, Stonyhurst (Jesuit) and Ampleforth (Benedictine), gained considerable reputations. Old grammar schools, such as Tonbridge and Uppingham, were being reshaped, the latter by a great educationalist, Thring, who was headmaster from 1853 to 1887. Two other great educational innovators, who influenced the whole public school system, were Thomas Arnold of Rugby (whose creed was stated in the words 'what we must look for here is (1) religious and moral principles, (2) gentlemanly conduct, (3) intellectual ability'),[16] and following him Sanderson of Oundle (1892-1922). Thus was built up a corporate sense of similar standards and similar ideals among all public schools. These were accepted as such by the attendance of their headmasters at the Headmasters' Conference, which by 1914 totalled 200 schools.

Notwithstanding differences in organization, social status of pupils and constitutional origins, these schools all produced a rather similar type and had very similar teaching methods. The aim they all shared was to inculcate in the future ruling class a common set of standards that emerged from the union of aristocratic and bourgeois values. Aristocratic influence appears in the 'élitism', the strong feeling of superiority and responsibility towards others, the conviction, carefully nurtured, of being a 'natural ruler', and withal a touch of chivalry and religious feeling. The ideal was the Christian English gentleman (so far as the use of both adjectives was not pleonastic!). Godliness and manliness, these were the two basic virtues to be cultivated, but the bourgeois virtues also played their part. For the young had to be prepared for a world of competition and enterprise, so great importance was attached to anything that encouraged competitiveness and personal rivalry, both in the classroom (examinations, prizes, debating societies) and on the playing field (athletics, school matches, and above all cricket and rowing). Although at Rugby in 1870 17 out of 22 hours of study were devoted to the classics, reflecting an aristocratic view of culture, modern subjects that conformed to more material and bourgeois needs were gradually introduced – mathematics, science and modern languages. The moral atmosphere, deriving from a system of 'prefects', group self-discipline and 'fagging', combined a cult of sturdy independence – self-control, courage, stoicism and the 'stiff upper lip' – with an ethic of sociability and 'fair play'. An evangelical exaltation of sacrifice and self-reliance thus went hand in hand with the boosting of each school's highly individualistic spirit. Since the aim was the formation of strong characters, it was constantly rubbed in that life was a struggle, calling for the pugnacious spirit of a medieval baron combined with the ruthless competitiveness of a modern bourgeois. Such was the lesson imbibed at the feet of Thomas Arnold by Hughes, the author of *Tom Brown's Schooldays*. Published in 1857, it became a bestseller, popularizing the current ideals of Rugby among the young. Such too was the atmosphere that pervaded Kipling's novel, *Stalky and Co.* (1899). Later on, his famous poem *If* was to celebrate manly courage as inculcated (with a certain degree of brutality and conformist pressure) in all the public schools of the kingdom.

In deep contrast to this world of education for rulers, organized teaching for the children of the lower classes was designed to instil obedience and acceptance of their lot, and to produce manual workers. The elementary school syllabus aimed at teaching the rudiments needed for performing the basic tasks of an industrial society. Not that every door to the advancement of freedom through education was closed. The tremendous efforts made after 1870 resulted in the opportunity of a place in school for every child of every class, street arab or respectable working class. They created an education that was gratis and compulsory. Truancy was reduced, though the 'half-time' system, common in northern industrial areas, persisted until its abolition in 1918. Another good result was the reduction of illiteracy, and England's record in this was good. By the end of the first half-century, two-thirds of all adult males could read and sign their names. In 1871 the Registrar-General recorded 80 per cent of males and 73 per cent of females able to read and write. By 1897 the number of illiterates had fallen to a mere 3 per cent.[17]

However the mission assigned to popular education was scarcely affected. From the time the education reform of 1870 – school for all – was set in train, to the beginning of the new century, the goal remained the same: to prepare the future worker by providing him with the necessary, but scanty, educational equipment. Hence the themes set out in 1861 by the Newcastle Commission on primary education, when it referred to 'the peremptory demands of the labour market'[18] or, a year later, by Robert Lowe, one of the pioneers of reform, who proclaimed 'we do not profess to give these children an education that will raise them above their station and business in life . . . but to give them an education that may fit them for that business'.[19] One finds much the same sentiments half a century later among the statements of the teachers' union, which, in the middle of the Edwardian era, stated as a self-evident aspect of primary education: 'Six million children are in the public elementary schools of England and Wales. They are the children of the workers, to be themselves England's workers a few years hence.'[20] The inescapable conclusion is that the whole system was avowedly geared to the perpetuation of the class system and social inequality.

It was the same with the Sunday schools, whose pupils came largely from the working class. In 1851 there were 2.4 million registered pupils, with an actual attendance of 1.8 million; in 1887 three out of four children were registered, a total of 5.2 million, with an attendance rate of two-thirds.[21] In these classes the emphasis was on religious instruction, play and general education, rather than on the three Rs, the need for which was by now fairly well met.

In a more positive sense portents of change were beginning to appear round about 1900: a movement towards local colleges of technical and further education; the undoubted growth of secondary education, which was beginning to be penetrated by the lower middle classes; and the birth of adult education, thanks to a triple alliance between the trade unions, the Co-operative Movement and the University Extension Boards, resulting in 1903 in the creation of the Workers' Educational Association. However these fragile innovations did very little to shake the cultural monopoly of the ruling class.

The idea of making education an instrument for planned social mobility was still in the womb of time. The vision of school as a ladder for surmounting the social strata, or as a series of stepping-stones from one sort of learning to another – all these bold dreams had to wait until the inter-war period for their fulfilment.

Sex and death

Nothing throws more light on the deep roots of a society than its attitude to sex and death. The Victorians, faced with these two great and mysterious forces, Eros and Thanatos, chose unequivocally to hush up sex and glorify death. Repression on one side, celebration on the other: a choice dictated as ever by the contrasting fears of the dark forces of creation and destruction. An attitude, one might point out, exactly the opposite of what prevails in England today where, in common with the rest of the western world, death is hushed up and sex glorified – this, too, a panic choice.

A century ago it was certainly difficult to avoid the omniprescence of death. Young and old were struck down, with a mortality rate twice that of today. Innumerable orphans, men and women stricken in the prime of life, mothers dying in childbirth, children in the cradle, a mass of widows and widowers, all helped to conjure up the vision of the abhorred Angel of Death. But as the poor would say, somebody did well out of it – the undertakers. In Great Britain 150,000 infants died annually before reaching their first birthday. Another significant statistic was the count of widows and widowers. The global proportion in the population (about 6 per cent) scarcely changed, but in less than a hundred years the age distribution altered strikingly. (It should be noted that the figure for those in the age group 15–44 would be considerably higher in 1871 were it not for the large number of second marriages.)

Death was not, however, accepted as just an inevitable feature of the daily scene. It was universally solemnized, indeed glorified, as part of the ritual of community life. Hence the scenes described in literature and popular art, interminable agonies, edifying ceremonies with the entire

Table 4 Distribution of the widowed population by age group, 1871–1966[22]

Age group (widows and widowers)	1871	1931	1951	1966
15–44 years	19	10	5	3
45–64 years	42	40	33	27
over 65 years	39	50	62	70
	100	100	100	100

family, children and servants, all gathered round the death bed; the hours spent in death chamber vigils, in lengthy funeral services and visits to the cemetery. Not to mention the deep and interminable mourning, so that, among the favourite colours of Victorian ladies, mauves, yellows and pastel greens, black unquestionably took pride of place. This was especially to be seen at funerals, which were always solemn and sometimes extravagant: huge baroque hearses, lavishly decked out with fancy harness and enormous draperies, followed by processions of mourners swathed in black crêpe veils. Such ostentatious display was not, we may observe, indulged in only by the wealthy. If the deceased was a person of some standing, the family of course excelled itself in funerary pomp; but even among the working classes, where burials were an occasion for colleagues and neighbours to congregate with the double aim of paying homage to the dead and asserting their own collective vitality, a lot of money was spent on the funeral, often the equivalent of several months' pay. Hence the attraction of Friendly Societies. 'Funeral benefits' were a prior charge, so great was the fear among the poor of being unable to afford a decent funeral. Another sign of the eternal presence of death lay in the great theological battles about the after-life which rolled on throughout the century. Controversy raged about the Day of Judgement. In 1853 F. D. Maurice, the Christian Socialist, was deprived of his professorship in the University of London for expressing doubts about the doctrine of eternal punishment. With God portrayed as a pitiless judge, the fear of eternal damnation was widespread, and the flames of hell haunted the humblest imagination.

Sexuality and death were both involved in a curious custom observed by London prostitutes, showing how some ritual traditions survived, more or less underground, into the industrial era. When one of them died, her fellow streetwalkers organized in her honour a funeral like that of a bride who died before her time. The hearse was decked with white plumes and followed by weeping prostitutes cloaked and veiled in black and adorned with white ribbons. The whole cortège would be protected by an escort of pimps to ward off the missiles and jeers of the respectable women of the neighbourhood.[23] For in Victorian and Edwardian England, where bourgeois morals were widely accepted among the working class, either silence or the double standard applied in matters of sex.

Let us begin with silence. Sex was taboo. It was surrounded with inhibitions and disapproval. It was tempting; it was shameful; it was better to say nothing about it. 'Sensual' meant 'animal'. In *Middlemarch*, George Eliot described how Doctor Lydgate's education had developed in him 'a general sense of secrecy and obscenity in connection with his internal structure'.[24] The body was taboo, and nakedness forbidden. Good form required that one should not talk about such things. One spoke of 'limbs', not 'legs', and rather than 'go to bed', one 'retired to rest'. An incredible degree of prudery and hypocrisy was attained. Triumphant respectability was personified in Mrs Grundy. There was some easing up toward the end of the century, but in social life and on the stage the moral code was strictly enforced. To be proved guilty of adultery in a court of law was enough to break a politician, be he as brilliant as Dilke or Parnell. In 1895 Oscar Wilde served a stiff term of imprisonment for homosexuality. Bernard Shaw's play, *Mrs Warren's Profession* (1893), all the more shocking for denouncing cant, was banned from the stage and remained so until 1925.

These prudish conventions drew additional force from their claim to have a spiritual sanction – the glorification of asceticism and chastity. Ideas about sex had undergone a great transposition. The diversion of Protestant religiosity into a narrow puritan morality caused sex to be treated as a secret and rather shamefaced affair, public reference to which was only justified by the legally sanctified production of children in the family setting. The family became the object of universal panegyric. There were, however, a few exceptions to this rigid code which are worth mentioning. Research into oral tradition shows that morals were rather more free and easy in some working-class circles and among country-folk. Language was more direct, and a more natural and permissive view was taken of relations between the sexes and their biological functions.

The alliance between strictness and hypocrisy bolstered the principle of the 'double standard'. This involved the creation of two separate worlds: in one, chastity and family life; in the other, pleasure and the gratification of the instincts. The first was bound up with the inheritance of property, marriage, and the legitimization of offspring. The second provided an outlet for the sexual impulses. The result was a separate set of morals for each sex. A woman was expected to adhere to a code of rigorous purity; chastity was considered to be a natural attribute, so she had to be sheltered from anything that might impair or defile it. Hence the utter contempt for the girl who had been seduced, and the 'fallen woman'. A man, on the other hand, was perfectly free to combine a happy family life with the pursuit of outside pleasures in the company of women from a different social class. The potency of the 'double standard' consisted in the fact that it not only gave a man unfettered freedom, but also satisfied the basic demands of a patriarchal and bourgeois society, where female chastity was enforced with the utmost strictness, while men were permitted any number of extra-marital affairs, so long as inheritances were not endangered. Moreover the lateness of marriage among the ruling classes provided a further incentive for this sort of behaviour. In short, collective morality, by establishing a clear-cut barrier between marriage and prostitution, established also their absolute interdependence.

This is why the seamy side of Victorian and Edwardian society, for long hidden but now fully exposed, served a profoundly logical purpose, instead of simply ministering to the needs of a few depraved and hypocritical characters. London's thousands of brothels and trysting places earned it the name of the 'whoreshop of the world'. It would have been simple to draw a map of its pleasures. Such a map would have stretched from St John's Wood in the north west where the cosy and discreet villas harboured mistresses and demi-mondaines, not to mention various perversions (especially 'le vice anglais' of flagellation), then across to the slum haunts of the port of London, after passing through the whole of the West End. There swarms of prostitutes walked the pavements of Piccadilly, Mayfair and Soho, and it was to these that Gladstone, on his way home from the House of Commons, addressed his exhortations to follow the paths of righteousness. There was pornography for sale, well concealed but now known to have been widely diffused, and a white slave trade, the cause of a resounding scandal in 1885. In fact London ran Paris close for the title 'the modern Babylon'.

The 'double standard' was accepted by many without a qualm. 'A French mistress and an English wife, that's the way to live', said an exponent of the theory to Hector Malot.[25] Lecky, a well-known liberal historian, sang the praise of the prostitute with a frankness verging on cynicism: 'Herself the supreme example of vice, she is ultimately the most efficient guardian of virtue. But for her the unchallenged purity of countless happy homes would be polluted . . . .'[26]

However, besides resort to prostitutes (called 'the great social evil'), there were plenty of other ways of enjoying the pleasures of the flesh. One has only to see the number of girls seduced, mostly servants, but working-class and farm girls too. An interesting sign of class differences in sexual behaviour was that illegitimate births were significantly higher in the West End than in the East End. In the working classes the young man usually married the girl he had put in the family way.

Among the aristocracy the libertine tradition was never quite stifled by bourgeois puritanism, but it was now carried on more discreetly. The middle-class ideal, on the other hand, was the 'blushing young maiden'. Woman was transformed into a sexless figure, and there was a lot of truth in the joke about Dickens' heroines – 'angels without legs'. There was also widespread ignorance of the facts of life. Current prejudices distorted even the utterances of scientists: from Dr Acton who, although he was a reputable scientist, remarked, 'Happily for them the majority of women are not much troubled by sexual desire: the best mothers, spouses and housewives know little or nothing of the pleasures of the senses; their strongest feelings are devoted to home life, children and their domestic duties',[27] down to the learned doctor who, just before 1914, told his students at Oxford: 'Speaking as a doctor, I can tell you that nine out of ten women are indifferent to sex or actively dislike it; the tenth, who enjoys it, will always be a harlot.'[28]

If English society chose to exorcize death by surrounding it with the most elaborate ceremonial possible, it did the opposite when it came to appeasing the demons of sexuality; for here repression was the rule. While the mystery of death was aired in endless discussion about survival – the certainty of the life hereafter and of eternal damnation – the mystery of sex was buried in silence. An extraordinary contrast with the England of today. Obscenity has a new meaning: yesterday it was sex, today it's death. Publicity a new object: yesterday death, today sex.

Up till 1914 change came slowly, but, as belief weakened, death became secularized. Cremation was becoming more common, but burial services changed very little. Soon the holocaust of 1914 provided an unexpected chance for funeral pomp at countless ceremonies in which patriotic fervour was combined with a desire to honour the absent dead. The more rapid change in sexual behaviour owed less to new-fangled theories, such as those of Havelock Ellis, the pioneer of sexology, than to social pressures and the struggle for female emancipation.

The end of *Pax Britannica*

Safe in their island world, immune to invasion, the British had enjoyed a peaceful century. True, it was not entirely peaceful, since there had been quite a spate of colonial wars, nicknamed 'Queen Victoria's little wars'. Most of these had been expeditions rather than wars. Only two had been of any seriousness, waged against foes of some size and strength and engaging the attention of the whole nation: the Crimean War and, fifty years later, the Boer War. In spite of heavy casualties (largely due to sickness) most people saw these campaigns as nothing more than routine punishments administered to bring temporarily recalcitrant partners to reason. After 1905 the clouds began to gather in Europe, but the carefree mood continued. Even on the morning after Sarajevo, Monday 29 June 1914, the *Daily Mail* carried the headline, 'The best week-end of the year', and quoted 'the general verdict of holiday-makers' returning from sea-side or country, speaking in euphoric terms of 'the golden sunshine and the elastic quality of the air' on that gorgeous Sunday. Who could dream that the English might soon be involved in a European war?

Ten years had passed since England had begun to lose her comfortable and advantageous position of non-involvement. For a hundred years her European policy had been based on two factors which she had manipu-lated with consummate skill – the strategic position of Britain as an island, and the multipolar system on the Continent. The Foreign Office had devoted all its skill to keeping this situation in equilibrium. Eternal vigil-ance and incessant effort were needed to keep the balance of forces and remain in an independent but commanding position. The idea behind this exercise in geopolitics was that 'the key to success in diplomacy lay in freedom of action, not in a system of formal alliances' (as Henry Kissinger remarks in his book on Metternich[29]). This kind of freedom gave more protection than an alliance, for it left all options open against the day of need. It had given the English a strong sense of security which lasted right up to the outbreak of war, and even after. The web of arrangements woven by Palmerston, Salisbury, Lansdowne and Grey seemed to hold fairly well, and when cracks began to show they were gradually patched up. The *Pax Britannica* had lasted so long, and people were so proud of its many successes over the century that they thought it could last for ever. Admittedly 'splendid isolation' had had to be abandoned at the begin-ning of the century. Faced with the threat offered by dynamic German imperialism to their naval and economic supremacy, England had signed an *entente* with France and had even held staff talks. The Triple Entente with Russia had also been formed. But even though English diplomacy had changed course decisively, and prudently, in moving towards a military alliance in Europe, the nation remained psychologically an island, its gaze fixed on distant seas. There were very few capable of believing that some day soon the country might be dragged into a great Continental war.

In other words the British continued to see themselves as a race apart. They felt no need to boast about this, or give themselves airs about their insular carapace, or behave condescendingly towards other countries. It was simply that for them *Pax Britannica* was upheld by three apparently indestructible forces: the sea, the fleet and the Empire. The first was a force of nature, the other two were forces of their own creation. This was why Germany's new naval ambitions not merely alarmed a people that firmly believed 'there could only be one ruler of the waves,' but shook their whole sense of national security. As Churchill said in a speech in

1912, a fleet was a necessity for Britain, but a luxury for Germany. It was the British Navy, he said, that made Britain a great power, while Germany was already a great power, respected and honoured all over the world, before she had a single ship.[30] Such was the pride and affection in which the Royal Navy was held; and such were the reasons behind the enthusiastic support from all parties – Conservative, Liberal and even Labour – for a massive shipbuilding programme aimed at maintaining Britain's naval supremacy. In July 1914, a few days before the outbreak of war, the crowds were treated to the thrilling spectacle of a 45-mile long line of warships at Spithead, the most formidable concentration of sea-power the world had ever seen.

With its many peoples, its great material resources, its political unity, the Empire stood as the pledge and symbol of a power that stretched across the world. The British were utterly confident in its strength, its permanence, its ability to stand up to any shock – an assurance well expressed in George V's message to his people at the outbreak of war: 'I shall be strengthened in the discharge of the great responsibility which rests upon me by the confident belief that in the time of trial my Empire will be united, calm and resolute and trusting in God.'[31]

But in spite of eloquent statements and bellicose cries of 'Down with Germany!' from excited crowds, there was deep anxiety. It was the end of *Pax Britannica*, the end of *Pax Europaea*. 'The lamps are going out all over Europe; we shall not see them lit again in our lifetime', said Lord Grey on 3 August, and when Britain's ultimatum to Germany expired, the mood changed from *insouciance* to stupefaction. Behind the almost forgotten shadow of war lay a terrifying plunge into the unknown. That afternoon, in a peaceful country village, a farmer's wife drove her pony-cart to the nearest market town to read the latest telegrams pinned up in the post office. She returned in the evening and told her husband the gist of what she had read. After a long silence, her husband, a veteran countryman, a self-made man of independent and pacific opinions, made this prophetic utterance: 'Now nothing will ever be the same again'.[32]

III *Through Storms and Crises to Recovery: 1914–55*

7 *The search for security and stability*

Twentieth-century blues

> And England over
> Advanced the lofty shade . . .

The shadow that A. E. Housman saw looming up over England was not just the shadow of war, for other clouds were piling up in Albion's sky. The year 1914 saw the beginning of a long and troubled period for English society. For forty years there was one shock after another, and it was not until the early 1950s that the country found a tolerable way of life again, social, economic and international. This is why we have chosen to organize this book in a rather unusual way as regards dates. For these forty years seem to us to have a definite unity. Through wars, depressions and reconstructions we watch the birth of a new society – a society in search of self-improvement, dominated on the one hand by the fight against poverty and on the other by its changed status in the world. At first the troubled islanders try to resist the forces of change; then, slowly adapting to them, they find their efforts faced with further crises. Finally peace is restored (the peace of the 'cold war') and prosperity returns (the dawn of the 'affluent society') with a new and rather precarious harmony established between classes, based on a remodelled distribution of wealth and power. Throughout the period, English society, armed with the traditional values and community feeling that permeated all classes, managed to resist the forces of disruption. These forty years fall between the easy and sheltered pre-1914 period and the mid-1950s, when consensus starts to crumble.

Right up to the First World War, England had enjoyed fortune's favours to an extraordinary degree. Geography and history had combined to shower her with so many blessings that her people had come to see themselves as divinely set apart. Thanks to their island home and their industrial and technological primacy, they had benefited from the incomparable advantages of immunity to invasion, civil harmony, a stable constitution and relatively high personal incomes (in 1900 average incomes were, for the British £43, the French £35, the Germans £30, and the Italians £17[1]). But now the English were reduced to the ranks. The crises of the twentieth century meant the end of their privileged position; and there was worse in store. Under the pressures of war (the 'locomotive of history', as Trotsky called it) movement prevailed over stability. Victorian society, and in many respects Edwardian as well, was founded on a well-defined social order with a fixed division of labour, and with the classes and the sexes knowing their proper roles. This state of affairs, already being called into question by 1900, was roughly shaken by the internal and external blows of war. The period of 'established disorder' began. The good ship Albion ran into rough seas, and fearful efforts were needed from her crew to pilot her through to calmer waters, where there might be at least a partial return to balanced order.

To begin with, the atmosphere had changed considerably in this country which once seemed a model of tolerance and conformity. International discord was reflected in increasing tension at home and in a general scepticism about established institutions. In 1929, after describing several generations of Forsytes, Galsworthy remarked ironically: 'Everything being relative now, there is no longer absolute dependence to be placed on God, Free Trade, Marriage, Consols, Coal, or Caste.'[2] Social and political change was accompanied by bitterness and achieved through brutal and vindictive confrontations. Fear of 'Reds' and 'workers' control' had taken the place of fear of the 'mob'. The political demands of Labour were to split the traditional party system which had provided government by the right and left wings of the middle-class set-up in turn. Two decades were to pass before the almost total elimination of the Liberals restored the old bipartisan game. Liberalism was in full retreat, both as an ideology and as an attitude. It seemed ill-adapted to modern needs which called for organization, regimentation and interventionism. Despite the protests of individualists the State, like a new Leviathan, was gradually interfering more and more in every aspect of life. The public resented this, preferring to trust to instinct and the amateur spirit. Improvisation and 'muddling through' were a national sport raised to the level of a fine art. After 1940 there was a change: planning and rationalization began to infiltrate ministries, local government, big business and industry. Technocracy was looming up. Little by little England adapted herself to the constraints of the modern world. Above all, in the second post-war period, she managed to widen the social basis of power and wealth. The result was a mitigation of social unease and a movement towards a less divisive, more conciliatory society – one that, in its own different way, recalled the harmony and integration of the latter half of the nineteenth century.

In spite of the traumas experienced by Britain in the twentieth century – the trenches, the blitz, the hunger marches, rearmament, the atom bomb, the shedding of the colonies, not to mention the impact of new inventions such as the cinema, the motor-car, psychoanalysis – there remained an internal strength sufficient to withstand the rudest shocks. There was an extraordinary cohesive force in the common fund of values which throughout history has been shared by the whole British community, regardless of political, religious or intellectual differences. When faced with a really serious crisis the English have recourse to their own unique form of defence, that of a national consensus. This was in striking contrast with the other great European nations, none of whom survived this period without domestic upheaval and even bloodshed. Once more England achieved peaceful change steadily without civil disturbance, slowing up from time to time, but never breaking down.

British consensus had three strands: political, national and moral. Politically, in spite of the decline of the Liberal Party, the English remained as attached as ever to individual liberty and parliamentary democracy. In the age of totalitarianism they remained totally unaffected, to the extent that even the strains of ruthless total war were not allowed to diminish the fundamental rights of citizens. With a stubborn confidence in representative government they never ceased to feel the same pride in and respect for the British constitution as did Bagehot and Mr Podsnap in the days of Queen Victoria – in somewhat different language. The same consensus existed at the national level, and under the threat of war there was no need of bellicose slogans to evoke a spontaneous and universal patriotism, combined with a condescending attitude towards foreigners. The nation's history bore witness to this consensus, and every Englishman was imbued with a sense of it; indeed there was almost an official version of it permeating works of scholarship, textbooks and newspapers. More generally, the institutions – schools, Civil Service, local government – perpetuated this feeling of civic community guided by tradition and the common weal. This nourished a powerful attachment to a firmly defined set of rules, observed by all, yet leaving people with a feeling of complete freedom of action. Finally, on the moral plane, the consensus drew strength from ancient Christian and evangelical sources. Even though the Churches' influence had declined the moral message of revivalism remained, either in its Anglican form or in an occasional resurgence of the Nonconformist conscience.

So, one asks, was the England of 1950 so very different from the England of 1920? In other words, did society change fundamentally in those years of instability? One must not be deceived by false appearances. Denis Brogan once said, with penetrating wit, that to 'change anything except the *appearance* of things is the favourite English political method'. This saying can equally well be applied to social change. Deciding what is actually going on – change or immobility, speed or gradualism, disruption or continuity – depends on the viewpoint and, in the end, on the character of the onlooker. At the end of the period a remark in John Osborne's play *Look Back in Anger* throws a vivid light on the foregoing analysis. Alison, the wife of the violently anti-social hero, says to her father, a retired colonel: 'You're hurt because everything's changed. Jimmy's hurt because everything's the same. And neither of you can face it.'

For King and Country: from Flanders' mud to the disillusion of peace

When England declared war on 4 August 1914, it was, to a far greater extent than for the other combatants, a profound break with the past. The liberal way of life, an insular independence, a tradition of peace, all were threatened. The country was unprepared for war, militarily, economically, and psychologically. The British Army consisted of 250,000 men, dispersed all over the world, and the actual expeditionary force sent to France only amounted to 100,000 men. But within a few months the huge machine was functioning and the peace-time industrial economy was mobilized for war. State control replaced *laissez-faire*. In 1916 conscription was imposed. Nine million men were called to the colours (6 million from Great Britain, 3 million from the Empire). It soon became clear how high the stakes were – total victory or annihilation – so that victory could only be won at the cost of a gigantic, almost superhuman effort by the entire nation. Everyone was struck by the apocalyptic nature of the conflict. Some years later, Winston Churchill, in his book *The World Crisis*, recalled its unmitigated violence. The 'Great War', he wrote, had no parallel in history: it differed from all previous wars because of the terrible power of the weapons of destruction employed. The rights of civilians and neutrals were brushed aside. Merchant ships, public buildings, hospitals were shelled or bombed. Poison gas, aerial bombardment, blockade – no weapon was too awful to use. 'In short', he concludes, 'all the horrors of all the ages were brought together.'[3]

It was those actually engaged in the fighting who were the first to realize with anguish that a relapse into utter barbarism was taking place. Their sort of war had nothing in it of 'the sport of kings', as Arnold Toynbee described ancient warfare.[4] For a whole generation the memory of the front remained a frightful nightmare that haunted them for years to come, right up to the outbreak of the Second World War. The whole country was shaken by the stream of pictures and descriptions of the horrors of the front line. How could they ever forget that for four years tens of thousands of their fellow-countrymen had lived in bestial discomfort, in muddy trenches, verminous, exposed to all kinds of weather, risking their lives daily? It was a war fought by the infantry ('the man in the street dressed as a soldier', in the words of Paul Valéry[5]) crouched on the ground, constantly on watch, bombarded and shelled, and in attack lacerated by barbed wire and slaughtered by machine guns. For 'Tommies' and their families the names of obscure places in France and Belgium suddenly acquired a sinister fame. Those peaks of suffering and sacrifice – Ypres and Loos, the Somme and Passchendaele, Vimy and the Chemin des Dames – were the scene of terrible carnage. On the first day of the Battle of the Somme British casualties were 57,000, of whom a third were killed. At Passchendaele in 1917 they reached a quarter of a million, for an advance of five miles.[6]

> England mourns for her dead across the sea . . .
> Fallen for the cause of the free,

so Laurence Binyon in his famous poem, words often inscribed on the memorials erected in every town and village after the war;[7] while in many an overseas cemetery, devotedly maintained by the Imperial War Graves Commission, one may find the words of Rupert Brooke, himself a casualty of the Dardanelles expedition:

> If I should die, think only this of me:
> That there's some corner of a foreign field
> That is for ever England.

Every year at 11 o'clock on 11 November during the inter-war period the whole nation was to honour the memory of its dead. All work, all movement stopped for two minutes in memory of the 723,000 men cut down in the prime of life between 1914 and 1918.[8]

Britain began the war in a mood of wild patriotic enthusiasm and impressive national unity. In the face of a foreign enemy all divisions were forgotten, all shades of opinion were merged in the conviction of the rightness of her cause. Yesterday's revolutionaries, Marxists like Hyndman, trade-union leaders like Ben Tillett, all unhesitatingly supported the war. Recruits poured in, from the green fields of Tipperary and the mining villages of Wales no less than from Oxford colleges and East End slums. The pacifists, swamped by patriotic fervour, formed a small group apart, isolated, ostracized, abused. Pacifism drew such strength as it had from three sources: Cobdenite radicalism, the Nonconformist conscience, and the Labour movement. But it had little influence on public opinion. To the bitter end of the long conflict national solidarity was to prevail over all appeals to international class feeling or the unity of the Christian world. People were not inspired by patriotism alone. From the very first morale was sustained by moral feelings, the absolute conviction that England was fighting for a just cause. To help little Belgium was to stand up for the right, for justice and civilized values. Writing from the front just before he was killed, a young officer explained to his parents that he could not have a more fitting death: 'You . . . will know that I died doing my duty to my God, my Country and my King.'[9] After a time the appalling bloodshed caused some to doubt these certainties. In the hell of the trenches the 'Tommy' stood fast; he stuck it down to the last minute, but with increasing doubt and with the feeling that the whole war was absurd, a grotesque reversion to barbarism. Disgust and lassitude were voiced by the poet Siegfried Sassoon, and Wilfred Owen's melancholy lines bewail

> The pity of war, the pity war distilled.[10]

Another soldier confessed that 'any faith in religion I ever had is most frightfully shaken by the things I've seen'.[11] As for the rank and file, their philosophy was summed up in the words 'fed up'.

In spite of universal exhaustion and longing for peace, people's hopes and expectations were dashed when peace actually came. The return to civilian life and the adaptation to the daily round seemed fraught with difficulty and frustration for the homecoming warriors. Some found unsatisfactory employment, others none at all. They had been treated like heroes: Lloyd George had promised them 'homes fit for heroes', and now they felt ignored and treated like dirt. The ideas of universal brotherhood and prosperity they had cherished in the trenches were, for all their altruism, found to be hopelessly anarchic and at odds with the most elementary political and diplomatic realities. The depth of their disillusions showed how lofty had been their illusions. Everyone dreamed of peace and concord, but in the 1920s international relations were ill-tempered and insecure, while the 1930s brought wars of nerves and the beginnings of aggression. How remote seemed the popular slogans of 1914–20, and how mocking in retrospect: 'the war to end war', 'never again'. The sad lines of Herbert Read written in 1940 reflect the tragic disenchantment of the old soldiers:

> We gave what you will give – our brains and our blood.
> We think we gave it in vain. The world was not renewed.

There was hope in the homestead and anger in the streets
But the old world was restored and we returned
To the dreary field and workshop, and the immemorial feud
Of rich and poor. Our victory was our defeat. . . .[12]

If in the world at large the sacrifice of so many lives appeared to have
been in vain, since neither peace nor security had been gained, internally
the bitter aftermath of war and its attendant vexations were graver still.
No new day of justice and prosperity had dawned; on the contrary, a
general feeling of gloom pervaded the whole of society. As Lewis Namier
well said, 'it is not a generation which seems to have perished in the last
war, but an atmosphere, an inspiration, an *élan vital*'.[13]
This was mainly because so many people thought life would go on just
as it did before the war, or rather better. Yet as early as 1919 Keynes had
warned his fellow countrymen with contemptuous lucidity that instead
of realizing that

an age is over, we are busy picking up the threads of our life where we
dropped them, with this difference only, that many of us seem a good
deal richer than we were before . . . We look, therefore, not only to a
return to the comforts of 1914, but to an immense broadening and
intensification of them. All classes alike build up their plans, the rich to
spend more and save less, the poor to spend more and work less.[14]

Furthermore when one considered how thin was the veneer of civilization, how enfeebled the economy, how embittered the state of industrial
relations, one began to lose confidence in the marvels of progress and
science; and belief in Britain's primacy was beginning to shake. John
Bull's self-assurance was far from dead, but the days of 'England *über
alles*' seemed to have faded and a mood of misgiving had supervened.
T. S. Eliot's *The Waste Land* (1922), expressing the anxiety of a country
threatened with ruin, is symbolic of the feeling of the age.
Deliverance from sudden death had also induced moods of hectic
gaiety, frantic affirmations of the search for life and pleasure after all the
privations and sacrifices of war. One need not take too seriously as a
portrait of the age the misleading and superficial literature of 'the roaring
twenties' with its giddy and snobbish characters – Noel Coward's 'bright
young things'. But fundamentally and in a less garish way the moral code
was changing at all levels of society. The straitjacket of puritanism was
loosening, and the audience for the admonitions of the Church was
smaller. In spite of the seriousness of industrial troubles and the stagnation of the economy, a novel factor now appeared – a strong urge towards
hedonism.

Economic vicissitudes

At first sight the balance sheet for the economy bears a rather negative appearance, and contemporaries painted a pretty bleak picture of England at this time. In a period which endured two world wars within twenty years, with economic dislocation after the first one and an arduous industrial reconstruction after the second, it is hardly surprising that Britain's standards of living and international status should have diminished, or that destruction and loss should have deeply shaken the nation which had recently been the richest in the world.

There was however a more serious ailment. A whole chorus of Jeremiahs at home and abroad rose up to denounce Britain's fatal economic apathy and her degenerate lack of dynamism. One of the severest of her numerous critics was the French writer André Siegfried in his well-known book, *England's Crisis* (1931). Employing a semi-economic, semi-psychological technique in his analysis of Britain's decline, he concluded that, having got thoroughly set in the comfortable habits of her pre-eminence, she had let success lull her to sleep and had lost all sense of the need for effort. Consequently she had become one of the spent powers, and to indulge in complacent optimism would simply lead to worse disappointment. Siegfried gave Britain credit for craftsmanship and know-how, but wages were too high: a comfortable existence and easy money had impaired her traditional qualities – energy and the spirit of enterprise. From his rather puritanical viewpoint Siegfried saw thrift supplanted by idleness, and echoed the alarm sounded much earlier by George V, 'Wake up, England!'

Siegfried's view now seems rather outmoded, and nobody would repeat them word for word today. All the same there were good reasons for pessimism. In the first place there was simply the damage resulting from the two wars, particularly the 1914 war. It is pointless to indulge in utterly conjectural calculations of the actual costs of the war (someone once worked out the monetary value of every dead soldier, a British corpse being valued at $4,140 – double that of a Russian![15]). One can only emphasize the vulnerability of the British economy, based as it was on trade, i.e. exports and financial liquidity. Any large-scale international conflict was bound to cause catastrophic dislocation of trade. T. C. Barker, comparing the situation of France with that of England, maintained that though the former had suffered far more heavily in loss of human lives, England had been harder hit in terms of her delicately balanced economy.[16] The brutal and unexpected shock of war had disorganized world markets, interrupted the attempts to adjust to the pre-war developments of the world economy and given a boost to England's rivals, the USA and Japan (the 'England of Asia'), who had stepped in and smartly grabbed much of her share of world trade.

1

2

3

4

847 Liverpool Railway Station

5

6

THE GREAT SOCIAL EVIL.

TIME:—Midnight. A Sketch not a Hundred Miles from the Haymarket.

Bella. "AH! FANNY! HOW LONG HAVE YOU BEEN *GAY*?"

7

8

EXCELSIOR!

SUFFRAGIST. "IT'S NO GOOD TALKING TO ME ABOUT SISYPHUS; HE WAS ONLY A MAN!"

9

10

11

12

13

14

ERDAY–THE TRENCHES

16

DAY–UNEMPLOYED

15

17

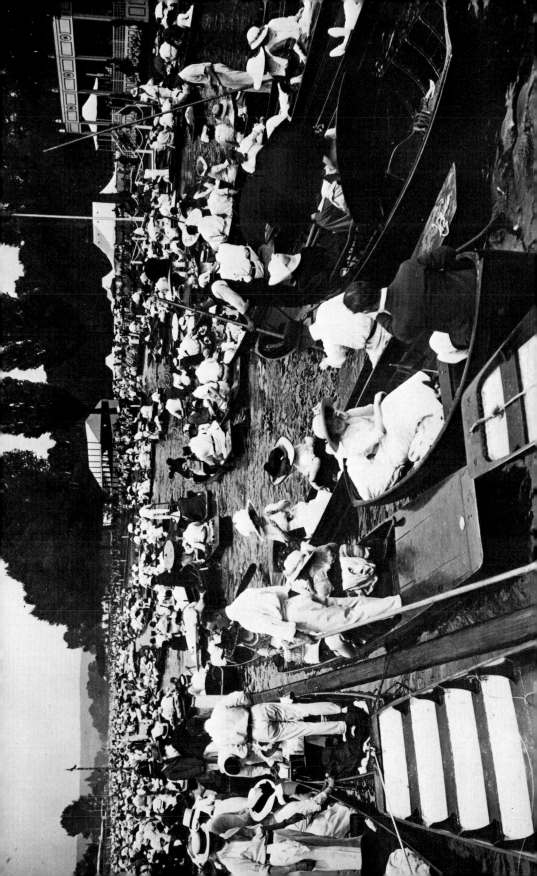

21

22

23

24

25   26

27

28

29

30

31

32   33

34 overleaf →

In 1918 most people thought that return to peace meant a return to a pre-war way of life, a form of blindness that also afflicted those who directed economic policy. They thought that by restoring the role of sterling as the pre-eminent international medium of exchange Britain could resume her traditional function of international broker. So the pound was revalued in 1925 in order to help the financial and commercial activities of the City of London. But a return to the gold exchange standard and the convertibility of the pound meant not only choosing to make profits on the world money market at the expense of industrial production, but assuming presumptuously that nothing had happened in the world since 1914 – a serious political error which raised production costs for industry, damaging exports and creating unemployment and industrial stagnation. This lasted until the Great Depression forced Britain to face facts by devaluing the pound by 30 per cent and abandoning free trade, which was a grave shock to confidence.

A further cause for anxiety was the decline of Britain's traditional bases of prosperity. The activities which had been the most flourishing all through the nineteenth century were now the most menaced. The three 'giants' of Victorian industry – coal, textiles and shipbuilding – were now in jeopardy. Coal production fell from 287 million tons in 1913 to 227 million in 1938, at which date there were 400,000 fewer miners than in 1923. In 1913 the shipyards produced a million tons of shipping, in 1938 only half a million. Cotton was the worst hit part of the textile industry. In 1913 yarn output was around 2,000 million pounds of thread; in 1930 it had fallen to 1,000 million, though by 1937 it was 1,400 million.[17] Those regions which had formerly been the most productive – Lancashire, the North East, South Wales and Central Scotland – became 'distressed areas', later to be euphemistically rechristened 'special areas'. Enforced idleness and poverty were widespread – scenes of desolation evoked by W. H. Auden:

Get there if you can and see the land you once were proud to own.
Though the roads have almost vanished the expresses never run:
Smokeless chimneys, damaged bridges, rotting wharves and choked canals . . .[18]

Poverty like a leaden cloak enveloped large parts of the country: their inhabitants felt doomed and without hope. England was ravaged by massive unemployment on a scale hitherto unknown. Throughout the entire inter-war period unemployment never fell below one million (one worker in ten) and in 1932 it reached the record figure of 2,700,000 (one worker in five). In that year more than a third of all miners were unemployed, 43 per cent of cotton workers, 48 per cent of iron and steel workers and 62 per cent of shipyard workers.[19] Comparing the years

1921–38 with the period 1856–1914, when unemployment averaged between 2 and 10 per cent of the nation's workforce, Beveridge concluded that for the inter-war period this evil had been 'just about three times as severe as before the First World War'.[20]

So the 1930s saw the demise of the traditional British economy – the system that had prevailed since the great 'take-off' of the Industrial Revolution and the invention of the railway. It meant the end of *laissez-faire* and free trade, the advance of State intervention, the assumption by governments of the defence of the currency and the protection of industry, the revival of agriculture and the use of income tax as an instrument for regulating society and the economy. The Victorian Age was well and truly dead. At the same time there were plenty of encouraging signs of change and adaptation to new conditions. The picture was not so black as has been painted and these dismal accounts (recently submitted to 'revisionist' criticism, itself perhaps carried too far) should give way to a more balanced view that takes account of both decline and revival.

As early as 1933 J. B. Priestley in *English Journey*, an acute piece of reportage on the English scene, had thrown a vivid light on these contrasts, this diversity which was so characteristic of the country, plunged as it was in the throes of the Depression. His conclusion, which became famous, was that there were three different Englands. First there was the old country of history, the England of cathedrals, manor-houses, ancient churches, thatched cottages: 'old England', green and peaceful, far from the madding crowd, just as it existed in the guides and history books. The squire and the parson were always in the forefront, and on the whole it did not seem to have changed much since the days of Shakespeare and Goldsmith. The second was the England of nineteenth-century industrialism, of coal and iron and cotton, machinery, railways and ports trading with the world. This was an England blackened with soot, with rows and rows of murky little houses, broken by occasional chapels in Victorian Gothic, Renaissance town halls, Mechanics' Institutes, fish and chip shops, railway stations and grill-rooms, gasworks and factory chimneys. Its streets were sad and dull, full of the sound of factory sirens and the clatter of trams. This was where one found the slums. But in spite of the soot and the ugliness, it had an impressive character of a sort and its own tradition. Finally Priestley's voyage of discovery led him to delineate a third England, that of the twentieth century. This was sprouting up all over the place, unplanned and shapeless. New factories, gleaming and white like exhibition halls, shiny petrol stations along by-pass roads, enormous cinemas and dance-halls, thousands of little semi-detached houses – and advertisement hoardings everywhere, for this was the age of publicity. A symbol of this new Americanized England was the ubiquitous Woolworth, itself a symbol of cheapjack commercialism, of stan-

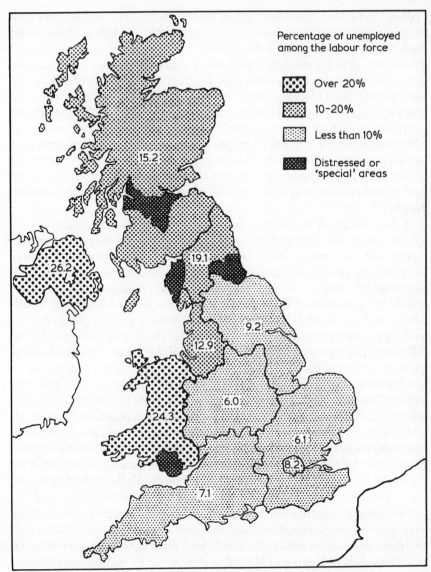

Map 6.   Unemployment in the UK, 1937: regional contrasts

dardized and depersonalized mediocrity. After describing these three aspects of his country, Priestley finds a fourth one, 'the England of the dole'. Where the scourge of unemployment is at its worst, nothing is to be seen but dejected and disheartened faces, and this usually where there was once the most activity. In short, the 'nation's tragedy'.[21]

However the paradox of the inter-war period was that, beside the 'palaeo-industrial' sites doomed to decay, there were new sectors constantly expanding. Ever since the war the former workshop of the world had been specializing and diversifying, so that there were pockets of prosperity side by side with distressed areas. What was extraordinary was that mass unemployment was accompanied by a rapid rise in the average standard of living, since the wages of those actually at work and the salaries of the middle classes rose proportionately with productivity and the growth of the economy. Between 1920 and 1938 the rise in national product was 2.1 per cent per annum, similar to that of 1870–1913 which was 2.3 per cent. Gross domestic product rose by 2.3 per cent in the years 1924–37 as against 2 per cent in 1856–99. Output per head grew by one third between 1924 and 1935, i.e. more rapidly than in the Victorian heyday.[22]

A fact of capital importance was that, right across the British Isles a geographical redistribution of industries and people was taking place. The north and south poles of development were being completely reversed; for the traditional centre of industry was in decay, while a new one was growing up. In 1924 half of the national output had been produced in Lancashire, West Riding, Northumberland-Durham, South Wales and the Scottish Lowlands. By 1935 these regions were producing only 37 per cent of the total, scarcely more than the London region and the Midlands put together. In 1937, 41 per cent of the Welsh workforce and 35 per cent of that of the North East belonged to industries in decline; but in the Midlands the proportion was only 7 per cent and in London only 1 per cent.[23] The Barlow Commission, set up to inquire into the huge movements of people and wealth, found that between 1921 and 1937, although the average overall increase in population was 7.5 per cent, that of the Scottish Lowlands had increased by only 4 per cent and Lancashire by less than 1 per cent. Northumberland-Durham had actually diminished by 1 per cent and South Wales by 9 per cent, while the Midlands had increased by 11 per cent and London and the Home Counties by 18 per cent.[24]

Ever since the eighteenth century it had been the North that had led the way in economic dynamism, technological advance, urbanization, and overseas expansion, while the South had remained rural, conservative and conscious of lagging behind. But after 1918 the regional equilibrium that had prevailed before the Industrial Revolution was restored. From the Middle Ages to the days of the Stuarts, the South had been the most populated and the most prosperous part of the country and was characterized by its progressive spirit and taste for overseas enterprise. In that period the North was impoverished, feudal and backward. Now the South, more bourgeois, was still a stronghold of Conservatism, while the proletarian North overwhelmingly voted Labour. On the economic front the North, hit by the depression, had to yield to its rival the lead in

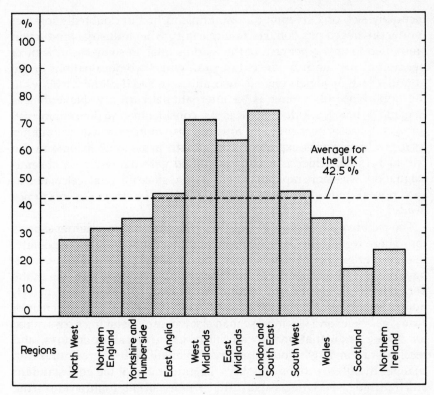

Figure 5. Percentage growth of the population in the UK by standard regions, 1901–71

innovation, scientific research and control of economic development. The 'golden triangle' of the South East tended more and more to accumulate population, power and decision-making. The Second World War certainly halted this drift south for a time, since it was too exposed to aerial bombardment; but the process was again accelerated in the years 1945–50.

England was divided as never before, economically, socially and politically by a line running from Bristol to Hull. It was a repetition, one might say, of 'the Two Nations' of Disraeli, though a geographical rather than a social division. In contrast to the North West with its obsolescent plant, the landscape dotted with Victorian survivals, the people puritan and mainly working-class, stood the South, prosperous and expansionist, green and tidy, a land of bourgeois and white-collar workers, devotees of individualism and Conservatism.

One must not be led into adopting one-sided or dogmatic views, for it would be a grave abuse of the truth to write off the post-1918 economy as incurably sick of a creeping decay. England had undoubtedly lost her former privileged position. For example in 1938 her industrial production amounted to only 9 per cent of the world's total, in comparison with 14 per cent in 1913 and 19 per cent in 1900, while two devaluations of the pound – each of 30 per cent – in 1931 and 1949 had dealt heavy blows to the importance of sterling as an international currency. Nevertheless England's share of world trade was still considerable: 19 per cent in 1938 (in 1913 it was 25 per cent), and towards 1950 more than a quarter of her total production was exported. The growth in national income in the period 1913–38, which is usually identified with depression and semi-stagnation, was more rapid than before 1913, since the total (calculated at 1900 prices), moved up from £2 to £2.7 billion, i.e. from £44 to £57 per head.[25]

The picture was certainly gloomy in parts, but it had its brighter aspects too. There were three particular signs of the economy's great flexibility: the rapid growth of new industries, mostly based on advanced technology, the revival of agriculture, and the general economic recovery in the period immediately after the Second World War. There had been, in fact, quite a strong recovery in the 1930s (it should be noted that the crisis of 1929 was briefer and less intense than elsewhere). Assuming a base of 100 for 1925–9, industrial production fell to 92 in 1931, rose in 1933, and reached 147 in 1937. Contemporary explanations laid great stress on changes in official economic policy – abandonment of the gold standard and free trade, special legislation in aid of rationalization and a veto on the export of capital. The recovery was really due to the rise in demand for consumer goods and a boom in new light industries. These last were involved in the manufacture of electric and electronic devices (145,000 employees in 1923, 340,000 in 1938); the motor vehicles, cycles and aircraft industry (200,000 employees in 1923, 400,000 in 1938 – a workforce equal to that of the cotton industry, although in 1923 the latter had employed 560,000); pharmaceuticals, photographics, plastics, rubber and artificial fibres.[26] Household equipment was among the fastest growing sectors: annual production of vacuum cleaners grew from 38,000 in 1930 to 410,000 in 1935. These new and sophisticated industries formed an entirely new growth point, catering as they did for mass consumption and drawing on the great scientific and technical advances made in England, advances reinforced after 1933 by the influx of scientists escaping from Nazi Germany. One only has to think of inventions with immense strategic and industrial importance, such as radar and the jet engine, and the spectacular advance in nuclear physics, computer science, biochemistry, all of which formed a springboard for industrial expansion after 1945.

Agriculture too gained a new lease of life. Already hard hit at the end of

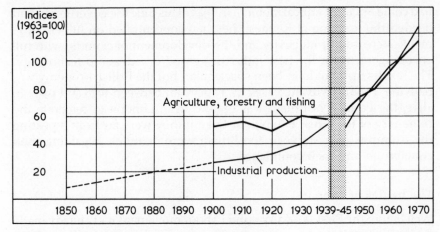

Figure 6.   Development of output in the UK

the nineteenth century, it had had during the 1920s to struggle against
adversity, increased competition from overseas and the doubling of
agricultural wages. The only helpful innovation had been the introduction of sugar beet during the First World War. Then had come the
depression of 1929–32, bringing more disasters such as market gluts and
falling prices. But then came the moment of recovery. With the introduction of protectionism and, soon, the threat of war, government policy
began to encourage and help home production. The method chosen was
to organize markets by means of guaranteed prices. 'Marketing boards'
were set up for the main products: meat, cereals and milk. With this
encouragement farmers took heart and started to diversify with renewed
energy. During the war they prospered to an almost shameful degree.
Their incomes were multiplied by two and a half, and their farm-hands
benefited likewise. Huge strides were made in mechanization. In 1939
there were only 150 combine harvesters in the entire country, but 650,000
farm-horses. Fifteen years later the horses had all but disappeared,
replaced everywhere by tractors. English agriculture had become one of
the most highly mechanized in the world. By 1951 its production, standardized, subsidized, with guaranteed markets, was 50 per cent more
efficient than before the war. For the countryside a half-century of lean
cattle had been replaced by an era of fat ones.

In short, Britain's economic recovery after the Second World War, in
spite of enormous problems caused by physical destruction, balance of
payment crises and shortage of dollars, contrasts very favourably with
the black years immediately after the First World War. Externally circumstances were more propitious. Two of her most formidable trade rivals,
Germany and Japan, were eliminated for the moment, and Marshall Aid

had come at a most critical moment in 1947. This time the government had heeded the teaching of Keynes: they had concentrated on full employment, increased productivity and the development of exports, with full encouragement for the new industries based on advanced technology. The results may not have been spectacular, but the British economy was reviving. Productivity increased by 25 per cent between 1938 and 1950. In 1951, the Festival of Britain was organized in London to celebrate the centenary of the Great Exhibition. Even if they were far from repeating the triumphs of yesteryear, the British were definitely regaining their equilibrium and their confidence.

The battles of Labour

Well before the First World War the Labour movement had already made itself widely felt. It was now everywhere, its growing power one of the main features of the years 1914–24. However, in spite of its newly acquired power it met with more setbacks than gains in its successive struggles, and the inter-war period was a series of disappointments. It was not until 1945 that Labour, with a solid electoral majority, was in a position to run the State machine and start fulfilling its programme of social reform and change.

The first thing to notice in the confrontations of the years 1920–45 is at the beginning of the period the rebirth of revolutionary feeling, followed by its rebuff. Towards the end of the First World War there was a revival of anti-capitalist forces, which came together with a view to establishing genuine worker power. Following on the labour unrest of the years 1910 to 1914, this phase of working-class history, lasting from 1914 to 1926 was marked by a return to extremism, a bitterness of class feeling, a violence in the revolt against injustice, such as had not been seen since the days of Chartism. A deeply rooted antagonism was at work, manifesting itself in two different ways: on the one hand in industrial strategy – direct action – on the other in a political form – the construction of a genuinely revolutionary workers' party.

Once the shock of entering into war had subsided, militancy revived. Starting from the factory floor and inspired and organized by the shop stewards, the movement, whose storm-centre was Glasgow ('Red Clydeside'), made simultaneous claims for better working conditions and a stop to the war. There was a whiff of revolution in the air; but it was the news from Russia that really fired the workers. The echo of the Russian Revolution resounded across Britain, bringing with it little sympathy for Bolshevik ideology, but a feeling of solidarity with the proletarian society that was struggling in its birth-pangs. In the eyes of the British working class the overthrow of the Tsarist regime and the installation of a revolutionary State proved that the capitalist system was neither inevitable nor indestructible. Under the stimulus of these events the word went round to form 'soviets' under the guise of workers' committees. The result was an industrial offensive across a wide front, lasting from 1918 to 1921, whose tactics varied from action by small aggressive minorities to large-scale action by the well-organized and disciplined masses of the big unions, in particular the Triple Alliance of miners, railwaymen and transport workers. Fear of the 'Reds' reached its peak at this time.

The year 1921 however saw a major setback to the industrial no less than to the political wing of this revolutionary movement. The climb-down of the unions on 'Black Friday' (15 April 1921) showed up the rift between the intransigent minority of active militants, all set for unremitting class warfare, and the more moderate majority who preferred compromise to confrontation, and social peace to social war. In the political arena the young Communist Party of Great Britain, formed between August 1920 and January 1921, had little success in attracting the more dynamic members of either the various socialist organizations or of the trade unions. Subjected to the brusque directives and untimely interference of the Third International, rejected by the Labour Party, which would have nothing to do with any Communist-inspired affiliation, and developing a sort of minority sectarianism, English Communism was never to take root in significant numbers in the working-class movement or have any real influence on the social and political life of the country. In 1939 its total membership amounted to only 18,000.[27] But it would be wrong to underestimate its role, as many have done. Its influence inside the unions has been profound, persistent and often effective. During the 1930s it acquired a certain cachet among intellectuals, amounting to a mild form of snobbery, and won the support of some distinguished literary figures and a great many students. By the same token the cause of anti-Fascism, Popular Front tactics, the Spanish Civil War, and during the Second World War the heroism of the Soviet Army, recruited a good many 'fellow-travellers' to Communism. All the same, with no parliamentary base, with no place among the big battalions of politics, English Communism has never got over its initial disadvantage appearing as a foreign body in the labour movement as well as in the nation.

After the twofold setback of 1921 for the revolutionary left, on both the industrial and the political fronts, it was the turn of the trade-union movement to suffer an even worse one in 1926, just as the gap between moderates and revolutionaries in the labour movement was widening. This was the *débâcle* of the General Strike, a crucial landmark in Labour's history. The call to a general strike, issued out of solidarity with the miners (a fascinating possibility to a generation of trade unionists) ended in total fiasco within a week. The result of this clumsy confrontation between the workers and the State (the latter backed by the leaders of industry and supported by all the forces of law and order) was total capitulation by the unions, followed by their submission to the whips and scorpions of the Conservative government. They paid in full, for their adversaries' revenge took the form of punitive legislation. The 'Trade Disputes and Trades Union Act' of 1927 (which was repealed by the Labour government in 1946) made any general strike illegal, banned

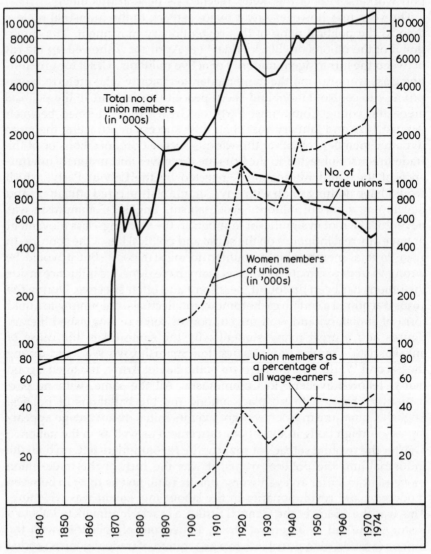

Figure 7. Trade union and trade unionists from the mid-nineteenth century

sympathetic strikes or attempts to coerce the government, imposed severe restrictions on picketing, forbade civil servants' associations to affiliate with the TUC and substituted a 'contracting in' system to the 'contracting out' for the payment of the political levy to the Labour Party, thereby severely damaging the Party's finances. Already in decline, trade-union membership fell by a fifth, and went on falling until 1934, by which time a million members had been lost. This was not made up until 1938 when total membership of the TUC finally passed the level of 1926.[28] The spirit of militancy was broken. The discouragement resulting from failure, followed by world depression, put a stop to strife in most industries for years. For example, while industrial disputes had caused an average loss of 45 million working days a year between 1919 and 1926, the number lost annually between 1927 and 1939 averaged only 3 million.[29] Above all the defeat of 1926 dealt a fatal blow to revolutionary unionism, especially the strategy of direct action and 'workers' control'. Beatrice Webb had good reason to prophesy in her *Diaries* that May 1926 would be seen as 'one of the most significant landmarks in the history of the British working class'.[30] In this spectacular engagement between the forces of Capital and Labour we may discern the last great attempt at revolution in English history. It was five years too late, for the crest of the revolutionary wave had been in the years 1919–20. Henceforward the idea of revolution that had buoyed up the hopes and rallied the forces of the extreme left faded to the realm of myth.

The road to 'reformism' seemed the only way clear, and the trade-union movement painfully recovered itself and set out again. Its leaders now followed a very different policy. Their tactics, relying on collective bargaining and avoiding revolutionist terminology, were realistic, geared to negotiation, long-term agreements that promised material benefits for workers, cooperation instead of conflict. Retreating from a strategy of all-out offensive to gain everything at once through workers' control and self-management, they now fell back on a quest for unambiguously economic objectives, short- or long-term. This was a choice fraught with serious consequences, because for nearly half a century trade-union activity was to be directed towards quantitative gains. Not until the 1970s did they divert their attention to qualitative aspects. This new conciliatory posture of the TUC coincided with a vogue among management in the 1920s for the scientific organization of labour, and in the 1930s for 'human relations' in industry. For the unions a truce in the class war was far from signifying an identity of interests between management and labour: it was simply to avoid expensive confrontations and win solid benefits for their members by judicious use of that on which their bargaining powers depended – numbers, discipline and organization. Along with absolute loyalty to traditional organizations there went a basic mistrust of the 'bosses'. Even the least committed and the least politically minded workers were conscious of a labour 'movement', a huge collective effort, patiently defending the poor and the humble against the encroachments of the privileged classes.

Reformism prevailed also in the political arena. The decision had really been taken in the early years of the century, when the path of parliamentary democracy was chosen. During the period from just before the First World War to just after, there had been a brief move in favour of Guild socialism. This represented an attempt to escape from the vagaries of the electoral system and the rigours of a collectivist State by adopting a form of autarchic and libertarian socialism. But the great mass of voters disliked these enterprising ideas, preferring the official prudent and moderate line of the Labour Party. Its doctrine was nevertheless set out in unequivocally socialist terms, for the Labour programme, *Labour and the New Social Order*, elaborated in 1918 by Sidney Webb, the inventor of the phrase 'the inevitability of gradualism', promised the abolition of capitalism and the installation of 'a new social order' – collectivist, egalitarian and fraternal. This change was to be brought about in Parliament, democratically, thanks to the supreme power of universal suffrage. So, faithful to its Fabian inspiration, but drawing equally on its liberal (intellectual as well as electoral) heritage, Labour aspired to a persuasive and gradual social transformation, achieved legally and without violence by means of a parliamentary majority. Even after the discouraging experience of two abortive terms of office, in 1924 and 1929–31, Labour leaders continued through the difficult 1930s to fight for a humane and democratic form of socialism.

'Their finest hour': from Armageddon to the New Jerusalem

In 1939, for the second time in one generation, England was plunged into war. But this time, although once again it was to be total war, longer, more destructive than the last, and with the homeland itself the scene of action, public opinion was neither so shaken nor so unsettled as it was in 1914. There was not so much bitterness engendered as in 1918. The reason for this was partly to be found in the difference between the two post-war periods, but also in the moral and strategic background of the conflicts. A. J. P. Taylor has written that

> in the Second World War the British people came of age. This was a people's war . . . Future historians may see the war as a last struggle for the European balance of power or for the maintenance of Empire. This was not how it appeared to those who lived through it. The British people had set out to destroy Hitler and National Socialism.[31]

That is why for all those to whom Churchill promised 'blood, toil, sweat and tears', it was truly 'their finest hour'.

When the British Government declared war on 3 September 1939, it was solidly backed by a calm and resolute public opinion. There were few dissenting voices; only tiny minorities here and there, Communist, Fascist or pacifist. There was nothing comparable with 1914, even less with 1917–18. On the contrary, national unity was accentuated as the war dragged on, with the Communists too lending their support after 1941. One interesting psychological change: the English found their tongues. Observers noticed that, after the outbreak of war, people of all classes started talking to each other in public places, on buses, in trains.[32] Everyone was dominated by the awareness of a common destiny.

Every individual, every household was affected by the war to a far greater extent than in the First World War. Civilians played a no less vital part than the fighting forces. Often they risked their lives as much, and it was not until 1942 that the number of combatants killed exceeded that of civilian victims.[33] It was to a far greater extent a 'world' war, being waged simultaneously over three continents, in the air and across every sea. It raged from Norway to Eritrea, from the lowlands of Belgium to the desert of Cyrenaica, from the Normandy 'bocage' to the Burmese jungle, from the skies of Kent to those of Hamburg and Berlin. Its high points bore the names Dunkirk, Tobruk, El Alamein, the Battle of the Atlantic, Caen and Arnhem. Above all, for the first time for centuries, one battle, whose outcome was decisive for the war, was given the name of 'the Battle of Britain'. The island, 'this fortress built by nature for herself', was no longer immune. Battles raged through the skies of Albion. Hardly had the threat of invasion been averted in the autumn of 1940 than English cities were subjected to continuous and devastating air raids from September 1940 to June 1941, which caused one Free French observer to remark, 'Londres c'est le front' ('London is in the front line').[34]

Two noteworthy features of the British attitude during these years left a lasting mark on national memories. First, there was a new sort of patriotism. People were fighting for mankind and civilized values as well as their own land and liberty, and their aim was to be loyal in the sense of Shakespeare's

> . . . Naught shall make us rue
> If England to itself do rest but true.

Were not the English people, inspired by the spirit of Dunkirk and solidly behind Churchill, the very symbol of resistance, on the way to fulfilling their predestined mission – 'this happy breed of men'? So in 1940 every Englishman felt that his country, which single-handed and with calm tenacity had beaten off a reputedly invincible enemy, was bathed in imperishable glory. Soon the island fortress, the home of a solidly united people, and London, the nerve centre and headquarters of the fight against Hitler, became the star of hope towards which all the enslaved peoples of Europe lifted their eyes. As the surrealist poet Robert Desnos wrote:

> Je vous salue sur les bords de la Tamise,
> Camarades de toutes les nations présents au rendez-vous,
> Dans la vieille capitale anglaise,
> Dans le vieux Londres et la vieille Bretagne . . . [35]

Anglophile sentiment had never before reached such an extraordinary pitch of intensity.

The other feature of note was that, after thirty years of bitter social confrontation in a climate of suspicion and hostility, the atmosphere had undergone a radical change, transformed by national solidarity. What caused this phenomenon to be much more than an outburst of national feeling was the certainty that the country was involved in a new sort of war. It was not a war of nameless masses like 1914–18, nor was it like the battles between handfuls of knights (or handfuls of airmen, as in the Battle of Britain, where 'never . . . had so many owed so much to so few'), but, in Priestley's words, it was a 'citizen's war'. Churchill called it 'a war of unknown soldiers'.

In the army, the Home Guard, and the Civil Defence, in offices and workshops, in canteens and air-raid shelters, a new community spirit was born. It was a society with its 'back to the wall', sharing the same sacrifices, the same restrictions, the same dangers. The wealthy gave up their luxuries and even their comforts. Their domestic servants vanished into factories, taxation became heavier, with basic income tax reaching 50 per cent. In his diary Harold Nicolson records his feeling of shock at the idea of having to go shopping on foot after the war ('we shall have to walk and live a Woolworth life hereafter').[36] Most people felt that social distinctions were being rapidly eroded, and that the class war, if not quite forgotten, had been put into cold storage until better times. In 1940 an American journalist wrote in the *New York Herald Tribune*: 'Hitler is doing what centuries of English history have not accomplished – he is breaking down the class structure of England.'[37] An illusion; for ephemeral impressions of this kind are always exaggerated. Social differences are more enduring than Panzers, and conflicting interests cannot be spirited away. On the factory floor shop stewards continued determinedly to support their colleagues' pay claims. In 1943, 1,800,000 working days were lost by strike action – 40 per cent more than in 1938.[38] The workers were far better at grabbing their chances than in 1914–18. Thanks to full employment and the need of their labour for the war effort, they did far better out of the war than their predecessors had done.

Even with these qualifications it remains true that everyone was inspired by the same spirit. Civilians and fighting men, young and old, men and women, privileged and underdogs, all shared the same will to victory and the same public-spiritedness – the latter a quality which particularly impressed the European exiles in England. To this same spirit was owed the willingness to submit to severe rationing (with a very limited black market) and to accept many restrictions. Innovations such as the British Restaurants, an invention of Churchill's, where it was impossible to spend more than 5 shillings, and cheap utility clothes, were all signs that the government was really trying to provide the minimum necessities of life for everyone. The religious leaders were quick to preach that the Christian traditions of the nation were at stake. Everyone knew where he stood and what he was fighting for. The suicide rate fell by a third of its pre-war average.[39] In retrospect it seemed an extraordinary interlude in the country's history, one of great social harmony – in the words of A. J. P. Taylor, 'a brief period in which the English people felt they belonged to a truly democratic community'.[40]

In other ways the war had formidable consequences for Britain's future. The British at the time hardly realized that they had reached a turning-point in their history. In the first place the advent of the two 'super powers' greatly diminished Britain's status as a world power, and in the second place she was to lose most of her overseas empire. Churchill was one of the first to recognize this change at Teheran in 1943, well ahead of his compatriots. He told Lady Violet Bonham-Carter,

> I realized . . . for the first time, what a small nation we are. There I sat with the great Russian bear on one side of me, with paws outstretched, and on the other side the great American buffalo, and between the two sat the poor little English donkey who was the only one, the only one of the three, who knew the right way home.[41]

In the same year another observer, General Smuts, prophesied that after the war Britain's position would be 'one of enormous prestige and respect . . . but she will be poor'.[42]

Long before victory was even in sight both fighting men and civilians started thinking about the post-war world, dreaming of a new order, quite different from the old one. Out of total war and all its horrors enormous hope was born. Even in the darkest hours of the endless struggle people thought they could see dawn breaking over a New Jerusalem, embodying in splendid confusion their generous, almost millenarian, aspirations. There was an enormous ferment of ideas and thousands of new projects were dreamed up. To take only a few examples of this impassioned determination to build a new and more just world, there were the plans for reform ventilated by the Army Bureau of Current Affairs, the Beveridge Report (which, in its shortened version, sold over 600,000 copies), and the sudden appearance of a new party, the Common Wealth Party, formed by socialist intellectuals and radicals. There was unanimous agreement on two points. Firstly, no repetition of the pre-war nightmare of government by 'little men', or small-minded 'capitulators', to use an expression from the Left Book Club's bestseller, *Guilty Men* (partly written by Michael Foot). Secondly, a set of very basic requirements was laid down: work for all, social security, a right to a decent standard of living, and genuine international cooperation. It was not just Labour, but the Liberal and even Tory middle class who were behind this desire for change and reform. The inventor of the term 'Welfare State' was none other than William Temple, the Archbishop of Canterbury, a pillar of the Establishment.[43] Conversely, the expression 'revolution by consent' came from that theoretician of advanced socialism, Harold Laski. As early as the summer of 1940 a famous editorial in *The Times* defined the social policy that should be followed after the war:

> If we speak of democracy, we do not mean a democracy which maintains the right to vote but forgets the right to work and the right to live. If we speak of freedom, we do not mean a rugged individualism which excludes social organization and economic planning. If we speak of equality, we do not mean a political equality nullified by social and economic privelege. If we speak of economic reconstruction, we think less of maximum production (though this too will be required) than of equitable distribution . . . The new order cannot be based on the preservation of privilege, whether the privilege be that of a country, of a class, or of an individual.[44]

Words and phrases can be deceptive. 'Social revolution' has been used and misused in connection with the years 1940–5, and the years that followed have shown up the exaggeration. It is however undeniable that democracy took a big step forward, even if achievements did not measure up to ambitions, even if vested interests and long-established customs succeeded in hampering the progress and reducing the victories of egalitarianism. For the whole great process of democratic debate caused a healthy dissemination of ideas, and in the long run it was impossible to disavow this generous will to change for the common good, these plans for building a new world, a world without hunger and fear, unemployment and poverty, insecurity and hate. 'Warfare had necessitated welfare', as Asa Briggs put it. Besides, war-time conditions had encouraged a leftward tendency, had given a boost for Labour and conferred respectability on planning and socialization. To say that capitalist civilization was on trial would be an exaggeration, but after 1942 all opinion polls pointed to a shift towards Labour.

Based on the work of the sociologist Andrzejewski, a law has been invoked that assesses the transformation of societies under the stress of war in proportion to the degree of mass popular involvement ('the military participation ratio'). Richard Titmuss has pursued the same theme with a different perspective and greater subtlety. A. Marwick has argued – incontestably – that war exerts a double action of rupture and acceleration. These are not quite the terms in which we formulate the problem. The real question for the historian, still unresolved, is as follows: Was the limited, though definite, transformation of England in the years 1940–50 caused by the phenomenon of war, in which case the turning-point came in the years 1940–4, or did this 'people's war' simply prepare the ground for the crucial changes made by the Labour government in the years 1945–50?

The Welfare State

'We are the masters now!', shouted, it is said, a Labour Member during a debate in the House of Commons in 1946, a significant demonstration of Labour's confidence and determination to act after its electoral success in July 1945.[45] They had a very large majority – 393 members (of whom 168 were of working-class origin) as against 213 Conservatives and a mere handful of Liberals. This was an unequivocal popular mandate for the construction of a new world – just, egalitarian and peaceful. So began a five-year period of structural reform, the 'peaceful revolution'.

The socialists attained power in a state of total euphoria. John Freeman went so far as to call it 'D-Day' in the battle for the new Britain. Hugh Dalton, describing in his memoirs the state of mind of the victors, says: 'There was exhilaration among us, joy and hope, determination and confidence. We felt exalted, dedicated, walking on air, walking with destiny.'[46] How dazzling it seemed to all those who had endured the setbacks of the years between the wars, and even more so to those who remembered the heroic age before 1914. After the years of effort and trial, after the long years in the wilderness, suddenly they saw the Promised Land. But the land of Canaan, so far from flowing with milk and honey, had no luscious fruits for a general share-out, but only the Dead Sea fruit of work, privation and reconstruction. The pillar of fire that led them was rapidly doused, and Labour's term of office took place in an atmosphere of grey austerity. The socialist team turned out to be moderate in their policies, and spectacular objectives had to be eschewed in favour of quiet competence.

They had started with boundless ambition. They had envisaged a total transformation of society, but they were only able to fulfil a fraction of their programme, namely the achievement of what came to be known as the Welfare State, i.e. a new social set-up that guaranteed a minimum of security and benefit to all. The expression soon acquired official status, appearing in the Oxford English Dictionary as early as 1955 as 'a polity so organized that every member of the community is assured of his due maintenance with the most advantageous conditions possible for all'. It is open to two definitions. For a rather narrow interpretation one may take the five points enunciated by M. Bruce at the end of his book, *The Coming of the Welfare State*. According to Bruce the five objectives are as follows: (1) to guarantee to everyone, in any circumstances, a decent standard of living, without this minimum income being necessarily earned through employment (thanks to the dual notion of insurance and assistance); (2) to protect everyone against the vicissitudes of daily life (illness, unemployment, etc.); (3) to help family life develop and thrive (hence family allowances); (4) to treat health and education as public services, so as to raise material and intellectual standards for all; and (5) to develop and improve all public establishments and equipment that may conduce to the betterment of personal life (housing, the environment, leisure activities).[47] Seen in this light, the Welfare State appears as the end-product of a long history, its origins far back in the past. This view considerably reduces the originality of Labour's initiatives in the years 1945–50. In fact it was towards something like this that the whole social policy of the inter-war years, and earlier that of the Liberal governments of 1906–14, had gradually been working. It has even been alleged by some historians that it was possible to trace State intervention in aid of the poor and feeble back to the Victorian age, if not to the Elizabethan Poor Law.

But this is a narrow, rather technical definition of Welfare State (though it is the one given in the *Concise Oxford Dictionary of Current English*, 1964 edition), amounting to little more than an enlargement of the social services. The phrase may be allowed a rather wider sense. In this it stands as the symbol of the structure of post-war Britain – a society with a mixed economy and full employment, where individualism is tempered by State intervention, where the right to work and a basic standard of living are guaranteed, and the working-class movement, now accepted and recognized, finds its rightful place in the nation.

By its own admission Labour's 'revolution' must be seen in the perspective of 'evolution'. The key word is 'social justice'. Without in the least denying the collectivist principles inscribed on Labour's tablets, the revolution found its main inspiration in two Liberals: first Beveridge, then Keynes. These were the two master-minds whose ideas guided Labour's actions. Sir Roy Harrod justly observes: 'The Welfare State is derived from a socialist philosophy, but it is associated with the liberal tradition.'[48] It is impossible to underestimate the enormous effect of the 'Beveridge Report' (*Report on Social Insurance and Allied Services*, 1942) which sets out in clear, simple language, intelligible by all, the basic principles on which all post-war reform was to be based. According to Beveridge, society should be guided by three ruling principles: (1) no privileged classes or sectional interests; (2) as social progress is a single entity it must slay, on the road to reconstruction, the five wicked giants: Want, Disease, Ignorance, Squalor and Idleness; (3) social security rests on cooperation between the State and the individual: so the State should provide the necessary social services, but without encroaching on voluntary initiative or personal responsibility. During the Labour Government the Chancellor of the Exchequer, Sir Stafford Cripps, who was the embodiment of austere egalitarianism and devoted public spirit, laid down similar norms. The problem, he explained, was 'to combine a free democracy with a planned economy', and to build 'a happy country in which there is equality of opportunity and not too great a disparity of personal incomes'.[49] One may well ask in what way such a philosophy differed from the radical democratic doctrines of the past. The very phrases echo the slogans of the Levellers, the Jacobins and the Chartists, refurbished to suit contemporary fashion.

This may well be so, but one must not ignore the degree to which the ideology of the Welfare State was determined by the conditions that prevailed at the time of its inception. What were these conditions? Liberal grandparents indeed, but Labour parents; a powerful urge towards a 'new deal' so that victory could have a real meaning; a new feeling of national unity; a genuine belief in the common weal; Disraeli's 'Two Nations' made one; a fairer division of labour and sacrifice for a common war effort; a truce in the class war, and a new spirit of conciliation. Apart from all this it was noticeable that one never heard exaggerated stories of the 'good old days', as one had in the earlier post-war period. This time the tendency was to disparage those days – the 'gloomy thirties', the 'devil's decade', when, according to George Orwell, England was 'a land of snobbery and privilege, ruled largely by the old and the silly'. What perhaps contributed most to the popularity and renown of the Welfare State was the principle of universality on which it was based. This principle was egalitarian, all inclusive, aiming at the greatest happiness of the greatest number, without any discrimination. This was in marked contrast with former social policy which was paternalistic, coldly dissuasive and condescending, when the poor were treated as 'paupers', subjected to the detested Poor Law and Means Test. In real terms the coming of the Welfare State was accompanied by a rise in the standard of living of the masses. In the ten years from 1938 to 1948 wage-earners (five-sixths of

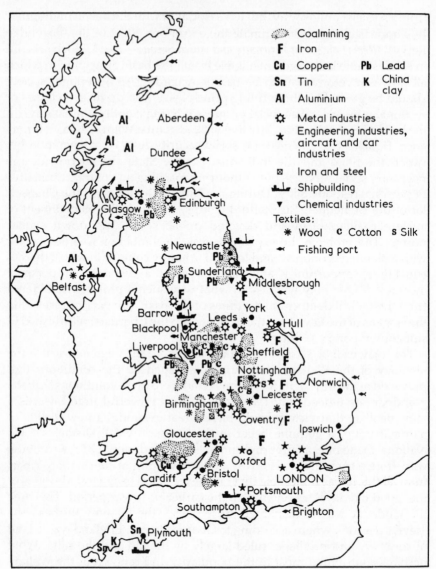

Map 7. Economic geography of the UK, 1951

the population) benefited by 25 per cent and pensioners by 50 per cent.

The innovations were carried out in two main areas. The first was nationalization. There was a steady stream of measures following the principle of public control of the main activities and services that were vital to the life of the nation: in 1946 the Bank of England and the coal mining industry; in 1947 transport (railways and canals); in 1948 gas and electricity; in 1949 steel. The method of running these industries was supposed to avoid the dangers and disadvantages of direct State owner-ship. Instead of being administered by Whitehall the nationalized enter-prises were managed by boards, councils or corporations. Other, much more popular, measures concerned the social services and set up a very comprehensive social security organization. These were the National Insurance Act of 1946 (pay and allowances for the sick, the aged, the unemployed); the National Health Service Act, also in 1946, which, in the face of frenzied opposition from the medical profession, created a national health scheme, completely free, financed by the national budget without any personal contributions; and the National Assistance Act of 1948 which abolished the old Poor Law and reorganized public assist-ance, thus benefiting a million people. The government's activities were not confined to social welfare, but took in many other aspects of human development: city life and the environment, (the New Towns Act of 1946, the National Parks and National Conservancy Act of 1949), housing, the arts (the Arts Council was formed in 1946), education and the family. For measures covering the last two, credit is due to the war-time coalition government (the Education Act of 1944 and the Family Allowances Act of 1945, the former owing much to the Conservative Minister, R. A. Butler). One point of vital importance was that, in the minds of its creators, the Welfare State was inseparably bound up with full employment, Labour's first commandment. Much of Labour's policy derived from the teaching of Keynes, notably the use of taxation to regulate the economy and redistribute income. Its achievement was a remarkably comprehensive series of measures which had the effect of fixing the shape of British society for years ahead. Some sort of timidity, however, inhibited Labour from laying hands on two institutions, the public schools and the City of London, thus leaving intact two keystones of bourgeois capitalist society, educational separatism and big business.

In seeking to determine the significance of the Welfare State one must bear three points in mind. Firstly, to use the word 'revolution' is to devalue its meaning. To speak of 'the quiet revolution', 'the cautious revolution' or even, with Beveridge, 'the British revolution',[50] i.e. as the outcome of a natural historical process, is simply an abuse of English. The language used by Labour in 1945 was certainly misleading. The party manifesto *Let us Face the Future* went so far as to promise a 'Socialist Commonwealth of Great Britain' which would be 'free, democratic, effi-cient and progressive', with its resources placed 'at the service of the people'. It is always wise to be suspicious about the use of words, especially where the Left is concerned, and the most suitable expression might have been 'social democracy', at most 'democratic socialism', but no further. Woodrow Wyatt, then a young Labour MP, was perspicacious enough to say as early as September 1945: 'What's the use of having an orderly revolution if there turns out not to be a revolution at all?'[51]

In the second place, the arrival of the Welfare State was situated in the mainstream of the history of democratic freedom, linking the pioneers of the London Corresponding Society with the militants of the Independent Labour Party, the Benthamites with the Fabians, the Nonconformist conscience with Christian Socialism. Without going so far as to agree with Anthony Howard that the Labour victory of 1945 had brought about 'the greatest restoration of traditional social values since 1660',[52] it is fair to say that the Labour movement through its evangelical roots and its radical ideology embodied a social creed that harked back to the great traditional ideals of social justice and brotherhood. Furthermore its policy of social reform marked the end of one period rather than the beginning of a new one. Like generals planning for yesterday's war, the Welfare State was redeeming the faults of its predecessors. This is not to disparage its merits, which were enormous. It would be unfair to minimize achievements which were quickly appreciated by those who benefited from them, and it would be pointless hindsight to reproach the governments of a world in ruins for not having planned for the affluent society.

Finally, if the Welfare State was the grandchild of Beveridge and Keynes, it was no less the child of the Fabians, since it concentrated on legislative, administrative and centralizing methods to the detriment of 'workers' control'. But in thus stamping on any frail aspiration towards a libertarian organization of society, Labour laid itself open to a charge that would weigh heavily on it in the future, namely of wanting to impose a bureaucratic form of socialism.

In the long run the establishment of the Welfare State must, in our opinion, be seen as a decisive episode in the evolution of modern Britain. It marks a turning-point in the history of socio-political relations which has shaped the country's destiny in the third quarter of this century, and probably the last as well. Peel's introduction of free trade in 1846 aimed at an accomodation between the old and the new ruling class, thus eliminating any risk of revolutionary upsets; and it also obliged the working class to conform with the social norms established by their 'betters'. In the same way the advent of the Welfare State in 1945 effected a similar *modus vivendi* between labour, whose full power was now manifested through universal suffrage, and the erstwhile ruling class; for the latter was now compelled to share the heritage it had kept as its exclusive right. This national consensus was founded on the principles of full employment, a minimum standard of living and social security for all. The Labour Party, which up till now had enjoyed more or less the status of a junior partner, now exerted its full influence and, although it was ready to discipline its forces and moderate its demands, it had established a new political balance of power.

So, after the confrontations of 1910–39, which were unusually heated by English standards, the harmony established during and after the Second World War ended in an unwritten agreement to share the cake and the seats of power in a new way. Labour was accorded the social advantages of State welfare and the right to be consulted on all major political questions. The middle class was assured of being able to go on running private business and also a good deal of the business of State. Thanks to this arrangement, pragmatically reached, disputes could once again be dealt with by traditional methods – a sign that a viable and pacific society was now established on the rock of consensus. The result was that, exactly a century after Peel's 'historic compromise' between the aristocracy and the middle class, a new compromise was effected under the name of the Welfare State, this time between the ruling middle class and the world of labour. The terms were largely devised by the Labour Party and the Trades Union Congress. Under these conditions social security and welfare were the price paid by the middle class to preserve its influence, just as formerly the abolition of the Corn Laws was the price paid by the aristocracy. Thanks to these accommodations with Labour, the way was paved for a stable society free of the troubles of 1918–39.

In other words, the topdogs and the underdogs, the 'Establishment' and the masses, had accepted a settlement dictated by the nature of the country's historic evolution. Each side was hoping to turn the deal to its own advantage, and all subsequent disagreements were to derive from just this question of who got the lion's share of power and the fruits of affluence. Members of the upper classes had their own ideas about the arrangement and expressed themselves unequivocally. Thus Robert Boothby, a distinguished member of the Tory Left, after pointing out that 'England had undergone one of the greatest social revolutions in her history', maintained that

> the strength of the Tory Party in Britain and its continuance as a major force in British politics lie in its empirical approach to current problems and its readiness to accept facts not as we should like them to be, but as they are. We accepted the revolution of 1832 and governed England for a considerable part of the nineteenth century in consequence . . . We have accepted the revolution of 1945 and are looking forward to governing England again for a good part of the rest of this century.[53]

Once the most blatant forms of social injustice had been eliminated, the way was open, under the aegis of the 'mixed economy', for what in the 1950s was called 'Butskellism' (an elision of the names Butler and

Gaitskell, respectively the actual and the shadow Chancellor of the Exchequer of the time), i.e. a middle-of-the-road policy, avoiding in a rational way the extreme policies of either side, considered to be danger-ously perverse and un-English. As for the mixed economy itself, in 1950 only 20 per cent of the national economy was in the public sector, with two million employees. As Richard Crossman very relevantly observed, Labour had abolished neither free enterprise nor competition, but had adapted them 'to meet the social and economic demands of organized labour'. On the whole, Crossman continued, the achievements of the Labour Govern-ment in 1945–50 formed the culminating point of a lengthy process by which capitalism had been 'civilized' and to a large extent reconciled to the principles of democracy.[54] So, by rejecting Marxism, class war and all the various theories postulating the fundamentally contentious character of neo-capitalist society, the British prided themselves on having con-structed a new and stable form of society. This was a society in which labour and capital, justice and democracy could live together in harmony – later to be called 'the Swedish way'.

The ideological principles of the Welfare State were far from winning universal acceptance. They came under heavy fire from the champions of individualism, who accused the State of stifling all enterprise by constant interference, of encouraging improvidence, of denying all right of inde-pendent choice to the individual, contrasting the vices of the Welfare State with the virtues of the Opportunity State. Despite all this the system as a whole has never been put in question. That is why the Conservatives, when they returned to power in 1951, made it clear that they would hardly touch the nationalized industries and certainly not the social services, which by then were extremely popular. Subsequently there were demands for repeal from a few diehards and intellectual Tories such as Enoch Powell. Their argument was that at a certain stage of its development capitalism had had to agree to certain limitations and con-cessions that were forced on it, but once the age of affluence arrived such a policy became anachronistic, and a good deal of the legislation of 1945–50 would have to be repealed. The first part of this line of reasoning bears a curious resemblance to that of the Labour left, exemplified by Crossman arguing in New Fabian Essays that 'the planned Welfare State is really the adaptation of capitalism to the demands of modern trade unionism'.[55]

No responsible Conservative politician yielded to these pressures. On the contrary, all initiatives from the Tory rank and file that might threaten the delicate balance of the 'historic compromise' were squashed. The control of business and industry remained in the same hands, and the Welfare State showed itself absolutely compatible with the survival of oligarchy. The much vaunted social mobility and democratization were soon shown to be illusory, so perhaps there was nothing surprising in the rage and the passion for destruction of the 'angry young men' who, after 1950, started banging their heads against the wall of the 'blocked society'.

8 *The immutable class system*

The Establishment

Although it seems to have been used for the first time by Ford Madox Ford around 1920, the expression 'the Establishment' only became current usage in 1954 when Henry Fairlie's use of it in his political column in *The Spectator* suddenly made it popular. Since then it has been used quite at random, often in an offensive sense, so that its meaning has become obscured. The word in its original, historic sense was used to designate the officially 'established' Church of England, but in its extended, secular sense it has come to mean the group of traditionally ruling bodies entrenched in the citadels of their institutions and quasi-hereditary privileges. Such are the Crown, the Court, the aristocracy, the Church, the judicature, the senior civil servants, Oxbridge, the General Staff, the City, the heads of the banking world and of industry, the big public corporations . . .

The term may seem useful and even evocative (a vision of entrenched privilege, of the weight of tradition), but it is imprecise. The same objection applies to another stock phrase: 'power élite'. In fact one comes back to the traditional, more precise and always valid idea of 'the ruling class', even to the term 'upper class'. This last phrase came back into favour in the 1950s as a result of the celebrated distinction originated by Professor Alan Ross and popularized by Nancy Mitford, according to which the English fall into two categories – U (upper class) and non-U (all the rest).

However, one needs to get away from snobbish distinctions of language, vocabulary and accent, important though they are in showing up class differences. In seeking to analyse the structure of the ruling class in the twentieth century one has to distinguish several different components. There has been considerable diversification since 1914 and one may discern three principal elements, historically superimposed on one another, but with a thousand subtle interconnections within their closed world.

At this base one always finds the old aristocratic families, their wealth and their power based traditionally on landed property though their influence, but not their prestige, was in sharp decline. The second element consisted of the plutocrats, the heads of industry, business and finance, whose irresistible ascent had continued all through the Victorian and Edwardian periods. From quite early on they had managed to ally themselves – matrimonially, financially and politically – with the aristocracy, and it was they who through the Conservative Party led the way politically between 1918 and 1939. Finally, during the two World Wars, and especially in the Second, another element appeared. They too were oligarchically inclined, born of the call for rationalization and industrial concentration, favoured by the growing intervention of the State in all sectors of the nation's life – bureaucrats and professional administrators, who derived their power from their expertise. Professionalism, efficiency, organizing ability were their assets; and their recruitment – success in examinations, and performance – won them the name of 'meritocrats'. The strength and the original character of the British ruling class sprang from the mingling of these three streams, successful combination of aristocracy, plutocracy and meritocracy. So formed, the 'Establishment' has survived threats and shocks, jealously keeping its place at the head of the State and of society.

After 1918 the aristocracy suffered decided setbacks in their two principal spheres of influence, landed property and political patronage. Many large estates were broken up. Early on in the First World War death duties and taxation were increased, land soared in price and many large properties went up for sale. This trend increased rapidly between 1919 and 1921 so that nearly a quarter of all English land changed hands, the purchasers being mostly tenant farmers who now acquired the land for themselves. This revolution in land ownership brought about a situation reminiscent of the days of yeoman farmers before the enclosures. In 1914 owner-farmers occupied 16 per cent of English cultivated land; in 1927 more than 36 per cent. A change of ownership of this size and speed was unparalleled since the confiscations of the Civil War, or the dissolution of the monasteries, or even the Norman Conquest![1] Such a move was greatly to the advantage of the former owners and was skilfully carried out at top prices just before the long decline in the price of produce and in farm rents had set in, reaching in 1936 the lowest figures since 1870. Aristocratic wealth was thus not affected, the capital being reinvested in trade and industry or in landed property overseas. This at least was true of the upper crust of patricians who knew how to look after themselves, but rather less so for the landed gentry, who suffered more from dwindling rent-rolls and various other difficulties such as lack of servants and the high cost of maintenance. This made it hard for them to keep up their old standards of agreeable country-house life.

It was these families, the traditional breeding-ground of officers, imbued with patriotism and the spirit of leadership, that had suffered most heavily in the holocaust of the trenches. It would be an exaggeration to speak of decadence, but a certain disenchantment with ancestral values did set in after the violent upsets of the war, and faced with the ostentation of the *nouveaux riches* aristocratic morale declined somewhat. Their political influence passed into hands of the plutocrats. A significant and symbolic event was the choice of Stanley Baldwin, a provincial industrialist (or, euphemistically, a 'countrified businessman') in 1923 for the leadership of the Conservative Party in preference to Lord Curzon, the proud heir apparent of the aristocracy. Thenceforward it was to be impossible for a peer to become Prime Minister. Socially the life of the aristocracy lost much of its glitter, and the lights gradually went out in the country houses. In London, Devonshire House, the splendid town house of the Cavendish family, became a car show-room; Grosvenor House, the home of the Dukes of Westminster, was pulled down and replaced by a hotel. The fact that many of the great country houses ceased to be inhabited was not entirely disastrous, since their owners, one after another threw them open to the sightseeing herd to pay for the costs of upkeep. During the 1950s it became quite usual for the bearers of the highest names in the land to lend their names to activities which might appear rather beneath their dignity. A Lord Tennyson was director of an advertising agency, a Duke of Argyll lent his name to a brand of socks and stockings, a Lord Montagu of Beaulieu specialized in motor cars and jazz, running a car museum and holding jazz festivals. Increasingly, without stigma, peers, baronets, knights and country squires were offered directorships in the City, in banks, large companies and even in the nationalized industries.

If however ancient families were being overtaken by commercialism, it showed that blue blood still commanded respect – and a price. Respect was always paid to the scion of an ancient family, as well as to the established tradition. Come riot or revolution, the name of 'gentleman' still conferred distinction. So did the title 'amateur'; the quality implied qualities. These were utterly traditional habits of thought, biological absurdities, but widely held throughout all classes, so visceral was the Englishman's love for a lord. Although landed property counted no more than mere lucre, and the town ruled the country, society still bore the indelible stamp of aristocracy. This is how it is in Osbert Sitwell's *England Reclaimed?* (1927) where 'the Great House' casts its portentous shadow over every cottage. On the very eve of the Second World War Hilaire Belloc describes the character of England as threefold: aristocratic, commercial and Protestant. And in this aristocratic country, the only one left in Western civilization, where oligarchy is not merely tolerated but revered, Belloc remarks paradoxically that 'Aristocracy comes from below', for it derives from the very preference of the governed.[2] Its strength is that it rests on a 'mystical and sacramental element', and one is inevitably reminded of Bagehot's description of the monarchy. Thus it came about that the aristocracy, the small group of titled families (950 peers in 1950) and the few thousand descendants of the gentry, survived the war and the years under Labour in good shape. Even those who bewailed its imminent demise, like Evelyn Waugh in *Brideshead Revisited* (1945), had to revise their opinion. In the preface to a later edition (1960) Waugh had to admit that the aristocracy had not merely survived decadence and punitive taxation but had managed to maintain its identity to a degree that in earlier days had seemed impossible. In 1955 Nancy Mitford, at that time living in Versailles, rejoiced in this talent for survival: 'The English aristocracy may seem on the verge of decadence, but it is the only real aristocracy left in the world today.'[3] That is why foreign observers continued to be struck by this distinctive trait persisting in English society – first the French and Americans like Taine and Emerson around 1860 or Halévy and Lowell in the Edwardian period, and later, in the middle of the twentieth century, the Dutchman Huizinga, who called the system 'aristo-democracy'.[4]

The quality that kept the aristocracy from being relegated to the shelves of a museum and gave the top class the power of constant renewal and adaptation to change was its capacity to absorb and assimilate. It welcomed outsiders and, by investing them with its own aura, perpetuated itself. It knew how to inculcate its own norms and values on those it took under its wing, converting and assimilating them, while they, profiting in their turn from the prestige conferred on them, then played their part in the hereditary process. Quite unlike a cast, the Establishment had no fixed rules for admission or disqualification. It was an oligarchy with half-hidden openings and paths of approach, a subtle combination of heredity and adoption. Hence a ruling class relatively united and coherent, mainly self-propagating, but exogenous as well; a complex fabric woven of numerous personal ties, of birth, education and social relations. Heredity, family connections, going to the same schools, belonging to the same clubs, the same social circle, going to the same parties, such were the conditions that enabled the 'charmed circle' to survive all change, unscathed, whether economic, political, religious or cultural.

Since the First World War two groups from the 'upper middle class' had come to play an increasingly important part in the governing stratum of society, the world of big business and the top ranks of the Civil Service. These were no longer in completely separate camps. Though one stood for the private sector and the other for the public, the distinction, a sharp one in 1914, was now obscured, and the two worlds with their countless overlapping interests tended to intermingle – all the more so as their members were mostly recruited from the same milieu, the narrow world of heredity and guarded preserves, a world where there was more succession than accession.

To safeguard his influence the aristocrat had two assets, his title and his title-deeds. The plutocrat only had wealth, but money was sufficient to gain power, prosperity and respect. The growth of big business had two characteristics. First, concentration: at the head of giant enterprises such as ICI, Unilever, Shell, BP, Imperial Tobacco, Hawker Siddeley, GEC, the giants of the business tribe sat in state. The 'tycoon' had superseded the captain of industry. The founding in 1916 of a powerful association of business chiefs, the Federation of British Industries, led to greatly improved cooperation and communication between industrialists. Second, between the wars, the big firms gradually ceased to be run by their proprietors. The managerial revolution was under way. After 1950 the tendency accelerated. Henceforward the decisions were made by top management, the directors of finance and the managing directors.

The number of company directors that composed the 'business élite' was about 30,000, but this gives a false impression of the extent of business concentration. In 1955, according to Sargant Florence, 1,700 concerns, 1 per cent of the total number, generated 60 per cent of the total turnover of all companies.[5] In fact, one finds the same names on the boards of the principal banks and insurance companies, of big financial and industrial firms and even on the boards of the nationalized industries. All in all they formed a close network, woven of a thousand strands of family, fortune, education and social relations, that controlled the economy and the centres of decision – an oligopolis of wealth and power, firmly resisting the inroads of democracy.

Finally, the world of top management grew in importance with the increase in State takeovers, as the State bureaucracy constituted a fully-grown new power group. It too was a closed world. In 1956 there were only 3,000 higher civil servants, a number which has remained fairly steady, since any growth that takes place is in the middle and lower ranks of the public service. Recruitment at the very highest level was often from other sectors of the Establishment, where there was a fair amount of mutual exchange; but there was also some penetration by members of the meritocracy. What was novel was the growth of the Treasury's financial muscle alongside that of the City.

Bourgeois and petit-bourgeois

A phenomenon common to all industrial societies is the growth of the middle classes. In England in the middle of the nineteenth century they formed about 15–20 per cent of the population. Bowley reckoned 23 per cent in 1921 and 26 per cent in 1931; and on the basis of the census returns he calculated that workers in middle-class occupations were increasing in number more rapidly than manual workers. He was counting male workers only; the increase is even more marked if female workers are included.[6] Towards 1950 the middle class was reckoned at 30 per cent, and some would put it as high as 35 per cent.

This increase was related to the growth of the tertiary sector. The expansion of the distributive and service industries favoured the growth of the middle classes in three ways. First, as the standard of living rose and the machinery of social life became more and more complex, so there was an increasing call for the services of professionals and specialists. While the higher branches of the professions (doctors, lawyers and so on) increased, lower down there was another branch flourishing, namely their staffs and assistants. Therefore the middle classes were playing a larger and larger part in running and organizing the lives of their fellow-citizens. Secondly, as central administration and local authorities were ceaselessly extending their fields of activity, they needed more and more staff. When the Civil Service started in 1854, it employed 42,000 people; in 1900, 100,000; in 1939, 387,000 (of whom a quarter were woman); and in 1953, 666,000 (of whom half were women).[7] Finally, in the private as well as in the public sector, office work was becoming more labour-intensive, which involved a professional regrouping, to the detriment of manual employment. Thus there was an 'inflationary' white-collar situation. Some were administrative staff, people with certain skills. The rest, the most numerous, were ordinary employees – a category whose rapid growth caused the authors of an important social survey of the mid-1950s to write, 'We are . . . increasingly becoming a nation of clerks'.[8] Indeed, between the census of 1931 and that of 1951, the proportion of clerical employees in the labour force had grown from 7 per cent to 10.5 per cent. In addition, the creation of the great 'corporations' between the wars and the nationalizations after 1945 created a semi-public sector which grew very rapidly. Careers in the public, semi-public and private sectors frequently offered similar pay, conditions of work and quality of life, and there were new opportunities for merit, knowledge and proficiency. Some professions experienced boom conditions – science, for example. In 1921 there were 48,000 scientists and engineers; in 1951 there were 187,000; in 1966, 483,000. Laboratory technicians increased from 5,000 in 1921 to 69,000 in 1951 and 113,000 in 1966. Draughtsmen increased over the same period from 38,000 to 130,000 and then to 171,000.[9]

In the solid middle class reasonable incomes (£500 to £2,000 a year between the wars, twice those sums around 1950) guaranteed the continuation of their privileged standards of education and material comfort. Certainly their way of life had changed, with fewer servants after 1918 and none after 1945 (except for an au pair girl in families with children), though household work had been enormously lightened by labour-saving inventions. Travel and outings became a habit, and social life was far less formal. Tennis, that supreme symbol of middle-class life, was

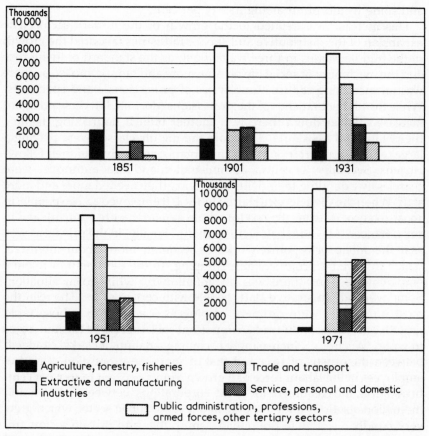

Figure 8. Changes in occupational distribution in Great Britain, 1851–1971

very popular – unlike traditional team games it could be played by both sexes. The great innovation, however, was the motor-car. By 1939 almost every middle-class household had one. Contemporary novelists such as Richard Aldington *(The Colonel's Daughter)* and Christopher Isherwood *(All the Conspirators, The Memorial)* competed in criticism of the middle classes, accusing them of being prudish, at once snobbish and philistine, and swollen with class prejudice. The bourgeois were convinced that, in addition to their financial strength, they had a monopoly of talent and judgement. They flattered themselves that they were the brain-power of the nation, that the qualities of leadership and enterprise were theirs alone. To their class they ascribed the moral and religious qualities that had made their nation great. In short, they were inclined to be prejudiced and self-satisfied.

The middle class maintained itself strongly, but without much recruitment from below. Social betterment was slow; there were middle-class dynasties, but not much mobility. Even after the Second World War, research into the social origins of the managerial classes (businessmen, managers, civil servants, professional people) showed that less than a quarter of their members were the sons of manual workers or wage-earners, and that more than half came from the established middle class.[10]

Situated as they were at the nation's centre of gravity, the middle class adopted a variety of attitudes towards the working class. There were roughly three phases. After the First World War and all through the 1920s, in the face of a growing and militant Labour movement, whose demands seemed insolent and excessive, the bourgeois were alarmed, closed their ranks and called for repressive measures. In a spirit of peevish conservatism they talked of putting the working class in its place and breaking the unions. They changed their tone during the economic crises of the 1930s, but without entirely losing their suspicions. Many of them felt profound disquiet at the sufferings of the unemployed. Anyone with any liberal or humanitarian feeling was horrified at the sight of so much poverty and injustice. Hence arose a call for reform, which grew in strength during the war and was partly responsible for the planning in 1943–4 of much more generous social legislation. There was a new phase in 1945. After Labour's election victory in 1945 and the enactment of more egalitarian measures, the middle classes had another fit of the sulks. They felt that they were being victimized by doctrinaire socialists and were being made to pay for the costs of peace and reconstruction. When two Conservative intellectuals, Roy Lewis and Angus Maude, published a book on the subject in 1949, they first thought of calling it *The Decline and Fall of the Middle Classes*. A Gallup poll showed that the worried reaction of a class on the defensive was to seek refuge in the bosom of the Conservative Party. While in 1945 not more than 76 per cent of the 'well-to-do' income group voted Conservative, in 1951 the proportion rose to 90 per cent. Of those moderately well-off (the 'middle income group'), 61 per cent voted Conservative in 1945, and 73 per cent in 1951.[11] However, this change in party allegiance took place in an atmosphere of calm and relative social harmony.

Below the class we have been describing came the ill-defined world of the 'lower middle class'. It was hybrid and complex, ever on the increase thanks to the growth in numbers of employees, civil servants and technicians, while at the same time all its traditional occupations – tradesmen, small businessmen, shop assistants, commercial travellers – continued to flourish. Although they benefited more than any other group from the improvements in state education, their mentality had hardly changed since the days when the Grossmith brothers, in *The Diary of a Nobody*, depicted the ordinariness of their empty conventional lives, entirely devoted to keeping up appearances. Yet this world did experience a slight rise in its standard of living. If the domestic servant, a ritual figure before 1914, had vanished, the 'home', the supreme object of attention, was embellished with labour-saving devices (vacuum-cleaner, refrigerator, etc.), with a radio, a gramophone, records, sometimes a car. The family took an annual holiday away from home, yet their lives remained constricted. Social convention ruled their behaviour, their thoughts, their language. The petit-bourgeois mind thought in terms of banal and parrot-like catch-phrases, derived at second hand from the small change of ideas in common currency.

What was particularly characteristic of lower middle-class psychology was a strong sense of class distinctions whether it was a feeling of being superior to the proletariat or inferior to the established middle class. In spite of their central position in the social scale they were acutely conscious of having no influence in the world of politics, society or the press, where all the seats of power were pre-empted by the middle or upper middle classes. They were conscious too of their powerlessness in the face of economic forces which they were quite unable to influence (the sort of insecurity described by the old clerk in Priestley's novel *Angel Pavement*). Their reaction to these frustrations was a wide adoption of various kinds of conformity: political – hence their unfailing support for the Conservative Party between the wars; social – the cult of respectability was a fetish; moral – adherence to a puritanical strictness of behaviour; religious – assiduous attendance at an Anglican church or a Nonconformist chapel. Even more than in 1914 they made desperate and absurd efforts to ape their betters, in their houses, furnishings, dress, reading habits and general way of life, and to be recognized by them – without ever succeeding. Their attitude and outlook were quite inconsistent, for they rejected the idea of class and pretended that what mattered was the nation as a whole, in which all social groups should be merged into one. Yet they lost no opportunity to emphasize the gap between lower middle-class respectability and the dreadful stigma of being labelled 'working class'.

The working class

Manual workers gained no advantage from forming a majority of the population, for, as ever in the past, theirs was a world apart, socially isolated and the victim of two basic laws, insecurity and dependence. In it one submitted and toed the line. Here were to be found all those to whom an industrialized society delegated the material tasks of manufacture and distribution. Their world was bounded by the inert matter they handled. They felt segregated from other social categories whom they judged to be above them and 'privileged' ('white-collar' workers and 'gentlemen'). Their outlook was confined by factory discipline to the dull performance of dull repetitive tasks. In this world of unchanging monotony consciousness of class, of belonging to a community that shared identical work and, even more, an identical destiny, was keen and enduring. The depth and fervour of such feelings are well described in D. H. Lawrence's account of the Nottinghamshire coalminers in *Sons and Lovers* (1913), in Llewellyn's Welsh miners in *How Green was my Valley* (1940), and in Richard Hoggart's *The Uses of Literacy* (1957) on West Riding. There were, of course, blatant regional differences. There were, especially between the wars, cases where contrasts between declining and expanding regions were superimposed on contrasts between traditional local peculiarities. As Peter Mathias has justly remarked, one's ideas about England's social situation in this period depended entirely on where the spotlight was turned.[12] There was a wide difference between the shipbuilding yards of Jarrow on the Tyne – 'the town that was murdered', in the vengeful words of its Labour MP, Ellen Wilkinson – and the light industries of Slough on the outskirts of London. Similarly, there was an enormous difference between the standard of living of the workers of Merthyr Tydfil or Greenock and those of Oxford or Coventry. But in spite of these quite wide differences there was a solid community of feeling, a consciousness of rejection and neglect, which persisted unassuaged right up to the 1950s.

During this third of a century, one can distinguish two periods in working-class history. The first, from 1921 to 1940, was dominated by the spectre of unemployment. There was nothing new about unemployment and its hazards, which had been a concomitant of working-class life since the beginnings of industrialism. But now unemployment assumed massive proportions, far greater than anything the world of labour had ever experienced, so that these two decades were of crucial and far-reaching importance. Not only did unemployment seem like some dire plague from which none could escape, the spectacle of millions of people condemned to the utmost distress being felt as the worst sort of scandal; but in addition this historic experience was to leave lasting marks, even beyond the generation of those who had suffered. The fear of losing their jobs haunted people long after the policy of full employment had been

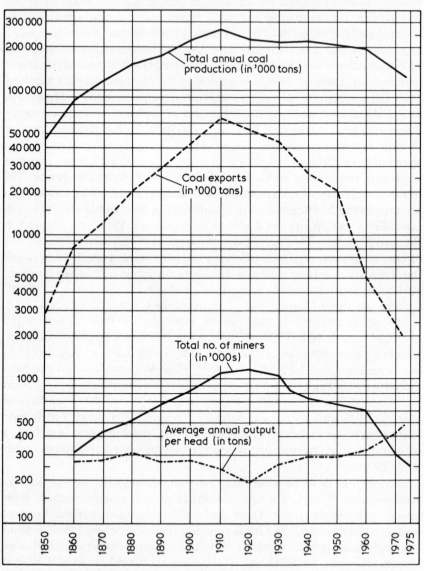

Figure 9. The coal industry in Great Britain, 1850–1974

implemented. Even today many restrictive practices and much trade-union behaviour are due to the recollection of those dark years, deeply engraved on the collective memory.

What gave this particular epidemic of unemployment its intolerable character was that it was as widespread as it was lasting. Whole regions were devastated: the Welsh mining valleys, Lancashire (in Wigan one man in three was 'on the dole'), the steel industry, the shipyards of Tyne and Tees, the Scottish Lowlands (in Glasgow nearly half the population was affected by unemployment). In the coalmines of Bishop Auckland (County Durham), out of 33 pits normally employing 28,000 miners, only 13 were working – and then not continuously – giving employment to 7,000 only. Alongside those lucky ones who were only jobless for a short time, there were two groups who had no hope of escape. On the one hand the young: some had never worked because there was no work for them, others had found unskilled jobs between the ages of 15 and 20, paid at juvenile rates, only to find themselves on the streets when they were adult and had acquired some qualification. On the other hand there were the quasi-permanently unemployed: in 1932 there were 300,000 who had been without work for over a year, and in 1933 there were 500,000. By 1936 there were still 340,000 in that situation, i.e. one man in every four; in that year 53,000 had had no work for more than five years and 205,000 for between two and five years.[13] In all the distressed areas there was a gloomy atmosphere of sadness, of bored resignation and despair. Forced inaction led to demoralization. In the streets of towns, large and small, the unemployed walked aimlessly up and down:

> They lounge at corners of the street
> And greet friends with a shrug of the shoulder
> And they empty pockets out,
> The cynical gestures of the poor . . .
> They sleep long nights and rise at ten
> To watch the hours that drain away.
>
> (Stephen Spender)[14]

Beggars in rags sold matches, boot-polish, boot-laces; pilferers took bits of coal from railway trucks in sidings. In little Welsh towns one saw miners sitting on the pavements endlessly singing songs such as 'Land of our Fathers' to pass the time. Everywhere one found shops closed and houses shut with their windows boarded up. Long queues formed alternately outside labour exchanges and cinemas. The only thriving businesses were pawnbrokers and bookmakers; for in this pointless life of unending idleness and waste people took desperately to betting, in the pathetic hope of the piece of luck that never turns up. Instead of the miracle came demoralization and a feeling of helplessness, witness

Walter Greenwood's *Love on the Dole*, a proletarian novel about life near Manchester, or George Orwell's *The Road to Wigan Pier* about Lancashire and the Sheffield area. Working-class life was not all unemployment, and there were some sheltered and prosperous regions like the South East where workers in expanding industries experienced a sharp rise in their standard of living. All the same the memory of unemployment left its mark on all alike.

This is why the policy of full employment, which started in 1940 and was more fully implemented after the war, represented a fundamental change in working-class life. Henceforward people felt that they would not lose their jobs, or if they did want a change they would find another job. There was also an all-round rise in the standard of living and near-extinction of 'primary poverty', that is poverty due to a lack of the basic necessities of life. The Rowntree social surveys based on research in the city of York showed that the proportion of the working-class population living below the poverty line had fallen from 31.1 per cent in 1936 to 2.8 per cent in 1950. In 1936 unemployment was the cause in 29 per cent of the cases; in 1950 there were none in that category, but two cases of poverty out of three were due to old age.[15]

This transformation of working-class life in the 1940s had three causes: the principal one was full employment, but there were also movements in the level of wages and there was the extension of the social services. The Welfare State gave really effective protection against the major hazards of existence. The real wage of the manual worker increased, but those at the bottom of the ladder, the worst paid, gained proportionately more than the rest. The difference between the pay of the unskilled and the skilled worker, which up till then had been substantial, was markedly reduced. This was partly because the advance of technology, with the development of the mechanized and later automated production line, had introduced intermediate categories of semi-skilled workers so that there was no longer any sharp distinction between those who were highly skilled through apprenticeship or training and those who had no skill at all. It was largely due to pressure from the big unions and public opinion that wide differences in pay disappeared – nominal pay at least, for the skilled worker got round this change by winning bonuses. Women's pay evolved along the same lines as that of men. They were heavily discriminated against, earning about half a man's pay in the years 1930–5. As a general rule the wages of all the lower-paid workers rose more sharply than that of the medium- and higher-paid.

As regards hours of work, 1919 was the key year. There was a major reduction at that date: from the 9-hour day and 54-hour week to the 8-hour day and a week that was sometimes of 46½ hours and sometimes of 48. This was the moment when the steel industry changed from two shifts

of 12 hours to three shifts of 8. But it took thirty years to reach the next
stage. The working week remained the same until after the Second World
War; then it fell to 44½ hours, and round about 1968 to 40½. In contrast
improvements in holidays came earlier, in the inter-war period. The
granting of holidays with pay became more common, and almost universal after 1945 (a fortnight on average). Leisure activities remained much
the same until the invasion of the working man's home by television
during the 1950s. The sacred trio – pub, sport and betting – had almost
acquired the status of a religion. Occupational hobbies also remained
much the same: miners continued to breed whippets and railwaymen
cultivated their allotments. Pigeon racing, football matches, trips to
Southend or Blackpool were widespread pleasures.

It can be said that there was a twofold process at work after the Second
World War. On the one hand, in contrast to the bitter conflicts of the
inter-war years, the world of the manual worker was found to be more
integrated with the life of the nation, sharing more of its main values.
Proletarian poverty seemed to be a thing of the past, since everyone had
food and work, a reasonable standard of living, genuine social security
and considerate treatment by the powers that be. On the other hand the
climate of working-class thought, its culture, language, family life and
collective institutions, such as the trade unions, were little changed. As
Ferdynand Zweig and Richard Hoggart found, the working class was still
deeply imbued with its own exclusive class culture and with the conviction of belonging to a distinct community that was quite apart from the
middle-class universe. It was the feeling of having a status rather than an
ideology that drew this reply of a timber porter to a sociological inquiry: 'I
am not a Socialist, I am Labour.'[16]

Rich and poor: an island of lords or a country of Mr Smiths?

If one is to draw any long-term conclusions about a society as stratified as
the English, it is essential to try to find out how class differences have
arisen. In other words, what have we to learn from the study of the
distribution and amount of wealth in different social groups at different
periods? Nobody will deny that the Great Britain of the pre-1914 era, with
its glaring social contrasts, well deserved the title of 'a paradise for the
rich'. Disraeli's 'Two Nations' lived on, side by side, separated by an
almost unbridgeable gulf. However, following two world wars, some
democratic pressure and great economic change, there were some signs
after 1918 and many more after 1945 of a narrowing of social differences
and some cracks in the stratification. The key question of twentieth-
century society is this: has there been a reduction of inequality or has
it continued, unchanged but skilfully disguised? One can see great

Table 5 Social hierarchy and size of income from the seventeenth to the twentieth century (in numbers)[17] 1688–1867: England and Wales 1908–70: the UK

Social class	1688			1803		
	Average income per family (£)	No. of families (in '000s)	Total income received (£ million)	Average income per family (£)	No. of families (in '000s)	Total income received (£ million)
1. Aristocracy	370	17	6	1,220	27	33
2. Middle ranks	60	435	26	195	640	125
Agriculture	52	330	17	119	320	38
Industry and						
commerce	80	50	4	279	240	67
Professions	91	55	5	250	80	20
3. Lower orders	13	920	12	39	1,350	52
Total	—	1,372	44	—	2,017	210

Social class	1929			1938		
	Personal income (£)	No. of incomes (in '000s)	Total income received (£ million)	Personal income (£)	No. of incomes (in '000s)	Total income received (£ million)
Aristocracy and upper middle class	10,000 + 2,000– 10,000	10 100	221 378	10,000 + 2000– 10,000	8 97	163 361
Middle class	1,000–2,000 500–1,000	199 508	237 312	1,000–2,000 500–1,000	183 539	247 361
Lower middle class	250–500	1,527	404	250-500	1,890	631
Lower middle class, skilled workers	125–250	4,925	980	250 –	20,300	2,613
Semi-skilled, unskilled, unemployed	125 –	11,600	1,170			
Total	—	18,869	3,702	—	23,017	4,376

* Average income per family or household
1,000 + : more than £1,000
  500 − : less than £500

	1867			1908		
Social class	Personal income (£)	No. of families (in '000s)	Total income received (£ million)	Personal income (£)	No. of households (in '000s)	Total income received (£ million)
Upper class	1,000 +	30	181	1,000 +	200	566
Top nobility	5,000 +	5	111			
Gentry and upper middle class	1,000–5,000	25	70			
Middle class						
Middle middle class	300–1,000	90	73	400–1,000	220	138
Lower middle class	100–300	510	94	160–400	680	205
	100	950	71	160 –	1,300	232
Manual labour class	58*	4,600	268	108*	6,500	703
Skilled	86*	840	72			
Lower skilled (or semi-skilled)	70*	1,600	112			
Unskilled and agricultural labourers	47*	1,500	71			
Paupers	22*	600	13			
Total	—	6,180	687	—	8,900	1,844

	1949			1969–1970		
Size of income	Personal income (£)	No. of incomes (in '000s)	Total income received (£ million)	Personal income (£)	No. of incomes (in '000s)	Total income received (£ million)
Very high	20,000 +	2	70	8,000 +	114	1,167
	4,000– 20,000	76	454			
High	2,000–4,000	152	397	4,000–8,000	322	1,500
Comfortable	1,000–2,000	550	735	2,000–4,000	1,522	3,868
Modest	500–1,000	2,690	1,740	1,000–2,000	10,058	14,114
Low	500 –	22,030	5,432	1,000 –	10,172	6,572
Total	—	25,500	8,827	—	22,188	27,221

Table 6 Social hierarchy and size of income from the seventeenth to the twentieth century (percentages)[17] 1688–1867: England and Wales; 1908–70: the UK

Social class	1688			1803		
	Average income per family (£)	No. of families (%)	Total income received (%)	Average income per family (£)	No. of families (%)	Total income received (%)
1. Aristocracy	370	1.2	14.1	1,220	1.4	15.7
2. Middle ranks	60	31.7	59.0	195	31.7	59.4
Agriculture	52	24.0	38.6	119	15.8	18.0
Industry and commerce	80	3.7	9.0	279	11.9	31.9
Professions	91	4.0	11.4	250	4.0	9.5
3. Lower orders	13	67.1	26.9	39	66.9	24.9
Total	—	100.0	100.0	—	100.0	100.0

Social class	1929			1938		
	Personal income (£)	No. of incomes (%)	Total income received (%)	Personal income (£)	No. of incomes (%)	Total income received (%)
Aristocracy and upper middle class	10,000 +	0.05	6.0	10,000 +	0.04	3.7
	2,000– 10,000	0.5	10.2	2,000– 10,000	0.4	8.2
Middle class	1,000–2,000	1.0	6.4	1,000–2,000	0.8	5.7
	500–1,000	2.7	8.4	500–1,000	2.3	8.3
Lower middle class	250–500	8.1	10.9	250–500	8.2	14.4
Lower middle class, skilled workers	125–250	26.1	26.5	250 –	88.3	59.7
Semi-skilled, unskilled, unemployed	125 –	61.5	31.6			
Total	—	100.0	100.0	—	100.0	100.0

* Average income per family or household
1,000 + : more than £1,000
500 – : less than £500

	1867			1908		
Social class	Personal income (£)	No. of families (%)	Total income received (%)	Personal income (£)	No. of households (%)	Total income received (%)
. Upper class	1,000 +	0.5	26.3	1,000 +	2.2	30.7
Top nobility	5,000 +	0.1	16.2			
Gentry and upper middle class	1,000–5,000	0.4	10.1			
. Middle class						
Middle middle class	300–1,000	1.5	10.6	400–1,000	2.5	7.5
Lower middle class	{ 100–300	8.3	13.7	160–400	7.7	11.1
	100 –	15.3	10.3	160 –	14.6	12.6
. Manual labour class	58*	74.4	39.1	108*	73.0	38.1
Skilled	86*	13.8	10.5			
Lower skilled (or semi-skilled)	70*	26.1	16.3			
Unskilled and agricultural labourers	47*	24.6	10.3			
Paupers	22*	9.9	2.0			
Total	—	100.0	100.0	—	100.0	100.0

	1949			1969–1970		
Size of income	Personal income (£)	No. of incomes (%)	Total income received (%)	Personal income (£)	No. of incomes (%)	Total income received (%)
Very high	{ 20,000 +	0.01	0.8	8,000	0.5	4.3
	4,000– 20,000	0.3	5.1			
High	2,000–4,000	0.6	4.5	4,000–8,000	1.5	5.5
Comfortable	1,000–2,000	2.1	8.3	2,000–4,000	6.9	14.2
Modest	500–1,000	10.6	19.7	1,000–2,000	45.3	51.9
Low	500 –	86.4	61.6	1,000 –	45.8	24.1
Total	—	100.0	100.0	—	100.0	100.0

psychological changes between the middle of the nineteenth and the middle of the twentieth century: a class-ridden society changed into a more egalitarian one. But did egalitarianism lead to more equality? We have two indicators to help us solve this burning question – the differences in income and the distribution of capital.

Let us start with incomes, since they relate directly to social classification and living standards. The two sets of tables (Tables 5 and 6)[17] show the evolution of incomes by social classes from the end of the seventeenth century to the present decade, the first in totals, the second in percentages. A very long period is needed to show social trends. The first two columns show the structure of pre-industrial England, starting in 1688 and using the figures given by that great statistician, Gregory King, in his *Natural and Political Observations and Conclusions upon the State and Conditions of England*, and going on to 1803 and the early days of industrialism, the figures taken from Patrick Colquhoun's *Treaty on Indigents* and *Treatise on the Wealth, Power and Resources of the British Empire* (using, in a simplified form, Harold Perkin's statistical presentation). Three facts emerge clearly: a concentration of high incomes in a small number of aristocratic families; the affluence of the middle classes (it is interesting that in the early years the highest proportion is formed of freeholders and tenant farmers, but later they are overtaken by the growing number of businessmen, manufacturers, merchants, etc., who together with members of the professions constitute the real middle class); finally comes the mass of labourers, artisans and paupers, lumped together as 'lower classes', who form two-thirds of all income-earners but only receive one-quarter of all income.

What emerges from a study of the two later columns (1867 and 1908), which represent the expansionist period of capitalism and *laissez-faire* (one, the 1867 column, is based on Dudley Baxter's calculations in his study *National Income*, 1868; the other, for 1908, was worked out by us on the basis of Chiozza Money's figures in his book *Riches and Poverty*, revised edition 1911), is the extent to which the social scale has stretched and wealth has become concentrated in fewer hands. For example, while the average proportional difference of income between the lowest level (labourers) and the highest (aristocracy) was formerly 1 to 30, in 1867 it was 1 to 100. The social pyramid had got thinner and higher. The share of those with middling incomes had diminished, while that of the top section had swollen; a few tens of thousands of people took between them almost a third of all incomes, while three-quarters of all families had to share out less than two-fifths of the available resources. One can well understand Ruskin's ironic modern version of the Beatitudes:

Blessed are the Rich in Flesh, for theirs is the Kingdom of Earth:
Blessed are the Proud, in that they have inherited the Earth:
Blessed are the Merciless, for they shall obtain Money.[18]

Chiozza Money's figures for the period before 1914 are confirmed by
the results attained by Bowley and Mallet for the years 1910–13. The
1 million families composing the upper and middle classes (11 per cent of
all families) shared two-fifths of available income, about the same as that
taken by the 8 million lower-class families (80 per cent of the population),
the rest going to the lower middle classes.[19]

On reaching the inter-war years one is at first surprised at how little
seems to have changed since the 'belle époque'. Although there was slightly
less inequality, the structure of incomes in 1929 showed little change from
that of 1908. At that date 2 per cent of the population received one-third of
all income, while another third went to three-quarters of the population.
By 1929, 4 per cent received about a third, while 60 per cent received a
little less than a third. The still considerable concentration of wealth may
be summed up in one set of figures: 16 per cent of all income went to 0.5
per cent of the total population of the United Kingdom. Other statistics
show a similar degree of inequality in the sharing-out of the national cake.
While 8.6 million families (73.5 per cent of all) earned less than £4 a week
and 2.5 million (21.3 per cent) between £4 and £10, there were only
600,000 families with a weekly income of over £10.[20] The enormous
disparity that existed in this period was such that Keynes in his *General
Theory* severely criticized the prevailing system as unjust and socially
unacceptable, although he believed in the inevitability of a certain amount
of inequality.[21]

On turning to the question of the proportion between earned and
unearned income between the wars, we find that, according to Bowley, it
remained unchanged between 1913 and 1924, at 65 per cent and 35 per
cent respectively.[22] Then followed a slight fall in unearned income due to
the halving of returns on overseas investments and a reduction of rents
from properties. By contrast, returns on capital invested at home resisted
prevailing trends better than is commonly believed. All in all, by 1938
unearned incomes had fallen to 22 per cent of all income.[23] The Second
World War gravely affected them, for they dropped to 12 per cent in 1948,
and by 1956 they represented only 11 per cent of total income – half the
1938 figure.[24] Earned income, on the other hand, continued to rise: it was
less than 50 per cent in 1914, 60 per cent in 1938, and 72 per cent in 1956.

Up to this point there has been little difficulty in interpreting our tables.
There is general agreement about the main lines of economic evolution.
This is no longer the case with the period beginning with the Second
World War, particularly as there is disagreement over the statistics for the

apportionment of income for 1938, 1949 and 1969. There is a great debate about their interpretation on the outcome of which depends the answer to the whole question of the social evolution of contemporary England.

The widely accepted theory is that the levelling effects of the war, then the policy followed by the Labour Government after 1945, and to some extent by the Conservatives in the 1950s, brought about a massive transformation in British society, annihilating the wealthy upper crust and, over the years, redistributing income to a degree quite out of proportion with the slow changes of the past. This theory, rather smugly propagated both by the Right and the Left (though for different reasons), is based on powerful arguments and has been widely supported. It can hardly be denied that the profusion of social services provided by the Welfare State gave a step-up to those at the bottom of the ladder and, in effect, increased their purchasing power. Nor can it be denied that the policy of full employment abolished the root causes of the chronic working-class poverty of the nineteenth century and the inter-war period by guaranteeing work and a decent wage for all. One should also add that unremitting trade-union pressure won pay increases for the lowest earners, and this did much to reduce some big discrepancies in wage scales.

But others have gone much further than Bertrand de Jouvenel's 'ethics of redistribution'.[25] It has been alleged that the incomes of the middle class – entrepreneurs, shareholders, members of the professions – were dramatically reduced as a result of socialist policies in the 1940s and inflation in the 1950s, by comparison with those of skilled and unskilled manual labour. This reduction was aggravated by heavy taxation (income tax and death duties) which ruthlessly whittled away the purchasing power and wealth of these shipwrecked survivors of old privilege, the 'new poor'. This is not to mention those theoreticians of neo-liberalism like Lionel Robbins, (who saw the post-war fiscal system as pushing relentlessly, year by year, 'towards collectivism and propertyless uniformity')[26] or Enoch Powell,[27] for whom the post-war years were a time of ceaseless levelling down. Hence the idea spread that the rich were a species doomed to extinction. There arose an optimistic vision of England moving slowly but surely – amid loud applause from many who saw in this the apotheosis of free democracy – towards an undifferentiated society in which the progressive levelling out of incomes would become a permanent feature and the installation of a universal middle class would almost totally eliminate both the really rich and the really poor. All this was to be achieved through semi-spontaneous, semi-planned mechanisms, by economic evolution, by labour organization, by socialization, and of course the advent of national affluence after the 1950s, all combining to steer the country towards the classless society.

These ideas, totally misleading in our opinion, are based on various illusions. The first, and commonest, concerns taxation – the tax on incomes which was designed as a major corrective, reducing higher incomes by progressive steps from a half to nine-tenths of their total. In actual fact, all authorities who have studied the question closely (even the most optimistic defenders of the idea of a progressive reduction of inequality) consider that the results of taxation were relatively unimpressive (which is why all comparative studies deal with incomes before tax).[28] The reason was that apart from fraud (far from negligible, incidentally) tax avoidance in the shape of various completely legal loop-holes, such as expense allowances, helped a great deal of income to pass through unscathed. The higher the income bracket, the greater the discrepancy between declared income and actual purchasing power. It was no accident that one of the most flourishing professions to appear in recent times was that of the 'tax consultant', the inventor of a new science – 'tax planning'.

The money was there, but it did not appear in the tables published by the Inland Revenue. For proof one only has to compare the number of taxpayers in the top band in 1938 and in 1958. Prices tripled between those dates, so for incomes of more than £6,000 in 1938 the equivalent in 1958 would be £18,000. On the first date there were 19,000 taxpayers, but on the second only 4,000.[29] Considering the growth in general and personal prosperity it is unimaginable that this group should have dwindled to such an extent: what had happened was simply that potential taxpayers had wriggled out of the bands most exposed to the tax-collector's axe. This is why one cannot altogether rely on the Inland Revenue's statistics, since the incomes of the privileged classes were not properly recorded. This deficiency falsifies all the relativities, and particularly the whole idea of equalization, the illusion of which depends on the apparent cutting down of higher incomes. For according to the record the top 1 per cent now received 8 per cent of all income in place of the pre-war percentage of 16 per cent, thereby raising the lowest by 8 per cent. In addition, however spectacular may have been the increases in income tax – for the rate quintupled between 1938 and 1954 – one should bear in mind that in the same period indirect taxation, levied on consumer goods, hence on the greatest number of taxpayers, on the lowest as well as the highest, increased just as much. Between 1938 and 1954 taxes on beer and spirits were multiplied by 3.5 and on tobacco by 6.5.[30]

Another deficiency in the official presentation of tax figures lay in the actual unit taxed, that is the taxpayer or the taxable household. In reality, as Titmuss rightly remarked, the only proper unit from the point of view of purchasing power was the family as a whole.[31] For a process of diminishing inequality between the actual physical receivers of income can easily hide an increase of inequality between one family and another. In addition demographic factors ought to be taken into account (marriage, age structure, etc.) as well as transfers of income via untaxed capital, capital gains, etc. This would show how mythical was the phenomenon of levelling. There was certainly a reduction in the number of the very poor – the ending of unemployment and the so-called affluent society having raised those at the bottom of the scale to the level of an only moderately inferior category. That does not mean that the apex of the pyramid had been sliced off. The 'income revolution' never happened, and inequality lived on.

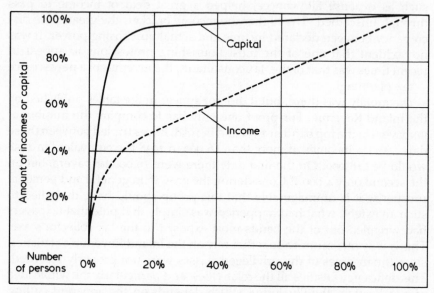

Figure 10. Distribution of incomes and estates in the UK, 1937[32]

The picture was very much the same for capital wealth after 1914. We have already emphasized the extreme inequality that prevailed in the period before the First World War. Thirty years later the situation had hardly changed. Tibor Barna's very careful calculations for the year 1937 show that at that date the 12 million families of Great Britain fell into three numerically equal categories: the first had no capital; the second owned only 4 per cent of the amount of all personal estates; the remaining 4 million thus owned almost all the nation's wealth. So, far from the democratization of society caused by war and its aftermath having brought about a redistribution, the reduction of wealth was a complete myth. Its concentration remained unchanged and just as it was in 1914.[33] Of course there had been some reduction of inequality, but in a very minor way and without seriously affecting the general balance. The gulf between the haves and the have-nots had hardly narrowed at all since the

Edwardian 'golden age'. In 1908, according to Leo Chiozza Money, 66 per cent of capital wealth was in the hands of 1.4 per cent of all families. In 1938, 2 per cent of the population owned capital sums of £5,000 and over, representing *in toto* 66 per cent of all capital wealth. In 1950 the equivalent capital sums of £10,000 and over – 54 per cent of all capital wealth – were owned by 1.5 per cent of the population.

The crux of the argument concerns the years 1939–50. Was the distribution of wealth seriously changed by the drive for egalitarianism? One is obliged to say No. Table 7 bears eloquent witness to this.

Table 7 Distribution of private capital* in Great Britain, 1936–8, 1946–50[34]

	1936–8				1946–50			
Size of holding	Number (in '000s)	%	Value (£ million)	%	Number (in '000s)	%	Value (£ million)	%
Under £100	21,421	75.5	1,015	5.3	19,633	62.4	883	3.0
£100 –	4,983	17.6	2,208	11.4	8,448	26.8	3,479	11.6
£1,000 –	1,688	6.0	5,279	27.3	2,899	9.2	9,461	31.6
£10,000 –	249	0.9	6,507	33.7	475	1.5	11,682	39.0
More than £100,000	15	0.1	4,304	22.3	19	0.06	4,402	14.7
Total	28,356	100	19,313	100	31,474	100	29,907	100

* Figures relate to persons aged 25 and over

As for more recent times, a basis for calculation was provided in the Labour Government's 'Green paper' of August 1974, prepared with a view to a possible wealth tax. It would seem that some dispersal of capital took place after 1960, for up till then there had been little change since the 1946–50 period. The wealthiest 1 per cent of the population, who owned 38 per cent of the total in 1960, had 30 per cent in 1970 and 25 per cent in 1974 (reckoning capital sums of £44,000 or more); but the wealthiest 5 per cent had suffered rather less, owning 64 per cent in 1960, 56 per cent in 1970, and probably 53 per cent in 1974. One must interpret these figures cautiously, and in any case they hardly add up to a march towards equality. For one thing, of all the people who died in 1970, 50 per cent had no estate to bequeath. Such change as there had been since 1960 was due principally to an increase in the size of the middle group (those whose capital amounted to between £5,000 and £20,000). Just as the escalation of income tax resulted in legal methods of disguising the extent of the very top incomes, so the severity of death duties provoked a crop of ingenious arrangements (gifts, discretionary trusts, settlements and so on) for their avoidance, particularly among the very rich. This at one stroke eliminated the largest accumulations of wealth from the official statistics. The results of an inquiry carried out in the 1950s provide an interesting illustration of this. If one calculates the average capital owned by different age groups among the wealthy, one finds that the totals are much higher in the 20–25 age group (about £16,000 per head) than among the 45-year-olds (about £10,000 per head), which is odd, since wealth normally increases with age. It shows that parents started transferring sizeable capital sums to their children as soon as they came of age. In this way the heirs to great estates always managed to get the better of Chancellors of the Exchequer by adopting the principle enunciated by Burke: 'the power of perpetuating our property in our families is one of the most valuable and interesting circumstances belonging to it and that which tends the most to the perpetuation of society itself.'[35]

In conclusion, not only was the class structure maintained in a much more rigid form than most people cared to admit, but the defence mechanisms of privilege and their ability to resist change triumphed over all legislative obstacles put in their way. In the economic as in the social sphere, deeply entrenched forces over a long period resisted the egalitarian trend and sought to perpetuate ancient inequalities. All that changed was that in later years they invented subtler and less obvious devices.

There are therefore two stages to be distinguished in the development of English society. Up to the beginning of World War II, Disraeli's 'Two Nations' lived on, fairly unchanged. That is to say the old society retained, almost unaltered, its outstanding features – masses of poor, a handful of rich, extreme inequality displayed in graphic form by a tall pyramid. After 1945 came a new factor – the defeat of poverty. Up till then at least a quarter of the population had lived below the poverty line; henceforward, according to the most careful calculations, there would be not more than one-tenth in that situation. Under the combined effects of socialization and 'the affluent society', the deprived classes attained a decent, sometimes even comfortable level. In this way the bottom layer of society achieved a substantial lift. But the ranks of the rich stood fast; for the neo-liberal system remained firmly based on the twin notions of class and inequality. One has only to compare the social structure of 1931 with that of 1961. The 1931 structure differs very little at the top from that of 1867 when Class I included 2 per cent of the population and Class II 16 per cent, whereas at the bottom of the scale Classes IV and V (60 per cent in 1867) had been considerably reduced by 1931 and even more in 1961.

Table 8, illustrating the distribution of the male occupied population according to socio-economic categories, brings out very clearly the change that had come about at the base of the social pyramid. It shows how the very poor moved up into the ranks of those with some income and some social status. But the top changed very little, though it became slightly larger. So one can only infer a very slight easing of the rigidities of the hierarchy, corresponding to the slow changes in the social landscape.

Table 8 The social structure of England and Wales, 1931–61 (After the classification given by the Registrar General)[36]

	Class	1931 (%)	1961 (%)
Class I	Higher professional and managerial	2	4
Class II	Intermediate non-manual	13	15
Class III	Skilled manual and routine non-manual	49	51
Class IV	Semi-skilled	18	21
Class V	Unskilled	18	9

9 *The slowly changing social landscape*

Neo-Malthusian fluctuations

It may seem paradoxical to maintain that the losses caused by the two world wars (considerably more than 1 million dead) have only had a limited effect on Britain's demographic evolution. Did not the loss of so many young men cut off in the prime of life cause grave imbalance – on the birth-rate, for a start? In the First World War, 9 per cent of the male population aged between 20 and 45, i.e. 5 per cent of the labour force, died on the battlefield. And even if in the Second World War the losses were only half those of the First World War, and differently distributed by sex and age (of the 60,000 civilians killed in air raids, 25,000 were women and 8,000 children), wasn't the loss of 300,000 combatants likely to affect a population that had been facing decline during the 1930s? The revealed facts state otherwise. The Royal Commission on Population, a monumental inquiry into every aspect of British demography over half a century, was able to report in 1949 that even the heavy losses of the First World War had only slightly influenced the already falling birth-rate. Cynics remarked that compared with the rate of emigration before 1914 the number of dead was less than the number who would have left the country for good. The Commission pointed out that fears expressed in the 1930s on the dangers of depopulation were unfounded. Hadn't one eminent demographer prophesied in 1933 that as a result of the falling birth-rate the population would fall to 36 million in 1965 and to 5 million in

2035 – equal to the population of Denmark! Although it would be wrong to underestimate the social, economic and cultural consequences of the two wars on society, it must be said that the psychological effect was incomparably greater than the demographic. The concept of the 'lost generation', so poignantly felt by those who had lived through the trenches had, in fact, little statistical reality.

Table 9 War losses in the UK[1]

	1914–1918	*1939–1945*
Deaths on active service		
Total (killed, or dead of wounds)	745,000	270,000
Army	(714,000)	(149,000)
Navy	(27,000)	(51,000)
Air Force	(4,000)	(70,000)
Civilian deaths		
Civilians killed in air-raids	1,100	60,000
Merchant navy	15,000	35,000
Total war losses	761,000	365,000
Percentage of total UK population	1.7 %	0.8 %

The truth was that England, pursuing and confirming a trend that had been at work over thirty years, settled down to a moderate and controlled rate of reproduction. After 1920 people thought and behaved in a spirit of Neo-Malthusianism. Fewer children, smaller families and birth control were the characteristics of population movements.

The population was no longer growing rapidly. Leaving out Ireland, which is a special case, the number of inhabitants in Great Britain rose from 40.8 million in 1911 to 44.8 million in 1931 and 48.9 million in 1951. In 1971 it reached the figure or 53.8 million. What a contrast with the nineteenth century when it nearly doubled in each fifty-year period! The annual rate of increase, which in England and Wales, was 1.5 per cent between 1831 and 1851, fell to 0.8 per cent from 1901 to 1921 and to 0.5 per cent between 1931 and 1951. And in this last period a positive balance of migration helped to support a growth rate that was regularly diminishing. The cause was a fall in the birth-rate. This was 22 per '000 from 1910 to 1920, fell to 18 per '000 in the 1920s and 15 per '000 in the 1930s, rose during the war and round about 1955 settled down at 16 per '000. It was the day of the small family. Of couples married in 1925, 16 per cent had no children, 25 per cent one only, 25 per cent two children, 14 per cent three, 8 per cent four, 5 per cent five and 7 per cent six or more.[2] The result was that in 1934 the number of children under 5 years old was smaller than in

1871, while the population was greater by 20 million. Alongside this, the net reproduction rate fell in a rather alarming way to below unity during the inter-war period. It fell from 1.1 in 1911–21 to 0.97 in 1923, and to 0.80 in 1938. It only passed unity again after 1950 (1.01 in 1950–4, and 1.25 in 1960) thanks to the moderate recovery of the birth-rate after the war. The average number of children per family followed the same curve: 2.82 for the cohorts of marriages celebrated in 1910–14, 2.31 for 1920–4, 2.07 for 1930–4, 2.08 for 1940–4 and 2.31 for 1950–4.[3] As often happens in demography, the record, instead of being straightforwardly linear, is studded with minor irregularities which interrupt the general trend.

There are two noticeable anomalies. Firstly there are the variations in the birth-rate curve, which are due less to the 'baby booms' which followed immediately after the two world wars (quite brief, 1919–1920 and 1945–8, and equivalent mainly to 'deferred births') than to the alteration of periods of low birth-rate (1921–9 and 1945–55) and of recovery (1941–5 and, especially, 1956–64). The other anomaly is the differential rate of fertility varying with social class. The use of contraceptives had started among the comfortably-off, spreading after 1900 to the lower middle classes, and then to the masses. There was a marked fall in the birth-rate among the working class between the wars. Nevertheless, up to the eve of the Second World War there was a definite negative correlation between reproduction rate and social (and income) level. Thus the families of mineworkers, agricultural labourers and unskilled workers produced 25 to 30 per cent more children than those of other social groups. But since the Second World War the social profile of fertility has changed. Instead of decreasing as one mounted the social scale, the birth-rate was found to have increased in the higher social groups (employers and managers, members of the professions, etc.). Thus the size of families was now largest at the two extremes of the social spectrum. Conversely the fertility rate was lowest in the intermediate groups, the lower middle classes and skilled workers.

Cutting across the whole movement and its minor fluctuations was the fact of a massive spread of the practice of contraception. Whereas in the middle of the nineteenth century probably one married woman in six used some method, between 1920 and 1940 it was three out of four. Neo-Malthusian ideas had permeated all social milieux (except the Roman Catholics) and overcome all moral and religious opposition. Strongly influenced by wars, depressions and unemployment, public opinion was convinced, collectively, of the dangers of overpopulation. Individually people took to the idea of voluntary family planning, rather than just trusting to luck, or accepting the arrival of another child as a sign of the divine will. Now it was those with large families who became the ones to be pitied. As babies became scarcer, domestic animals – dogs and cats –

ruled the home. The ubiquity of pets became a feature of civilized life.

Many factors contributed to this profound mental and moral revolution: the recognized association of poverty with large numbers of children; the needs of feminine emancipation (was not the release from constant child-bearing a prime condition for liberation?); the desire for a fuller extension of woman's physical and mental satisfactions (Dr Marie Stopes' *Married Love* had an enormous influence); anxieties about children's careers and education; a taste for comfort and good living (contemporaries used to say they wanted 'a Baby Austin rather than a baby'); a philosophy of life that demanded both more individualism and more mobility. Peter Laslett has shown that the average household of 4.5 persons which remained absolutely constant all through the eighteenth and nineteenth centuries began to get smaller towards the First World War, fell to 4.1 in 1921, 3.7 in 1931, and 3.2 in 1951, thus proving that the nuclear family was getting smaller.[4]

However, in spite of the attempts at education through the now rapidly spreading birth-control clinics, the use of contraceptives did not keep up with the spread of contraceptive ideas. Only a minority among the privileged classes used condoms, diaphragms or spermicides. The vast majority resorted to coitus interruptus. A. J. P. Taylor has rightly remarked that between the end of the nineteenth century – the beginning of contraceptive practices – and the Second World War, when more satisfactory methods became widespread, English men and women were 'frustrated people'.[5] This was something which could hardly fail to have a deep effect on personal and national behaviour. One might add another source of frustration – an uneasy collective attitude towards sexuality which hedged it around with a censorious puritanism, labelling talk about the taboo subject as 'indecent' or 'un-English'. Is it entirely by chance that the condom is known as a 'French letter' and diaphragm as a 'Dutch cap'?

Two other aspects of demographic change deserve mention, for they show how profoundly the England of the mid-twentieth century differed from Victorian England. First, the progressive ageing of the population, a feature common to all advanced European cities. This explains why the death-rate hardly changed. Having fallen to 12.4 per '000 in 1921 it stayed around that figure, at times decreasing to just below 12 per '000. Infant mortality, however, fell spectacularly. From 150 to 160 per '000 at the end of the nineteenth century, it fell to 110 per '000 on the eve of the First World War, then to 66 in 1931 and 30 in 1951, i.e. a reduction by half between 1901 and 1931, and by another half between 1931 and 1951. In addition the expectation of life rose rapidly since the beginning of the century. While in 1910 it was 52 for men and 54 for women, by 1960 it had risen to 68 and 74 respectively.

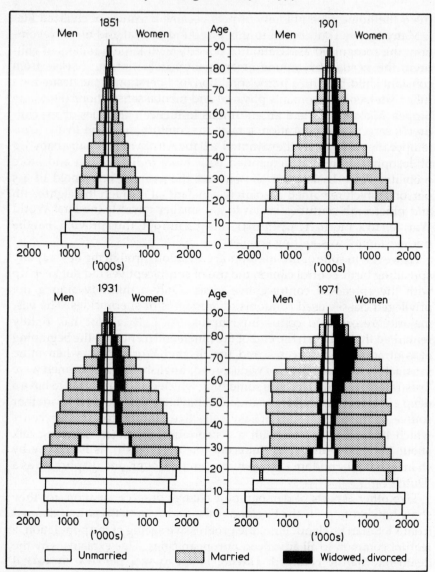

Figure 11. Age pyramids in England and Wales, 1851, 1901, 1931, 1971

As for emigration, the traditional stream of departures overseas continued unabated, with a temporary acceleration after each of the two wars. Between 1911 and 1931 Great Britain lost 1.5 million subjects, but the stream dried up in the 1930s as distant El Dorados became less attractive during the Depression. Between 1952 and 1957 emigration returned to its previous high level, 200,000 a year. Henceforward it was to be directed towards the Commonwealth – only one emigrant out of ten went to the USA. Most went to Australia and New Zealand, and a substantial number to Canada. What was most remarkable was that after the 1930s England became as much an immigrant as an emigrant country. This was something that had not been seen for centuries. For the first time, between 1931 and 1951, there was more inward than outward migration. The Scots continued to expatriate themselves (to England among other places), but England and Wales gained three-quarters of a million inhabitants, which included refugees from Nazi Germany and other totalitarian States, returning emigrants, the Irish (drawn back by the needs of war-time industries and post-war reconstruction), former Polish servicemen and so on. Over the decade 1951–61 as a whole, Britain showed a slight gain in population, there was a decline until 1957, then an excess of immigrants, but of a different kind – coloured people from the Commonwealth. As a result the country was to face problems of a size and character hitherto unknown.

Urbanization, suburbanization and town-planning

In *Anticipations*, H. G. Wells prophesied that the day would come when the whole of Great Britain, from south of the Scottish Highlands to the English Channel, would consist of one vast urban region, a sort of nebula, whose citizens, now all commuters, could choose their home anywhere within 100 miles of where they worked.[6] In fact, without actually being realized, the prophecy began to look much less futuristic in the middle of the twentieth century. For decades the advance of urbanization had dominated the lives of the British; now the last stage had arrived. Four out of five were town-dwellers. Of those who still lived in the country, only half cultivated the soil. The 1951 census showed less than a million people working on the land, 5 per cent of the total labour force.

This urban predominance resulted in some extraordinary concentrations of population. In 1951, one-third of the land surface of Great Britain (mostly mountain, moor and forest) was occupied by 2 per cent of the population, while 40 per cent were clustered in the six largest conurbations – Greater London, the West Midlands round Birmingham, Merseyside, South-East Lancashire round Manchester, West Yorkshire round Leeds, Newcastle and Tyneside; while more than one-third of the population of Scotland lived in the Glasgow conurbation. In France people talk of Paris and the 'desert of France', but the London concentration is far greater. In 1801 one-tenth of the population lived there, in 1851 one-eighth, and one-sixth after the beginning of the twentieth century. Paris contains only one-eighth of the population of France. Having reached 8,700,000 inhabitants in 1939, Greater London ceased to grow, but after

that an urban region sprung up which covered most of South-East England. Between 1914 and 1951 a million people left the heart of the agglomeration – the County of London – to live on the edge. Then after 1951 the
Londoners who departed, at the rate of 30,000 a year, to beyond that limit,
formed a sort of outer ring around the agglomeration.

This development had two features. The first was a new kind of
urbanization – the 'urban region', a composite but variegated phenomenon. Moving on from the small town to the large town, from the large
town to the agglomeration, from the agglomeration to the conurbation,
we arrive finally to the 'megalopolis'! What was new about this was that it
enfolded ancient townships, middle-sized cities – old and recent – and
even semi-rural areas (hence the new term 'rurban' appeared). The second feature was the enormous growth of suburbs, accelerated by the
centrifugal effect of city centres. The new Leviathan of the megalopolis
rested on the more ancient authority of suburbia.

Suburbs had been growing rapidly ever since the last quarter of the
nineteenth century, but it was only after the First World War that the
disease of 'urban sprawl' became an epidemic. For instance, the built-up
area of Greater London was tripled between 1919 and 1939.[7] This spread
was as much a social as a spatial phenomenon, linked with middle-class
habits and progress. Setting up house in the suburbs was a way of
moving up the social scale. Just as a country house on the green outskirts
of a town was the ideal for many of the established middle class, so for the
lower middle class and the upper strata of the working class a 'semi-
detached' in the suburbs seemed the ideal way to independence and
social consideration. Hence the proliferation of suburban outgrowths that
characterized the inter-war way of life: 'ribbon development', interminable rows of little two-storey houses all alike with brick walls, bow
windows, little gardens full of rose-bushes and neatly mown grass
patches – a dull, narrow, restricted world, cruelly described by George
Orwell ('Do you know the road I live in. . . ? Even if you don't you know
fifty others exactly like it. You know how these streets fester all over the
inner-outer suburbs. Always the same. Long, long rows of little semi-
detached houses . . . as much alike as council houses and generally
uglier. The stucco front, the creosoted gate, the privet hedge, the green
front door. The Laurels, the Myrtles, the Hawthorns, Mon Abri, Mon
Repos, Belle Vue . . .').[8]

The widespread ownership of cars, beginning between the wars but
vastly increasing in the 1950s, gave a further impetus to this suburban
dispersion. As Asa Briggs has pointed out, the railways created the towns
(at least those of the nineteenth century) and the motor car has 'blown
them up'; after the 'urban' comes the 'suburban', the 'conurban' and the
'exurban'.

However, disillusion with suburban life soon set in. Not only did it fail to live up to the hopes of its protagonists as a synthesis of fresh air, greenery and country calm with the life of the city with its jobs, shops, trades and entertainments; but constant travel between the two was found to be costly, exhausting and time-consuming. Worse still, suburban life had peculiar frustrations on the psychological plane. One derived from the privacy imposed by suburban villadom, not just the frigid and selfish privacy of 'we like to keep ourselves to ourselves', but a privacy of loneliness and tedium. The other frustration lay in the standardization of interiors and exteriors and the people who lived in them – the endlessly repeated humdrum pattern of existence creating its own form of anonymity, unlike the one found in towns but no less pernicious in its depersonalizing effect.

Planning came into being partly in reaction to the imperfections of old towns with their slums, insanitary dwellings and overcrowding, and partly to avoid the proliferation of dreary suburbs. The need had been seen early on because of the rapid development of urban sprawl, so that England may rightly be called the cradle of town-planning. The earliest, timid measure to regulate town development was the Town Planning Act of 1909, though the word 'town-planning' first appeared in the Oxford English Dictionary in 1906. Between the wars there was a whole series of regulations concerning building standards and planned housing. It was a period during which a great deal of building went on, much of it as social provision by municipal enterprise. Out of 4 million houses built between 1919 and 1939, 2.5 million were produced by the private sector, but 1.5 were municipally provided 'council houses'.

The really decisive phase came after the Second World War, with the creation of a 'Ministry of Town and Country Planning' in 1943. In 1947 the Labour Government passed the Town and County Planning Act, which for the first time formulated a uniform system of planning for the whole country. In addition, widespread bomb damage had necessitated urgent reconstruction of a planned kind, particularly in London, Birmingham, Coventry, Bristol and Plymouth. Meanwhile public opinion had given a warm welcome to the imaginative schemes of town-planners and architects for new towns. In 1946 the New Towns Act was passed, a vast project drawing off surplus population from ancient urban centres, by creating new balanced urban communities, which were to provide both employment and homes. This ambitious programme resulted in 29 'new towns' (23 in England and Wales, 6 in Scotland, plus 4 in Northern Ireland). The first generation of these (1947–50) comprised a dozen towns, mostly situated round London. The second generation, benefiting from the experiences of the first, was completed between 1961 and 1971. Between 1947 and 1970 the new towns attracted 700,000 inhabitants in all.

Elsewhere, in the country as a whole, more housing was provided by the
public authorities than by private enterprise: 57 per cent of new housing
built between 1945 and 1970 was the result of action by local authorities or
the State.

All post-war town-planning was dominated by two principles: first the
creation of 'neighbourhood units', so as to have local districts of human

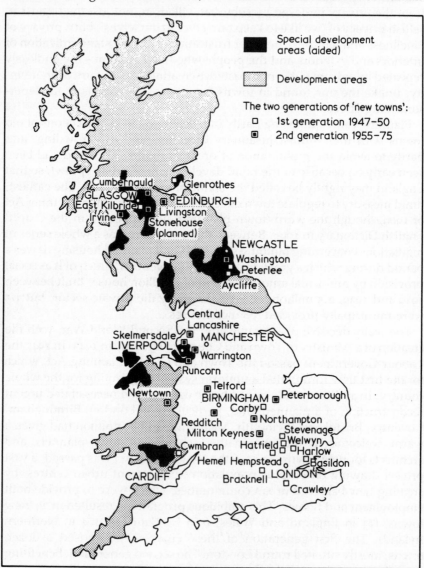

Map 8. Town and country planning: the new towns

dimensions; secondly the formation of 'balanced communities', which could provide, as did the traditional village, home life as well as both work and play, and could inspire the sort of civic spirit one associated with a medieval town. This should be seen as an attempt to create 'micro-societies' that would provide the means for everyone to develop individually without suffering the ills of mass society; the background of a pre-ordained plan was not to interfere with the spontaneity of the individual. Scrupulous attention was paid to the environment and the natural setting (hence the number of parks and 'green belts') and there was determined opposition to overdevelopment, wastage of land and ugliness. In its devotion to horizontal rather than upward spread, town planning showed its attachment to a cultural tradition going back to the teaching of Ruskin, William Morris, Ebenezer Howard (the father of the 'garden city', whose book *Garden Cities for Tomorrow* had a tremendous influence) and of Patrick Geddes, the apostle of the community spirit and the quality of life.

The schools: democratization or élitism

Before 1914 the British educational system was guided by two basic principles. One was the idea that a ruling class needed a special education adapted to the needs of future leadership. The other was the need in a modern, progressive society for a growing number of workers with a modest level of educational attainment. Hence, within the system, a double segregation – one between primary and secondary, the other between paid, private education for the élite, and free, public education, provided by the State or the Churches, for the masses. Education was thus firmly enmeshed in the class system. After the First World War the demands of society for higher standards and parents' demands for more education for their children, coupled with the spread of egalitarian ideas, led to an enlargement of schooling, especially at secondary level, leading finally to the Education Act of 1944. Just as in the nineteenth century primary education for all was the goal, so in the twentieth the prize to be won was universal secondary education and the raising of the school-leaving age. Between the wars the biggest gulf was that which divided primary from secondary schooling, but after 1944 the social cleavage appeared between the different sectors of secondary education. In 1914 this was provided in England and Wales for 300,000 pupils, of whom 200,000 were in state secondary schools. By 1935 the total was 600,000 (the so-called 'public' schools and other fee-paying establishments accounted for one-quarter of this total), and by 1955 2 million. Of these pupils there were 500,000 in secondary grammar schools, 1.25 million in secondary modern schools (which provided a less academic schooling) while the remaining 250,000 were in 'public' and other types of fee-paying schools.[9]

It was all too hastily concluded that, thanks to the new school system, a 'silent social revolution' had been achieved. It was repeatedly stated, smugly and *ad nauseam*, that universal secondary education had broken down one of the toughest class barriers and transformed English society. Up till then this particular class barrier concerned the name of the school one had attended and the sort of education one had had. One was marked for life, and it was something either proudly to boast of or quietly not to mention. But indeed it was a delusion to pretend that this exclusiveness had been broken down. All the reforms, with their liberal and benevolent intentions – the Fisher Act of 1918, and above all the Butler Act of 1944, besides innumerable reports of commissions and experts – however hard they tried to contribute to social mobility and equal chances for all, ran their heads up against the harsh realities of intellectual and institutional exclusiveness that functioned, almost unaffected by change, for the benefit of the rich, the cultured and the privileged classes. Tawney's description of the English educational atmosphere in 1939 remains true today: 'a not unkindly attitude to individuals with a strong sentiment of class and a deep reverence for wealth.'[10] The reforms, important though they were, did more to preserve an élitist system of education than to democratize society. The only permanent change that had been effected was the ending of the lively and continuous bickering about religious instruction. This had in any case declined in the course of the twentieth century, and the 1944 Act, although it made the teaching of religion compulsory, insisted that it should be 'undenominational': a victory for the Church of England, allied on this point at least with the Church of Rome, and, as always, a steady pressure group.

Clearly it was not by chance that the great reform movements in education – in 1902, 1918 and 1944 – took place just after major wars, when the education of the next generation seemed of the first importance. Hence the need for better quality schooling which, in its turn, involved the raising of the school-leaving age, fixed at 14 in 1918, raised to 15 in 1944, and later to 16, though this was not implemented until 1972. After 1918 the feminists were prominent among the champions of egalitarianism, for they saw in improved education for girls the best guarantee of female emancipation, and did all in their power to promote it. At the same time after the war other currents pushed forward in favour of more equality for children. Thus the Labour slogan 'Secondary education for all' was taken up officially by the Hadow Report in 1926. These aspirations found a ready hearing among the enlightened, for liberal opinion was imbued with the reforming idealism of thinkers like John Stuart Mill and Matthew Arnold, for whom school meant social even more than

economic progress. Some saw in equality of opportunity a way of breaking down class barriers. A start was made on the grammar schools. The
clever children of families in the lower income bracket were provided
with scholarships and 'free places', later to be called 'special places', of
which there were 250,000 free or partly free in 1935.[11] Curricula were
modernized, English taking the place of Latin as the basic subject. There
was an increased number of school places and a general widening of aims
– the Spens Report of 1938 proclaimed that school was 'to be regarded as
not merely a "place of learning", but as a social unit or society'.[12] The
Butler Act of 1944 was a dramatic step forward. It involved the principle of
a two-stage education, through which every child had to pass – primary
for the under-11s and secondary for those over 11. Every child was to be
directed according to his or her abilities either towards a long-term
academic education ('secondary grammar') or to a shorter, more modern,
practically or technically orientated education ('secondary modern' or
'secondary technical'). At the time it was seriously believed that this
would break down all the old barriers and give a worth-while fillip to
social mobility.

   However, disenchantment swiftly followed with the realization that
the new educational set-up had quite failed to eliminate traditional class
distinctions. There were three reasons for this: firstly, the indisputable
pre-eminence of the public schools; secondly the social and intellectual
values inculcated by the grammar schools; and thirdly the criteria for
selection.

   Let us first take the public schools, which the reforms of the educational
system had left untouched. The Labour Government of the years 1945–51
had been too timid to touch them – a serious mistake, given their ambitions. Hot-houses for the élite, the public schools went on just as before,
faithful to their traditions and leaving their educational principles
unchanged. They were there to turn out gentlemen, the nation's future
rulers and administrators. They were subjected to withering criticism (the
young emerge from them, said E. M. Forster, with 'well developed
bodies, reasonably developed minds and underdeveloped hearts');
nevertheless they lorded it with imperturbable ease at the summit of the
educational system. They still managed to corner the lion's share of the
'Establishment': they survived, unshaken, all the nation's crises and any
outward signs of democratization imposed on them. Thus, in 1937, 19 of
the 21 members of Chamberlain's Cabinet had been to public schools; in
1961 Macmillan's Cabinet had 17 out of 21. Earlier, Baldwin had described
how, when he was called upon to become Prime Minister, one of his first
thoughts was that he should form a government worthy of his old school
Harrow; and in fact his Cabinet contained no fewer than six old Harro-
vians.[13] Not only were the Foreign Service, the Bar, the Army and the

Navy largely manned, as by tradition, by public-school men, but also business, the City, public relations. . . . In 1944 the Fleming Commission reported that out of 830 top civil servants, bishops, judges, members of the Indian Civil Service, dominion and colonial governors, directors of banks and railway companies, three-quarters had been to public schools (half of them to the 'sacred nine'). Ten years later the situation had hardly changed. During the period 1950–70 the proportion of Conservative MPs who had been to public schools, namely three-quarters, was exactly the same as it had been between the wars. If one took Conservative and Socialists together one still found that in 1970, as in 1951, almost half of all MPs had been to public schools (see Figure 15).[14]

So the power of the public schools survived intact, and with it certain caste privileges: a special kind of education, as befitted an élite, and a special language. Public-school men can recognize others of their kind, *The Times* once remarked, by certain indefinable turns of speech; but although the hallmark was indelibly stamped on the character, it was adaptable to changing times. For instance, as Raymond Williams has acutely observed, instead of openly developing a sense of superiority in these 'natural leaders', the idea of rank gets camouflaged under the disguise of 'service'. Another characteristic of public schools that gave them an ineradicable strength was that even the most open-minded parents, who disliked the system and wanted to escape from it, felt obliged to send their children to them so as to give them the best start in life. In this way inequality was perpetuated from generation to generation. In 1953, for instance, it was calculated that 90 per cent of all those with incomes of over £1000 a year gave their children a private fee-paying education.[15] Thanks to the undeniably superior quality of the education they provided, the public schools, the appanage of a privileged minority (in 1939 Tawney calculated 3 per cent of all families)[16] maintained their ascendancy, based on wealth, culture, prestige and power. All told, not one educational reform succeeded in infringing in the slightest way the educational monopoly constituted by this powerful network of private schools, reserved (apart from a few scholarship pupils) for the children of the upper and upper middle classes.

The grammar schools, though recruited from rather lower down the social and financial scale, were strongly influenced by the public schools. The latter seemed such patterns of scholastic excellence (just as Oxford and Cambridge served as patterns to other universities) that grammar-school life became gradually impregnated with the traditions and customs of the public schools. Such were the daily religious service ('school assembly'), the emphasis on community and group loyalty, the system of giving responsibility for discipline to older pupils (monitors, prefects, head-boys, head-girls), team games, sport and the competitive spirit (e.g.

the encouragement of rivalry between 'houses'). The teachers in these establishments, since they came mainly from the middle and lower middle classes, were well disposed to this kind of imitation of a model handed down from above. Some such schools, too strenuously 'aping their betters', managed only to caricature them, achieving sort of 'poor men's public schools'.

Furthermore the result of educational practice was to inculcate a middle-class mentality, a middle-class speech and a middle-class ethic. Wasn't conformity with current social attitudes the surest way to success? Consequently a school, even when it had a proportion of working-class children, would act as an integrating force, impressing on the pupils the prevailing values of the middle class. This was so much the case that Labour, which all through the inter-war period had pinned its hopes on the opening of the grammar schools to the children of the working classes (and its own future militants), started to back-pedal on the idea when they found that what it was really doing was to encourage individual ambition and absorption into the middle class. Democratization at that stage was mainly benefiting the lower middle classes.

The secondary educational system, as envisaged by governments and the planners of education between the wars, depended on a method of selection that was supposed to give every child the chance his or her abilities deserved. All depended on the criteria determining the way in which the selection and guidance of the children were carried out. It was widely believed that, thanks to the discoveries of psychology and pedagogy, 'scentific' and hence impartial criteria were available. Experience showed, however, that instead of measuring aptitudes they unwittingly reflected the child's socio-cultural background. There were three stages in this educational development. Between the wars official policy was concentrated on finding out which of the children of the masses were fittest to be offered places in grammar schools, while the rest were to be provided with a post-elementary education. The system thus consisted of two levels – élite and masses – not much different from the Victorian system, except that there was more scope for assisted and scholarship pupils at the secondary level, and hence intelligence tests and various selection methods were designed to reveal latent talent. After 1944 there was a second stage. Every child went to a primary school up to the age of 11; after that each one went to one of three different types of secondary school, according to his or her abilities: academic ('grammar'), modern or technical. It soon became evident that this system had two major shortcomings. On the one hand the three separate types gave rise to a new social hierarchy, for in spite of all the promises of equality of level and status ('parity of esteem') the secondary grammar schools were immediately invested with a superior status, while the 'secondary moderns' suggested second best. This appearance of inequality was given reality not only by the results of selection – middle-class children going to secondary grammar schools, working-class children to secondary moderns – but also by the qualifications of the teachers. Direction to a secondary modern involved the double stigma of social and academic failure. So a new idea came into being in the early 1950s. The basic concept was a single school with pupils of all abilities under one roof, and able to offer every variety of educational choice. This was the 'comprehensive school'. Unification seemed to be the only way to achieve democratization, though it may be remarked that the private education provided by the 'public' schools stayed outside . . . and above. Although some advance had been made, there was still an inherent élitism in the educational scene, not to mention the fact that teaching methods and selection systems continued to favour the new middle-class meritocracy at the expense of the socially deprived.

Higher education expanded proportionately with secondary. In 1900 there were 20,000 university students, in 1938, 50,000, in 1955, 82,000, and by 1962 the total had jumped to 118,000 (see Figure 13).[17] But most of the new students came from the middle and lower middle classes rather than from the working class. Only 25 per cent were sons or daughters of manual workers, though the manual workers formed 75 per cent of the population. This percentage remained unchanged from 1928 to 1960. Once again the children of the masses had benefited less than those of the better-off.

Finally, mention must be made of two educational sectors where democratization and the diffusion of culture were undoubtedly more successful. One was that of adult education. Partly as a result of the strength of working-class organizations and partly, no doubt, in reaction against the avowed élitism of national education, the English pioneered popular education of a cultural kind. The principal organizations were 'extra-mural studies', run by the universities, and the 'Workers' Educational Association', which had about 60,000 students in the 1930s, and some 100,000 in 1948. In general the movement for adult education accelerated during and after the 1939–45 war; so much so that at the beginning of the 1950s there were about 2 million people taking evening courses, technical training and so on.

There was also a tremendous expansion in the production of books. The number of titles published at the beginning of the century was very rapidly doubled: 6,000 in 1901, 12,400 in 1914. In 1937 it reached 17,000 and was doubled again after the war (there were 35,000 titles in 1973).[18] More and more people used the public libraries: in 1949 the number of books lent out in the whole of Great Britain was nearly 300 million.[19] To take one example – at Plymouth the total went from over 365,000 in 1924 to 1.1. million in 1948. The first paperbacks appeared in 1935 when Allen Lane launched 'Penguins', followed two years later by his 'Pelicans', low-priced and aimed at a wide market. In fifteen years 250 million copies were sold.[20] Besides this there was radio (1 million sets in 1925, 9 million in 1935, 12 million in 1950)[21] and the BBC's cultural programmes. The beginning of the 1950s saw a great increase in television: some tens of thousands of sets in 1950, 4 million in 1955, 10 million in 1960, and by 1970 the total was to reach 16 million (see Figure 13).[22] Henceforward school was to be neither the sole nor the most privileged instrument for the diffusion of culture. The age of 'mass media' had begun.

Secular encroachment on religion

As early as the last quarter of the nineteenth century the edifice of religion was beginning to show cracks, and even signs of eventual collapse. After 1914 the position of the Churches took on an even more alarming aspect. Except in the Roman Catholic minority, religious observance seemed to be increasingly confined to women, the elderly and the lower middle class. There was widespread dissatisfaction not only with devotional and ritual practices but also with the beliefs and the moral instruction dispensed by the various sects. For the perspicacious the symptoms were all too clear. The less the Churches counted on having a future the more they dwelt on the past. So it was that indifference was more strongly resisted and the faith more stoutly maintained in the country than in the town, by women more than by men, by the aged more than by the young. Would it be wrong to talk of the decay of Christianity? It would certainly be an exaggeration, in that time-honoured religious sentiments did partly continue to colour people's mental outlook.

However, collective and personal behaviour both became secularized. Gradually human consciousness became adapted to a laicized world, a world that rejected the supernatural, a world 'without enchantment' (Max Weber's expression), where religion merely provided moral and social sanctions and was thus further deprived of meaning, except to those minorities of believers who still hoped to find in Christianity the answer to their questions on salvation and the future life. The change came about quite gently; no strife, no strong anti-clerical feeling. The decline of religious feeling brought about a decline in sectarian bitterness. The process was not a single movement but had many streams. In spite of a small active minority of atheists the militancy of former days that one associates with the names of Holyoake and Bradlaugh, was entirely lacking. Rejection of religion tended to be confined to the fairly frequent reactions against the odious tyranny of hypocrisy and the conventions.

The great 'sea of faith', which once covered the country, had ebbed until nothing was left but little pools in the midst of deserts of indifference or of marshlands where religion survived only in the shape of religiosity. This inexorable retreat of traditional religious practice was characterized by three different phenomena: first, a rapid falling-off of religious observance, helped by a decline of belief in the basic tenets of Christianity; secondly, the reduction of Christian faith to a rather woolly social ethic; thirdly, a wide gulf between the religious institutions – Churches and sects – and the actual aspirations cherished by the great majority of people.

On the first point, thanks to various pieces of research, we now have data which, however approximate, all point in the same direction, namely a massive decline in church attendance. This, it must be admitted, had already been pretty low among the urban masses ever since the Industrial Revolution. Three surveys in York, carried out by Rowntree, all on the same lines, in the years 1901, 1935 and 1948, enable one to measure the change in a typical medium-sized town over half a century.[23]

Table 10 Number of attendances at places of worship in York by adults in 1901, 1935, 1948

Denomination	No. of attendants			Percentage of members of each denomination		
	1901	1935	1948	1901	1935	1948
Anglican	7,453	5,395	3,384	43.7	42.2	33.1
Nonconformist	6,447	3,883	3,514	37.8	30.4	34.4
Roman Catholic	2,360	2,989	3,073	13.8	23.4	30.1
Salvation Army (indoor services)	800	503	249	4.7	4.0	2.4
Total	17,060	12,770	10,220	100	100	100
Total population of York	48,000	72,000	78,000			
Percentage of population	35.5	17.7	13.0			

Figures relate to persons aged 18 and over

It will be seen that in 1948 churchgoers numbered only one-third of those in 1901. This more or less corresponds with the results of research carried out by Geoffrey Gorer in 1955. He concluded that about 16 per cent of the population were regular churchgoers and 45 per cent intermittent ones (i.e. they attended at least one or two services a year). The remainder, of whom half were adults males, never went into a place of worship, except for funerals and weddings.[24] Another inquiry on Sunday observance carried out in 1957 by the News Chronicle produced an average of 14 per cent composed of 9 per cent from among Anglicans, 20 per cent from among Nonconformists and Presbyterians (Church of Scotland) and 44 per cent from among Roman Catholics.[25]

Still more disturbing for the faithful was the muddle-headedness that prevailed over questions of belief. Soon after the Second World War *Mass Observation* did some fairly intensive research in a representative part of London. The results, published in 1948 under the appropriate title *Puzzled People*, showed that although two-thirds of the men and four-fifths of the women believed more or less in God (only 5 per cent were atheists – a figure confirmed by other inquiries) only one out of three had been into a church in the preceding six months, one out of five did not believe in eternal life, and one out of four never prayed. Furthermore, of the agnostics one-quarter occasionally prayed to a God of whose existence they were not sure; one out of twelve sometimes went to church; one out of four thought that Christ was 'more than human', and half of them favoured religious education in schools. In contrast, of the regularly or intermittently practising followers of the Church of England one-quarter believed neither in life after death nor in the divinity of Christ. For many people religion simply boiled down to maxims like 'doing as much good as you can', or 'helping one another' and so on – all of which corresponds to the age-old working-class saying, 'You don't have to go to church to be a good Christian'.[26]

Behind these various symptoms of change one feels a certain personalization of religious feeling. Henceforward it became a matter of free individual choice rather than of melting into the ranks of a conformist body. Another sign of the waning of the Churches' influence was the habit of reducing faith to a collection of humanitarian precepts, or a moral exhortation, or some form of rather sentimental 'do-gooding'. A neo-morality, so widely and thinly spread as to be rather pallid, had taken the place of the austere morality of evangelism. 'The value of any religion depends upon the ethical dividend that it pays', said Sir George Newman, a distinguished Quaker physician. It is true that, worlds apart from this commercial terminology, one often found genuine fervour among the small number of true believers. But in most cases religion, both as belief and practice, became stale. This was due to the liberalism that abolished the absolute, and the desire for a comfortable life that blunted the old imperatives. Gone was the traditional ascetic ideal with its sublimation of desire. But the force of puritanism was so strong that desire had not been liberated. The attempt to find a way between humanism and Christian tradition resulted in a hybrid ethic, with a taint of hypocrisy. This explains why controversy erupted where the two traditions clashed, e.g. on divorce and contraception. Curiously enough rather less was heard about temperance being the highway to salvation. The spirit of evangelicalism was dying. All that was left of it, except among the few who had an inner life, was an outward show of moral respectability.

No sweeping revivalist movement came to the rescue of the Churches either in the Church of England, where defection, in spite of some missionary endeavour, had been strongest, or from the Nonconformist bodies which were all in full retreat. The only such movements (all, significantly, from America) such as Moral Rearmament (introduced in the 1920s by Frank Buchman's Oxford Group) Christian Science, the Jehovah's Witnesses, and Billy Graham's giant interdenominational meetings, all met with a very small response.

The result was a twofold separation: first between the religious institutions, which were often relegated to the role of a hollow façade, and people's religious needs; secondly between the various groups of genuine believers (becoming smaller and smaller) and society as a whole, which paid less and less regard to all forms of organized religion. This caused much lamentation, especially among traditionalists. Some of the more discerning of the faithful saw a positive side to this clear distinction between belief and religion. T. S. Eliot expressed the opinion that the Churches would in future draw their supporters solely from the small section of the population who were dissatisfied with the spiritual emptiness of a hand-to-mouth existence. These would guard and keep their faith and their liturgy alive, apart from the multitude. Graham Greene said much the same from a Roman Catholic point of view about 'Post-christianity' in England.

All through this period only the Roman Catholic Church managed to avoid falling back, and even increased its numbers. The total number in Great Britain increased from about 2 million in 1914 to 5 million in 1955. The figures were even more significant over a longer period. In 1850 there were 600 churches and chapels and 840 priests; in 1913 1,800 and 3,800 respectively; in 1940, 2,600 and 5,900; in 1955, 3,000 and 7,000. In spite of persistent cries of 'Papistry', the allure of the Church of Rome was demonstrated by the number of its converts – a steady 12,000 a year from 1920 to 1955, whereas the figure was only 7,500 before 1914.[27] In addition, the resumption of Irish immigration during and after the Second World War, and the fact that many Poles had settled on English soil, swelled the numbers of the Roman Catholic community. With all this there was still a feeling of isolation, and the community retained the outlook of a minority.

One must not, however, exaggerate the extent of English irreligion, for it was tempered in two ways. One was institutional pressure: public life continued under the aegis of a State Church, and, more importantly, this Church was closely interwoven with the whole fabric of national existence. Even if it got harder and harder to describe the content of orthodoxy – if only because of the diversity of currents within the established Church itself* – the religious trappings of everyday national life (public thanksgivings, official religious ceremonies, religious education for all schoolchildren) all combined to maintain the pressure, felt or unfelt, of an atmosphere that was coloured by Christian tradition.

The other curb on the move to secularization – if it was a curb – was the abundance of religious feeling, partly cerebral and partly sentimental, that was found deeply ingrained in all social classes. Was this a structural component of society that transcended the sphere of primitive myth as well as that of the Christian tradition – what Corbon, the 1848 militant, called 'the imperishable religious faculty in man's nature' – or was it rather a degraded form of religion, just adequate to provide an answer, albeit in a very elementary way, to the need for some ritual event (e.g. the family Christmas and royal coronations) and involving an escape from organized and institutional religion? Various new kinds of attitudes flowed from this, in which humanism acquired religious overtones – a kind of socially respectable spirituality composed of smooth, uncontroversial beliefs adding up to a reasonable and benevolent consensus. On the other hand this general retreat from orthodox faith and Christian observance was accompanied by surviving superstition and magical beliefs. The inquiry carried out by Geoffrey Gorer in 1955, and cited above, brought out some surprising facts about the hold these obscure forces had on people. Gorer found that one adult in six believed in ghosts and one in ten in reincarnation. One out of three servicemen in the Second World War admitted carrying a mascot for self-protection. All this goes to show that, after eighteen centuries of Christianity and one of secularization, the ramparts of both Christian faith and its rival Free Thought could still be breached by the resurgence of sacred primitivism.

*BBC religious broadcasts were subjected to a sort of ecclesiastical censorhip, and it was only after 1947 that dissenting and non-Christian voices could be heard.

IV A Disrupted Society 1955–75

The end of
the old England?

Around 1955–6 English society was suddenly hit by a wave of change and from then onwards driven on a new course that was to transform the atmosphere of the country within a few years. This happened without warning. 1954 had seen the end of post-war reconstruction: the nation had regained its equilibrium, thanks to full employment, the Welfare State and economic expansion. After the great shocks of 1917–20, 1931 and 1945, political consensus seemed restored with traditional Labour–Tory confrontation temporarily becalmed in 'centrism'. The historic leaders, Churchill and Attlee, had just left the scene with their missions completed, and everything seemed to point to calm and stability. It was at this moment that the new lines of cleavage suddenly came to light, putting all the nation's conventional values in question. The ingrained conformism of decades was riven by shocks both from without and within. While the young rebelled, literature and the arts were seized with a new creative spirit. In the midst of the calm the country suddenly burst out in all directions.

Externally the Suez *débâcle* caused a national crisis of conscience and put an end to illusions of national power. Internally there was the irruption of the 'angry young men', the arrival of commercial television, rock'n'roll, the blasphemy of the characters in *Waiting for Godot*. Old England's mask of formality was undergoing radical change. New generations, new manners, new morals: straitlaced austerity was giving way to the bread and circuses of the new age of prosperity. Under the disruptive influence of the 'permissive society' old values and points of reference were shaken off. Yet so much remained – social classes, oligarchic groups, the distribution of power and wealth – that one might well ask what had really changed in this fragmented society. In any case hadn't the change been grossly exaggerated by the mass media which, having grabbed the idea with enthusiasm, exploited and trivialized it, all the while contributing their own raucous accompaniment?

Three factors appear to have contributed to this change. Firstly, the country's entry into an era of abundance. The years 1954–5 were a vital turning-point; they were the moment of take-off into prosperity and good living. To pass in a few years from human society's traditional state of endemic scarcity to one that seemed to promise unlimited prospects of growth involved a real mental revolution. Wasn't this odour of opulence enough to intoxicate even the most phlegmatic people of the Western world? Time would show that behind the philosophy of growth lay the ills that accompanied excessive wealth, and people came to realize that behind the fiction of the consumer as king lurked the reality of the consumer as slave.

No less significant was the transformation that took place in collective moral standards. Two value systems were confronting each other. On the one side was the moral code inherited from the nineteenth century, impregnated with puritanism; on the other, a longing to be free, to cast off the shabby garments of worn-out convention. This clash had been looming for some time. As we have seen, the erosion of the old order started before 1914. The façade of respectability and hypocrisy did not prevent loose living, and ostentatious good citizenship was an inadequate cover-up for the pursuit of grossly selfish interests. But the essential point about 1955–60 was not so much the change in behaviour as the change in standards. England had formerly been characterized by an unyielding framework of tradition and conformity, a structure which had been slowly built up and had kept national consensus alive, confined in a sort of moral corset. This crumbled because it was no longer accepted, and indeed was often violently rejected. So the break was very abrupt, and from now on, instead of living in the integrated society to which they were accustomed, the British had to find their way through one that was fragmented and devoid of signposts. Malcolm Muggeridge has described in striking images the chaos and cacophony that resulted:

One feels today that things are out of sync. The conductor is working from one score and the orchestra from another, with consequent total confusion in the resultant performance. The players have learnt their lines from a play other than the one which is being performed; they make false entrances and exits, stumble over unfamiliar scenery, and turn in vain to the prompter. There is no correlation between word and deed, between the aspirations ostensibly entertained and what actually happens, between (to use Blake's dichotomy) what is seen with, and what is seen through, the eye.[1]

To go back further still, we would attribute the collapse of standards that took place between 1955 and 1965 to the repudiation of that strict code of behaviour that the evangelical movement had so deeply impressed on the nation during the first half of the nineteenth century. It was this which had formed and sustained England for over a century, and it survived to the end of the Second World War. In this partly moral, partly religious code, the ideas of duty, honesty, respectability, hard work, and above all self-respect were central to life. This conduced to a voluntary self-discipline which made adherence to the law, whether the law of the land or the social code, a matter of individual personal responsibility. In this austere code of evangelical morality one might find a union of altruism and repression, discipline and hypocrisy, respect for authority and devotion to the public good. In it, too, one might find the source of all those varieties of social virtue of which the English used to be so proud, and which astonished generations of visiting foreigners: civic feeling, loyalty to institutions, personal honesty, mutual confidence, all instilled in the classroom, in church and chapel and indeed through every organ of social indoctrination. This explained the social cohesion that so struck Elie Halévy, and which he rightly attributed to the influence of liberal and evangelical Protestantism. It generated a spirit of independence no less than one of self-imposed discipline.

The anti-Victorian reaction swept aside this time-honoured heritage. The pillars of the temple crashed under the iconoclastic tug of a multitude of Samsons. Conformism and idealism in their traditional forms were shattered by the storm, and the whole moral fabric of the nation was affected. With the growth of indifferentism and the decline of the Churches, the religious foundations of the national edifice had disappeared, and the moralism that survived seemed no more than a jumble of abstract obligations and tedious inhibitions of no intrinsic significance. It had become 'the letter that killeth', lacking 'the spirit that giveth life'. Henceforward the craving for liberation was given free rein. People talked of spontaneity, genuineness, with an accent on freedom of expression and the right to happiness. It was hardly surprising if behind these demands one detected the reflection of the 'affluent society', which tended to increase needs and consumption, just as the 'indigent society' put a premium on asceticism and deprivation. There was, too, a noticeable decline in voluntary (including charitable) organizations, the profusion of which had formerly borne witness to an evangelical concern for 'works', no less than to the necessity of having a clear conscience.

The socially orientated individualism of earlier days had been succeeded by a new sort of individualism, symptomatic of the general social fragmentation. People were tending to confine themselves to the narrow world of their family, the circle of their acquaintances, following their own individual line of conduct, not concerning themselves or interfering with the behaviour of others, or bothering about setting an example. Everyone now had to invent his (or her) own norms.

Thirdly, the break with the past was in nothing more manifest than in national pride and patriotic feeling. The proud sense of superiority enjoyed by the English for generations (what Jules Romains, in *Les Hommes de Bonne Volonté*, called 'their calm and solid megalomania'[2]) had endured until the middle of the twentieth century. John Bull had emerged from the second great world conflict with an actual enhancement of the feeling that he belonged to a race apart. As the only great European State to have escaped invasion and internal convulsion, hadn't Great Britain every reason to go on seeing herself as an impregnable fortress and the leader of a world empire? Even when circumstances forced the British to realize their impoverished condition, they could still console themselves with the memory of their heroism in 1940 and in comfortable contemplation of their pacific record of international co-operation and rather generous decolonization. Quite soon this self-assurance faltered however. As the memory of the war gradually faded, as the nature of world problems changed, as a new generation knowing little of the glory of the past grew up, the accumulation of self-confidence began to drain away and self-doubt to take its place. The Suez crisis of 1956 was the turning-point. Glaringly and pitilessly it revealed that not only was England no longer a first-class power, but she also suffered from a fatal weakness. Forthwith the 'smallest of the great powers' was reduced to the 'greatest of the small powers'. If this were so, how could one believe in the future of a tiny overpopulated island with a feeble economic growth, distrustful and jealous of its European neighbours, happy to be towed along in the wake of American power, and, whatever happened, doomed to inevitable withdrawal? In other words, had the nation entered the age of abundance only to follow the road of surrender?

10 The fruits of affluence

The cornucopia of neo-capitalism

In 1954 the then Chancellor of the Exchequer, R. A. Butler, an exponent of enlightened Conservatism, put up the apparently chimerical idea that the country should aim at doubling its standard of living within the next twenty-five years. This was in 1954 when war-time rationing had just ended. Many people saw in this only a piece of politician's bombast, yet three years later Harold Macmillan made his famous remark which everybody took seriously, that England 'had never had it so good'.[1] Two years later, in 1959, the Tories won a resounding electoral victory and a cartoonist depicted Macmillan in the aftermath of battle talking to four of his agents, personified respectively by a refrigerator, a television set, a washing-machine and a motor-car, and thanking them in these terms: 'Well, gentlemen, together we have fought the good fight.'

Having entered the land of plenty the English gathered its fruits with enthusiasm. The years 1953–4 saw the arrival of a new civlization – the 'affluent society'. Growth and prosperity went hand in hand. Although there are now good reasons for rating Britain's economic dynamism unfavourably in comparison with the performance of her European rivals, there was some real growth. In 1970 industrial production was 30 per cent greater than in 1960 and 80 per cent greater than in 1950; it was two and a half times the production of 1938 and five times that of 1900.[2] The annual rate of growth of the national product, averaging 2.6 per cent from 1953 to 1973, was higher than in the celebrated years of the Victorian age. The driving force behind this neo-capitalist prosperity was the total mobilization of society for the purpose of producing and acquiring. It was this half-collectivized and half-individualistic impulse which conditioned people's outlook and won their co-operation through the stimulus of growth and enrichment.

It may be objected that there was nothing new about all this; that there was no difference between the neo-liberalism of 1950–60 and the orthodox liberalism of 1850–60. That period, too, had been obsessed with productivity and progress, but the psychological background was quite different. In nineteenth-century society the growth of productivity came up against a variety of obstacles, cultural and economic, such as vested interests, archaic ways, a ruling class preferring leisure and safe steady incomes, and among the masses such deprivation as made it impossible for them to enjoy the fruits of prosperity. At an even deeper level the pre-1914 world obeyed one supreme law – the law of thrift. This thrift was not just an economic habit but was caught up in a whole tissue of moral and religious overtones, with the various rewards and returns which ensued. On the other hand, by the middle of the secularized twentieth century, inflation had eroded the spirit of thrift. Doing without was no longer a virtue, but a misfortune; instant enjoyment and conspicuous acquisition, egged on by advertising and the mass media, became the paramount consideration. The sole and openly avowed aim was happiness. An uplifting idea, no doubt, but one which risked being soon found illusory, so limited and materialistic was the philosophy of 'consumer-dom'. Disappointment and revolt were liable to follow, as time was to show.

Inequality remained, in fact it was the motive power of the whole system. The secret of neo-capitalistic growth was to get inequality accepted in the hope and promise of a better future. Galbraith has pointed out that the traditional aim of reducing economic and social differences is forgotten when increased production eliminates their most acute tensions. In other words, increase in productivity becomes a substitute for redistribution and even for social justice.[3]

Social tension was also as much eased by full employment as by gains in productivity. In 1944 Beveridge in his book *Full Employment in a Free Society*, defined the maximum tolerable limit of unemployment, not to be exceeded in any circumstances, as 3 per cent. Not only was his golden rule observed, but for over twenty years after the Second World War the rate stayed under 2 per cent, the total number of unemployed ranging from the irreducible core of 300,000 to a maximum of 600,000. Altogether, from 1945 to 1974 unemployment remained below the limit fixed by Beveridge, except in the years 1971 and 1972. Governments had learnt

Keynes' lesson and had managed the economy in such a way that the effective level of demand was high enough to provide work for all. Prosperity was thus the child of the Keynesian revolution.

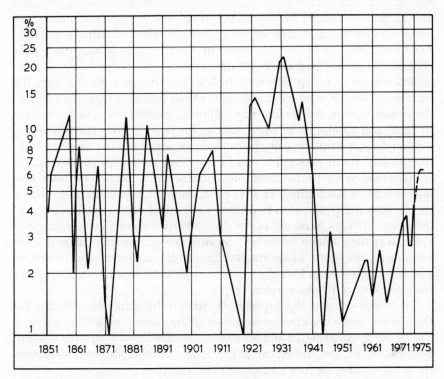

Figure 12. Unemployment in the UK, 1851–1974

In such conditions the road to welfare was taken at a gallop – or more exactly the road to consumer goods. Food improved: there was more variety, with less bread and farinaceous foods, more vegetables, cheese, and eggs (an annual average of 240 eggs per head in 1964, compared with 152 thirty years earlier, and 104 in 1909–13)[4] More luxury foods came from abroad. Food was still the chief expense in family budgets, but its relative proportion gradually declined. It was the same with clothing. Housing, the car, and leisure activities began to assume importance. In the twenty years from 1953 to 1972, 7 million houses were built in the United Kingdom.[5] At the same time the quality of housing improved greatly. The General Household Survey of 1971 showed that 88 per cent of all dwellings had a bathroom or a shower (only 62 per cent in 1951); 96 per cent had their own toilet (80 per cent in 1951); 34 per cent had central heating –

an innovation that only gathered momentum towards the end of the 1950s, and a revolution for Britain, the home of draughts and the open fire. The number of owner-occupiers doubled between 1951 and 1972. At the latter date half of all dwellings were owner-occupied, one-third were rented and belonged to some public body, usually a local authority, and one-sixth were rented from private individuals. In 1975 nine out of ten homes had a vacuum cleaner, more than two out of three a washing machine, three out of four a refrigerator. On the other hand, only 0.5 per cent of all families had a servant or servants.

Other signs of prosperity were holidays. Between 1951 and 1970 the number of British who went abroad for their holidays was quadrupled. As for telephones, there were 3.25 million subscribers in 1939, 8.5 million in 1962, and 20 million in 1975. And as for pets, in 1971 there were 5.2 million dogs, 3.6 million cats, 3.2 million canaries;[6] and the total expenditure on food for all these pets was £150 million, or two-thirds of Britain's overseas aid to the underdeveloped countries. The figures for television are even more astounding. In 1951 hardly one household in fifteen had a set; in 1955 the proportion had risen to one in four; in 1960 two out of three, and by 1975, nine out of ten. In 1969 a quarter of all spare time was spent watching television[7] – an absolute revolution, that turned *homo britannicus*, the open-air sportsman, into a stay-at-home *homo televidens*. The rise of television brought about a huge drop in cinema attendance from the end of the war onwards.

The motor-car was the supreme symbol of the consumer society. Far from being just a convenient means of getting about or getting away, it conferred personal status and prestige, as well as providing an extension, both spatial and psychological, of the home. Table 11 shows how rapidly the total number of cars had grown since 1955.

Table 11 Number of cars in Great Britain[8]

Date	No. of cars	No. of people per car
1904	8,000	4,750
1910	53,000	770
1913	106,000	390
1920	187,000	229
1930	1,050,000	43
1938	1,950,000	24
1945	1,500,000	32
1950	2,250,000	21
1955	3,500,000	14
1960	5,500,000	9.3
1965	8,900,000	5.9
1970	11,500,000	4.7
1973	13,500,000	4.0

There are some who object to the expressions 'consumer society' and 'age of opulence'. In our opinion it is useless to deny the success of neo-liberalism, which within twenty years undoubtedly brought about a complete transformation, from penury to plenty. One can only agree with Andrew Shonfield, who refers in his book *Modern Capitalism* to a new economic order, thanks to which capitalism was converted from 'the cataclysmic failure' that it appeared to be in the 1930s, into 'the great engine of prosperity' of the post-war world.[9] But one cannot escape the fact that this neo-capitalist world, based on the maximization of private profit, is suffused with a complex commercial ideology which taints all social and moral values. Neighbourly relations, family life, and in general every medium of social communication are indissolubly impregnated with it. This ideology, which finds its ultimate expression in advertising, is simply based on the philosophy of getting and having. In this sense England had returned wholeheartedly – if she had ever left it – to the 'acquisitive society' that Tawney denounced so vehemently and so pertinently in his book of that title fifty years earlier.

During the 1960s, amid all the euphoria of growth, it began to seem that opulence had its limits and the logic of productivity its dangers. Poverty, believed to have been abolished, reappeared, 'rediscovered' by economists and sociologists such as Abel-Smith, Townsend, Atkinson, Coates, Silburn, etc. They brought to light great 'patches of poverty', a whole unseen and unheard world living below the poverty line. Any definition of poverty is of course relative, and standards of need, as of things needed, change all the time, as society changes. Nevertheless the results of research showed with blinding clarity that, in the midst of abundance and state welfare, at least 5 million people, about 10 per cent of the population, lacked the means for a reasonable minimal standard of living. The ones 'whom growth forgot' formed a serious blot on the image of the 'affluent society'. In another sphere it soon became evident that technological advance risked causing catastrophic damage to the environment, and that rapid action must be taken to stop the free-for-all that was leading to waste and pollution.

Winds of revolt and spiritual quests

That Man does not live by bread alone and is not to be satisfied by a paltry mixture of bread and circuses was startlingly demonstrated in the years 1955–75. As soon as the British set foot in the promised land they found that its much vaunted fruit had an unexpectedly bitter taste. For neither the undeniable improvement in the standard of living nor the vast increase in material benefits available could resolve the eternal problem of the individual and the community – the achievement of happiness, the ever-elusive prize. Even worse, the affluent society was developing its own pathology. An uneasy state of well-being led to new twinges of conscience and fears of being suffocated by the all-enveloping materialism. In face of the glorification of bourgeois values and appetites glutted with selfish satisfactions, there arose a mood of rejection, even of revolt. Behind this repudiation of the world of goods and pleasures one may see a perpetually self-renewing idealism. Far from having disappeared, the old yearning for the absolute persisted, transmuting deep-seated ethical feelings of Christian or humanistic origin. Behind the scenes of material affluence and the mask of febrile self-indulgence, there was a ferment of self-questioning.

The first waves of protest came in the middle of the 1950s, and took the form of a revolt against all the traditional conventions of society, denouncing the whole existing system – the Establishment, politicians and authority, traditions and institutions. Inchoate in its aims, rancorous and trenchant in expression, the revolt manifested itself in three different ways: literary, social and political. In literature it was represented by the 'angry young men' (1955–9), typified by their leaders, whose success was meteoric – John Osborne (*Look back in Anger*), Kingsley Amis (*Lucky Jim*), John Wain (*Hurry on Down*) and John Braine (*Room at the Top*). They expressed their ideas through the novel, the cinema and the theatre. They were mostly left-wingers disappointed by the dullness and deferential smugness engendered by a mating of the Acquisitive Society with the Welfare State. They felt that there had been no change in the seats of power – 'the old gang are back'. This was not an outburst of adolescent emotion such as occurred in the 1960s: it sprang from the intellectual dissent of young men of 25 to 30 years of age. As Kenneth Tynan, one of them, explained, they were people whose childhood and adolescence had been scarred by economic crisis and war, who had grown up under a socialist government only to find that the class system remained mysteriously intact.

The 'teddy-boys' (1953–7) were a very different phenomenon, a form of social protest, confused and imprecise, rising from the tribal setting of 'the gang'. It was an adolescent phenomenon and marked the first appearance on the scene of a new social entity – 'teenagers' – but it was also a popular movement. It made its first appearance in the southern suburbs of London among the children of poor parents. Wearing pseudo-Edwardian clothes (hence their name) – narrow stove-pipe trousers, long jackets, fancy waistcoats – they flaunted their social alienation, which they resented and cultivated at the same time, not without occasional bouts of violence, in a world of juke-boxes and snack-bars. In particular they were deeply suspicious of the outside world – a feeling strongly reciprocated.

There was a third form of revolt, this time deliberate, organized and politically orientated. This was the Campaign for Nuclear Disarmament (CND) which flourished between 1958 and 1962. Prompted by guilt and fear concerning the atom bomb, it harked back to the great moral tradition of nineteenth- and early twentieth-century radical protest. It was a genuine moral crusade driven by the inspiration of an almost religious revivalist movement, with its ritual Aldermaston March at Eastertime. One of its leaders, Canon Collins, went so far as to say that it seemed to him 'more religious and more reverent than many church services' he had attended.[10] Though the movement mainly comprised the left-wing young of the middle classes, it made a deep impression on a whole generation, comparable with the effect of the Spanish Civil War. The march itself was like a mixture of pilgrimage – with an almost mystical atmosphere of community feeling and good fellowship – and a pop festival, with its disregard for bourgeois conventionality, the fantastic variety of clothes worn by the marchers, and the enthusiastic display of fraternal feeling. In line with the CND movement another political trend was finding expression, the New Left (1957–61). Born of a demand for a revival of culture and thought, it channelled the energies of young left-wing intellectuals into a form of socialism that was interested in ethical and aesthetic as well as social questions.

Such were the starting points for the revival of ideology that characterized the 1960s. During this period the revolt against society took two distinct forms. One, purely individual, was a continuation of the 'teddy-boy' movement: same social alienation, same gang organization, same taste for rock'n'roll and fancy clothes, same rejection of the adult world. Such, from 1960 to 1965, were the 'mods', then the 'rockers' (who added a taste for violence and fighting). Later, at the end of the decade, came the 'skinheads', themselves a reaction against the 'hippies' with their long hair, 'flower-power' and pacifist views, who appeared around 1965.

There was yet another movement, which was limited to young intellectuals. Their stance was forthrightly revolutionary and their chosen ground was the universities, then expanding rapidly (228,000 university students in 1971, as against 113,000 in 1961, 82,000 in 1955 and 50,000 in 1939[11]). With a great show of demonstrations and 'sit-ins' they bawled out their rejection of neo-capitalist society and demanded a live, 'relevant', not to say militant culture. They objected to the cold, rationalist socialism of the bureaucrats and even more to the pseudo-socialism of the Wilson administration. Their ideal was a hard, pure socialism, innovatory as well as renovatory, a kingdom-come socialism of the joy of living: 'Socialism isn't talking all the time, it's living, it's singing, it's dancing, it's being interested in what goes on around you, it's being concerned about people and the world.'[12]

Map 9. The historical development of British universities

But although student agitation, which reached its height between 1967 and 1970, evoked some sort of public response, politically it led nowhere. For all the effect it had, the revolutionary uproar might have been a whisper. On the other hand, in the realm of theory, after the 1950s when the sham of consensus had pointed to 'the end of ideology', the 1960s heralded ideology's resounding comeback. For disputes at home and disagreements over foreign affairs brought reality back with a jolt and shattered any beautiful certainties à la Talcott Parsons about social stability and harmony. At the same time the spread of social studies helped to restore the influence of ideology as a potential guide through the problems of a perplexing and rudderless world.

Finally, even before the student troubles had quietened down, other movements started up, this time against the structure imposed by technocracy. The first one was among the workers who ever since the end of the 1960s had been showing signs of renewed and sometimes violent militancy. Discontent had been growing in a rather inchoate way, and factory floor disputes, usually aimed at union machinery, were on the increase. Unofficial strikes, factory occupations, 'work-ins', an unexpected revival of direct action and the idea of workers' control – all these were symptoms, even though only small numbers were involved, of a revulsion against the crushing pressure of the 'techno-structure' on the individual. Elsewhere the movement for the defence of the natural environment, just started between 1965 and 1970, grew very rapidly into a veritable ecological crusade. Finally there was another movement of revolt around 1970 – the radical, militant, neo-feminist movement of 'Women's Lib', which attacked the social order of 'male chauvinism'. Their ambitious aim was a fundamental transformation of relations between the sexes and complete freedom and equality.

Significant though they may seem, one should not make too much of these successive and endlessly recurring movements of protest. Some fell by the wayside, isolated by their own eccentricity; others got taken up by the mass media or passing fashion. All were minority movements, which is why none succeeded in being a serious threat to the social status quo, or even bending it more than a little from its appointed course. Once more England had displayed her ability to absorb her dissident elements.

In contrast there was what might be called majority movements that effected profound changes in habits, values and behaviour. Care is needed in assessing them, for the most hasty and misleading generalizations have been made about them. They concern the famous so-called 'permissive society'. Has it not been said that the new permissiveness swept across Britain, destroying at one blow all traditional values in favour of unbridled licence? Mary Quant, Vanessa Redgrave, 'swinging London', the mini-skirt, the 'youth cult', the 'androgynous sixties', violent denunciations by Malcolm Muggeridge of a generation hooked on dope and sex,[13] the mounting figures of delinquency (283,000 cases in 1939, 1,489,000 in 1969): this farrago of examples has been endlessly served up to show that a moral revolution occurred in England which changed the country more in the decade 1959–69 than it had been changed in the previous half-century. Similarly, patron figures for this period have been found in Aphrodite, in Dionysus, in Baal, though others have preferred Calvin, Savonarola and Joanna Southcott.[14] The truth is that throughout this phase there were liberating, messianic aspirations mingling with the cult of pleasure, and a yearning for a true spirit of community combined inextricably with a passionate desire to proclaim one's freedom. One must not be misled by appearances. In the convulsions of youth, in the neglect of established religion for sects and made-up cults, it is probably right to see a hungry spiritual search, which often found neither solution nor response. In short these were groping, faltering steps in pursuit of a humanism that could cope with the challenge of an overpowering technical civilization.

Youth, family life, religion

One has to pick one's way through a jungle of clichés about the 'youth cult', 'obsession with sex', 'Women's Lib' and the break-up of morals and religion, and it is important to judge lucidly. In particular one has to extract what is hidden behind the blaze of light flooding the more sensational aspects of these phenomena. Elucidation is needed of the development's varied character in which appearances were very deceptive. Among the issues that we shall consider in turn – youth, sex, children and the birth-rate; the role of the Churches, the family, spiritual aspirations, the place of women in society – some were moving towards crisis and disintegration (the first ones for example), others embodied forces of permanence (the family and the 'new' religions). But all were in a state of ambivalence, with the weight of tradition resisting the explosive force of innovation.

One fact is clear. During the 1950s there was a very decided break between generations (well described in Colin MacInnes' novel, *Absolute Beginners*), and as time went on this became more marked. Simultaneously the 15–20 age group acquired a privileged niche in society, whence it proceeded to assert its independence, energetically and sometimes aggressively. This change in the situation of the young had various causes, such as the earlier maturity of teenagers, the massive redistribution of earnings in the consumer society to the advantage of the young, and the considerable increase in mobility thanks to the development of individual transport. So there came into being a whole cultural world peculiar to the young. Following Frank Musgrove, one may identify this 'youth culture' (which sometimes assumed the character of a counter-culture) by the following characteristics: lack of interest in political or economic power, lack of respect for authority, disregard of frontiers and labels, desire for utter authenticity, freedom and unpossessiveness in sexual relations, a taste for art and music and states of ecstasy, community feeling and an urge to share, a passion for leisure and liberty, repudiation of the idea of property – 'all one needs is a sleeping-bag'.[15] The aim was clear, a revolution born of a romantic dream mixed with a utopian vision. Neither a violent revolution nor an institutional one, for neither would change anything, but a revolution in man's relations with man, a revolution in hearts, bodies and minds: a revolution that would break down all barriers, establish real communication and harmony between minds, making the richness of humanity available to all.

Secondly, so far as sex was concerned, the casting-off of the heavy hand of Victorian morality had left scope for a wild free-for-all. Prudery, of course, and convention and taboos all went by the board. The imposed orthodoxies were replaced by a demand for absolute freedom, a licence for enjoyment and flights of fancy and at the same time a serious attempt to discover and establish new standards of behaviour. One should therefore talk of a moral crisis rather than a crisis in moral standards. The spirit of conformity had not disappeared; where formerly it had followed ready-made rules, it now expressed itself through spontaneous behaviour. Nor can one say that so-called 'liberation' had done away with traditional aspirations, such as the well-being and even stability of the married – or unmarried – couple.

Thirdly, as far as the couple and its offspring were concerned, the 'moral revolution' speeded up the long-term demographic trend rather than changed its direction. Since the beginning of the 1970s there was (as in other Western countries) a short decline in the birth-rate. After reaching 18 per '000 in the period 1960–5, it fell gradually to 16 per '000 in 1970–1. After that it fell rapidly to 13 per '000 in 1974, during which year there were only 674,000 births in England and Wales, a decline of one-quarter in ten years. The fertility rate fell in 1974 to 2.04, which was below the level necessary for replacement (2.1). In 1975 the excess of births over deaths fell to an insignificant figure, while the death-rate, since 1920, had remained stationary at 12 per '000. As, since 1964, the number of emigrants had exceeded that of immigrants, it seemed that Britain was reversing the long-established trend and was in danger of a decline in population. There were various demographic factors that helped to explain this process, such as the widespread use of 'the pill', easier abortion, and more married women taking jobs; but these 'technical' reasons do not entirely account for the phenomenon. Clearly it had something to do with new ideas about having children, resulting from the ethical and psychological turmoil in society.

These changes in social outlook had severe repercussions on the Churches and on belief. Dissatisfaction with institutionalized religion had been evident for about fifty years, but it increased sharply during the course of the 1960s. Even the Roman Catholic Church was affected – a

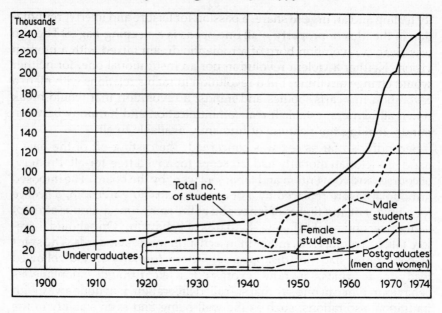

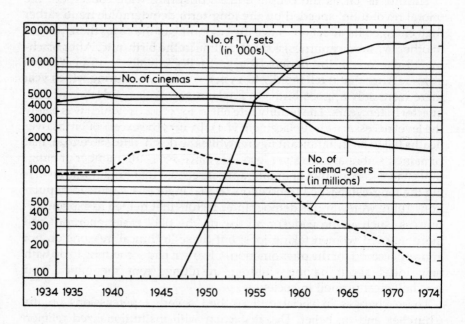

Figure 13. Three aspects of contemporary society: higher education, cinema and television, delinquency

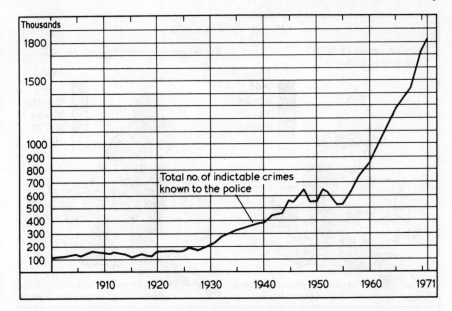

definite sign of the times. Up till then its steady increase in numbers (partly due, it must be admitted, to Irish immigration) had been in sharp contrast to the sad state of the Protestant sects; but round about 1970 the numbers of its flock diminished for the first time. There were other worrying symptoms: fewer recruits to the priesthood, many fewer conversions, a fall in church attendance. In addition there were internal upheavals, controversy between clerics as well as laymen. So in the 1960s, as a result of sharp criticism, a radical Catholic movement centred on the review *Slant* got under way. The Church of England also came under fire. Pressure for modernization was growing, and the very real progress of the oecumenical movement was no compensation for setbacks in the field of faith and works. Hence the moves towards pastoral and theological reveval, such as the attempt by John Robinson, the Bishop of Woolwich, in *Honest to God* (1963) to put across a new image of God. Hence too the active steps that were taken for the relief of suffering all over the world: Oxfam for the Third World, Shelter for the homeless, Christian Action against apartheid. The Nonconformists were no better off. In the twenty years 1950–70 the Baptists and Congregationalists lost one-sixth of their followers.[17] As Table 12 shows, the all-round decline from the beginning of the century had been most serious.[18]

Summing up the situation of the Churches in 1966, Bryan Wilson concluded that fewer than 25 per cent of the adult population of England and Wales had any real claim to be 'members' of any religious denomination.[19]

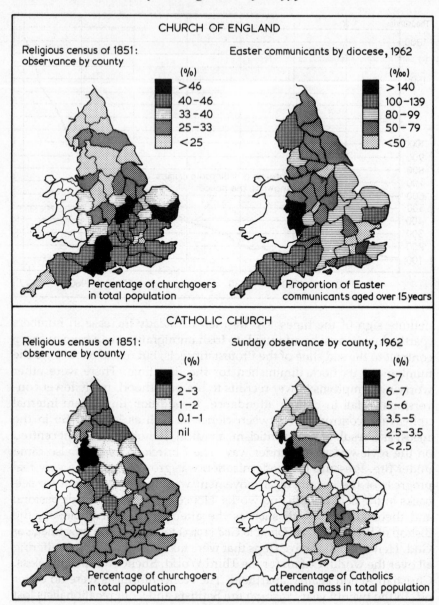

Map 10. The geography of religious observance in England, 1851–1961/2[16]

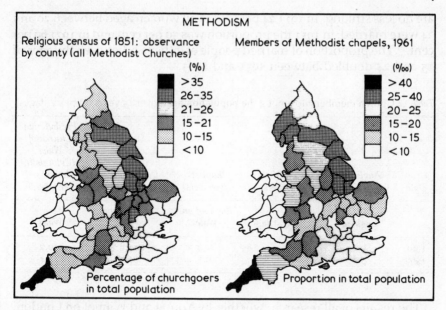

METHODISM

Religious census of 1851: observance by county (all Methodist Churches)

(%)
>35
26–35
21–26
15–21
10–15
<10

Percentage of churchgoers in total population

Members of Methodist chapels, 1961

(%o)
>40
25–40
20–25
15–20
10–15
<10

Proportion in total population

As to actual religious belief, recent research has shown a dramatic falling-off, even allowing for any doubts one may feel about findings based on questionnaires whose formulations are not always reliable or satisfactory. According to one carried out in 1974, only 29 per cent of the population believed in a personal God, compared with 38 per cent in 1963; and only two out of five believed in a future life (one out of two in 1963). It is true that atheism remained at the rather low level of 6 per cent. Of especial significance was the widespread indifference – worrying both for the Church militant and for the atheists – and the prevalence of various forms of vague belief, such as the conviction held by a third of the British people that somewhere there is a 'spirit' or 'life force'.[20]

As regards the family, there were plenty of pessimistic predictions, both from the traditionalists, who raised a chorus of moans about general immorality, and from *avant-garde* circles who never ceased to attack this suffocatingly bourgeois institution. In spite of these gloomy prognostications, everything goes to show that the family was more popular than ever. More people got married; they married younger; most divorced people married again. Statistics bear eloquent witness to the rise in the number of marriages since the First World War. Out of every hundred women between 20 and 40 years of age, 55 were married in 1911 and 57 in 1931; between 1961 and 1971 the figure reached 80. While in 1939 52 per cent of the adult population of Britain were or had been married, in 1973 the percentage had risen to 59 per cent. The figures for the age of marriage are no less striking. In 1911 24 per cent of all women aged between 20 and 24 were married; in 1951 the proportion was 50 per cent and in 1971 60 per cent.[21] The proportion of married people of either sex between the ages of 15 and 24 doubled between 1931 and 1965.

Table 12 Church membership among the population aged over 15 years (in percentages)

Date	Anglicans (churchgoers)	Methodists (members)	Baptists (members)	Congregation-alists (members)	Presbyterian Church of Wales (Calvinistic Methodists) (members)
	England	Great Britain	England and Wales	England and Wales	Wales
1961	9.9	3.1	1.6	1.8	10.7
1966	5.4	1.6	0.7	0.5	5.4

The results of all research, whether by Young and Wilmot on London, Rosser and Harris on Swansea, or more recently by Geoffrey Gorer on England (*Sex and Marriage in England*) not only unanimously confirmed the stability of marriage and the nuclear family – a nucleus of unquestioned popularity – but they also emphasized how much more demanding married couples had become. Their ideals of married life had become much higher; they saw marriage as a partnership leading to a joint enhancement of personal development. An apparent objection to this optimistic interpretation was the spectacular increase in the number of divorces, which at first sight would suggest the increasing instability of family life. There were 4,800 divorces annually in 1931–5, 28,000 annually in 1955–60, increasing rapidly to 55,000 in 1968 and 110,000 in 1972.[22] But it should be noted, firstly, that many divorces, previously impossible or unthinkable, resulted as much from changes in the law (chiefly the Legal Aid Act of 1960 and the Divorce Law Reform Act of 1969) as from any moral reason. Secondly, two-thirds to three-quarters of all divorcees married again. Thirdly, the large number of divorces provided additional proof that more stress was laid on the partners' individual happiness – more divorce meaning higher expectations of marriage – than on the institution of marriage itself. Furthermore it is significant that now, in two cases out of three, it was the wife who sought divorce, while twenty years earlier the initiative came from either party.

Another survivor was man's yearning for the divine. Like family feeling this ancient instinct, changed almost out of recognition, retained its hold on men's hearts. In his inaugural Reith Lecture in 1968, the anthropologist Edmund Leach spoke of the obstacles that rationalism still faced: 'Men have become gods,' he said, 'science offers us total mastery over our environment and over our destiny, and yet instead of rejoicing we feel deeply afraid.'[23]

How then can one possibly talk about the end of religion? Just as the death of God was being announced, the millenarianists were flourishing. It was a fact that the official Churches were losing their congregations, but never were the sects so prosperous – the Christian sects invoking strict biblical precepts, such as Jehovah's Witnesses, the Latter Day Saints, the Plymouth Brethren, the Seventh-Day Adventists, the Pentecostal Churches; or the semi-oriental sects, in which all the spiritual teachings of Asia from Zen and Yoga to Sufism and Transcendental Meditation ran riot. What a retaliation of the religious spirit in a so-called sceptical age to see the faithful – beginning with university students – flocking to these neo-mystical encounters! Weren't these all signs that the yearning for the divine rejected temples and altars and sought refuge in homes and the meeting-places of groups, always looking for fresh incarnations provided only that they did not reveal themselves in church. Even so one must not minimize the power of traditionalism and even conformism. Thus an inquiry undertaken by *Mass Observation* in 1965 showed that the majority of the population had no hesitation in expressing its desire for the established Church to go on providing, in the name of the nation its services and ritual for official functions, public prayers, coronations and so on. Alisdair MacIntyre was very near the truth when he said jokingly: 'The creed of the English is that there is no God, and that it is wise to pray to him from time to time.'[24]

The emancipation of women: progress or stagnation?

When one comes to consider the condition of women in our period one finds a perfect example of the contradictions that arose when an innovatory force came up against the strength of tradition. Much ground had been won since the days when the suffragettes made their gallant fight, but on the whole less than is usually maintained. In spite of some showy but not very significant progress (the legend started with the 'emancipated' flapper of the 1920s), the long march of women during the forty years since 1914 achieved only a partial success. In view of these fragmentary results, the sense of frustration and impatience of contemporary 'radical feminism' is quite understandable.

But, to be fair, there were a good many positive aspects. First there was the progress in political rights. The vote was conceded partially in 1918, then totally in 1928. The first woman MP, Lady Astor, was elected in 1919, and the first woman, Margaret Bondfield, entered the Cabinet in 1929, as

Labour Minister of Labour. In 1958 the first women life peers entered the House of Lords. Secondly, on the civil rights side, changes in the law of property in 1926 and 1935 gave women, married and unmarried, equality of rights in the management and disposal of their property. In family matters the rights of women were gradually levelled up with those of men. The Sex Disqualification Act of 1919 opened all the doors to the professions and the universities. Above all, the Equal Pay Act of 1970 abolished all differences in treatment over jobs and pay, and in 1975 the Sex Discrimination Act did away with all remaining distinctions based on sex. Equally positive was the change in behaviour resulting from the independence that was gradually conceded to women – an independence symbolically reflected in clothing and lifestyle. A further result was a considerable advance in women's education, especially at the secondary level.

Table 13 Working women in Great Britain, 1851–1971

	Women in total labour force (%)	Women at work in total female population (%)	Women at work in total female population aged between 15 and 64 years (%)	Working women in total labour force (%)	Married women at work out of all married women (%)
1851	30.1	35.2	–	–	–
1881	30.5	33.9	–	–	–
1901	29.1	31.6	–	–	–
1911	29.3	31.9	34.9	13.6	9.6
1921	29.4	32.2	32.6	12.9	8.7
1931	31.2	34.2	33.9	15.2	10.0
1951	30.8	34.7	41.3	38.2	21.7
1961	32.5	37.5	46.0	50.2	29.4
1971	34.6	41.7	52.4	62.6	40.8

Total female population aged over 10 years for 1851–1911, over 12 for 1921, over 15 from 1951 onwards

More significant still was the massive influx of women into occupations and professions that were previously closed to them, but there are some common confusions that must be avoided. In Table 13 we have collected the basic percentages illustrating the long-term evolution of the female occupied population. It shows beyond any doubt (and contrary to what has so often been said) first that female labour corresponds to an extremely ancient economic reality, as ancient as work itself; and secondly that the First World War did not cause a decisive increase in the female labour force. What the first column of our table shows very clearly is the extraordinary stability of the figures between the middle of the nineteenth and the middle of the twentieth centuries. It also shows that changes only started very recently, since the increase took place in the third quarter of the twentieth century, rising from 30.8 per cent in 1951 to 36 per cent in 1975. On the other hand it would be wrong to underestimate the apparently small changes, for they had decisive consequences. They must also be carefully distinguished, for since 1914 there had been three different kinds of change: (1) a great diversification of female employment as a result of women doing work (including responsible work) that was previously done only by men; (2) the gradual entry of middle-class women into employment; and (3) a great influx of married women into gainful occupations since the Second World War.

As regards our first point, one should note that in the two sectors where in the nineteenth century the majority of the female labour force was to be found, there was a sharp drop after 1918. One was the textile and clothing industry, which employed two out of five women in 1851, and was only employing one in four in 1921, and one in eight in 1951. The other was domestic service, in which were to be found 45 per cent of occupied women in 1900, 32 per cent in 1921, and after that there was a falling-off which ended in their almost total disappearance. In contrast women poured into offices (21 per cent of all office employees in 1911, 45 per cent in 1921, 60 per cent in 1951, 69 per cent in 1966), into teaching and, in more limited numbers, into the professions, the Civil Service, the universities and management. As a result of female labour being no longer restricted to the lower classes, distinctions in prestige started to appear. The occupational hierarchy was subtly changed and the arrival in force of women from the middle classes conferred a certain cachet on the jobs they undertook. Finally, the great new phenomenon of the years 1940–70 was the vast and rapid increase in the number of married women at work, for up to 1939 spinsters and widows were in an overwhelming majority. The turning-point was 1961, when for the first time it was the married women who formed the majority. The movement has continued unabated, and the prediction is that by 1980 two-thirds of all women at work will be married.

Demographic change had, in the course of two generations, transformed the condition of women in another way. And here we must underline that the transformation affected the women of the lower classes as much as, or even more than those of the middle class or the lower middle class, whereas in other respects – law, education and jobs – it was the lower middle class who benefited the most. As Titmuss has remarked, the fall in the birth-rate and the advent of voluntary child-bearing, combined with a longer average life expectancy, had many wide-reaching effects on family and individual life. Where on average, at the end of the nineteenth century, a working-class wife married, as a rule, between the ages of 18 and 23, spent at least fifteen years (about a third of her total expectation of life) burdened by pregnancies, suckling and tending her younger children, by the middle of the twentieth century the average had fallen to four years, or 6 per cent of her total expectation of life.[25] This average mother would have completed her cycle of maturity and still have thirty-five or forty years of life ahead of her. If, further, we take into consideration the improvement in the family's standard of living as a result of fewer children, medical advances in the care of married women and the various inducements to take a job, we cannot fail to see how all these new factors must have had a transforming effect on the family economy, domestic life, the idea of 'home', and all the roles and functions of womanhood.

In spite of all this the age-old inferior status of women remained, at all levels of society and in all social institutions. This was certainly the debit side of the account. In an epoch of allegedly total emancipation signs of inequality were to be found everywhere – in public life, education, and work. In politics, either parliamentary or municipal, women played a very small part. From 1945 to 1970 there were never more than 24 women in the House of Commons, or 4 per cent of all Members (admittedly better than in the 1930s, when the proportion was 2 per cent). If Parliament continued to be a 'club for gentlemen', the situation in local government was no better. In 1972, out of the 141 county councils and county boroughs, only 14 had a woman for mayor or chairman, and the overall proportion was one woman councillor to ten men councillors. (It is only fair to mention at this point the choice of Margaret Thatcher as leader of the Conservative Party.*) In the realm of higher education masculine predominance was maintained, unbroken, for half a century. In the years 1919–20 women formed 27 per cent of the total student number; in 1967–8 the percentage was unchanged, and by 1971–2 had only reached 29 per cent.[26] In every occupation the dice was systematically loaded against women. Most of the time they found themselves restricted to particular kinds of work, where they had to accept inferior jobs. Between the years 1911 and 1966 the proportion of female heads of businesses remained unchanged (about one-tenth). They made less progress in the professions than was generally believed: they succeeded in moving from 5 to 9 per cent of the total in the forty-five years from 1921 to 1966. By contrast the number of female operatives remained high, one-third of the manual labour force. As for pay, the principle 'equal pay for equal work' continued to be as unobtainable as it was desirable, such was the persistence of disparity, even in teaching and the Civil Service. It is true that in 1970 a theoretically decisive reform was brought in with the passing of the Equal

* And now, in 1979, her election as Prime Minister.

Pay Act, which came into force in 1975. Nevertheless it was noticeable that in the decade 1965–75 the salaries of women increased less rapidly on average than those of men. In conclusion let us quote one figure which alone denotes the startling difference that remained between the sexes in the matter of pay and jobs. In 1975 the average earnings of women were just a little more than half of those of men.

11 *Decadence or wisdom?*

Sic transit gloria Britanniae . . .

When, in 1963, *Encounter* devoted a special number to England 'face to face with its destiny', it gave it the provocative but significant title 'Suicide of a Nation?'[1] National introspection was then the fashion, and in some quarters the wind of masochism was blowing at gale force. There was a mood of anxious self-questioning. Was John Bull getting like the character in John Osborne's *The Entertainer* whose jokes nobody laughed at and whose opinions nobody wanted to hear? Even those who refused to look back nostalgically at the past were gloomy and worried about the future. The death of Churchill in 1965 seemed an event of symbolic significance. It brought the islanders brutally up against the fact that a page of their national and imperial history had been turned over, whose glory could never return. While the enormous cortège wound its way through London to the tolling of the bells of St. Paul's, the whole country mournfully reflected that it had lost a part of itself for ever. Since the calamitous setback of Suez in 1956 the British had been troubled with a painful sense of lost identity. They had experienced a series of disappointments after the hollow euphoria of victory in 1945. The vision of the 'new Elizabethan age' that everyone had hoped for at the Queen's coronation had vanished, and cries of 'decadence' were heard instead. People recalled the words of Matthew Arnold, who at the very apogee of the Victorian era was haunted by the idea of a Great Britain reduced to the role of 'a sort of greater Holland'. Sir Geoffrey Crowther said publicly that England in the twenty-first century would be like Spain in the eighteenth. It was about this time that the Germans invented the contemptuous phrase *'die englische Krankheit'*. That 'the sick man of Europe', the phrase once used to describe the Ottoman Empire, Britain's former client and protégé, should be applied to Britain herself was the very depth of humiliation.

The British were demoralized, not just because of their country's nuclear inferiority at a time when nuclear power meant world power, nor because of the growing evidence of economic weakness, but mainly because they felt that what had been destroyed could never be replaced. They had liquidated their past without planning or even defining their future.

One can discern three reasons for this disenchantment. Loss of the Empire naturally came first, and it was more than just sadness. For a country whose greatness and prosperity had been so dependent on imperial expansion, it was hard to get used to being confined within 90,000 square miles. Even though decolonization had not involved such drama and near-revolution as it had in France, how could the man in the street not be struck by the contrast with the glorious time when, as Ian MacLeod put it, 'at school a third or a quarter of the map was coloured red, and you did get some sort of consolation for being in this bright little, tight little island, and all the old jingo phrases, because of the very vastness of the empire, of which Britain was not only the head but the owner'.[2]

Another reason was that the idea of insularity, isolationism, the 'chosen nation, not like others' gradually lost all credibility. Over the years the British had been deceiving themselves with self-satisfied slogans like 'our world leadership', 'our special position', all aimed at perpetuating the idea that England was a country set apart. They boasted of their privileged position *vis-à-vis* the Commonwealth, and the 'special relationship' with the United States. Even before the Second World War André Siegfried had been amazed at the docility with which the British gave in to all American demands, to the extent that they 'seemed to have decided always to give in'.[3] After the war this dependence was accentuated, the faithful British ally moving more or less openly to the position of a US satellite. Round about 1960, however, the illusion of partnership faded, and all attempts at artificial respiration only led to pointlessly servile behaviour. So England now shared the common lot, and what a shock it was for her to discover that she was just like everyone else! Suddenly she found that she no longer knew her position in the world pecking-order. Old certainties had turned into uncertainties that were all the more painful because 'la nature, la structure, la conjoncture qui sont propres à la Grande-Bretagne' (the character, the structure and the situation of Great Britain), to use de Gaulle's words,[4] made it very uncomfortable for her both to define her new vocation and to discover the joys of being like everyone else. As the years went by, Dean Acheson's cruel epigram about the country 'that had lost an empire and not yet found a role' became more and more pertinent. So it was that, as her myths faded, England learnt resignation. This did not stop her from looking west; for between Europe and America the heart did not always follow the path dictated by reason. C. Le Saché put it well: 'if British xenophobia sets up a barrier the length of the Channel, there is no such barrier on the side of the Atlantic Ocean.'[5]

Yet reason had to prevail. Every analysis, every calculation went to show that England's future lay with Europe. Hence the third cause of dismay – how to manage the difficult re-orientation towards the European community. Apart from a few small groups long convinced of the idea, the move encountered great resistance. This was exacerbated by the tedious sequence of snubs and humiliations imposed by the abrasive character of French diplomacy. However feelings had to bow to facts; and the year 1962 saw a decisive turning-point in the history of Britain's overseas trade. For the first time her exports to Western Europe exceeded those to the sterling area, which roughly meant the Commonwealth. The proportions were: in 1950, 26 per cent and 50 per cent; in 1958, 27 per cent and 37 per cent; in 1970, 41 per cent and 21 per cent; and in 1974, 50 per cent and 18 per cent. The English gradually realized that they were condemned to become Europeans. Thereafter steady progress was made in negotiating the concessions Britain needed before joining the Common Market, leading to the Heath-Pompidou agreement of 1971 and the official entry on 1 January 1973. Finally in June 1975 came the referendum that massively confirmed Britain's entry into Europe.

The threat of stagnation and disruption

One of the arguments in favour of joining Europe concerned the threatening clouds that gathered on Britain's economic horizon. Many saw the Common Market as a sort of life-saving raft. They saw it as an unexpected means of stimulating the flagging economy, which had been going downhill ever since the 1950s. 'Stop-go', 'stagflation', the instability of the currency (closely dependent on the dollar – the pound had been twice devalued, officially in 1967 and *de facto* in 1974), a disastrous balance of payments due to the deficit on foreign trade, and the export of capital giving rise to an increasing external debt – all these adverse trends gave rise to alarm and despondency. There were endless warnings. Among the various Cassandras prophesying doom, Arnold Toynbee raised his voice in denunciation of the typical English vice of always letting things slide until the last minute. All this failed to stir public opinion unduly, unless one bears in mind Arthur Murphy's remark dating from the eighteenth century, when he said with caustic Irish wit: 'People in England are never so happy as when you tell them they are ruined.'

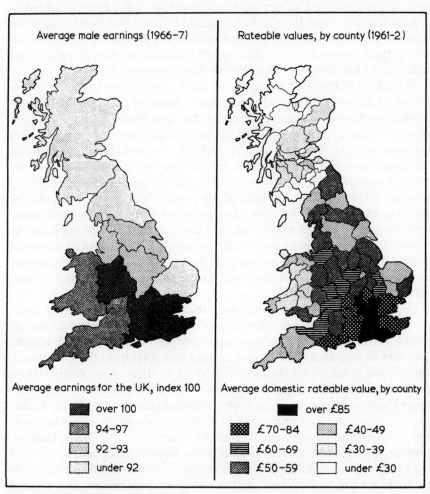

Average male earnings (1966-7)

Rateable values, by county (1961-2)

Average earnings for the UK, index 100

- ██ over 100
- ▨ 94-97
- ░ 92-93
- ☐ under 92

Average domestic rateable value, by county

- ██ over £85
- ▨ £70-84
- ▤ £60-69
- ▨ £50-59
- ░ £40-49
- ☐ £30-39
- ☐ under £30

Map 11. The geographical distribution of wealth: differences in the standard of living, by region

Whatever criteria were used to compare national economies, Britain came out badly. From 1950 to 1970 her rate of growth was only three-fifths that of the average of other industrialized countries.[6] The same with her rate of productivity. The second decade (post-1960) was worse than the previous ten years. For example, in 1960–74 the productivity of the United

Kingdom increased by only 30 per cent, in comparision with 90 per cent for Germany and 100 per cent for France. In 1961 the Gross National Product was 26 per cent of the total of what were to be the 'Nine'; by the time Britain had joined them in 1973 it had fallen to 19 per cent; in 1975 it was 16 per cent; and 14 per cent is forecast for 1980. Here is a further comparison. In 1950 the Gross Domestic Product per head was twice what it was in the future community of Six; in 1958 when this community was actually formed it was still more than a third higher; in 1974 it had fallen to 27 per cent less than the per head average of the Six.

In the light of this depressing performance, should one to despair of the future of Britain, now become the 'black sheep' of Europe? There were some who hoped for a great national effort that would drag the country from its lethargy; but in spite of appeals to the 'spirit of Dunkirk' this seemed unlikely. Others, more realistically, pinned their hopes on the enormous energy resources discovered in the North Sea. That was certainly a splendid gift to Britain from Nature. Only discovered in 1965, natural gas provided 57 per cent of the country's needs by 1970, and 90 per cent by 1975. Oil deposits, first found in 1970, seemed even more promising. Oil started to flow in 1975 and production was expected to reach 120 million tons by 1980, a figure definitely in excess of domestic needs. But was this bonanza going to shake the 'stagnant society' out of its obsolescence and into dynamic life? One was, alas, bound to feel certain doubts about this.

On another front, calm until now – that of national unity – two problems had arisen to disturb internal peace and threaten serious divisions. First there was coloured immigration. From 1953 onwards British society had had to face an influx of poor immigrants, first from the Caribbean, then from India and Pakistan. The West Indians came mainly from Jamaica, the Indians were 80 per cent Sikhs, the Pakistanis came either from Pakistan proper or from Eastern Bengal (later Bangladesh). Immigrants rapidly grew so numerous that, under pressure from public opinion, successive governments, first Conservative and then Labour, imposed restrictions on entry. Finally the legislation of 1962, 1968 and 1971 put very strict limits on immigration. This was an absolutely new problem for the British, who, in the course of a few years, saw several towns turning into multiracial communities. Up to the war the coloured population had been negligible – 100,000 in 1931 – but by 1961 it was over 400,000 and by 1971 1.5 million, or 2.5 per cent of the total population of Great Britain. As British subjects they were certainly entitled to all civil and political rights. Moreover, since the Race Relations Acts of 1965 and especially of 1968, all discrimination in matters of employment, housing, services and education was forbidden by law. But the vast flux of coloured people, the differences in standards of living and culture, problems of

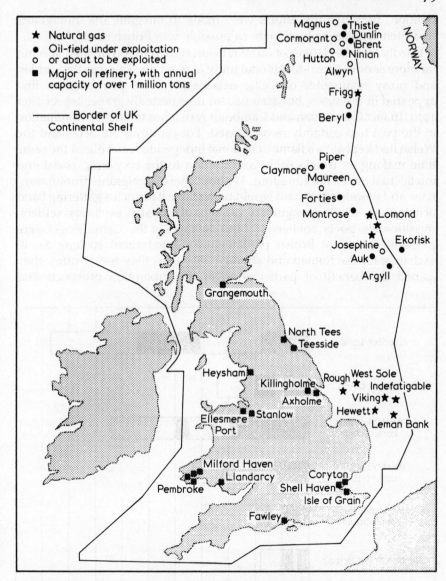

Natural gas (★)
Oil-field under exploitation (●)
or about to be exploited (○)
Major oil refinery, with annual capacity of over 1 million tons (■)

———— Border of UK Continental Shelf

NORWAY

Magnus ○ ●Thistle
Cormorant ○ ●Dunlin
○ ●Brent
Hutton ○ ●Ninian
Alwyn ○
Frigg ★
○
Beryl ●

Piper ●
Claymore ○ Maureen ○
Forties ●
Montrose ● ★Lomond
Josephine ★ ★Ekofisk
Auk ●
Argyll ●

Grangemouth ■

North Tees ■
Teesside ■

Heysham ■ Rough West Sole
Killingholme ■ ★ Indefatigable
Axholme ■ Viking ★ ★
Ellesmere ■ Stanlow Hewett ★ ★
Port Leman Bank

Milford Haven ■ Coryton ■
Llandarcy ■ Shell Haven ■
Pembroke ■ Isle of Grain ■
Fawley ●

Map 12. Discovery of North Sea oil and natural gas, 1965–75

health, work and family life caused much friction between newcomers and locals, and even outbreaks of racism. The problem was aggravated by the unequal geographical distribution of immigrants, who were mainly concentrated in the six great conurbations, and especially in London and Birmingham. It should be remarked, however, that under the three-fold influence of local authorities, voluntary organizations and public opinion, praiseworthy efforts were made to integrate the immigrants and their families as humanely as possible into British society.

Hardly had the danger of racial tension started to recede than another far more serious threat to national unity loomed up. This was the sudden and noisy resurgence of Celtic nationalism. This phenomenon first appeared in the 1960s, but assumed an unexpectedly graver aspect after 1970. In fact Caledonian and Cambrian resistance to English domination in the past had certainly never ceased. For centuries the Scots and the Welsh had kept alive a flame of national independence, while at the same time making an irreplaceable contribution to the economic, social and intellectual life of the Kingdom. Without these immigrants from mountains and moorlands Britain would never have had such a glittering band of inventors, scholars, engineers, captains of industry, explorers, settlers, missionaries, poets, soldiers. . . . But the races of the 'Celtic fringe' were prepared to accept British parliamentary government so long as, in exchange for the human and strategic resources they had to offer, they gained the benefit of participating in the promotion prospects and

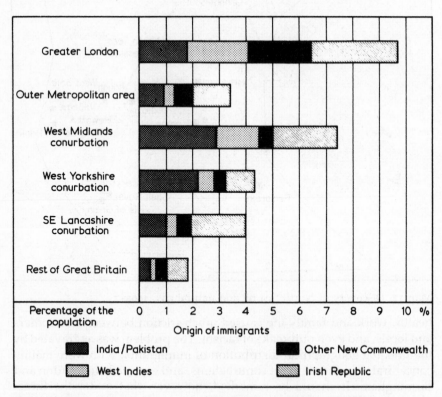

Figure 14. The concentration of immigrants in conurbations, 1971[7]

economic power of a vigorous nation with a vast empire overseas. But after the 1950s the situation had changed fundamentally. Already conscious of being poor relations, ill-favoured by geography, they had been sharply affected by English economic decline, since stagnation worsened the neglect which they already felt was their lot. With all this went feelings of cultural frustration, so that the nationalist movements began to snowball rapidly, particularly among the younger generation. They gained some success at the polls. The first Welsh Nationalist reached the House of Commons in 1966 and the first Scottish Nationalist in 1967. In the parliamentary elections of 1974 the hopes of both parties were encouraged by many more candidates being elected. Neither Welsh nor Scottish separatism seemed in a position to go to the limits of their programme, but they looked as if they might turn the United Kingdom into the Disunited Kingdom.

Class, State and power

During the euphoric expansionist days of the 1950s, a chorus of authoritative voices proclaimed that the days of traditional class and ideological conflicts were over. The country had entered its 'post-capitalist' phase, a dynamic, 'fluid' period heralding the arrival of an 'open' mobile society, ruled by consensus and offering equality of opportunity, where the living standards were middle-range without necessarily being middle class. At the same time, it was claimed, the growing homogeneity of society (itself a result of mass consumption), the unifying power of the techno-structure and the mass media would eventually cut down social distinctions through the standardization of behaviour and leisure activities, and through the universal sharing of common cultural values. The nation was treading the path of social peace – essential, according to Galbraith, if it sought economic growth. This integration process went together with a passive acceptance of the economic system and 'cultural democratization' resulting from mass schooling and mass leisure activities.

This short-term view, contradicted at the very moment that it was formulated, did not stand up to experience, and by the beginning of the 1960s there was a return to earth. Later developments were to show that it was simple-minded to think that growth would lead to an upheaval of the class structure and that affluence would bring general contentment. The truth was that boundaries between social groups had become hazier and less easy to define. These differences, confused by much overlapping, had none of the sharpness and simplicity of Victorian times (though these were relative, as we have seen). Gone was the dichotomy between a working class haunted by pauperism because it lived in a subsistence economy (and often below the subsistence level) and a higher class, bourgeois and aristocratic, with a monopoly of wealth, well-being and leisure. However, to take one example, two excellent social surveys on Banbury (conducted by Margaret Stacey at nearly twenty years' interval, in 1948–51 and 1966–68, and published in 1960 and 1975) show very clearly that in this small but expanding Midland town the differences not only of income and power but particularly of socio-cultural interconnections survived, intact, the arrival of successive layers of population. The research results show very clearly the heterogeneity of two different worlds, each with its own network of social and institutional relationships. On one side there was the middle-class with its Conservative organizations, Anglican churchgoers, Rotarians and Arts Council members; on the other side the world of the masses – Labour bodies, the Trades & Labour Club, the WEA and the Friends of Banbury Hospitals.[8] To take another small example, Arthur Marwick has pointed out that, in the buffets of the House of Commons, one still sees Labour Members taking their cups of tea while the Conservatives treat themselves to gin-and-tonics.[9]

So the whole of the class set-up, sophisticated to the last degree, went cheerfully on its way, just as elaborately stratified as ever. Since the war it had brought itself up to date and adapted itself to the needs of a technological output-minded world. But underneath there always remained the age-old confederacy of birth, money and power. In other words the psychological factor – status and prestige – continued to be allied with the economic – property, income and standard of living. As the crowning triumph of the aristocratic principle, the distinction conferred by name and family was still very much alive. A century before, Disraeli had remarked correctly that England was governed, not by an aristocracy but by the aristocratic principle. This was deeply embedded in the national consciousness and perpetuated itself in a powerful group of forces, institutions and customs, labelled monarchy, House of Lords, honours lists, titles and so on. The strength of the system lay in its capacity for endless extension. From the top to the bottom of the ladder there was a lively consciousness of status. The characteristic that was peculiar to England was that the criterion for discrimination was not related simply to money, as in the United States, but to birth, breeding, occupation, way of life and education. Class was symbolized by a way of being, behaviour, gestures and, above all, accent. People had only to open their mouths to be identified as 'them' or 'us': social origin was betrayed by the first word uttered. In no other country did language, pronunciation and intonation play such a role. A model of social acceptability and good manners was constructed round the 'Oxford' accent, backed up by the BBC accent. The entire educational system, by conforming to the model, added its support.

However, alongside these subjective criteria for determining class affiliations, there were objective inequalities – inequalities of wealth and income, of security and culture. They came under fire, but they continued to flourish in spite of the successes of the Welfare State in reducing extremes of wealth and poverty. As John Westergaard has written: 'Despite a good deal of individual movement up and down the socio-economic scale, most of it short-distance and more of it than before channelled through educational institutions, the substantial inequalities of opportunity arising from social origin have hardly changed over a number of decades.'[10] In these circumstances one feels that for such a society 'opaque' would be more descriptive than 'open'.

At the heart of this society there were two categories deserving closer attention, for it was the interplay of their respective strengths that determined the shifts in real power. On top was the controlling upper class, and more particularly the body of technocrats; and below were the manual workers supported by their unions. Each was backed (though in far from equal strength) by a whole network of institutions and pressure groups, and a precarious equilibrium resulted from the ensuing trials of strength. In short, the power of the State and the techno-structure was faced by its classic opponent – labour.

There were also internal changes in the ruling class. Its influence derived less from its traditional power bases – property, inherited wealth, ability to lead a life of leisure, and conspicuous consumption – than from knowledge, contacts and power of decision. These were the key qualities needed for the management, on a global scale, of giant organizations, as well as for the enjoyment of the advantages and pleasures that went with money and power. A new sort of man was on the increase – the merito-crat. This brought a shake-up in the ranks of the 'charmed circle', and a debate of some importance. Two concepts of the élite were competing, and one was gaining on the other. On the one side, the old aristocratic ideal held good, the ideal of the amateur, born with a gift for leadership, the 'effortless superiority' of the Oxford man. On the other side, the modern ideal was in the ascendant: the competent professional, hard-working and efficient, whose worth was underwritten by merit and good paper qualifications gained in hard competition. In a prophetic book, *The Rise of the Meritocracy*, which caused some sensation when it was published in 1958, Michael Young forecast an awe-inspiring future when, in the name of pure efficiency and by a ruthless system of selection, only the ablest would rise to the top. Was this to be the end of the regime of amateurs, the sudden death of snobbery in its peculiarly English form – which has been called the *Pox Britannica*? Was this to be the triumph of the diploma and the degree? Certainly the change of attitude due to the requirements of technical management, the growth of universities and the multiplication of graduates (the annual number doubled between 1960 and 1970) pointed to a happy future for the meritocrats. All the same, even the new merit-based élite was shaped by the self-same schools and universities that bore, either by tradition or by imitation, the irradicable stamp of upper-class origin. It would appear from recent research, such as that carried out by the Nuffield Foundation on the family and school background of top members of the Civil Service, that even there, where meritocrats abounded, there was still a marked weakness for the semi-aristocratic charms of the public schools and Oxbridge.[11]

The working class found itself up against the twin power of State and Capital, consisting of a huge array of corporate institutions, banks, insurance companies, investment trusts and giant industrial complexes, not to mention the little world of personal connections and interlocking directorships. But even more it found itself up against the privileged holders of knowledge, who had the key to the control of society's future and who had introduced a new version of the division of labour – 'the eggheads and the serfs' in the words of Sir John Newsom.[12] Faced with this alliance of the City and the Treasury, the workers turned to their traditional weapon – trade-union power, in the form of wage claims and by exerting pressure. This was particularly true of the new labour aristocracy, which drew its power both from the technological growth sectors and its key professional positions in the labour hierarchy.

However, for a clear understanding of the deep-seated feelings behind working-class strategy, one needs to shed two widely believed fallacies: one concerns *'embourgeoisement'*, the other 'integration'. On the first, the work of J. Goldthorpe and D. Lockwood has disposed of a belief that was too hastily deduced from undeniable improvement in standards of living and even what might be called working-class prosperity. One can say unequivocally that there was no *'embourgeoisement'* of manual workers any more than there was 'proletarianization' of white-collar workers. As for 'integration', it has been alleged that the philosophy of mass consumption and the brainwashing action of the mass media led to a sameness of outlook. This in its turn engendered an illusion of participation that was really dependence and stifled any creative challenge. In actual fact the working class remained firmly apart, socially, culturally and even materially. The contrast of 'them' and 'us' was still strongly felt. In any case, as Frank Parkin has shown, participation in the dominant system of values was far from preventing the continuation of individual minor cultures. This plurality of sub-cultures was related to particular social or occupational milieux, regional traditions, ideologies, etc. This separateness was further emphasized by two new features: diminishing work satisfaction among a majority of manual workers, and an increasingly home-centred existence. Even so, in the heart of this partially fragmented

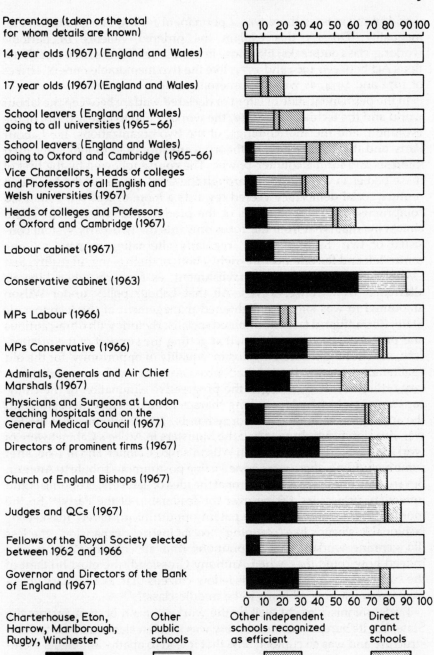

Figure 15. Educational background of leading citizens[12]

world of the masses there was a permanent feeling of exploitation and inequality. Doesn't this explain the ordered violence of periodic working-class outbreaks, like those in protest against the Industrial Relations Act between 1969 and 1974, like the two memorable miners' strikes of 1972 and 1974, as well as numerous smaller eruptions?

In the permanent state of latent or declared warfare between the labour world and the technocratic State, the workers had to take account of the evolution, and the shortcomings, of the two organizations, the Labour Party and the TUC, which in theory were supposed to look after their interests and form a counter-power. The course followed by the first of these bodies is very clear: all through the third quarter of the twentieth century social democracy veered towards a more or less self-confessed compromise with the oligarchs of the productivist system. One could almost maintain that from the 1950s onwards the two-party system consisted of two 'Establishments' regularly alternating in power – one centre-left and the other centre-right – both of them being, in reality, just two branches of the same Establishment, as formerly when Liberals alternated with Conservatives. All that Labour policy under Wilson amounted to was simply enlightened management of the technocratic State. Its traditional tactics combined socialist rhetoric with ultra-cautious and pragmatic measures; it aimed at getting the support of the meritocracy, substituting the modest slogan 'equality of opportunity' for the old egalitarian war-cries. It combined mixed economy with pure parliamentary orthodoxy. It encouraged the progressive elimination of the cloth-cap element which had for so long characterized the Party: henceforward the appeal was to brains, not horny hands. The development at the top was also significant. In 1945 half the Ministers in Attlee's Cabinet were of working-class origin; a quarter in Wilson's 1964 Cabinet; and in 1969, after some reshuffling, there were none – a fine posthumous tribute to Aneurin Bevan, who once expressed horror at the idea of 'lawyers, economists and university professors' taking over the leadership of the Party![13] So the more official Labour sank into patent opportunism, barely masked by fashionable slogans like 'planning', 'social justice', 'expansion', the less did genuine working-class aspirations find an echo in Party policy. Indeed how could they when Anthony Crossland, the most brilliant of the Party's theoreticians, told his fellow-citizens that, as a primary objective, 'we must now all learn to be middle-class'?

Trade unionism might well be the workers' main bastion against the State, but its bureaucratic machinery was itself an element in the techno-structure and was so cumbersome that it lead to apathy among its members. Nor should the importance of this apathy be minimized, for it was a significant feature of the current social situation. At various levels members' participation in decision-making was minimal, most of them doing no more than taking their card and paying their dues. It has been reckoned that, just as in earlier times many workers voted Tory, so after 1945 about 30 per cent of manual workers regularly voted Conservative, and 20–5 per cent of actual trade-union members either Conservative or Liberal. In spite of all this, and however stiff in the joints the unions might be, their claims backed by action made them, in the actual state of society, the principal counter-power. This power was exerted, it is true, in a variable manner, at once progressive and conservative. Their stick-in-the-mud approach was epitomized by their old-fashioned, not to say obtuse habit of aiming at quantitative objectives, often limited to small groups, almost always simply seeking pay increases. At the same time, thanks to a well-tried strike technique capable of causing the maximum disruption of industrial production with the minimum inconvenience to the workforce, the working class was able to give full vent to their sense of alienation and injustice. This is what enabled the workers to keep the Establishment in check, because the latter was warned that it could not misuse its power without suffering for it, and that therefore it would be better to come to terms with the world of labour.

However, alongside this classic instrument of worker power, sturdy but slow-thinking as it was, there arose in the years 1965–75 other forces hoping to form a genuine counterpoise to the weight of the ruling oligarchy. These sniping operations, conducted by determined, inventive and forward-looking minorities, usually operated from the flanks rather than from the front, and their attacks were directed at key-points. The activists tended to be a mixed collection – workers who wanted to see some direct action for a change, young people and women in revolt, intellectuals, technicians on the loose. . . . This sort of action (all part of the 'wind of revolt' mentioned earlier) ran the risk of being defused by the Establishment (to which many of the activists belonged) or by the commercialism of the mass media. However the forces thus set in motion sometimes managed to plant pinpricks in the body of the technocratic State, and so hold the power of neo-capitalism partially in check, but without ever succeeding in shaking the passive conformism of the herd.

An art of living?

'We must cultivate our garden.' No one nowadays seems to have paid more heed to Candide's advice than the English. In renouncing growth at all costs, rejecting the productivity rat race, and in choosing to work less and live more, have the islanders stolen a march on the rest of the world and found a way of wisdom, a quiet shady lane, away from the hellish din of by-passes and motorways? In many ways the present state of England – a calm, well-to-do, relaxed community – seems to bear out John Stuart

Mill's prediction that the slowing-down of growth at the advanced stage of industrial society would lead inevitably to stabilization: within the framework of the 'Stationary State' everyone would accept their place in the economic order because they would rather devote their time to more attractive activities such as culture and the arts.[14] Indeed one only has to re-read Keynes to find that he was the first to proclaim that life was more important than the economy: 'The day is not far off when the economic problem will take the back seat where it belongs, and the arena of the heart and the head will be occupied or reoccupied by our real problems – the problems of life and of human relations, of creation and behaviour and religion.'[15]

There has undoubtedly been a revulsion from purely economic criteria, from an infatuation with technology, from the motivation of pure gain. A passionate acquisitiveness has been replaced by a retreat into one's own garden, or by pursuits of an aesthetic and cultural nature, but everywhere there is a feeling for the importance of calmness, well-being and good sense. In other words, from having been the paragons of industrialization and urbanization in the nineteenth century, the English seem to be moving towards a different model, a cosy genial society, quite unlike the tough conquering race of earlier days. Increasingly the accent is on happiness, but not any sort of happiness. The chosen kind is what one might call the English brand of happiness – leisurely, relaxed, sheltered, not overstrenuous – an existence enjoying equal measures of security and freedom. It is certainly not easy to measure this happiness, nor to discover how far the English think they are blessed with it. But the satisfaction with the way of life they proclaim to the world is plain to see. Witness an inquiry published by the Social Science Research Council in 1974 which put them at the top of the European league for satisfaction with their lot: 85 per cent said they were 'satisfied'; one-third of these were 'very satisfied'.

One can even go further. In showing so much enthusiasm for their 'quality of life', the English have found a new source of national pride; and, curiously enough, there are signs of a resurgence of the old superiority complex. Deeming that they have travelled further along this road than other nations, the islanders are eager to find there new causes for hope. In this way they see themselves fulfilling the proud boast of John Milton: 'Let not England forget her precedence of teaching nations how to live.'[16] In fact in this revival of cultural and spiritual values, in this rediscovery of beauty, simplicity and the importance of human relations, the idea is not simply to drive out Mammon by refusing to become the slave of the money machine and the cash nexus. It functions at a deeper level, as the affirmation of a new ideal, benefiting the community as well as the individual. It is what *The Times*, in a series of articles devoted to the future of England in 1971, expressed in these terms: in this 'post-imperial' age one can define a new objective,

> the ideal of a country which has raised the real standard of life, rather than the statistical standard of life, higher than any other country. The values which should come first are the human and aesthetic values. Some nations make civilization a by-product of the creation of wealth; Britain is more likely to make wealth a by-product of the creation of a worthwhile civilization.[17]

So, little by little, the mist of failure clears and a modicum of optimism shines through. It is the point made by John Boorman in his film *Leo the Last*: when, at the end, the hero, a prince who has taken up the defence of the oppressed, meets with one failure after another, one of the characters makes the splendid remark that although he has not changed the world, he has changed his neighbourhood!

So the new England of the 1970s is, in many ways, turning its back on its past. Is this the end of Prometheus, and the rebirth of Orpheus? Certainly the new art of living that is emerging has a markedly aesthetic content. Culture and beauty have become major preoccupations of the new generation. The striking burst of creativity that the country has seen since the 1950s in the theatre, in the cinema, in music, classical and popular, art and fashion bears witness to a freedom of expression and a new spontaneity, which show a determination to venture outside well-trodden paths.

In addition, the English are more proud than ever of the tolerance and freedom that are found in their midst, for these qualities form an essential part of the background of their existence. To quote one symbolic fact, the 1887 edition of Baedeker, under the heading 'Passports', says: 'These documents are not necessary in England, except for the purpose of retrieving a letter from a *poste restante*.' Today the identity card is still unknown in Britain. A pluralist society resisting the abuse of power, always ready to fight against any encroachment on the rights of the individual, this is a basic asset of the English art of living. In short, a world that is at once polite and even polished, whose ambition it is to be 'civilized'. Finally, even though England is far from being a paradise, it is undoubtedly a place where it is good to live.

Conclusion

Our book has reached its end. In it we have tried, scrupulously and, we hope, fairly, to evoke the multifold movements of a society over a century and a quarter. At the same time we have sought to outline a general picture – the evolution of England herself in the course of these 125 years. It was certainly a period full of every kind of change, not to mention reversals of fortune. Now that we have reached the limits of what can be seen, what conclusions can we draw? At first sight the British people of 1975 seem very different from the insular folk of 1851. But after all can we be so certain that change has ousted permanence, that the new has triumphed over the old, and innovation over tradition? We propose to end by disentangling from the vicissitudes of successive phases certain major trends which have influenced the historic march of English society – always being aware, of course, of the inevitably summary character of such a general approach.

1

From one end of the period to the other, from the triumph of Victorianism to the Edwardian Age, from the inter-war years to the affluent society, the acceptance of social stratification has vigorously survived all change. *Class* and *hierarchy* are the two twin notions which we must regard as the keystones of English society. Without them we cannot fathom how this society works. 'Them' and 'Us' – the division is still fundamental. Class consciousness breaks through at every opportunity. To prove this we need only to pick at random from the wealth of testimony running from the mid-nineteenth century to today. In 1852 the Director of HM Convict Prisons, giving evidence before a Commons' Select Committee, declared: 'With us the distinction of classes is a national characteristic. There may be considerable kindness between classes, but there is no cordiality.'[1] This impression was corroborated by Cobden who, at the same period, lamented loudly that class distinction was a national trait. It was Cobden too who cited the case of the chimney-sweep who refused to allow his daughter to marry a fish-and-chips seller on the grounds that the latter's origins were too lowly![2] In *The Lion and the Unicorn* (1941), George Orwell fulminated against this same attachement to hierarchy that was so deeply rooted among his compatriots: 'England is the most class-ridden country under the sun.'[3] And more recently it was one of the champions of 'revisionism' within the Labour Party, Anthony Crosland, who felt obliged to admit: 'Never have class divisions been so acute and anguished as since they were theoretically abolished'[4] – an attitude excellently conveyed by John Betjeman in this sly couplet:

> That topic all absorbing, as it was,
> Is now and ever shall be, to us – CLASS.

2

One of the paradoxes of British social development is that the march of democracy has gone hand in hand with the ruling oligarchy's maintenance of its position. It would be pointless to deny the reality of democratization. Progress has been made in all directions – the working of the political system, recognition of workers' rights, the development of thought and ideas. Yet, as we have seen, there has also been a strong concentration of power, often in the hands of families privileged by inheritance. Amazing resilience has been shown by that closed circle, aristocratic and élitist, which has calmly resisted every assault! For one very much has the feeling that the Establishment today is only a direct extension of that little world of privileged people which Cobbett abominated and denounced, calling it 'the Thing'; or it could be considered simply a continuation of what Thackeray half a century later termed 'the Great World'. Nowdays, to be sure, 'the élite' is much less aristocratic in its recruitment and more diluted with meritocrats; but it is always the same small world which holds the money and the power, the education and the know-how, and hence the chief levers of decision.

Thus the social life of England never ceased to divide itself into two circuits which only rarely impinged on one another. On the one side was the world of crowds and of appearances – the world of representative democracy: Parliament, elections, universal suffrage, in short the majority. On the other side we have the 'magic circle', discreet and effective, where a small minority's controlling power was exercised. In a statement of unusual frankness Anthony Eden at the outset of his political career described this double process: 'We have not got democratic government in this country today. We never had it and I venture to suggest . . . that we shall never have it. What we have done, in all the progress of reform and evolution of politics, is to broaden the basis of our oligarchy.'[5]

3

One can even go further. If England has enjoyed such social stability, such political continuity and such an unbroken survival of the established order, in spite of the threats of revolutions, wars and totalitarianism, we must look in two directions for the reasons.

First of all, for more than a century there existed a consensus that was both national and social. It was a consensus which succeeded in rallying the vast majority of the country around a few simple principles and values. Among its basic elements was the fact that the ruling classes began very early on to believe that it was better to govern by persuasion than by force, or according to R. G. Collingwood's formula, that in politics, it is essential to recruit the governed class as partners in the art of government. Thanks to this cooperation freely expressed and freely accepted, the status quo was guaranteed more effectively than by any other device, for it resulted in the people conferring upon the oligarchy a legitimacy that no one could challenge. In this situation not only did the electoral and parliamentary process present no threat, but it played a vital role by expressing the majority's support of the existing order.

Let us not imagine for one moment that this picture amounts simply to an historian's *a posteriori* reconstruction. The rulers of Victorian England were the first to be aware of this phenomenon, and, what is more, they spoke about it very openly. Listen for example to Lord Cairns, Conservative Lord Chancellor in the Disraeli Cabinet of 1868, proclaiming that it was 'utterly impossible for the country to be governed by any party otherwise than in accordance with the opinion of the great majority of householders in this country'.[6] And Gladstone, in 1865, expressed a similar view from a Liberal Party standpoint: 'Please to recollect that we have got to govern millions of hard hands; that it must be done by force, fraud or good will; that the latter has been tried and is answering. . . .'[7] Or again the Positivist Frederic Harrison, supporter of advanced radicalism, who explained that the British system of government rested on the 'rule by consent, and not by force', and consequently on the ability of the governing classes 'to maintain their supremacy by their social power and their skill in working the constitutional machine'.[8] So the oligarchy, by expanding somewhat, was simply reinforcing its power. For, instead of having recourse to compulsion, it internalized its channels of support ('deference') which were nourished by prevailing ideologies and values, themselves diffused by every means of communication and social intercourse.

Secondly, the Establishment showed extraordinary tactical ability in perpetuating its influence and indeed its existence. These tactics were at once far-seeing and flexible, showing consummate skill in the art of judicious sharing. Here one finds, well integrated but immediately recognizable, the famous British 'compromise' the old habit of a trading nation for whom, on the collective as well as the individual level, a bargain was always more profitable than a fight. These tactics likewise showed masterly skill in the art of defusing problems, to the point of reducing them to banality or harmlessness, without letting them take too dramatic a turn, and certainly not allowing them to get out of control. 'The English', quipped Oscar Wilde, 'have a miraculous ability to turn wine into water'. Hence there was no longer any need for repression, for the explosive nature of a problem tended to vanish. Finally they were tactics that knew how to use all the magic of snobbery and convention to cash in on situations, to integrate and to assimilate. Not to mention the great attraction of traditions, all the resources of that grandiose, unchanging pageantry which old England keeps at her disposal – the monarchy, the aristocracy, Parliament, civic and academic institutions with their rites, their ceremonies and their decorum.

4

Chateaubriand maintained once that the French thirsted more for equality than liberty. The history of England since the nineteenth century, on the contrary, shows clearly (and John Stuart Mill complained bitterly about it) that liberty appeared more important than equality. This passion for liberty is certainly a distinctive trait of English society, and one comes across it constantly. Today no less than yesterday, Emerson's saying remains true: 'The English stand for liberty.' It amounts to an innate requirement in each 'free-born' Englishman, hungry for personal liberty in all its forms, as well as political liberty. Furthermore the demand is so deep-rooted that no one, so to speak, notices it any more, apart from foreigners who continue to register astonishment and admiration at its strength. One finds this admiration expressed, of course, in the writings of liberals such as Emile Boutmy and Jacques Bardoux, but one discovers it also in the *communards* Louis Michel and Jules Vallès, who were amazed to find a country without a secret police. (Before leaving London after nine years of exile, Jules Vallès saluted the English capital: 'I took off my hat to the black city to thank these people . . . for having taught me, the native of a republican country, what liberty was.'[9]) Indeed liberal England welcomed all those who sought refuge: Esterhazy as well as Zola, Lenin no less than Kropotkin, in our day Kolakowski and Koestler.

Liberty and *individualism* – these are two permanent characteristics of English society. A pair that are as essential as the pair *class* and *hierarchy*. But what in practice is particularly original about English individualism is that it combines the recognition of an almost unlimited liberty for the individual with the habit of voluntary association, that is, the possibility of joining all kinds of groups and societies: hence a myriad of small communities where one finds oneself accepted instead of feeling isolated and abandoned.

5

In its relations with the outside world the whole of English society has had to undergo a radical conversion in order to pass from the allure of Victorian supremacy, when prosperity and optimism reigned, to the disappointments and setbacks of the twentieth century. Now it was this process that forced England to become European, a change which she had hitherto obstinately resisted. Just after the First World War, Keynes underlined the contrast that was then so evident between the position of the islanders and the 'compact block' of Europeans, stating in his usual trenchant manner: 'England still stands outside Europe. Europe's voiceless tremors do not reach her. Europe is apart and England is not her flesh and body.'[10] This same conclusion was reached shortly afterwards by André Siegfried when he compared England in a famous phrase to a 'ship anchored in European waters, but always ready to set sail'.[11]

Yet as one now looks at English society in the process of joining the European block, one begins to wonder. Shouldn't one see this more as a sign of decadence of an obsolescent country, living on its past, and incapable of rediscovering that aggressive – and isolationist – dynamism that created its growth, its expansion and its greatness? Undeniably there are signs that point in this direction. How for example can one deny the change in moral climate and the absence of any common long-term aims? A disappointed General de Gaulle confided to André Malraux in 1970: 'Even the English no longer have any national ambition.'[12]

So must one despair and say 'the game's over', proclaiming the inevitable decline of a nation whose glory must now belong to the past? All in all, we feel that it would be wrong to give too much credence to the countless prophecies that periodically announce imminent catastrophe. Let us remember that there was no lack of earlier Cassandras and they were invariably wrong, starting with Ledru-Rollin who as early as 1850 saw fit to devote two volumes to *The Decadence of England!* 1850! The very date when this history starts, in a period full of success and glory. . . . The very fact that English society has survived in the face of such pessimism should make us hesitate before accepting such cynical proclamations. This caution does not of course prevent one from observing and even underlining the extent to which the British position *vis-à-vis* the world has diminished and deteriorated since the middle of the twentieth century. The British are now reduced to the common lot, to the level of a decent European average. We must agree, however, that the islanders do hold some important cards in their hand. The asset of a civilization going back many centuries is unlikely to fade away in quite such a fleeting manner. The creativity of the last twenty years in the sphere of culture and the art of living are a sign of various untapped resources. In the world of today England has definitely ceased to be a great power strutting proudly in the first rank of nations, but it is up to the English to continue to be a great people.

Postscript
1975–9

The writing of this book was completed just four years ago. Since then English society has proceeded on its way and enriched itself with new experience. What have these years 1975–9 brought with them? And does the new data serve to round off, modify or revise the views set out in the book, particularly in the last part, the most contemporary section?

Let us first note that the year 1979 does not seem to mark a major turning-point, any more than 1975 was a key date. It is true, of course, that the economic crisis, which erupted at the end of 1973, has continued to become progressively worse, all the more so in Britain where this world crisis struck an economy that had for some years been suffering from a sluggish anaemia. However, in this period, galloping inflation has been mastered; the 'social contract' has played a calming role for three years; the party system, even if it brought some friction and no glory, has survived the danger of collapse; the menace of Scottish and Welsh separatism has receded and the unity of the kingdom has been maintained; racial difficulties, instead of worsening, have tended to stabilize; finally the general pessimism prevalent at the end of the 1960s and beginning of the 1970s (wasn't it thought in many circles that Britain was sliding down a steady slope of decline from which there wasn't the slightest hope of recovery?) gave way to some renewal of confidence and hope for a respectable future. On many counts the 1977 Jubilee coincided with a stocktaking that was on the whole optimistic. It was felt that, in her search for a new way of communal living and a new relationship between society and culture, well-being and basic values, Britain, peaceful haven of contradictions and a people civilized and rich in humanity, had once more in her history managed to find the way of balance; she had achieved this without rupture or breakdown, absorbing the shocks, avoiding violence and respecting the individual's right to choose.

In connection with this, rather than speaking of a 'mixed economy' – a term which merely attempts to conceal a neo-liberalism nervously tempered by the existence of a number of public or semi-public sectors – it would be better to speak of the progress of a 'mixed society'. This is a development which was sparked off after the Second World War but which has gained impetus in recent years. It is a development which leads not to social democracy, but to a socialized democracy where respect of the law of the majority, the right to well-being, the primacy of legality and the rejection of totalitarianism in all its forms are promoted to universally accepted principles. There is also built into this system a balance, limited but none the less real, between the power of the State, the power of capital and the power of the workers. In fact, just as it is wrong to describe, as is often done, the leaders of the large trade unions as 'new barons' cutting the State set-up down to size and foisting on the public the feudal law of their groups, it is equally important to underline just how much the trade-union organization, strengthened by the laws passed in 1974–6, and further supported at the base by militant shop stewards, has provided effective opposition to the economic and political Establishment. This is less true with respect to the cultural and educational Establishment. Hence a subtle interplay of powers and counter-powers has given rise to a renewed spirit of emancipation, independence and individual liberty.

Moreover one concludes that British society seems to have finally absorbed, without permanent damage, the shock of permissiveness which suddenly arrived twenty years ago to undermine the age-old puritan heritage. The shattering of traditional codes certainly did constitute, as we have seen, a grave danger of disruption. Now the transition seems to have been successfully made from a society with a strict morality, well ordered and defined for the community as a whole, to a splintered society in which each individual discovers his own rules arising from his own choice. As the summit has been scaled in the space of one generation, one can now look forward with confidence to the future of the 'tolerant society' which has asserted itself.

Furthermore the opinion polls show a high degree of satisfaction with life among the British, for in spite of the clouds massed on the horizon they unhesitatingly express a collective contentment, whether the current government or housing or standard and mode of living are in question. What is more, traditional values persist despite the changes in the social and moral context. So, for those interviewed, the things that count most for the quality of life are (in this order) the home, family life, standard of living, personal beliefs and religion, personal relationships, health, work and freedom. Then come nature and the environment, education, and, finally, at the end, equality.

However, side by side with these indicators that favour the pursuit of a peaceful evolution, one cannot altogether ignore negative factors. To begin with, there are the deficiencies in growth, in investment and in productivity that have been confirmed year after year. For the pressures surrounding the division of the national cake to remain vigorous, but not violent, as has been the case until now, that cake must be large enough to offer the satisfaction judged necessary by the different partners.

Many of the islanders certainly console themselves by declaring that they prefer quality to quantity, 'spiritual' wealth to material wealth. But how can one fail to see the simplistic illusions of such arguments if they are pushed too far? As if one could separate production from consumption, the cultural from the economic, the private from the public with such ease! Furthermore, in wanting to avoid the outrages and excesses of yesterday's Promethean universe, there is the great danger of falling into the banality and boredom of the 'mediocracy'. What one can say, however, is that the British capacity for invention, such as has been evident during the last twenty years, has shown that its great strength lies in social practice much more than in theoretical constructs and pre-established doctrines. Before being translated into ideology, social processes have to be discovered and tried by practical experiment, and it is only by slow degrees that it can be transformed into reasoned and conscious organization. At the same time one can rely on the Establishment, now diversified and enlarged but still strong, to show its capacity for assimilation and absorption, and to carry out necessary modernization. It may do this by embodying in prudent reform aspirations that do not take kindly to change, so that English society may preserve its orderly style, both stable and hierarchic, in accordance with the well-tried and reassuring principles of a democracy skillfully blending socialization, individualism and 'meritocracy'.

February 1979

Notes to
the text

PREFACE

1 Halévy Papers, Letter to Célestin Bouglé, 28 April 1898: 'I seek to decipher the most undecipherable of peoples, the most moral, the least family-minded, the most mobile, the best adapted, the most candid and the most hypocritical. What principle should I follow?'
2 Quoted by Charles de Franqueville in *Les institutions politiques, judiciaires et administratives de l'Angleterre*, Paris, 1863, p.v (Bülow was Prussian envoy in London from 1827 to 1842).
3 Quoted by L. Scheler in J. Vallès, *La rue à Londres*, 1951 edn, p. xii.
4 G. Orwell, 'The Lion and the Unicorn' in S. Orwell and T. Angus (eds.), *Collected Essays*, vol. II, London 1968, p. 57.
5 E. Halévy, *History of the English People in the Nineteenth Century*, vol. I, *England in 1815*, London 1924, p. xii.
6 J. Bardoux, *L'Angleterre radicale. Essai de psychologie sociale (1906–1913)*, Paris 1913, p. vii. (The reader may like to note that Jacques Bardoux was the grandfather of President Giscard d'Estaing.)
7 Cf. A. J. P. Taylor, *English History, 1914–1945*, Oxford 1965, p. v; W. J. Reader, *Life in Victorian England*, London 1964, p. 15; J. Ryder and H. Silver, *Modern English Society*, 2nd edn, London 1977, pp. xvi–xvii.
8 Daniel Defoe, *A Tour through the Whole Island of Great Britain*, vol. I, 1724, Preface.

Part I

1   INDUSTRIALISM TRIUMPHANT

1 *Letters of Queen Victoria*, 1st series, vol. II, London 1907, p. 383, 3 May 1851.
2 J. Ruskin, *The Seven Lamps of Architecture*, 1849.
3 C. H. Gibbs-Smith, Victoria and Albert Museum, *The Great Exhibition of 1851*, HMSO 1950, p. 33.
4 B. Texier, *Lettres sur l'Angleterre*, Paris 1851, p. 54.
5 Elihu Burritt, *Peace Papers for the People*, 1851, p. 125; *Thoughts and Things at Home and Abroad*, 1856.
6 Quoted in J. W. Dodds, *The Age of Paradox 1841–1851*, London 1953, p. 443.
7 A. de Valon, 'Le Tour du Monde à l'Exposition de Londres', *Revue des Deux Mondes*, III, 1851, p. 222.
8 Letter dated 14 October 1851, G. O. Trevelyan, *The Life and Letters of Lord Macaulay*, vol. II, London 1876, p. 206.
9 *Tallis's History and Description of the Crystal Palace*, London 1851.
10 B. R. Mitchell and P. Deane, *Abstract of British Historical Statistics*, Cambridge 1962, ch. XIII.
11 ibid., chs V, VIII, XI.
12 E. P. Hood, *The Age and its Architects*, London 1850, p. 17.
13 Quoted by S. G. Checkland, *The Rise of Industrial Society in England 1815–1885*, London 1965, p. 209.
14 F. Perroux, *L'Europe sans rivages*, Paris 1954, p. 39.
15 P. Laslett, 'The Size and Structure of the Household in England over Three Centuries', *Population Studies*, XXIII, 2, 1969; *Household and Family in Past Time*, Cambridge 1972.
16 M. Anderson, *Family Structure in Nineteenth-Century Lancashire*, Cambridge 1971.
17 Registrar-General, *Statistical Review for 1961*, III, 70, Table XLII.
18 J. Stuart Mill, *Principles of Political Economy*, Book V, ch. XI, §14.
19 H. Taine, *Notes sur l'Angleterre*, Paris 1872, p. 75.
20 Source of Table 2: C. M. Law, 'The Growth of Urban Population in England and Wales 1801–1911', *Transactions of the Institute of British Geographers*, vol. XLI, June 1967, pp. 141–2.
21 Census of 1851, Report of the Registrar-General, *Parliamentary Papers*, 1852–53, vol. 85, pp. XXXV–XXXVI.
22 E. Bernstein, *My Years of Exile*, London 1921, p. 155.
23 H. Mayhew and J. Binny, *The Criminal Prisons of London*, London 1862, p. 9.
24 Sources of Map 2: *Guide to London Excursions*, 1800, 1850, 1880, 1914, 1939, 1958, 20th International Congress, London 1964; R. Clayton (ed.), *The Geography of Greater London*, London 1964, pp. 2, 33, 'The South East Study', p. 27; E. J. Hobsbawm, *Industry and Empire*, London 1968; *Readers' Digest Atlas of the British Isles*, London 1965, p. 227.
25 B. Scott, *A Statistical Vindication of the City of London*, London 1867; Report by J. Salmon, *Ten Years' Growth of the City of London, 1881–1891*, London 1891.
26 T. C. Barker and M. Robbins, *History of London Transport*, vol. I, London 1963, pp. 57–8 (20,000 commuters by omnibus, 15,000 by steamboat, 6,000 by train, plus those travelling by private carriage).

27 C. Baudelaire (reviewing Whistler's etchings in 1862), *L'Art romantique*, ch. IV: 'Peintres et aquafortistes'.
28 J. Ruskin, *The Crown of Wild Olive*, London 1865.
29 J. Saville, *Rural Depopulation in England and Wales, 1851–1951*, London 1957, pp. 53ff.
30 A. L. Bowley, 'Rural Population in England and Wales: A Study of the Changes of Density, Occupations and Ages', *Journal of the Royal Statistical Society*, LXXVII, May 1914, pp. 597–645.
31 Source of Map 3: D. Friedlander and R. J. Roshier, 'A Study of Internal Migration in England and Wales', Part I, *Population Studies*, XIX, March 1966, p. 262.
32 F. M. L. Thompson, *English Landed Society in the Nineteenth Century*, London 1963, pp. 27–32; J. D. Chambers and G. E. Mingay, *The Agricultural Revolution 1750–1880*, London 1966, p. 162; P. Flavigny, *Le régime agraire de l'Angleterre au XIX° siècle*, Paris 1932, p. 172.
33 *Bulletin de statistique et de législation comparée*, I; 1877, p. 164; P. Flavigny, op.cit., p. 172.
34 Cf. J. Clapham, *An Economic History of Modern Britain*, vol. I, Cambridge 1926–38, p. 451; vol. II, pp. 263–4.
35 Title of a pamphlet published by J. Caird in 1848.
36 P. Anderson Graham, *The Rural Exodus*, London 1892, p. 38.
37 A. Rimbaud, 'Mouvement', *Les Illuminations*.
38 Mitchell and Deane, op. cit., pp. 225–6.
39 ibid., pp. 355–7; pp. 251–3.

2   THE MERITS OF HIERARCHY

1 Article in *The People's Paper*, cf. *Karl Marx and Frederick Engels on Britain*, Moscow 1962, p. 416.
2 Speech at the South London Industrial Exhibition. Quoted, after *The Illustrated London News*, 8 April 1865, by G. Best, *Mid-Victorian Britain 1851–1875*, London 1971, pp. 234–6.
3 On the word *class*, cf. A. Briggs, 'The Language of "Class" in Early Nineteenth-Century England' in A. Briggs and J. Saville (eds.), *Essays in Labour History*, vol. I, London 1960.
4 C. Hall, *The Effects of Civilisation on the People in European States*, London 1803, p. 3.
5 *Political Register*, vol. 39, 14 April 1821, p. 85.
6 See H. Perkin, *The Origins of Modern English Society 1780–1880*, London 1969, pp. 26–8, 257.
7 *Monthly Repository*, 1834, VIII, p. 320.
8 A. de Tocqueville, *Voyages en Angleterre, Irlande, Suisse et Algérie* in *Oeuvres complètes*, vol. V, 2, Paris 1958, p. 47. One finds exactly the same remark under the pen of another well-known French visitor, Léon Faucher, *Etudes sur l'Angleterre*, Paris 1845, vol. I, p. VII: 'L'Anglais se console d'avoir des supérieurs auxquels il doit le respect et l'obéissance, pourvu qu'il ait des inférieurs qui le respectent à leur tour; et quand il ne voit rien au-dessous de lui dans son propre pays, il s'exalte par comparaison avec l'Europe.'
9 M. Arnold, 'Equality', *Mixed Essays*, London 1878, p. 49.

10 H. James, 'London at Midsummer', *English Hours*.
11 E. Burke, *Letters to the Duke of Richmond*, 1772.
12 J. Morley, *Life of Richard Cobden*, vol. II, London 1903, p. 54.
13 Lord Willoughby de Broke, *The Passing Years*, London 1924.
14 *Essays, Political and Miscellaneous*, London 1868, vol. I, p. 100.
15 Cf. F. M. L. Thompson, *English Landed Society in the Nineteenth Century*, London 1963, chs. I and II.
16 On these figures see W. L. Burn, *The Age of Equipoise*, London 1964, pp. 306–8, and F. M. L. Thompson, op. cit. On the Marquis of Bredalbane, Taine, op. cit., p. 243.
17 Introduction to the second edition of *The English Constitution*.
18 The first sentence is dated 1849: cf. J. Morley, op. cit., vol. II, p. 53; the second assertion appeared in a letter from Cobden to Caird, 28 March 1857, quoted in R. Robson (ed.), *Ideas and Institutions of Victorian Britain*, London 1967, p. 113.
19 Taine, op. cit., p. 203.
20 Léonce de Lavergne, *Essai sur l'économie rurale de l'Angleterre, de l'Ecosse et de l'Irlande*, Paris 1854, p. 135.
21 Lord Brougham and Vaux, *Speeches on Social and Political Subjects*, London 1857, vol. II, p. 373.
22 W. Thackeray, *Letters*, vol. IV, p. 105.
23 J. Morley, op. cit., vol. II, p. 396: letter dated 7 February 1862.
24 J. A. Froude, 'England and her Colonies', *Short Studies on Great Subjects*, London 1878, vol. II, p. 206.
25 Taine, op. cit., ch. VII, pp. 294–5.
26 G. Best, *Mid-Victorian Britain*, pp. 81–4; J. A. Banks, *Prosperity and Parenthood*, London 1954, pp. 104–5; H. Perkin, *The Origins of Modern English Society*, pp. 417 ff.
27 J. Jaurès, *L'Armée Nouvelle*, Paris 1911, ch. X; 1977 edn, p. 271.
28 S. Smiles, *Self-Help*, Introduction to the 1st edn, 1859.
29 B. Webb, *My Apprenticeship*, London 1926, p. 13.
30 C. Kingsley, *Alton Locke*, London 1850, ch. X.
31 A. Barbier, 'Les mineurs de Newcastle', *Lazare*, Paris 1837.
32 H. Mayhew, *London Labour and the London Poor*, London 1861, vol. III, p. 233.
33 Thomas Wright, *Our New Masters*, London 1873, pp. 3–6.
34 F. Harrison, *Order and Progress*, London 1875, p. 171 and p. 274 (first sentence written in 1868, second in 1874).
35 *Hansard*, 3rd series, vol. C, col. 773–81.
36 A. L. Bowley, 'Changes in Average Wages (Nominal and Real) in the United Kingdom between 1860 and 1891', *Journal of the Royal Statistical Society*, LVIII, 2 June 1895, Table VII, p. 248.
37 G. Best, op. cit., pp. 80 ff and 91 ff, cf. also S. G. Checkland, *The Rise of Industrial Society in England 1815–1885*, London 1965, pp. 225 ff.
38 Sampson Low Jr, *The Charities of London*, London 1862, pp. xi and 86.
39 L. Levi, *Wages and Earnings of the Working Classes*, London 1885, p. 25.
40 S. Pollard, 'Nineteenth-Century Co-operation: From Community Building to Shopkeeping', A. Briggs and J. Saville (eds.), *Essays in Labour History*, vol. I, London 1960, p. 100; Perkin, op. cit., pp. 383–7.

41 Cf. P. H. J. H. Gosden, *The Friendly Societies in England 1815–1875*, Manchester 1961, pp. 7, 16, 22–4.
42 Letter of 30 November 1868, quoted by R. Harrison, *Before the Socialists*, London 1965, p. 21.
43 Harrison, op. cit., p. 7.
44 Address to Rochdale Co-operative Congress: cf. M. Cole, *Makers of the Labour Movement*, London 1948, p. 131.
45 G. Howell, *The Conflicts of Capital and Labour*, London 1878, p. 372.

3   POWER AND CONSENSUS

1 R. Dudley Baxter, *National Income*, London 1868, p. 1.
2 Cf. E. J. Hobsbawm, *Industry and Empire*, London 1968, p. 310.
3 Figures worked out from contemporary data gathered by L. de Lavergne, *Essai sur l'économie rurale de l'Angleterre*, Paris 1854.
4 In the last chapter of the book: 'The Attitude of the Bourgeoisie towards the Proletariat'.
5 F. E. Mineka and D. N. Lindley (eds.), *The Later Letters of John Stuart Mill 1849–1873*, vol. II, Toronto 1972, p. 553 (letter dated 15 April 1858).
6 Manuscript note left by E. Halévy and quoted by P. Vaucher, '1848 en Angleterre', *Actes du Congrès historique du centenaire de la Révolution de 1848*, Paris 1948, p. 95.
7 J. Morley, *Life of Richard Cobden*, vol. II, London 1903, p. 365: Letter written 1 March 1861.
8 Letter to Marx, 7 October 1858, in *Karl Marx and Frederick Engels on Britain*, Moscow 1962, p. 537.
9 Quoted in J. W. Dodds, *The Age of Paradox 1841–1851*, London 1953, p. 487.
10 *Culture and Anarchy*, ed. J. Dover Wilson, Cambridge 1932, p. 121.
11 Preface to *William Shakespeare*, 1864.
12 A. Briggs, 'Robert Applegarth and the Trade Unions', *Victorian People*, London 1954, p. 185.
13 J. Stuart Mill, *The Subjection of Women*, London 1869, ch. I.
14 A. V. Dicey, *Lectures on the Relation between Law and Public Opinion in England during the Nineteenth Century*, 2nd edn, London 1914, p. 198.
15 *Law Reports*, 2 Ex., 230, cf. W. L. Burn, *The Age of Equipoise*, London 1964, pp. 302–3.
16 G. Kitson Clark, *The Making of Victorian England*, London 1962, p. 193.
17 Source of Map 4: W. S. F. Pickering, 'The 1851 Religious Census', *British Journal of Sociology*, December 1967, p. 397.
18 A. Trollope, *An Autobiography*, 1950 edn, pp. 291–4.
19 A. Watkin, *Extracts from his Journal 1814–1856*, ed. A. E. Watkin, London 1920, p. 275.
20 H. Malot, *La vie moderne en Angleterre*, Paris 1862, pp. 5–6.
21 T. Carlyle, *Chartism*, 1839.
22 *Illustrated London News*, 22 July 1848 and 13 October 1849.
23 C. J. Bartlett (ed.), *Britain Pre-eminent*, London 1969, p. 186.
24 J. Vallès, *La rue à Londres*, Paris 1884; ed. L. Scheler, 1951, pp. 86–90.

Part II

4   THE CRISIS OF VICTORIAN VALUES

1 D. H. Aldcroft and H. W. Richardson, *The British Economy 1870–1939*, London 1969, p. 65; B. R. Mitchell and P. Deane, *Abstract of British Historical Statistics*, Cambridge 1962, pp. 367–8.

2 Aldcroft and Richardson, op. cit., pp. 65–6.

3 D. McCloskey, 'Did Victorian Britain Fail?', *Economic History Review*, XXIII, 3, December 1970, p. 458; 'Victorian Growth: A Rejoinder', ibid., XXVII, 2, May 1974, p. 277.

4 W. Booth, *In Darkest England*, London 1890, p. 78.

5 A. Toynbee, *'Progress and Poverty': A Criticism of Mr Henry George, being a lecture . . . delivered at St. Andrew's Hall, London, 18 January 1883*.

6 John Rae, *Contemporary Socialism*, London 1884, p. 61 (the book consists partly of articles reprinted from the *Contemporary Review* and the *British Quarterly Review*). The author was an economist and Provost of Edinburgh University.

7 Matthew Arnold, *Friendship's Garland*, 1903 edn, p. 141.

8 C. F. G. Masterman, 'What the Age Looks Like', *The Nation*, 26 December 1908, quoted by D. Read, *Edwardian England*, London 1972, p. 12.

9 J. A. Hobson, *The Crisis of Liberalism*, London 1909, p. 271.

10 V. Woolf, *Collected Essays*, vol. I, London 1966, pp. 320–1.

11 S. Webb, *English Progress Towards Social Democracy*, Fabian Tract no. 15, 1890, p. 1 (the sentence had actually been coined by William Whewell and applied to religion in its confrontation with scientific discoveries: cf. Aubrey Moore, *Science and the Faith*, London 1889, p. 83.

12 Source of Figure 2: H. McLeod, *Class and Religion in the Late Victorian City*, London 1974, p. 323.

13 A. H. Halsey (ed.), *Trends in British Society since 1900*, London 1972, pp. 415–17.

14 ibid., ch. XIII.

15 *Royal Commission on Population*, vol. VI, part I, (A Report on the Family Census of 1946 by D. V. Glass and E. Grebenik), London 1964, pp. 110–11.

16 Cf. N. Tranter, *Population since the Industrial Revolution: the Case of England and Wales*, London 1973, p. 100.

17 *Life of Hugh Price Hughes*, by his daughter, pp. 254–5.

18 Alfred Lord Tennyson, *The Princess*, Part V, lines 437–40.

19 J. Ruskin, *Sesame and Lilies: Of Queen's Gardens*, 1865.

20 G. K. Chesterton, *Autobiography*, London 1936, p. 20.

21 Quoted in J. Laver, *The Age of Optimism*, London 1966, p. 31, cf. J. Dunbar, *The Early Victorian Woman*, London 1953.

22 J. Stuart Mill, *The Subjection of Women*, 1869, Everyman edn, pp. 247–8.

23 M. G. Fawcett, *Women's Suffrage: A Short History of a Great Movement*, London and Edinburgh 1911, p. 23.

24 E. Halévy, *History of The English People in the Nineteenth Century*, vol. VI: *The Rule of Democracy* (1905–1914), pp. 500, 503.

5   FROM OLIGARCHY TO DEMOCRACY?

1 In his obituary tribute to the Queen in the House of Lords, Salisbury declared: 'She had an extraordinary knowledge of what her people would think –

extraordinary, because it could not come from any personal intercourse. . . . I always felt that when I knew what the Queen thought, I knew pretty certainly what view her subjects would take, and especially the middle class of her subjects', G. Cecil, *Life of Robert Marquis of Salisbury*, vol. III, London 1931, pp. 186–7. (25 January 1901).

2 P. Deane and W. A. Cole, *British Economic Growth 1688–1959*, Cambridge 1962, p. 142.
3 F. M. L. Thompson, *English Landed Society in the Nineteenth Century*, London 1963, p. 315.
4 Quoted by R. Lewis and A. Maude, *The English Middle Classes*, London 1949, Penguin edn, pp. 41–2.
5 On the process of ennoblement during the nineteenth century, see S. G. Checkland, *The Rise of Industrial Society in England 1815–1885*, London 1965; • Thompson, op. cit.; E. Halévy, *History of The English People in the Nineteenth Century*, vol. VI, Book II, ch. II.
6 Cf. W. L. Guttsman, *The British Political Elite*, 2nd edn, London 1965, pp. 41, 78, 104.
7 Speech at Newcastle-on-Tyne, 9 October 1909, *The Times*, 10 October 1909.
8 G. Kitson Clark, *The Making of Victorian England*, London 1962, p. 251.
9 Duke of Portland, *Men, Women and Things*, London 1937, pp. 228–9.
10 J. Morley, *Life of Richard Cobden*, vol. II, London 1903, p. 365.
11 Letter from Engels to Marx, 7 October 1858; letter from Marx to Liebknecht, 11 February 1878: *Karl Marx and Frederick Engels on Britain*, Moscow 1962, pp. 537, 554.
12 Cf. H. L. Beales, *The Industrial Revolution*, 2nd edn, New York 1967, New Introductory Essay, p. 17.
13 *Hammersmith Social Record*, May 1892, quoted by E. P. Thompson, *William Morris: Romantic to Revolutionary*, London 1955, p. 683.
14 J. Keir Hardie, *The I.L.P.: All about it*.
15 Lord Snell, *Men, Movements and Myself*, London 1936, p. 99.
16 *The Letters of Queen Victoria*, 2nd series, vol. III, London 1928, pp. 166, 130–1 (letters to Forster, 25 December 1880, and to Granville, 8 August 1880).
17 S. Pollard, *The Development of the British Economy 1914–1967*, 2nd edn, London 1969, p. 13.

6 THE SPLENDOUR AND SQUALOR OF A GOLDEN AGE

1 G. N. Curzon, *Problems of the Far East*, London 1894, p.v.
2 Speech at the Royal Colonial Institute, 2 March 1893.
3 H. F. Wyatt, 'The Ethics of Empire', *The Nineteenth Century*, XLI, April 1897, p. 529.
4 Quoted by C. H. D. Howard, *Splendid Isolation*, London 1967, pp. 17–18.
5 Letter from Engels to Kautsky, 12 September 1882, *Marx and Engels on Britain*, Moscow 1962, p. 560; article by Lenin, 20 October 1907, V. I. Lenin, *On Britain*, p.76.
6 J. Vallès, *La rue à Londres*, Paris 1884; ed. L. Scheler, p. 185.
7 J. Maynard Keynes, *The Economic Consequences of the Peace*, London 1919, pp. 9–10.
8 C. E. Montague, *Disenchantment*, London 1922.

9 B. Webb, *Our Partnership*, London 1948, p. 347.

10 Lady Dorothy Nevill, *Reminiscences*, London 1906, quoted by D. Read, *Edwardian England*, London 1972, p. 46.

11 Randolph Churchill, *Winston Churchill*, vol. I: *Youth 1874–1900*, London 1966, p. 371.

12 E. H. Phelps Brown, *The Growth of British Industrial Relations*, London 1959, p. 37.

13 *74th Annual Report of the Registrar-General* (for 1911), P.P., 1912–13, XIII, Cmd 6578, Table 28 B, p. 88.

14 L. Chiozza Money, *Riches and Poverty*, revised edn, London 1912, pp. 45–50, 60, 76, 79.

15 *Clarendon Report on the Public Schools*, P.P., 1864, XX, p. 66.

16 Quoted in W. J. Reader, *Life in Victorian England*, London 1964, p. 20.

17 L. Stone, 'Literacy and Education in England', *Past and Present*, 42, February 1969; J. Lawson and H. Silver, *A Social History of Education in England*, London 1973, p. 324.

18 *Report of the Commission on the State of Popular Education*, P.P. 1861 (2794), XXI, Part I.

19 *Hansard*, 3rd series, CLXV, col. 238, 13 February 1862.

20 Quoted by Lawson and Silver, op. cit., p. 318.

21 For 1851 see Lawson and Silver, op. cit., p. 281; for 1887 see O. Chadwick, *The Victorian Church*, vol. II, London 1970, p. 257.

22 Sources of Table 4: D. C. Marsh, *The Changing Social Structure of England and Wales 1871–1961*, London 1965, pp. 34, 38; A. H. Halsey (ed.), *Trends in British Society since 1900*, London 1972, p. 42.

23 Cf. Frederic Rogers, *Labour, Life and Literature*, London 1913.

24 George Eliot, *Middlemarch*, Book II, ch. XV.

25 H. Malot, *La vie moderne en Angleterre*, Paris 1862, p. 207.

26 W. E. H. Lecky, *History of European Morals*, vol. II, London 1869, pp. 299–300.

27 W. Acton, *Prostitution considered in its Moral, Social and Sanitary Aspects*, London 1858.

28 Sir Lawrence E. Jones, *An Edwardian Youth*, London 1956, pp. 162–3.

29 H. Kissinger, *A World Restored*, New York 1964, pp. 270–1.

30 Speech at Glasgow, 9 February 1912: Randolph Churchill, *Winston Churchill*, vol. II: *Young Statesman 1901–1914*, London 1967, p. 563.

31 Quoted in E. Grierson, *The Imperial Dream*, London 1972, p. 13.

32 M. K. Ashby, *Joseph Ashby of Tysoe 1859–1919*, London 1961, p. 290.

7   THE SEARCH FOR SECURITY AND STABILITY

1 Cf. also the figures in the *Cambridge Economic History of Europe*, vol. VI, *The Industrial Revolution and After*, Part I, Cambridge 1965, p.27.

2 J. Galsworthy, Preface to *A Modern Comedy*, London 1929.

3 W. S. Churchill, *The World Crisis*, Part I, London 1923, pp. 10–11.

4 A. Toynbee, *War and Civilization*, London 1951.

5 *Discours de réception du maréchal Pétain à l'Académie Française*, 1929.

6 Cf. A. J. P. Taylor, *English History 1914–1945*, Oxford 1965, pp. 60–1, 87.

7 L. Binyon, 'For the Fallen' (the poem appeared in *The Times*, 21 September 1914).

8 Estimates of the war losses differ considerably, the figures extending from under 600,000 to over 900,000. For a critical reappraisal, see J. M. Winter, 'Some Aspects of the Demographic Consequences of the First World War in Britain', *Population Studies*, XXX, 3, 1976, p. 541, who concludes that the most reliable figure is 723,000.

9 J. S. Engall, *A Subaltern's Letters*, 1918, pp. 119–20.

10 Wilfred Owen, 'Strange Meeting'.

11 Quoted by A. Marwick, *The Deluge*, London 1967, Pelican edn, p. 234.

12 H. Read, *Collected Poems*, London 1966, p. 152.

13 Lewis Namier, 'The Missing Generation', *Conflicts*, London 1942, pp. 74–5.

14 J. M. Keynes, *The Economic Consequences of the Peace*, London 1919, p. 2.

15 Cf. A. S. Milward, *The Economic Effects of the Two World Wars on Britain*, London 1970, p. 14.

16 T. C. Barker, 'L'économie britannique de 1900 à 1914: déclin ou progrès?', *Revue d'histoire économique et sociale*, vol. 52, 1974, p. 222.

17 For coal and shipbuilding, see E. J. Hobsbawm, *Industry and Empire*, London 1969, p. 174; for cotton, see P. Mathias, *The First Industrial Nation*, London 1969, p. 435.

18 W. H. Auden, *Poems*, London 1930.

19 Hobsbawm, op. cit., pp. 175–6.

20 W. H. Beveridge, *Full Employment in a Free Society*, London 1944, p. 72; see also pp. 47–72.

21 J. B. Priestley, *English Journey*, London 1934, pp. 397–407.

22 D. H. Aldcroft and H. W. Richardson, *The British Economy 1870–1939*, London 1969, p. 4.

23 Hobsbawm, op. cit., p. 189.

24 *Royal Commission on the Distribution of the Industrial Population* (Barlow Report), P.P. 1939–40, IV, Cmd 6153, pp. 36–7.

25 Aldcroft and Richardson, op. cit., p. 65; Mitchell and Deane, *Abstract of British Historical Statistics*, Cambridge 1962, pp. 367–8.

26 R. S. Sayers, *A History of Economic Change in England 1880–1939*, London 1967, p. 76.

27 H. Pelling, *The British Communist Party: A Historical Profile*, 2nd edn, London 1975, pp. 192–3.

28 D. Butler and A. Sloman, *British Political Facts 1900–1975*, 4th edn, London 1975, p. 299.

29 *British Labour Statistics: Historical Abstract 1886–1968*, HMSO 1971, Table 197, p. 396.

30 Margaret I. Cole (ed.), *Beatrice Webb's Diaries 1924–1932*, London 1956, p. 92.

31 A. J. P. Taylor, *English History 1914–1945*, Oxford 1965, p. 600.

32 A. Calder, *The People's War*, London 1969, Panther edn, p. 39.

33 R. M. Titmuss, *Problems of Social Policy*, HMSO 1950, pp. 335–6, 559–61.

34 A. Gillois, *Histoire secrète des Français à Londres de 1940 à 1944*, Paris 1973, p. 197.

35 R. Desnos, 'Le Veilleur du Pont au Change' (poem published by the clandestine Editions de Minuit in *Europe*).

36 H. Nicolson, *Diaries and Letters*, vol. II: *The War Years 1939–1945*, London 1967, p. 170 (entry dated 4 June 1941).

37 *New York Herald Tribune*, 21 September 1940. Quoted by A. Marwick, *Britain in the Century of Total War 1900–1967*, London 1969, Penguin edn, p. 298.

38 *British Labour Statistics. . . .*, p. 396.
39 Calder, op. cit., p. 412.
40 A. J. P. Taylor, op. cit., p. 550.
41 Quoted in J. Wheeler-Bennett (ed.), *Action This Day*, London 1968, p. 96.
42 N. Mansergh, *Documents and Speeches on British Commonwealth Affairs 1931–1952*, vol. I, London 1953, p. 570.
43 The word was actually used for the first time in 1941 by William Temple, then Archbishop of York, in his book, *Citizen and Churchman*, London p. 35: 'In place of the conception of the Power-State, we are led to that of the Welfare-State.'
44 *The Times*, 1 July 1940.
45 In fact the sentence uttered by Sir Hartley Shawcross, the Attorney-General, was: 'We are the masters for the moment – and not only for the moment, but for a long time to come.' Cf. M. Sissons and P. French (eds.), *Age of Austerity 1945–1951*, London 1963, Penguin edn, p. 29.
46 H. Dalton, *Memoirs*, vol. III: *High Tide and After*, London 1962, p.3.
47 M. Bruce, *The Coming of the Welfare State*, 4th edn, London 1968, pp. 331–2.
48 R. F. Harrod, *The Life of John Maynard Keynes*, London 1951.
49 *Hansard*, vol. 474, col. 39, 18 April 1950.
50 Cf. Herbert Morrison, *The Peaceful Revolution*, London 1949; E. I. Watkin, *The Cautious Revolution*, London 1951; Beveridge Report (*Social Insurance and Allied Services*) § 31 ('The scheme proposed here is in a way a revolution, but in more important ways it is a natural development from the past: it is a British revolution').
51 Sissons and French, op. cit., p.25.
52 ibid., p. 33.
53 Quoted by Marwick, *Britain in the Century of Total War 1900–1967*, p. 390.
54 R. Crossman (ed.), *New Fabian Essays*, London 1952, p.6.
55 ibid.

8   THE IMMUTABLE CLASS SYSTEM

1 F. M. L. Thompson, *English Landed Society in the Nineteenth Century*, London 1963, p. 333 (see also the whole of ch. XII).
2 H. Belloc, *An Essay on the Nature of Contemporary England*, London 1937, chs. I and II.
3 N. Mitford (ed.), *Noblesse Oblige*, London 1956, Penguin edn, p. 35.
4 J. H. Huizinga, *Confessions of a European in England*, London 1958, p. 101.
5 P. Sargant Florence, *Ownership, Control and Success of Large Companies*, London 1961, p. 13. See also W. L. Guttsman, *The British Political Elite*, London 1965, ch. XI.
6 A. L. Bowley, *Wages and Income since 1860*, Cambridge 1937, pp. 127 ff.
7 Wyn Griffith, *The British Civil Service 1854–1954*, HMSO 1955, pp. 14–19.
8 A. M. Carr-Saunders, D. Caradog Jones and C. A Moser, *A Survey of Social Conditions in England and Wales*, Oxford 1958, p. 106.
9 A. H. Halsey (ed.), *Trends in British Society since 1900*, London 1972, p. 114.
10 See D. V. Glass (ed.), *Social Mobility in Britain*, London 1954.
11 R. Lewis and A. Maude, *The English Middle Classes*, London 1949, Penguin edn, pp. 60–1.

12 P. Mathias, *The First Industrial Nation*, London 1969, p. 431.

13 On the extent and statistics of unemployment, see C. L. Mowat, *Britain between the Wars 1918–1940*, London 1955, pp. 481–3; G. D. H. Cole and M. I. Cole, *The Condition of Britain*, London 1937, pp. 219–33.

14 S. Spender, *Poems*, London 1933, p. 29.

15 B. S. Rowntree and G. R. Lavers, *Poverty and the Welfare State*, London 1951, pp. 30–1, 34–5.

16 F. Zweig, *The British Worker*, London 1952, p. 189.

17 Sources of Tables 5 and 6: for 1688–1867, H. Perkin, *The Origins of Modern English Society 1780–1880*, pp. 20–1, 420; for 1908, L. Chiozza Money, *Riches and Poverty*, London 1912; for 1929, Colin Clark, *The National Income 1924–1931*, 1932, and 'Further Data on the National Income', *Economic Journal*, September 1934; for 1938–49, G. D. H. Cole, *The Post-War Condition of Britain*, London 1956, and Carr-Saunders, Caradog Jones and Moser, op. cit.; for 1969–70, *Annual Abstract of Statistics*, 1972.

18 J. Ruskin, *Usury*, Preface. Republished in *On the Old Road*.

19 B. Mallet, *British Budgets 1887–1913*, London 1913, pp. 431–7.

20 Clark, op. cit.; G. Harrison and F. C. Mitchell, *The Home Market: A Handbook of Statistics*, London 1936.

21 J. M. Keynes, *The General Theory of Employment, Interest and Money*, London 1936, p. 374.

22 A. L. Bowley, *Wages and Income since 1860*, Cambridge 1937, p. 96.

23 Cole and Cole, op. cit., p. 67.

24 G. D. H. Cole, *The Post-War Condition of Britain*, London 1956, pp. 224–5; Carr-Saunders, Caradog Jones and Moser, op. cit., p. 140.

25 B. de Jouvenel, *The Ethics of Redistribution*, London 1951.

26 *Lloyds Bank Review*, October 1955, p. 18.

27 E. Powell, *Saving in a Free Society*, London 1960, pp. 126–7.

28 R. Titmuss, *Income Distribution and Social Change*, London 1962, pp. 19, 53.

29 ibid., pp. 186, 230.

30 G. D. H. Cole, op. cit., p. 296.

31 Titmuss, op. cit., chs. 3 and 9. Cf. also J. A. Brittain, 'Some Neglected Features of Britain's Income Levelling', *American Economic Review*, 50, 2, May 1960, and T. Stark, *Distribution of Personal Income in the United Kingdom 1949–1963*, Cambridge 1972; B. Atkinson, *The Economics of Inequality*, London 1975.

32 Source of Figure 10: 'Income', *Chambers' Encyclopaedia*, London 1955.

33 Cf. Chiozza Money, op. cit.; T. Barna, *Redistribution of Incomes through Public Finance in 1937*, London 1945, Tables 16 and 71; Cole and Cole, op. cit., pp. 72–80.

34 Source of Table 7: statistics of wealth in Carr-Saunders, Jones and Moser, op. cit., pp. 176–7.

35 E. Burke, *Reflections on the Revolution in France*, 1790.

36 Sources of Table 8: D. C. Marsh, *The Changing Social Structure of England and Wales 1871–1961*, London 1965, and J. Ryder and H. Silver, *Modern English Society: History and Structure 1850–1970*, 1st edn, London 1970, pp. 198, 215.

9 THE SLOWLY CHANGING SOCIAL LANDSCAPE

1 Sources of Table 9: For 1914–1918 figures, see the official statistics given in

Hansard, CXLI, col. 1033–4, 4 May 1921; A. Marwick, *The Deluge*, London 1967, p. 313; W. N. Medlicott, *Contemporary England 1914–1964*, London 1969, pp. 74–5; and the statistical reassessment by J. M. Winter, 'Some Aspects of the Demographic Consequences of the First World War in Britain', *Population Studies*, XXX, 3, 1976, pp. 539–41. For 1939–1945 figures, see *Strength and Casualties of the Armed Forces 1939–1945*, P.P. 1945–46, XV, pp. 89ff.; R. Titmuss, *Problems of Social Policy*, HMSO 1950, Appendix, p. 559; H. Pelling, *Britain and the Second World War*, London 1970, pp. 205, 273.

2 D. C. Marsh, *The Changing Social Structure of England and Wales 1871–1951*, London 1958, p. 43.

3 E. A. Wrigley, *Population and History*, London 1969, Table 35, p. 197.

4 P. Laslett, 'Size and Structure of the Household in England over three centuries', *Population Studies*, XXIII, 2, 1969; *Household and Family in Past Time*, Cambridge 1972.

5 A. J. P. Taylor, *English History 1914–1945*, Oxford 1965, p. 166.

6 H. G. Wells, *Anticipations of the Reaction of Mechanical and Scientific Progress upon Human Life and Thought*, revised edn, London 1901, pp. 46, 61.

7 J. Shepherd, J. W. Westaway and T. Lee, *A Social Atlas of London*, London 1975, p.13.

8 George Orwell, *Coming Up for Air*, London 1939, ch. II.

9 These figures can only be approximate, as the statistical data for public schools are inadequate.

10 Quoted by J. Lawson and H. Silver, *A Social History of Education in England*, London 1973, p. 395.

11 D. Wardle, *English Popular Education 1780–1970*, Cambridge 1970, pp. 132–3.

12 Board of Education, *Secondary Education* (Spens Report), London 1938, p. 147.

13 S. Haxey, *Tory M.P.*, London 1939, p. 180.

14 P. Stanworth and A. Giddens (eds), *Elites and Power in British Society*, Cambridge 1974, pp. 28, 35.

15 See J. Vaizey in Hugh Thomas (ed.), *The Establishment*, pp. 25–6.

16 R. H. Tawney, *The Radical Tradition*, London 1964, p. 65.

17 A. H. Halsey (ed.), *Trends in British Society since 1900*, London 1972, pp. 191, 206.

18 S. Nowell-Smith (ed.), *Edwardian England*, London 1964, p. 309; *Times Literary Supplement*, 4 January 1974.

19 B. S. Rowntree and G. Lavers, *English Life and Leisure*, London 1951, p. 301.

20 ibid., pp. 310–11.

21 J. A. R. Pimlott, *Recreations*, London 1968, ch. 5.

22 See *Annual Abstract of Statistics*, HMSO.

23 Source of Table 10: Rowntree and Lavers, op. cit., pp. 342–3.

24 G. Gorer, *Exploring English Character*, London 1955, pp. 241–2.

25 *News Chronicle*, 16 April 1957.

26 Mass Observation, *Puzzled People*, London 1948, p. 18.

27 Figures based on the *Catholic Directory*.

Part IV

THE END OF OLD ENGLAND

1 Arthur Koestler (ed.), *Suicide of a Nation?*, London 1963 p. 31.

2 Jules Romains, *Les Hommes de Bonne Volonté*, vol XIV, Paris 1923–7.

10 THE FRUITS OF AFFLUENCE

1 R. A. Butler, October 1954; H. Macmillan, speech at Bradford, July 1957.
2 See *The British Economy: Key Statistics 1900–1970*, London and Cambridge Economic Service, Table B, p. 5.
3 J. K. Galbraith, *The Affluent Society*, London 1958, p. 76.
4 J. Burnett, *Plenty and Want: A Social History of Diet in England from 1815 to the Present Day*, London 1966, Penguin edn, p. 340.
5 *The British Economy . . .* , Table J, p. 13; *Annual Abstract of Statistics*, HMSO.
6 *Britain 1975: An Official Handbook*, HMSO, p. 18.
7 A. H. Halsey (ed.), *Trends in British Society since 1900*, London 1972, p. 553.
8 Source of Tables 11: Left column, Number of motor cars, B. R. Mitchell and P. Dean, *Abstract of British Historical Statistics*, Cambridge 1962, p. 230, for 1904–1938; *Annual Abstract of Statistics* since 1945.
9 A. Shonfield, *Modern Capitalism*, 2nd edn, London 1969, p. 3.
10 L. J. Collins, *Faith under Fire*, London 1966, p. 298.
11 Halsey (ed.), op. cit., p. 206; *Annual Abstract of Statistics*.
12 A. Wesker, *Roots*, 1960, Act II, scene II.
13 Sermon in Edinburgh, *The Times*, 15 January 1968.
14 See B. Levin, *The Pendulum Years: Britain and the Sixties*, London 1970, p. 89.
15 F. Musgrove, *Ecstasy and Holiness: Counter Culture and the Open Society*, London 1974.
16 Source of Map 10: J. D. Gay, *The Geography of Religion in England*, London 1971, pp. 271, 273, 282, 284, 310, 311.
17 Halsey (ed.), op. cit., pp. 419, 426.
18 ibid., pp. 444–5, 447–8.
19 B. Wilson, *Religion in Secular Society*, London 1966, Penguin edn 1969, pp. 22, 25.
20 *The Times*, 14 October 1974.
21 For 1911–61, see R. K. Kelsall, *Population*, 2nd edn, London 1972, p. 21; for 1971, *Annual Abstract of Statistics*.
22 Halsey (ed.), op. cit., p. 47 for 1931–68; *Annual Abstract of Statistics* since 1970.
23 E. Leach, *A Runaway World?*, London, 1968, p. 1.
24 A. MacIntyre, 'God and the Theologians', *Encounter*, XXI, 3, September 1963, p. 10.
25 See R. Titmuss, 'The Position of Women: Some Vital Statistics', *Essays on the Welfare State*, London 1963, pp. 88–103.
26 For 1919–68, see Halsey (ed.), op. cit., p. 217; for 1971–2, *Annual Abstract of Statistics*, p. 126.

11 DECADENCE OR WISDOM?

1 Published afterwards in A. Koestler (ed.), *Suicide of a Nation?*, London 1963.
2 Quoted in A. Sampson, *Anatomy of Britain*, London 1962, p. 91.
3 A. Siegfried, *La crise britannique au XX⁰ siècle*, Paris 1931, p. 200 (English trans. *England's Crisis*, London 1931).
4 Press conference, 14 January 1963.
5 C. Le Saché, *La Grande-Bretagne en évolution*, Paris 1969, p. 126.
6 See G. A. Phillips and R. T. Maddock, *The Growth of the British Economy 1918–1968*, London 1973, p. 23.

312   A Social History of England 1851–1975

7 Source of Figure 14: *Social Trends*, No. 4, CSO, HMSO 1973, Table 13, p. 83.
8 Margaret Stacey, *Stability and Change: A Study of Banbury*, London 1960; M. Stacey, E. Batstone, C. Bell and A. Murcott, *Power, Persistence and Change: A Second Study of Banbury*, London 1975.
9 Open University, *Popular Politics 1870–1950*, p. 22.
10 J. Westergaard, 'The Myth of Classlessness' in R. Blackburn (ed.), *Ideology in Social Science*, London 1972, p. 158.
11 Nuffield Foundation for Educational Research, *Elites and their Education*, London 1973.
12 *Newsom Commission on the Public Schools Report*, HMSO 1968 (Source of Figure 15).
13 B. Hindess, *The Decline of Working-Class Politics*, London 1970, Paladin edn., p. 9; M. Foot, *Aneurin Bevan*, vol. II, p. 498.
14 J. S. Mill, *Principles of Political Economy*, 6th edn, vol. II, 1865, book IV, ch. 6 ('I am not charmed with the ideal of life held out by those who think the normal state of human beings is that of struggling to get on').
15 Lord Keynes, *First Annual Report of the Arts Council*, 1945–1946.
16 J. Milton, *Doctrine and Discipline of Divorce*, 1643.
17 'The Prospect of Britain', *The Times*, 28, 29, 30 April; 3 and 4 May 1971 (the quotation is from the 29 April article).

CONCLUSION

1 Cf. G. Best, *Mid-Victorian Britain 1851–1875*, London 1971, p. XV.
2 Quoted by Jacques Bardoux in *Le socialisme à l'étranger* (by various authors), Paris 1909, p. 40. Cf. also for the 1930s, Viscountess Rhondda, *Notes on the Way*, London 1937, p. 126: 'Caste after all survives in its worst form today only in India and England.'
3 S. Orwell and I. Angus (eds), *Collected Essays*, vol. II, p. 67.
4 Quoted by A. Sampson, *Anatomy of Britain*, London 1962, p. 16.
5 Speech at the House of Commons on the Representation of the People (Equal Franchise) Bill, *Hansard*, 5th series, vol. 215, col. 1436, 29 March 1928.
6 *Hansard*, 3rd series, vol. 188, col. 2007, 23 July 1867.
7 Letter to Lord Lyttelton, his brother-in-law: J. Morley, *The Life of William Ewart Gladstone*, 1908 edn, vol. I, p. 574.
8 F. Harrison, 'The Transit of Power', *Fortnightly Review*, III, 1 April 1868.
9 J. Vallès, *La rue à Londres*, 1951 edn, p. 250.
10 J. M. Keynes, *The Economic Consequences of the Peace*, London 1919, p. 3.
11 R. Siegfried, *La crise britannique au XX° siecle*, Paris 1931, p. 205.
12 A. Malraux, *Les chênes qu'on abat*, Paris 1971, p. 23.

Notes to the plates

1 Panorama of Leeds, seen from Richmond Hill (1885)

The triumph of industrialism, steam and manufacturing. Countless chimneys rising into the sky, belching forth smoke and mingling their silhouettes with the towers and gothic steeples of the churches. Industrial quarters straggling greyly along the River Aire. Masses of small working-class houses stretching out side by side. Here in Leeds, one of the capitals of the industrial North, all is black. The town, once a centre of the wool trade, gradually yielded this activity to Bradford and turned to the manufacture of ready-made clothing together with engineering, an industrial combination founded on the available work-force – female labour on the one hand, male labour on the other.

2 London Bridge in 1895 (Greater London Council Library)

In the heart of the City, a flood of humanity – on the river as well as on the bridge. This is indeed the giant *emporium* once celebrated by Schiller: 'Where the four corners of the world exchange their treasure/Along the Thames, on the world's market,/Thousands of ships take on their cargoes and depart/

There all that is precious is for sale/And on God's earth there reigns – Gold.'

Seeing this dense crowd in a hurry, reminds us of Heine who, seventy years earlier, was already stunned by this

motley tangle of men, women, children, horses, carriages, and even a hearse, which swirled around – rumbling, shrieking, cracking, creaking. So it seemed to me that all London was like a bridge over the Beresina on which each person, driven on by an anguished mania, wanted to beat a path forward at any price, where the bold rider crushed the poor pedestrian, where he who fell was lost for ever, where the best of comrades trod down mercilessly the dead body of his friend. . . .

3 Hydraulic presses for a ship's launching (National Maritime Museum, London)

The first Industrial Revolution, besides multiplying the number of machines, also increased the number of engines for mechanical transmission. Hence the profusion of wheels, cogs, winches, belts etc., which were for a long time a feature of the industrial landscape. The brothers Tangye, coming from Cornwall and specializing in engineering (one brother, Richard, appears on the photograph) managed a firm making hydraulic equipment of all kinds. They became famous in 1858 by successfully launching the largest ship ever built, the 'Great Eastern', weighing 19,000 tons.

4   Liverpool: Lime Street Station (about 1880)

The stations of the great Victorian cities are like cathedrals of the new civilization of railways and machines. Wasn't the Liverpool station justly christened a 'cathedral of steam'? With its double roof of cast-iron and glass spanning well over 200 feet (at the time it was the biggest glass roof in the world), this building, opened on a more modest scale in 1830 when Manchester and Liverpool were first linked by rail, was thoroughly remodelled and enlarged by Waterhouse in 1870.

5   Gustave Doré: 'A poor quarter of London'

Overcrowding of working-class families in their slums. In the background a railway and viaduct. In the hovels, all alike, one can see heaps of starving people in rags.

6   F. M. Sutcliffe: 'Old houses in Whitby' (The Sutcliffe Gallery, Whitby)

A slice of popular life in a small town on the north-east coast.

7   London prostitutes (Punch, 1857)

In the centre of the West End, around Piccadilly and the Haymarket, there were masses of prostitutes and brothels. Every evening rich clients went out on the pavements where the girls paraded to pick their choice without the slightest embarrassment. Periodically the press took up the theme of the 'great social evil' with much righteous indignation. (Note that the word 'gay' at the time was used to describe 'tarts'.)

8   Votes for Women: an endless labour

Punch cartoon. A suffragette with much effort pushes the stone of female suffrage right to the top of the parliamentary hill, but she consoles herself with the thought that after all 'Sisyphus was only a man'.

9   Arrest of a suffragette

In the Mall in front of Buckingham Palace, the forces of 'Law and Order' – on foot and on horseback – surround a militant feminist who had just been arrested for having tried to enter the royal residence by force (May 1914). 'Provocation-repression' tactics were one of the favourite weapons in the suffragettes' armoury.

10   Fin de siècle trip by bicycle

From its invention in 1885 the 'safety bicycle' spread with extraordinary speed. It soon caught on with the general public, but its success at first was due to its popularity in the middle classes. Combining sport and relaxation, the bicycle certainly contributed to female emancipation, for the young ladies who became ardent cyclists – either individually or in groups – found a way to independence as well as an agreeable pastime to occupy their long hours of leisure.

11   Haymaking in Berkshire (1910) (Museum of English Rural Life, Reading)

Country scene in which at the twentieth century's beginning 'the eternal order of the fields' seems to continue without much change. It is indeed a crowd of farmworkers and more particularly women workers, with their pitchforks and their hayrakes, who labour under the warm summer sun; but in this peaceful countryside, which looks like a park, everything is redolent of age-old rural labour.

12   The luxury of the aristocratic life: Harewood House (Photography by R. Fenton, 1860. Gernsheim Collection, University of Texas)

In its country houses spread all over England the high aristocracy led a luxurious life, sheltered from the din of the town. (Harewood House, seat of the Lascelles family, the Viscounts Harewood, who owned 32,000 acres, is only 8 miles from Leeds, the subject of Plate 1). An elegant edifice of the eighteenth century, built by Carr and Robert Adam, it has a collection of pictures which includes works by El Greco, Tintoretto, Veronese, Turner, etc. The photograph shows the view of the garden on the south side – terraces, fountains, parterres, lake and woods – while the northern façade looks out on a vast park in the English style, designed by Capability Brown.

13   The War in Flanders (1917)

The life of Tommies on the Belgian front in the course of the Third Battle of Ypres (Passchendaele). Stretcher-bearers evacuate a wounded man. Note the depth of the mud, even though it was the middle of August.

14 and 15   Tomorrows that bring disillusionment

These Labour Party posters (1923) summarize the experiences of many ex-servicemen who experienced the bitter disappointments of peace.

16   A 'hunger march'. The Jarrow workers on their way to London (1936)

The picture reflects both the utter despair of the workers and all the pride of a class which claimed its right to live. Among the various hunger marches of the inter-war period, the one organized by the workers of the Jarrow shipyards near Newcastle-upon-Tyne was the most famous – a long trek of over 300 miles which brought a delegation of 200 unemployed from the banks of the Tyne as far as London. When the pitiful group reached a built-up area – in this case a small Bedfordshire village – in spite of weariness and pouring rain, shoulders were braced, the pace quickened, and fifes and harmonicas started to play martial tunes to give the procession a purposeful air. On went the march to the next town, only to meet (on arrival at the capital) with the indifference of the government and the inexorable laws of economics. . . .

17   The 'Two Nations'

A snapshot taken at the entrance to Lords cricket ground during the Eton-Harrow match. On one side two Etonians, on the other two local cockney lads. One could take it as a caricature on the 'two worlds of youth'. In fact, when this photograph by Hutton appeared in *Picture Post* in 1937, there was a storm, so bitter was the social climate. Some went even so far as to say that the photograph was a fake.

18, 19 and 20   Leisure scenes: from the Edwardian to the inter-war period

Henley regatta under the warm summer sun of 1912 (18).
Hampstead Heath on a Bank Holiday in 1922 (19).
Middle-class picnic by Brooklands motor-racing track in 1923 – a leisurely lunch in the open air in the midst of gleaming roadsters (20).

21   Shelter in the Underground (1940)

In the centre of London, the Underground stations (Picadilly Circus in this case) were widely and effectively used, because of their great depth, during air raids. Apart from one tragic episode (in Bethnal Green station where in 1943 a panic led to 173 deaths), calm, sang-froid and even good humour generally reigned in these improvised refuges.

22   Churchill as war leader

The Prime Minister goes off to a meeting with Roosevelt – a meeting which resulted in the Atlantic Charter.

23   In the City of London

Or, the contrasts between yesterday and today. Victorian decor, bowler hats, rolled umbrellas, the coming and going of businessmen – the traditional City is still there. But in the fifteen years after 1960 large buildings of glass and steel soon transformed the historic Square Mile. Another contrast is the life by day and the life by night. After six in the evening the City is deserted and life only starts again the next day when the offices re-open.

24   Pub scene

Beer loosens tongues.

25   Two elders

The problems of ageing in a country where, according to the 1971 census, one inhabitant out of five is over 60 years old.

26   Open-air oratory

Speakers' Corner in Hyde Park. Liberty of expression for the citizen, and a sense of tolerance on the part of the listener and the passer-by.

27   Urban development in the 1970s: Thamesmead

An extensive, entirely new estate laid out on the site of the old Woolwich Arsenal by the Thames to the south-east of London. Thamesmead was destined for an urban community of 50,000 inhabitants. The whole scheme combines living quarters, towers, shops, pedestrian zones etc., with complete services and a series of lakes joined together by canals.

28   A traditional street

Repeated thousands of times, this type of

residential accommodation – small brick houses, bow windows, small gardens full of flowers – is to be found from one end of England to the other. On the borders of the middle class and the lower middle class it combines comfort and independence, monotony and a taste for home, and yet still leaves room for the personal touch.

29   Rural landscape in Yorkshire (1974)

A farmer and his sheep, small fields carefully enclosed, shallow valleys barely traced out. In the centre the church-tower and cottages of the village. The old rural England shows its permanence and its vitality.

30   In a Midlands mining town

The picture of this miner and his wife leaning on their garden fence reminds one that, in spite of the oil from the North Sea, coal remains one of the prime resources of Great Britain and that the miners continue to form a class apart, and always an influential one, in the world of labour.

31   Pop festival

Photograph taken in Windsor Park in 1973.

32   The Beatles

1966 appearance in the television programme *Top of the Pops*. It was on this occasion that the Beatles launched 'Paperback Writer' and 'Rain'.

33   Francis Bacon: 'Portrait of Isabel Rawsthorne standing in a Soho street' (1967) (Nationalgalerie, Berlin)

34   In the heart of London

A view of the capital's centre taken from the top of New Zealand House in the Haymarket. The photograph underlines to what extent the successive strata of London's architecture are jumbled together. In front, Admiralty Arch, a massive Edwardian construction separating Trafalgar Square from the Mall. In the next row the neo-classical alignments and cupolas of the Admiralty, then the War Office, all baroque and dotted with turrets. In the background, on the other side of the Thames, the pretentious Shell skyscraper, and County Hall, headquarters of the Greater London Council; and between the two, Waterloo Station.

Chronological table

Year	Political Life	International Relations and Empire
1846	Split in the Conservative Party Liberal supremacy	End of the first *Entente Cordiale*
1848	European revolutions, English stability	
1850		Don Pacifico affair
1851		Discovery of gold in Australia Livingstone reaches the Zambezi
1853	Reform of the Civil Service (1853–5)	
1854		Crimean War
1855	Palmerston Prime Minister	
1856		
1857		Indian Mutiny (1857–8)
1858	Property qualification for MPs removed	China War (1858–60) and Treaty of Tientsin
1859		
1860		Coben treaty with France Unification of Italy
1861	Death of Albert, the Prince Consort	American Civil War
1863		
1864		Schleswig-Holstein Question
1865	Deaths of Palmerston and Cobden	
1866	Radical agitation (1866–7)	
1867	Second Reform Act	Canada becomes a Dominion

Economy and Society	Culture and Religion	Year
Free Trade, 'Railway mania' Great Famine in Ireland		1846
Defeat of Chartism	Pre-Raphaelite Brotherhood, Christian Socialism Mrs Gaskell: *Mary Barton*	1848
	Roman Catholic hierarchy restored in England Alfred Lord Tennyson: *In Memoriam*	1850
Great Exhibition in London Dover-Calais cable Amalgamated Society of Engineers		1851
	Opening of Cheltenham Ladies' College	1853
	Charles Dickens: *Hard Times*	1854
Abolition of stamp duty on newspapers		1855
Invention of the Bessemer converter	Thomas Hughes: *Tom Brown's Schooldays*	1856
Matrimonial Causes Act		1857
		1858
	Charles Darwin: *Origin of the Species* John Stuart Mill: *On Liberty* Samual Smiles: *Self-Help*	1859
Foundation of London Trades Council	*Essays and Reviews*	1860
Abolition of paper duty	Newcastle Commission on elementary education	1861
Opening of first London underground railway		1863
Foundation of the First International in London	John Henry Newman: *Apologia pro Vita Sua* Clarendon Commission on the public schools	1864
	Lewis Carroll: *Alice in Wonderland* Ford Madox Brown: 'Work'	1865
Last cholera epidemic Transatlantic telegraph cable	George Eliot: *Felix Holt* John Ruskin: *The Crown of Wild Olive*	1866
	Walter Bagehot: *The English Constitution* Karl Marx: *Capital*	1867

Year	Political Life	International Relations and Empire
1868	Gladstone's first Cabinet (1868–74)	
1869		Opening of the Suez Canal
1870	Civil Service made open to competitive exams	Franco-Prussian War
1871	Purchase of commissions abolished	Unification of Germany
1872	Ballot Act	
1873		
1874	Disraeli's Cabinet (1874–80)	Annexation of the Gold Coast
1875	Irish Parliamentary Party	Purchase by England of the Suez Canal shares
1876		Victoria Empress of India
1877	National Liberal Federation	
1878		Balkan crisis, Berlin Congress Jingoism
1879	Agitation of the Land League in Ireland (1879–82)	Zulu War
1880	Gladstone's second Cabinet (1880–5)	
1881	Death of Disraeli	
1882		Occupation of Egypt
1883	Primrose League	John Seeley: The Expansion of England
1884	Third Reform Act (1884–5)	Conference of Berlin, Scramble for Africa
1885		Death of Gordon at Khartoum, Birth of Indian National Congress

Economy and Society	Culture and Religion	Year
Trades Union Congress		1868
	Matthew Arnold: *Culture and Anarchy* John Stuart Mill: *On the Subjection of Women*	1869
	Elementary Education Act	1870
Labour laws (1871–5)	Anglican tests abolished at Oxford and Cambridge	1871
Arch's National Agricultural Labourers' Union	Samuel Butler: *Erewhon*	1872
	Foundation of Girton College, Cambridge	1873
		1874
Cross's Housing Act Public Health Act		1875
	Primary education made compulsory	1876
First public electric lighting in London		1877
	Foundation of the Salvation Army *HMS Pinafore* starts vogue for Gilbert and Sullivan operas	1878
Agricultural and industrial depression Thomas-Gilchrist process in steel	Henry George: *Poverty and Progress*	1879
		1880
Hyndman introduces Marxism to England Married Women's Property Act		1881
	Robert Louis Stevenson: *Treasure Island*	1882
		1883
Foundation of the Fabian Society Parsons invents the turbine	Toynbee Hall and the Settlement Movement	1884
Rover safety bicycle		1885

Year	Political Life	International Relations and Empire
1886	Home Rule Bill, Liberal split, Unionist victory, Salisbury Prime Minister	
1887	Victoria's Golden Jubilee	First Colonial Conference 'Mediterranean agreement' with Italy and Austria
1888	County Councils Act	
1889	Creation of London County Council	Rhodesia under British rule
1890	Fall of Parnell	
1891		
1893		
1894	Gladstone's retirement District and Parish Councils Act	Annexation of Uganda
1895	Salisbury-Chamberlain Cabinet	Jameson raid
1896		
1897	Victoria's Diamond Jubilee	
1898		Kitchener reconquers the Sudan Fashoda crisis
1899		
1900	'Khaki Election'	Commonwealth of Australia Act
1901	Death of Victoria Accession of Edward VII	
1902		Anglo-Japanese treaty
1903	Tariff Reform controversy	Committee of Imperial Defence (1903–4)
1904		Entente Cordiale
1905	Foundation of Sinn Fein	

Economy and Society	Culture and Religion	Year
Demonstrations of unemployed in London (1886–7)		1886
	'Arts and Crafts' Movement	1887
Dr Dunlop invents the pneumatic tyre		1888
Dockers' strike, 'New unionism'	Charles Booth: *Life and Labour* Jerome K. Jerome: *Three Men in a Boat*	1889
Electrification of the tramways (1890–1900)	H. M. Stanley: *In Darkest Africa* General Booth: *In Darkest England*	1890
Free primary education	William Morris: *News from Nowhere* Conan Doyle: *Sherlock Holmes*	1891
Independent Labour Party		1893
	Rudyard Kipling: *The Jungle Book* Aubrey Beardsley: *Yellow Book*	1894
First Motor Show in London	Foundation of the London School of Economics Trial and sentence of Oscar Wilde	1895
Creation of the *Daily Mail*	Sunday opening of museums	1896
	The Tate Gallery	1897
Ebenezer Howard: Garden Cities		1898
	Foundation of Ruskin College Havelock Ellis: *Psychology of Sex*	1899
Labour Representation Committee First electric underground (*tuppenny tube*)		1900
Taff Vale Judgement	B. S. Rowntree: *Poverty*	1901
	Balfour Education Act	1902
Workers' Education Association (WEA)	Mrs Pankhurst creates WSPU Bernard Shaw: *Man and Superman*	1903
		1904
First motor buses in London Royal Commission on the Poor Law	Start of suffragette agitation	1905

Year	Political Life	International Relations and Empire
1906	Elections: Liberal victory; progress of the Labour Party	Launching of the first Dreadnought
1907		Anglo-Russian Convention Triple Entente
1908	Asquith Prime Minister	
1909	Lloyd George: 'The People's Budget'	
1910	Constitutional crisis over House of Lords Accession of George V	Union of South Africa
1911	Parliament Act	Agadir crisis
1912	Home Rule voted by House of Commons	Balkan crisis Scott at the South Pole
1914	Threat of civil war in Ireland	Invasion of Belgium, Great Britain joins the war
1915	Coalition government	Failure of the Dardanelles expedition
1916	Lloyd George War Cabinet	Battle of the Somme
1917		Russian Revolution, U-boats campaign Passchendaele
1918	Representation of the People Act Right to vote for all adult males and for females over the age of 30 'Coupon' election: victory of Lloyd George's coalition	
1919		Treaty of Versailles, League of Nations
1920		Palestine mandate
1921	Independence and partition of Ireland	Irak mandate
1922	Resignation of Lloyd George Final retreat of the Liberals	Chanak crisis, Anglo-French disagreement on reparations

Economy and Society	Culture and Religion	Year
	John Galsworthy: first volume of *The Forsyte Saga*	1906
Hampstead Garden Suburb		1907
Old Age Pensions	The Boy Scout Movement founded by Baden-Powell	1908
Bleriot flies the Channel Housing and Town Planning Act Labour Exchanges Act	H. G. Wells: *Ann Veronica*	1909
	Bertrand Russell and A. Whitehead: *Principia Mathematica* Norman Angell: *The Great Illusion*	1910
National Insurance Act		1911
Serious strikes and labour unrest (1912–13) Wreck of the *Titanic*	Foundation of the *Daily Herald*	1912
Trade unions Triple Alliance	Disestablishment of the Anglican Church in Wales	1914
Shop stewards movement Development of Guild Socialism	D. H. Lawrence: *The Rainbow*	1915
Conscription introduced		1916
	Wilfred Owen: *War Poems*	1917
New Labour Party constitution	Fisher Education Act	1918
Strikes and labour agitation	Arrival of jazz in England	1919
Communist Party of Great Britain		1920
Economic crisis: 2 million unemployed, Failure of the Triple Alliance (Black Friday)	Moral Rearmament	1921
	Creation of the BBC T. S Eliot: *The Waste Land* James Joyce: *Ulysses*	1922

Year	Political Life	International Relations and Empire
1924	January-October: first Labour government October: elections bring Conservatives to power Baldwin Prime Minister	
1925		Locarno Pact
1926		Imperial Conference: Balfour Report
1927		
1929	Second Labour Government	Agreement on reparations: Young plan
1931	MacDonald forms a coalition government	Statute of Westminster
1932	British Union of Fascists created by Mosley	Disarmament conference at Geneva Ottawa: Imperial Economic Conference
1934		Rearmament starts
1935	Jubilee of George V Baldwin Prime Minister again	Abyssinian war and sanctions policy
1936	Accession, then abdication of Edward VIII, George VI comes to the throne	Remilitarization of the Rhineland Spanish Civil War
1937	Neville Chamberlain Prime Minister	
1938		The Anschluss; Munich
1939		British guarantee to Poland (31 March) Declaration of war on Germany (3 September)
1940	Churchill Prime Minister (10 May)	Battle of Britain
1941		USSR joins war Atlantic Charter
1942		Victory at El Alamein, Fall of Singapore
1943		Battle of the Atlantic; Italian campaign

Economy and Society	Culture and Religion	Year
		1924
Return to the Gold Exchange Standard		1925
General Strike	T. E. Lawrence: *The Seven Pillars of Wisdom*	1926
Trade Disputes and Trade Union Act	First sound film Virginia Woolf: *To the Lighthouse*	1927
	Noel Coward: *Bittersweet*	1929
Mass unemployment Devaluation of the pound		1931
End of free trade (Import Duties Act)	Aldous Huxley: *Brave New World* Rutherford, Cockcroft, Chadwick: splitting the atom Shakespeare Memorial Theatre, Stratford	1932
	J. B. Priestley: *English Journey*	1934
Watson Watt invents the radar	T. S. Eliot: *Murder in the Cathedral*	1935
Jarrow hunger march Left Book Club	John Maynard Keynes: *General Theory* Deaths of Kipling and Chesterton	1936
	Ecumenical conferences at Oxford and Edinburgh	1937
	Spens Report on secondary education	1938
Conscription (April) Evacuation of civilians (September)	Agatha Christie: *Ten Little Niggers*	1939
Full employment Penicillin, discovered by Fleming in 1928, made effective by Florey	Graham Greene: *The Power and the Glory*	1940
		1941
Beveridge Report	William Temple appointed Archbishop of Canterbury and writes *Christianity and Social Order*	1942
		1943

Year	Political Life	International Relations and Empire
1944		Invasion of Normandy
1945	Labour election victory Attlee Prime Minister	Yalta conference, Surrender of Germany and Japan, Creation of the United Nations
1946	Nationalization of the Bank of England and of the mines	
1947	Nationalization of the railways	Independence of India Cold War begins
1948		Marshall Plan in operation
1949		The Atlantic Pact
1950	Second Attlee Cabinet	Korean War, Guerilla War in Malaya
1951	Conservatives return to power	
1952	Death of George VI Rise of Bevanism	Nationalist revolution in Egypt British atomic bomb
1953	Coronation of Elizabeth II	
1954		Evacuation of the Suez base
1955	Churchill retires, Eden Prime Minister	
1956		Suez crisis
1957	Macmillan Prime Minister	Independence of Ghana
1958	Campaign for Nuclear Disarmament	
1959	Third successive Conservative victory at the polls	Macmillan in Moscow
1960		Decolonization in Africa European Free Trade Association
1961		Britain asks to join EEC, South Africa leaves the Commonwealth
1962		Cuban rocket crisis

Economy and Society	Culture and Religion	Year
	Butler Education Act	1944
Atomic bomb Family Allowances Act	*Brief Encounter*, a film directed by David Lean	1945
National Insurance Act Creation of new towns	Creation of the Arts Council	1946
		1947
National Health Service End of the Poor Law	Formation of the World Council of Churches	1948
Devaluation of the pound	George Orwell: *1984*	1949
		1950
Festival of Britain	Introduction of the General Certificate of Education (GEC)	1951
Last tram in London The *Comet*: first passenger jet		1952
Ascent of Everest		1953
End of rationing introduced in 1940	Kingsley Amis: *Lucky Jim*	1954
	Start of commercial television	1955
First nuclear power station at Calder Hall	John Osborne: *Look Back in Anger* Alan Sillitoe: *Saturday Night and Sunday Morning*	1956
Consumers Association		1957
	J. K. Galbraith: *The Affluent Society*	1958
		1959
Opening of the M1, the first motorway	Harold Pinter: *The Caretaker* The 'new universities' (1960–5)	1960
		1961
Commonwealth Immigrants Act	Coventry Cathedral (Spence, Piper, Sutherland, Epstein) Benjamin Britten: *Requiem*	1962

Year	Political Life	International Relations and Empire
1963	Death of Gaitskell, Harold Wilson leader of the Labour Party	French veto British entry to Common Market
1964	Elections: Harold Wilson Prime Minister	
1965	Death of Churchill	Unilateral Declaration of Independence in Rhodesia
1966	Elections keep Labour in power	
1967		Decision to withdraw British troops East of Suez (1967–8)
1968		
1969	Violent troubles in Northern Ireland	
1970	Conservatives win General Election Heath Prime Minister	
1971		
1972	Northern Ireland under direct rule from London	Britain joins the Common Market
1974	Miners' strike, Two general elections, Wilson Prime Minister again	
1975	Margaret Thatcher leader of the Conservative Party	Referendum on Europe

Economy and Society	Culture and Religion	Year
	John Robinson: *Honest to God* Beatlemania	1963
	Mary Quant launches the mini-skirt	1964
Discovery of natural gas in the North Sea Abolition of death penalty	Edward Bond: *Saved* at the Royal Court Decision to convert secondary schools to comprehensives Creation of the Social Science Research Council (SSRC)	1965
Hovercraft (Cockerell, 1955) goes into operation Welsh Nationalist MP elected	Archbishop of Canterbury meets the Pope	1966
Devaluation of the pound Scottish Nationalist MP elected	Arts Laboratory	1967
Student unrest: LSE, Essex, etc. (1967–8)	Abolition of theatre censorship	1968
Age of majority brought down to 18	Isle of Wight Pop Festival	1969
Discovery of oil in North Sea Equal Pay Act	Start of Woman's Liberation Movement	1970
Decimalization of currency Industrial Relations Act		1971
	Stanley Kubrick: *A Clockwork Orange*	1972
Economic crisis: inflation and unemployment		1974
North Sea oil starts to flow	Sex Discrimination Act	1975

Bibliography

1. General works of reference

The most recent bibliographical guides are: W. H. Chaloner and R. C. Richardson (eds), *British Economic and Social History: a Bibliographical Guide*, Manchester 1976; H. J. Hanham, *Bibliography of British History 1851–1914*, London 1976; J. Altholz, *Victorian England 1837–1901*, Cambridge 1970; D. Nicholls, *Nineteenth-Century Britain*, Folkestone 1978; C. L. Mowatt, *Great Britain since 1914*, London 1971; J. Westergaard, A. Weyman and P. Wiles, *Modern British Society: a Bibliography*, 2nd edn, London 1977; G. S. Bain and G. B. Woolven, *Bibliography of British Industrial Relations*, Cambridge 1978; G. R. Elton, *Modern Historians on British History 1485–1945: a critical bibliography 1945–1969*, London 1970; Social Science Research Council, *Research in Economic and Social History*, London 1971. To which one should add the *Annual Bulletin of Historical Literature*, published each year by the Historical Association, and the lists of works on economic and social history which appears annually in the *Economic History Review*. In more specialist fields, there are the annual bibliographical lists drawn up by the *Bulletin of the Society for the study of Labour History*, the *Urban History Yearbook*, *Victorian Studies*, etc.

For historical dictionaries see: J. Brendon, *A Dictionary of British History*, London 1937; S. H. Steinberg and H. I. Evans (eds), *Steinberg's Dictionary of British History*, 2nd edn, London 1970; and of course the *Dictionary of National Biography*, Oxford. As far as the labour and working-class movement is concerned, one should add J. M. Bellamy and J. Saville (eds), *Dictionary of Labour Biography*, 5 vols, London 1972–9, F. M. Powicke and E. B. Fryde (eds), *Handbook of British Chronology*, 2nd edn, London 1961.

Statistical sources: if M. Mulhall, *Dictionary of Statistics*, 1892, is difficult to obtain, sound references are conveniently accessible in B. R. Mitchell and P. Deane, *Abstract of British Historical Statistics*, Cambridge 1962; for the more recent period, on the other hand, B. R. Mitchell and H. G. Jones, *Second Abstract of British Historical Statistics*, Cambridge 1971, is less useful. For the twentieth century, A. H. Halsey (ed.), *Trends in British Society since 1900*, London 1972, is indispensible. To which one should add, London and Cambridge Economic Service, *The British Economy Key Statistics 1900–1970*, London 1972, and A. Sillitoe, *Britain in Figures: A Handbook of Social Statistics*, 2nd edn, London 1973. Also very useful are P. Deane and W. A. Cole, *British Economic Growth 1688–1959*, 2nd edn, Cambridge 1976; C. H. Feinstein, *National Income, Expenditure and Output of the United Kingdom 1855–1965*, 2nd edn, Cambridge 1977; *British Labour Statistics: Historical Abstract 1886–1968*, London 1971. D. Butler and A. Sloman, *British Political Facts 1900–1974*, 4th edn, London 1975, covers a very wide field, as, for the nineteenth century, does C. Cook and B. Keith, *British Historical Facts 1830–1900*, London 1975. E. A. Wrigley (ed.), *Nineteenth Century Society: Essays in the Use of Quantitative Methods*, Cambridge 1972, presents a more methodological viewpoint.

For the most recent developments, consult Central Statistical Office, *Annual Abstract of Statistics*, London; Central Office of Information, *Britain: An Official Handbook*, London (annual).

HISTORY AND ENVIRONMENT

In the field of historical geography, one should note P. J. Perry, *A Geography of Nineteenth Century Britain*, London 1976; H. C. Darby (ed.), *A New Historical Geography of England After 1660*, Cambridge 1976.

In order to set the movement of society back in its context, one would do well to consult works of general English history, whether they be the elegant evocations of D. Thomson, *England in the Nineteenth Century 1815–1914*, London 1950, and *England in the Twentieth Century 1914–1963*, London 1964; H. Pelling, *Modern Britain 1885–1955*, Edinburgh 1960; or whether they be the more substantial volumes in the series 'The Oxford History of England', R. C. K. Ensor, *England 1870–1914*, Oxford 1936; A. J. P. Taylor, *English History 1914–1945*, Oxford 1965. Also to be recommended is the excellent book by C. L. Mowat, *Britain Between the Wars 1918–1940*, London 1955; as well as A. Marwick, *Britain in the Century of Total War*, London 1968.

PERIODICALS

In so far as the most interesting and the most recent contributions appear in the form of articles, this bibliography would be incomplete without mentioning the principal reviews to which the reader should turn for a deeper understanding of particular aspects of British society: *Economic History Review; Population Studies; Bulletin of the Society for the Study of Labour History; Social History; Urban History Yearbook* (formerly *Newcastle*); *Past and Present; History; English Historical Review; Historical Journal; History Workshop Journal; Victorian Studies; British Journal of Sociology; International Review of Social History*; etc.

2. Society

GENERAL TRENDS

The social history of England has recently been enriched by some excellent works. Along with G. D. H. Cole and R. Postgate, *The Common People 1746–1946*, London, 1st edn 1938, 4th edn 1962, which is now somewhat dated, one should mention three remarkable syntheses, each putting forward an original interpretation: one, E. J. Hobsbawm, *Industry and Empire*, London 1968, covers the whole period; the two others stop at the end of the nineteenth century: H. Perkin, *The Origins of Modern English Society 1780–1880*, London 1969; and S. G. Checkland, *The Rise of Industrial Society in England 1815–1885*, London 1965. J. Ryder and H. Silver, *Modern English Society: History and Structure 1850–1970*, 2nd edn, London 1977, successfully combines the historical and sociological approaches in one volume; J. Roebuck, *The Making of Modern English Society from 1850*, London 1973, on the other hand, is disappointing. As for G. M. Trevelyan, *English Social History*, London 1944, this has been entirely superseded and cannot be recommended. A clear and relatively well-informed textbook is P. Gregg, *A Social and Economic History of Britain 1760–1970*, 7th edn, London 1972. The lively evocations conjured up by W. J. Reader, *Life in Victorian England*, London 1964; R. Cecil, *Life in Edwardian England*, London 1969; and L. C. B. Seaman, *Life in Britain between the Wars*, London 1970, unfortunately have no sequel after 1939.

There is an equally rich crop of books for individual periods. For the mid-Victorian era, apart from the classics such as G. M. Young (ed.), *Early Victorian England*, 2 vols, London 1934, and *Portrait of an Age*, 2nd edn, London 1953, and A. Briggs, *Victorian People*, London 1954, G. Best has presented a brilliant analysis in *Mid-Victorian Britain 1851–1875*, London 1971. Also rich in observations are W. L. Burn, *The Age of Equipoise*, London 1964; G. Kitson Clark, *The Making of Victorian England*, London 1962, and *An Expanding Society: Britain 1830–1900*, Cambridge 1967.

For the late-Victorian and Edwardian periods, perceptive views are presented in H. M. Lynd, *England in the Eighteen-Eighties*, New York 1945, and H. Pelling, *Popular Politics and Society in Late-Victorian Britain*, London 1968. Sound analyses are given in: S. Nowell-Smith (ed.), *Edwardian England*, London 1964; D. Read, *Edwardian England: Society and Politics 1901–1915*, London 1972; P. Thompson, *The Edwardians*, London 1975.

For the twentieth century, a useful survey is M. Abrams, *The Condition of the British People 1911–1945*, London 1946. A. Marwick has specialized in a study of the changes in society following the two world wars: *The Deluge: British Society and the First World War*, 2nd edn, London 1973, *War and Social Change in the Twentieth Century*, London 1974, and *The Home Front*, London 1976. For the inter-war years, the impressionistic accounts by R. Graves and A. Hodge, *The Long Week-End: A Social History of Great Britain 1918–1939*, London 1940; R. Blythe, *The Age of Illusion: England in the Twenties and Thirties 1919–1940*, London 1963, give a good feeling of the 'Roaring Twenties' and the 'Bleak Thirties'. N. Branson, *Britain in the Nineteen Twenties*, London 1976; J. Stevenson (ed.), *Social Conditions in Britain between the Wars*, London 1976; J. Stevenson and C. Cook, *The Slump*, London 1977; S. Glynn and J. Oxborrow, *Interwar Britain*, London 1976, all provide sound accounts, while N. Branson and W. Heinemann, *Britain in the Nineteen Thirties*,

London 1971, is occasionally rather tendentious. For the Second World War, A. Calder, *The People's War*, London 1969, a rich and evocative book, should be linked with the intelligent study provided by H. Pelling, *Britain and the Second World War*, London 1970, as well as with the sound analyses of P. Addison, *The Road to 1945: British Policies and the Second World War*, London 1975. On Great Britain since 1945, the book by P. Gregg, *The Welfare State: An economic and social history of Great Britain from 1945 to the present*, London 1967, contains a wealth of information presented in a somewhat uncritical manner. One should, however, consult the more recent study by C. J. Bartlett, *History of Post-War Britain 1945–1974*, London 1977. Useful analyses can be gleaned from: M. Sissons and P. French (eds), *Age of Austerity 1945–1951*, London 1963; V. Bogdanov and R. Skidelsky (eds), *The Age of Affluence 1951–1964*, London 1970; D. McKie and C. Cook (eds), *The Decade of Disillusions: British Politics in the Sixties*, London 1972. For a severe warning against the inertia of English society, see M. Shanks, *The Stagnant Society*, 2nd edn, London 1972. A. Sampson has dissected in detail the organs of power and the structure of collective life in *Anatomy of Britain*, London 1962, and then in *New Anatomy of Britain*, London 1971. Finally a brilliant semi-historical semi-prophetic description is given in M. Young, *The Rise of the Meritocracy*, London 1958.

On the evolution of social policy – from the Poor Law to the Welfare State – one should consult the small book by M. Rose, *The Relief of Poverty 1834–1914*, London 1972, as well as the textbooks by M. Bruce, *The Coming of the Welfare State*, 4th edn, London 1968, and D. Fraser, *The Evolution of the British Welfare State*, London 1973.

TOWN AND COUNTRY

The development of agriculture has been well covered in: J. D. Chambers and G. E. Mingay, *The Agricultural Revolution 1750–1880*, London 1966; C. Orwin and E. H. Whitham, *History of British Agriculture 1846–1914*, London 1964; E. H. Whitham, *Agrarian History of England and Wales*, vol. 8: *1914–1939*, London 1978. Recent critical revisions are to be found in P. J. Perry, *British Agriculture 1875–1914*, London 1973, and *British Farming in the Great Depression 1870–1914*, Newton Abbot 1974. Lord Ernle, *English Farming Past and Present*, London, 1st edn 1912, new edn 1936, should, on the other hand, now be considered completely out of date. Valid information can still be obtained in two old French works: P. Besse, *la Crise et l'évolution de l'agriculture en Angleterre de 1875 à nos jours*, Paris 1910, and P. Flavigny, *le Régime agraire de l'Angleterre au XIXe siècle*, Paris 1932. Life for the country-dweller in the second half of the nineteenth century is admirably depicted in M. K. Ashby, *Joseph Ashby of Tysoe: A Study of English Village Life 1859–1919*, Cambridge 1961. Equally to be consulted is R. Samuel (ed.), *Village Life and Labour*, London 1975.

As far as the towns are concerned, although there are a great number of monographs, there is no synthesis dealing with English urban development as a whole. For the Victorian period, three excellent works are available: A. Briggs, *Victorian Cities*, London 1963; H. J. Dyos and M. Wolff (eds), *The Victorian City*, 2 vols, London 1973; D. Olsen, *The Growth of Victorian London*, London 1976. For the twentieth century, see the detailed study by C. A. Moser and W. Scott, *British Towns: a statistical study of their social and economic differences*, London 1961. T. W. Freeman, *The Conurbations of Great Britain*, 2nd edn, Manchester 1966, deals largely with historical geography. R. Williams, *The Country and the City*, London

1973, examines the image of the town. On the environment, consult A. Sutcliffe (ed.), *Multi-Storey Living*, London 1974; and E. Gauldie, *Cruel Habitations: a History of Working Class Housing 1780–1918*, London 1974. On development and planning, W. Ashworth, *The Genesis of Modern British Town Planning*, London 1954; and G. E. Cherry, *Urban Change and Planning*, Henley 1972.

POPULATION, FAMILY AND THE CONDITION OF WOMEN

A summary of the principal demographic features can be found in E. M. Hubback, *The Population of Britain*, London 1947, and R. K. Kelsall, *Population*, 2nd edn, London 1972. The more ambitious N. Tranter, *Population since the Industrial Revolution: the Case of England and Wales*, London 1973, is useful, but raises more questions than it answers. More recent studies are presented by R. Mitchinson, *British Population Changes since 1860*, London 1977; and M. Flinn (ed.), *Scottish Population History*, London 1978. On the birth-rate and the beginnings of birth-control, there are three interesting contributions: J. A. Banks, *Prosperity and Parenthood: a study of family planning among the Victorian middle classes*, London 1954; J. A. and O. Banks, *Feminism and Family Planning in Victorian England*, Liverpool 1964; and A. McLaren, *Birth-Control in Nineteenth-Century England*, London 1978. On emigration, see N. H. Carrier and J. R. Jeffery, *External Migration 1815–1950*, London 1953.

The family has been studied in monographs by M. Anderson, *Family Structure in Nineteenth Century Lancashire*, Cambridge 1971; M. Young and P. Wilmott, *Family and Kinship in East London*, London 1957, and *Family and Class in a London Suburb*, London 1960, and in a more global way by these same two authors in *The Symmetrical Family*, London 1973; and by R. Fletcher, *The Family and Marriage in Britain*, 3rd edn, London 1973. Also to be remembered is O. R. McGregor, *Divorce in England*, London 1957, as well as the contemporary inquiry by G. Gorer, *Sex and Marriage in England Today*, London 1971. The underworld of Victorian society appears in F. Henriques, *Modern Sexuality: Prostitution and Society*, vol. III, London 1968; S. Marcus, *The Other Victorians*, London 1966; R. Pearsall, *The Worm in the Bud: the World of Victorian Sexuality*, London 1969.

On the place of women in society, the growth of contemporary neo-feminism has given rise to a whole new crop of publications. To old works dealing with the struggle for rights, such as R. Strachey, *The Cause*, London 1928, new edn 1978, and E. Reiss, *Rights and Duties of English Women: a study in law and public opinion*, London 1934, one can now add various – and variously successful – attempts at syntheses: D. M. Stenton, *The English Woman in History*, London 1957; C. Rover, *Love, Morals and the Feminists*, London 1970; S. Rowbotham, *Hidden from History*, London 1973. On the Victorian period, see: M. Hewitt, *Women and Mothers in Victorian Industry*, London 1958; D. Crow, *The Victorian Woman*, London 1971; M. Vicinus (ed.), *Suffer and Be Still: Woman in the Victorian Age*, Bloomington 1972; P. Branca, *Silent Sisterhood*, London 1975; E. Trudgill, *Madonnas and Magdalens*, London 1976. On the suffragettes, whose bibliography is constantly on the increase, one should consult: R. Fulford, *Votes for Women*, London 1957; C. Rover, *Women's Suffrage and Party Politics 1866–1914*, London 1967; A. Rosen, *Rise Up Women!*, London 1974; J. Liddington and J. Norris, *One Hand Tied Behind Us: The Rise of the Women's Suffrage Movement*, London 1978; B. Harrison, *Separate Spheres:*

The Opposition to Women's Suffrage, London 1978. Cf. also A. Marwick, *Women at War 1914-1918*, London 1977. On the political role of women, see M. Currell, *Political Woman*, London 1974.

On the position of children in society, I. Pinchbeck and M. Hewitt, *Children in British Society*, vol. 2: *From the Eighteenth Century to the Children Act 1948*, is disappointing, as it confines itself to the legal aspects of the question.

On the attitude to death, note J. Morley, *Death, Heaven and the Victorians*, London 1971; J. S. Curl, *The Victorian Celebration of Death*, Newton Abbot 1972, and the study by G. Gorer, *Death, Grief and Mourning in Contemporary Britain*, London 1965.

SOCIAL STRUCTURE AND SOCIAL CLASS

There is a great amount of information available on the development of social structures: D. C. Marsh, *The Changing Social Structure of England and Wales 1871-1961*, 2nd edn, London 1965; G. D. H. Cole, *Studies in Class Structure*, London 1955; G. D. H. Cole and M. I. Cole, *The Condition of Britain*, London 1937; G. D. H. Cole, *The Post-War Condition of Britain*, London 1956; A. M. Carr-Saunders and D. C. Jones, *A Survey of the Social Structure of England and Wales*, Oxford, 1st edn 1927, 2nd edn 1937; A. M. Carr-Saunders, D. C. Jones and C. A. Moser, *A Survey of Social Conditions in England and Wales*, Oxford 1958; D. V. Glass (ed.), *Social Mobility in Britain*, London 1954; C. J. Richardson, *Contemporary Social Mobility*, London 1977.

The land-owning aristocracy has been excellently dealt with in F. M. L. Thompson, *English Landed Society in the Nineteenth Century*, London 1963; See also G. E. Mingay, *The Gentry*, London 1978. On the power élite, interesting analyses are given in W. L. Guttsman, *The British Political Elite*, 2nd edn, London 1965; and P. Stanworth and A. Giddens (eds), *Elites and Power in British Society*, Cambridge 1974. One should refer also to J. Blondel, *Voters, Parties and Leaders*, London, 1st edn 1963, revised edn 1974; R. Rose, *Politics in England Today*, London 1974.

There is no satisfactory study of the middle classes, but none the less it is worth noting W. J. Reader, *Professional Men: the Rise of the Professional Classes in the Nineteenth Century*, London 1966; and R. Lewis and A. Maude, *The Middle Classes*, London 1949. On the Army and officers, see C. Barnett, *Britain and her Army 1509-1970*, London 1970. There is, however, no equivalent for the Navy. The rise of white-collar workers has been dealt with in: F. D. Klingender, *The Condition of Clerical Labour in Great Britain*, London 1935; D. Lockwood, *The Blackcoated Worker*, London 1958; G. S. Bain, *The Growth of White-Collar Unionism*, Oxford 1970.

On the workers, sociological studies have been written by F. Zweig, *The British Worker*, London 1952, and *The Worker in an Affluent Society*, London 1961, and above all J. Goldthorpe *et al.*, *The Affluent Worker: Industrial Attitudes and Behaviour; Political Attitudes and Behaviour; The Affluent Worker in the Class Structure*, 3 vols, Cambridge 1968-9.

The redistribution of wealth and incomes has been the subject of several studies, from the pioneering L. G. Chiozza Money, *Riches and Poverty*, London 1905; Colin Clark, *National Income 1924-1931*, London 1932, and *National Income and Outlay*, London 1937; A. L. Bowley, *Wages and Income in the United Kingdom since 1860*, Cambridge 1937; right up to the recent works by R. Titmuss, *Income Distribution and Social Change*, London 1962; B. Abel-Smith and P. Townsend, *The*

Poor and the Poorest, London 1965; T. Stark, Distribution of Personal Income in the United Kingdom 1949–1963, Cambridge 1972; D. Wedderburn (ed.), Poverty, Inequality and Class Structure, Cambridge 1974; A. B. Atkinson, The Economics of Inequality, London 1975; A. B. Atkinson (ed.), Personal Distribution of Incomes, London 1976; A. B. Atkinson and A. J. Harrison, Distribution of Personal Wealth in Britain, Cambridge 1978. Attempts at an overall view of contemporary society are to be found in J. Westergaard and H. Ressler, Class in a Capitalist Society, London 1975; and A. H. Halsey, Change in British Society, London 1978.

THE LABOUR MOVEMENT

Here too, the bibliography is very rich. For an introduction to the history of trade-unionism, refer to H. Pelling, A History of British Trade Unionism, 3rd edn, London 1976; and J. Lovell and B. C. Roberts, A Short History of the TUC, London 1968. On a more detailed level, alongside traditional interpretations – S. and B. Webb, The History of Trade Unionism, London 1920 edn; G. D. H. Cole, A Short History of the British Working-Class Movement 1789–1947, London 1948; A. L. Morton and G. Tate, The British Labour Movement 1770–1920, London 1956 – one can find new points of view and new data in: A. Briggs and J. Saville (eds), Essays in Labour History, 3 vols, London 1960–77; E. J. Hobsbawm, Labouring Men, London 1964; T. Tholfsen, Working-Class Radicalism in Mid-Victorian England, London 1976; R. Harrison, Before the Socialists, London 1965; A. E. Musson, British Trade Unions 1800–1875, London 1972; H. A. Clegg, A. Fox, A. F. Thompson, A History of British Trade Unionism since 1889, vol. I: 1889–1910, Oxford 1964; D. Kynaston, King Labour: The British Working Class 1850–1914, London 1976; S. Lewenhak, Women and Trade Unions, London 1976; N. C. Solden, Women in British Trade Unions 1874–1976, London 1978; A. Clinton, Trade Union Rank and File: Trade Union Councils 1900–1940, Manchester 1977; J. Lovell, Trade Unions 1875–1933, London 1977.

On the development of socialist ideas and the labour movement, see: M. Beer, A History of British Socialism, London 1940; H. Pelling, The Origins of the Labour Party, 2nd edn, Oxford 1965, and A Short History of the Labour Party, 6th edn, London 1978; P. Adelman, The Rise of the Labour Party 1880–1945, London 1972; C. Brand, The British Labour Party: a short history, 2nd edn, Stanford 1974; R. Miliband, Parliamentary Socialism, 2nd edn, London 1973. On revolutionary movements and Communism, consult: W. Kendall, The Revolutionary Movement in Britain 1900–1921, London 1969; H. Pelling, The British Communist Party, 2nd edn, London 1976; and on the contemporary scene, L. Panitch, Social Democracy and Industrial Militancy 1945–1974, London 1976; R. Taylor, The Fifth Estate, London 1978.

For an overall view of the Labour and working-class movements, see F. Bédarida, 'le Socialisme en Angleterre de la fin du XVIIIe siècle à 1945' in J. Droz et al., Histoire générale du socialisme, 3 vols, Paris 1972–6.

VARIOUS ASPECTS OF SOCIAL LIFE

The following works provide an insight into different aspects of living conditions, ways of life, leisure, criminality, etc.:

J. C. Drummond and A. Wilbraham, The Englishman's Food: A History of Five

Centuries of English Diet, 2nd edn, London 1958; J. Burnett, *Plenty and Want: A social history of diet in England from 1815 to the present day*, 2nd edn, London 1968, and *A History of the Cost of Living*, London 1969; M. and C. H. B. Quennell, *A History of Everyday Things in England*, vol. IV: *1851–1914*, 5th edn, London 1950; vol. V: *1914–1968*, by S. E. Ellacott, London 1968; B. Harrison, *Drink and the Victorians*, London 1971; J. J. Tobias, *Crime and Industrial Society in the XIXth Century*, London 1967; J. A. R. Pimlott, *The Englishman's Holiday*, London 1947; J. Walvin, *Leisure and Society 1830–1950*, London 1978; J. K. Walton, *The Blackpool Landlady*, London 1978.

3. The economy

Three works stand out from the collection of economic histories of England: P. Mathias, *The First Industrial Nation*, London 1969, which covers the eighteenth century to 1939; W. Ashworth, *An Economic History of England 1870–1939*, London 1960; S. Pollard, *The Development of the British Economy 1914–1967*, 2nd edn, London 1969. J. H. Clapham, *An Economic History of Modern Britain*, 3 vols, Cambridge 1926–38 (vol. II: *1850–1886*; vol. III: *1886–1929*), remains an outstanding classic. More concentrated is W. H. B. Court, *A Concise Economic History of Britain from 1750 to Recent Times*, Cambridge 1954. Equally notable is the useful contribution made by D. H. Aldcroft and H. W. Richardson, *The British Economy 1870–1939*, London 1969. Contributions to the new economic history can be found in D. N. McCloskey (ed.), *Essays on a Mature Economy: Britain after 1840*, London 1971. An excellent synthesis is F. Cronzet, *L'économie de la Grande Bretagne victorienne*, Paris 1978 (English translation forthcoming).

Taking each period separately: J. D. Chambers, *The Workshop of the World 1820–1880*, London 1961, and R. Church, *The Great Victorian Boom 1851–1873*, London 1975, deal with the great expansion of the nineteenth century. From 1870 on, consult S. B. Saul, *The Myth of the Great Depression 1873–1896*, London 1969; R. S. Sayers, *A History of Economic Change in England 1880–1939*, London 1967.

On the First World War and its consequences, and on the inter-war years, see A. S. Milward, *The Economic Consequences of the Two World Wars on Britain*, London 1970; and B. W. E. Alford, *Depression and Recovery? British Economic Growth 1919–1939*, London 1970. (Both these works seriously call into question the views put forward by A. Siegfried, *la Crise britannique au XX*e *siècle*, Paris 1931.) On the problems of growth in the twentieth century, consult G. A. Philips and R. T. Maddock, *The Growth of the British Economy 1918–1968*, London 1973; and A. J. Youngson, *Britain's Economic Growth 1920–1966*, 2nd edn, London 1968.

For the period after 1945, see J. Leruez, *Economic Planning and Politics 1945–1974*, London 1975. The most recent data can be found in A. R. Prest and D. J. Coppock (eds), *The United Kingdom Economy: a Manual of Applied Economics*, 7th edn, London 1978.

Certain areas of economic life have been the subject of specialist studies. On the relationship between private enterprise and the State in the nineteenth century, it would be of benefit to consult the small books by A. J. Taylor, *Laissez-faire and State intervention in Nineteenth-Century Britain*, London 1972, and P. L. Payne, *British Entrepreneurship in the Nineteenth Century*, London 1974. On twentieth-century industry, see G. C. Allen, *The Structure of Industry in Britain*, 3rd edn, London 1970. Several sound works trace the development of transport: T. C. Barker and C. I. Savage, *An Economic History of Transport in Britain*, 3rd edn, London 1975;

H. J. Dyos and D. H. Aldcroft, *British Transport: an Economic Survey*, Leicester 1969; P. S. Bagwell, *The Transport Revolution since 1770*, London 1974.

4. Religion

A brief but relevant outline is given in A. Vidler, *The Church in an Age of Revolution*, London 1961. On the nineteenth century, L. E. Elliott-Binns, *Religion in the Victorian Era*, London 1936, remains valid, but O. Chadwick has produced an outstanding work in *The Victorian Church*, 2 vols, London 1966–1970. One should also mention A. D. Gilbert, *Religion and Society in Industrial England 1740–1914*, London 1976; and E. R. Norman, *Church and Society in England 1770–1970*, London 1976. Interesting suggestions are given in H. Davies, *Worship and Theology in England*, vol. IV: *From Newman to Martineau 1850–1900*, and vol. V: *The Ecumenical Century 1900–1965*, Princeton 1962–5. On the twentieth century, a useful but awkward work is G. S. Spinks, *Religion in Britain since 1900*, London 1952, and one should also consult K. Slack, *The British Churches Today*, London 1970. Two original works are to be recommended, one social, K. S. Inglis, *Churches and the Working Classes in Victorian England*, London 1963, the other geographical, J. D. Gay, *The Geography of Religion in England*, London 1971. More recent studies are S. Budd, *Varieties of Unbelief 1850–1960*, London 1977; and R. Currie, A. D. Gilbert, and L. S. Horsley, *Churches and Churchgoers*, Oxford 1978.

On Anglicanism, there are three books written from the Anglican point of view: S. C. Carpenter, *Church and People 1798–1889*, London 1933; J. W. C. Wand, *Anglicanism in History and Today*, London 1961; R. B. Lloyd, *The Church of England 1900–1965*, London 1966.

On the Nonconformists, see an introduction by H. Davis, *The English Free Churches*, 2nd edn, London 1963, and E. A. Payne, *The Free Church Tradition in the Life of England*, London 1944. More recently, a critical light has been shed on the subject by S. Koss, *Nonconformity and Modern British Politics*, London 1975.

Catholicism has mainly been dealt with by Catholic writers: D. Mathew, *Catholicism in England*, 2nd edn, London 1948; G. A. Beck (ed.), *The English Catholics 1850–1950*, London 1950; and in French, J. A. Lesourd, *Le Catholicisme dans la société anglaise 1765–1865*, 2 vols, Lille, 1978.

Works on religious sociology proliferate. Two works of synthesis should be noted: B. R. Wilson, *Religion in Secular Society*, London 1966, and D. Martin, *A Sociology of English Religion*, London 1967; and three good monographs: on Sheffield, E. R. Wickham, *Church and People in an Industrial City*, London 1957; on London, H. McLeod, *Class and Religion in the Late Victorian City*, London 1974; on Reading, S. Yeo, *Religious Organisations in Crisis*, London 1976.

5. Education

The institutional aspects are dealt with in J. W. Adamson, *English Education 1789–1902*, Cambridge 1930, a compact and classic book, and in S. J. Curtis, *History of Education in England*, 7th edn, London 1967, *Education in Britain since 1900*, London 1952, and, in collaboration with M. E. A. Boultwood, *An Introductory History of English Education since 1800*, 4th edn, London 1966. H. C. Barnard, *A History of English Education from 1760*, 2nd edn, London 1961, gives a clear and precise introduction to the subject. The social aspects are treated more extensively by J. Lawson and H. Silver, *A Social History of Education in England*, London 1973, and by D. Wardle, *English Popular Education 1780–1975*, Cambridge 1975. Note also: W. H. G. Armytage, *Four Centuries of English Education*, Cambridge 1964; J. Murphy, *Church, State and Schools in Britain 1800–1970*, London 1971; P. Horn, *Education in Rural England 1800–1914*, London 1978; H. C. Dent, *Education in England and Wales*, London 1977; I. G. Fenwick, *The Comprehensive School 1944–1970*, London 1976; W. K. Richmond, *Education in Britain since 1944*, London 1978.

On public schools, see T. W. Bamford, *The Rise of the Public Schools*, London 1967; and D. Newsome, *Godliness and Good Learning*, London 1961.

On teachers, note A. Tropp, *The School Teachers*, London 1957.

An excellent book on adult education and popular culture is J. F. C. Harrison, *Learning and Living 1790–1960: a study in the history of the English adult education movement*, London 1961.

6. Culture

Besides R. Williams' stimulating studies, *Culture and Society 1780–1950*, London 1958, and *The Long Revolution*, London 1961, one should consult the various studies on prevailing attitudes and values. In particular, for the Victorian period, see: *Ideas and Beliefs of the Victorians*, BBC Talks, London 1949; W. E. Houghton, *The Victorian Frame of Mind*, New Haven, Conn. 1957; and R. D. Altick, *Victorian People and Ideas*, New York 1973. On the dominant culture and popular literature, refer to R. D. Altick, *The English Common Reader: a social history of the mass reading-public 1800–1900*, Chicago 1957; and M. Vicinus, *The Industrial Muse*, London 1975.

For the twentieth century, there is an interesting contribution from S. Hynes, *The Edwardian Turn of Mind*, Princeton 1968; and one should also consult the small descriptive encyclopaedia by C. B. Cox and A. E. Dyson (eds), *The Twentieth Century Mind: History, Ideas and Literature in Britain 1900–1965*, 3 vols, London 1972. On the working-class world, R. Hoggart, *The Uses of Literacy*, London 1957, is a first-class book. Also to be recommended is the study by G. Gorer, *Exploring English Character*, London 1955. On youth and the counter-culture, see F. Musgrove, *Youth and the Social Order*, London 1964, and *Ecstasy and Holiness: Counter Culture and the Open Society*, London 1975; and S. Hall and T. Jefferson, *Resistance through Rituals: Youth Sub-cultures in Post-War Britain*, London 1977. On the political front, see B. Jessop, *Traditionalism, Conservatism and British Political Culture*, London 1974.

On the development of literature, good references are given in B. Ford (ed.), *Pelican Guide to English Literature*, vol. 6: *From Dickens to Hardy*; vol. 7: *The Modern Age*, London 1958–1961.

7. National and racial problems

Descriptions of Scottish society can be found in: R. H. Campbell, *Scotland since 1707: the Rise of an Industrial Society*, Oxford 1965; W. Ferguson, *Scotland: 1689 to the Present*, Edinburgh 1968; W. H. Marwick, *Scotland in Modern Times: An Outline of Economic and Social Development since 1707*, London 1964; C. Harvie, *Scotland and Nationalism*, London 1977; J. Brand, *The National Movement in Scotland*, London 1978.

On Wales, consult: parts of Brinley Thomas (ed.), *The Welsh Economy*, Cardiff 1962; A. Butt Philip, *The Welsh Question: Nationalism in Welsh Politics 1945–1970*, Cardiff 1976; D. Williams, *A History of Modern Wales*, London 1977.

Attempts at an overall view are presented in M. Hexter, *Internal Colonialism: The Celtic Fringe in British National Development 1536–1966*, London 1975; A. H. Birch, *Political Integration and Disintegration in the British Isles*, London 1978; and V. Bogdanov, *Devolution*, London 1979.

Whilst earlier immigration has been studied by J. A. Jackson, *The Irish in Britain*, London 1963, and L. P. Gartner, *The Jewish Immigrant in England 1870—1914*, London 1960 (note here too the relevant book by V. D. Lipman, *Social History of the Jews in England 1850–1950*, London 1954), and C. Holmes, *Anti-Semitism in Britain 1876–1939*, London 1979, coloured immigration from the 1950s on has given rise to a multitude of studies: E. J. B. Rose (ed.) *Colour and Citizenship: A Report on British Race Relations*, London 1969 (a detailed study); C. S. Hill, *Immigration and Integration: A study of the settlement of coloured minorities in Britain*, Oxford 1970 (precise and practical textbook); E. Krausz, *Ethnic Minorities in Britain*, London 1971 (a useful panorama); C. Holmes (ed.), *Immigrants and Minorities in British Society*, London 1978.

8. Foreign views: the English seen by the French

One should be very careful not to overlook the precious mine of information available in the accounts of the French who have stayed some time in England, whether simply as travellers, or else intending to work on some more detailed research, or even, because, wanted by the police in their own country, they sought refuge there (such as Martin Nadaud, Alfred Esquiros, Jules Vallès). A great many of these publications, made up of observations and impressions drawn from daily life, of reports and studies, cannot fail to be highly instructive about English society (unfortunately, since the Second World War, the seam has run out). Amongst the generations of visitors who thus succeeded one another, one should mention: at the beginning of the Victorian era, Flora Tristan, *Promenades dans Londres*, 1840, republished with an introduction by F. Bédarida, Paris 1978; Léon Faucher, *Etudes sur l'Angleterre*, 1845; and the illustrations of Gavarni. From the middle of the century, Léonce de Lavergne, *Essai sur l'Économie rurale de l'Angleterre*, 1854; Hector Malot, *la Vie Moderne en Angleterre*, 1862; Martin Nadaud, *Histoire des classes ouvrières en Angleterre*, 1872; A. Esquiros, *l'Angleterre et la vie anglaise*, 1869; Taine, *Notes sur l'Angleterre*, 1872; and Gustave Doré's realistic illustrations of London. In the 1880s, there are the writings of Jules Vallès, *la Rue à Londres*, 1884; and Max O'Rell (Paul Blouet), *John Bull et son île*, 1883. At the turn of the century, one finds: Paul de Rousiers, *la Question ouvrière en Angleterre*, 1895, and *le Trade-unionisme en Angleterre*, 1897; E. Boutmy, *Psychologie politique du peuple anglais au XIXe siècle*, 1901; Jacques Bardoux, *Psychologie de l'Angleterre contemporaine*, 3 vols, 1906–13, and *l'Ouvrier anglais aujourd'hui*, 1921. The inter-war years are represented by André Siegfried, André Philip, Pierre Bourdan: the last of which, *Perplexités et Grandeur de l'Angleterre*, published 1945 (in English, Pierre Maillaud, *The English Way*) represents the last noteworthy study in this long series.

Note, too, two collections made by particularly acute observers of social development in England: *Marx and Engels on Britain*, Moscow 1962, and *Lenin on Britain*, Moscow 1959.

Index

affluence, 221–4, 250–7, 281, 290
age pyramids, 12–13, 230
agriculture, 16, 25–31, 44–5, 103, 113,
  126–8, 176, 180–1, 231
Anglicanism, 39, 41, 50, 51, 83, 86–90,
  111–13, 132, 153, 155, 200, 208, 236, 242,
  244–5, 265–6
angry young men, 199, 249, 258
aristocracy, 7, 24, 27–30, 36, 41–7, 54,
  78–9, 103, 115, 125–32, 143, 155, 156,
  200–5, 282, 283, 291
Army, 50, 130, 132, 202, 237
Arnold, Matthew, 40, 56, 81, 104, 107–8,
  236
atheism, 112, 241, 243, 267

Bagehot, Walter, 46, 76
Beveridge, Sir William, 192, 193, 196, 254
Beveridge Report, 190
Bible, The, 7, 8, 26, 86, 93, 110
bicycles, 110, 122
birth control, 113–16, 228–9, 243
birth-rate, 12–13, 113–16, 226, 228–9, 263,
  271–2
bureaucracy, 201, 204–5
Burke, Edmund, 41, 135

capital, investment of, 10, 19, 65, 99–101,
  144–9, 151, 219, 221–4, 284
capitalism, xv, 8, 25, 27, 36, 37, 48, 70,
  101, 118, 121, 143, 149, 218
Catholicism, 83, 89–90, 111, 155, 236, 243,
  244, 265, 266
children, 52, 114, 206, 208, 271
Churchill, Winston, 150, 163–4, 170, 189
cinema, 256, 258, 264, 289
City of London, 10, 23–4, 127, 195, 200,
  205, 238
civic sense, 188–9, 235, 251–2
Civil Service, 50, 85, 130, 152, 169, 204,
  205, 238, 284
coal, 6, 9, 10, 11, 58, 175, 210, 211, 228
Cobden, Richard, 41, 46–7, 80–1

Common Wealth Party, 219
Communism, 183
comprehensive schools, 240
consensus, xvi, 73, 78, 80–1, 133, 169–70,
  188–9, 251, 261, 281, 292
Conservatives (Tories), 39, 77, 81, 84, 129,
  130, 140, 287
consumption, 34, 152, 256
cooperative movement, 67, 71
Corn Laws, 26, 41, 79, 197
cotton, 9, 10, 175
countryside, see agriculture
Crystal Palace, 3, 6–7, 107

death, 158–60, 162, 173
de-christianization, 86, 92, 110, 241–5,
  263–5
democracy, xv, 59, 68, 80, 138, 139–43,
  169, 189–91, 193, 196–9, 237, 240–2,
  291–2
demography, 12–15, 113–15, 178, 226–7,
  263, 271–2
Dicey, A. V., 84–5, 108
Dissent, see Nonconformism
distressed areas, 175–6
divorce, 121, 243, 268
double standard, 121, 160

education, 100, 115, 122, 133, 140, 153–8,
  169, 195, 235–41, 270, 271, 283; primary,
  157; secondary, 158, 235; adult, 158, 241
Edwardian age, 171–6, 223, 290
emigration, 15–16, 103, 152, 226, 230–1,
  263
Empire, 9, 108, 144–8, 163–4, 189, 275
employees, 52, 114, 206, 208, 271
Engels, Frederick, 53, 75, 81, 132
entrepreneurship, 9, 48, 53, 55, 100–1
environment, 235, 261
Equal Pay Act, 270, 272
Establishment, the, xv, 75, 131, 197,
  200–5, 238, 258, 286, 287, 291–3
exports, 9, 180, 182

Fabians, 130, 134–6, 142, 186, 195
family, 14, 113–15, 118, 120, 161, 195, 227–9, 262–3, 267, 272
farms and farmers, 27–31, 126–7
farmworkers, 28–9, 58, 63–4, 127–8, 130, 151
Federation of British Industries, 204
feminism, 115–24, 228–9, 236, 261
fertility, 14, 113, 115–16, 227–8, 263
Festival of Britain, 182
Friendly Societies, 67, 71, 159
full employment, 182, 192, 195, 212, 220, 249, 254

gentry, 42, 45, 85, 127, 129, 202–3
George, David Lloyd, 131, 143, 172
governing class, xv, xvii, 77, 78, 85, 103, 104, 113, 125, 146, 156
grammar schools, 235, 238–9
Great Exhibition of 1851, 3–8, 182
growth, 8–12, 99–100, 174, 178, 180, 253–4, 257, 276–8, 288, 298

Halévy, Elie, xiii, xiv, xvi, 77–9, 85, 108, 139
hierarchy, 29, 40–1, 46–7, 73–4, 78, 80, 91, 151, 153–4, 157, 213, 220, 224–5, 238–9, 281–2, 290–1
housing, 17–20, 32–3, 152, 232–5, 255–6
Hyndman, H. M., 135, 171

immigration, 231, 278–80
income: national, 8, 10, 100, 168, 178, 180, 254, 278; personal, 151, 168, 178, 238, 213–25
individualism, xv, 48, 54, 66, 81–5, 104, 108, 169, 198, 252, 293–4
industrialists, 54–6, 129, 151, 201–2, 204, 209, 212
industry, 4, 6, 24, 50, 57–8, 93, 101, 180–1, 253–4, 288
inequality, 40, 73–4, 78, 92, 105–6, 148, 151–3, 157, 188–9, 213–25, 238–40, 254, 281–4
integration, 8, 66–70, 81, 133–4, 188–9, 193, 198, 213, 239, 282, 286, 293

Keynes, John Maynard, 148, 182, 192, 195, 196, 219, 255

Labour movement, 135–9, 143, 168, 182–6, 190, 191, 193, 194–6, 207, 213, 236–7, 239, 259, 286
labour unrest, 103, 136, 152
laicization, 92, 162, 241–3

laissez-faire, 12, 19, 54, 74, 82, 103, 106–7, 108, 141
Lavergne, Léonce de, 26, 47
liberalism, 48, 77, 81–5, 104–5, 108, 140, 193, 254; neo-liberalism, 254, 256–7
Liberals (Whigs), 39, 56, 68, 81, 84, 140, 169
liberty, xv, 49, 76, 81–3, 85, 169, 250–1, 261, 262, 288–9, 293–5
Lib-Lab, 68, 79, 137
life expectancy, 14, 229

Macaulay, Lord, 8, 48, 75–6
machinery, use of, 4, 6, 8–10, 56
marriage, 113, 267
Married Woman's Property Acts, 122
Marx, Karl, 19, 36, 37, 39–40, 53, 80, 132
Marxism, 109, 135, 138
mass media, 241, 250, 254, 261, 281, 284
meritocracy, 205, 284, 291
middle class, 36–40, 48–56, 77–8, 79, 103, 105, 113, 117, 125, 127–9, 133, 143, 150, 152, 155, 190, 196–7, 205–9, 218, 219, 220, 232, 238–9, 271–2, 281–4; lower middle class, 52, 61, 208–9, 232, 271–2
Mill, John Stuart, 16, 81, 84, 121–2, 236
migrations: internal, 26–7, 178–9; daily, 233
miners, see coal
mobility, social, xv, 12, 36–7, 73, 84, 198, 207, 236, 283
morality, 4, 6, 7, 12, 34, 49, 50, 53–5, 86, 91–2, 107, 118, 124, 134, 156, 161, 172, 207, 208, 241, 243, 250–1, 254, 258, 261, 263
mortality, 14–15, 116, 158–9, 229, 263
motor-cars, 101, 110, 128, 150, 207, 229, 232, 256

national pride, xvi, 3, 8, 81, 92–5, 145–8, 164–5, 168, 171–2, 188, 274–6, 288–9, 294
nationalization, 194–5, 205
Nationalism (Scottish and Welsh), 280–1
Navy: merchant, 9, 10, 101; Royal, 94, 132, 163–4, 238
neo-capitalism, 254, 256–7
new towns, 233–4
Nonconformism, 39, 50, 51, 83, 87, 89, 111–12, 153, 208, 242, 244, 265, 268

officers, see Army

Palmerston, Lord, 3, 36–7, 94
patriotism, xvi, 81, 92–5, 133, 145–8, 169, 171, 187–8
Pax Britannica, 9, 162–4
Poor Law, 103, 142, 192, 195

population, 12–14, 17–18, 113–16, 178–9, 206, 226, 227, 270
poverty, 4, 8, 18–19, 24, 104–8, 142, 150–2, 175, 212–13, 224, 257, 281
Primrose League, 130
private wealth, 151, 221–4
productivity, 10, 24, 26, 99, 101, 178, 182, 254
professions, 50–1, 115, 122, 152, 155–6, 206
progress, 4, 7, 9, 24, 26, 107, 173, 237, 254
prostitution, 25, 107, 119, 161–2
Protestantism, 7, 84, 93, 251
public schools, 34, 154–7, 195, 235, 237–8, 240, 284–5
pubs, 111, 213
Puritanism, 50, 52, 53–4, 66, 71, 90–2, 110–11, 117, 124, 133, 160, 162, 173, 207, 229, 243, 250–1, 263

quality of life, xvi, 235–6, 288, 295

radicalism, 39, 41, 55, 59, 68, 79, 80, 109, 117, 140–1, 143
railways, 8–10, 32, 38, 44, 56, 107, 232
real estate, 20, 25, 27–8, 40–2, 46, 47, 126–7, 143, 201
religion, xvi, 4, 6, 7, 12, 29, 39, 69, 77, 78, 83, 85–92, 109, 110–13, 117, 118–19, 138–9, 144–5, 153, 156, 157, 159, 169–70, 236, 241–5, 251, 259, 262, 263–5, 268–9
rents, 27, 31, 39, 44–5, 74, 126–7, 149, 202, 219
revolution: absence of, xv, 5, 75–81, 169; spirit of, 183–5, 186, 299; 'revolution of 1945', 190–1, 195, 197; 'school revolution', 236; revolution of morals, 263
Ruskin, John, 5, 25, 118–19, 235

servants, 18, 46, 47, 50, 52, 58, 63, 120, 202, 206, 208, 256, 271
sexuality, 90, 159–62, 229, 261, 262–3
Siegfried, André, 174, 275
slums, 18–19, 24, 104, 107, 172, 176, 233
social classes, xv, 5, 8, 18, 24, 27–8, 36–40, 49–50, 61, 69, 73–4, 78–9, 151–2, 208, 213, 221, 224, 228–9, 235–6, 281, 290–1
Social-Democratic Federation, 109, 134, 137
social order, xv, 4–5, 54, 80, 104, 194, 207, 292
social services, 141, 192–3, 195, 213, 270
Socialism, 67–8, 80, 105, 106, 108–9, 117, 133–9, 141, 182–6, 193, 195, 259–61; Guild socialism, 138, 186
sport, 31–2, 34–5, 83, 122, 156, 213, 238

State, the, xv, 55, 68, 77, 81, 84–5, 86, 108–9, 134, 139–41, 153, 168, 170, 186, 193, 196, 198, 286, 288
strikes, 70–1, 136, 140, 183–5, 188, 261, 287
students, 259–61, 264, 269
suffragettes, 123–4
Sunday schools, 65, 154, 157
superiority, British, 3–4, 9–12, 21, 92–5, 100, 163, 168, 274–6, 288–9, 294

Taine, Hippolyte, xvi, 16, 25, 47
Taylor, A. J. P., 186, 189, 229
technocrats, 169, 283, 286
'teddy boys', 258
television, 213, 241, 249, 256, 264
Tocqueville, Alexis de, xvi, 40
tolerance, 83–4, 168, 289
town-planning, 195, 233–5
trade, 9–10, 12, 51–2, 100–2, 180
Trade Disputes and Trade Union Act, 184
trade unions, 64, 66–72, 133–8, 182–6, 220, 286–7

underworld, 4, 25, 65
unemployment, 62, 103, 106, 175–7, 209–12, 255
universities, 106, 122, 154, 240, 259–61, 283–4
unskilled workers, 60–1, 62, 71, 133, 136, 152, 212–13
urban life, 4, 14, 16–20, 39, 44, 63, 127, 231–5, 288

Vallès, Jules, xiv, 94, 147, 294
Victoria, Queen, 3, 125
Victorianism, 17, 36, 104, 176, 290

War: Crimean, 162; Boer, 162; First World, 150, 163, 164, 167–8, 170–3, 226–7; Second World, 186–91, 219, 227–8
Webb, Beatrice, 105, 150
white-collar workers, 205, 208, 284
Welfare State, 141, 190–9, 212, 220, 249, 258, 283
widowers and widows, 158–9, 230
women, 63, 116–24, 161, 269–73
worker control, 138, 168, 183, 185–6
Workers' Educational Association, 158, 240
working class, xv, 5, 38–40, 56–72, 78–9, 81, 104–5, 115, 120, 132–9, 143, 146, 150–2, 157, 161, 176–7, 182–6, 197, 207, 209–13, 218, 240, 271–2, 282, 284–7

youth, 13, 249, 258–63